JABOTINSKY AND THE REVISIONIST MOVEMENT
1925–1948

JABOTINSKY
AND THE
REVISIONIST
MOVEMENT
1925–1948

YAACOV SHAVIT
Department of the History of the Jewish People
Tel Aviv University

FRANK CASS

First published 1988 in Great Britain by
FRANK CASS & CO. LTD.
Gainsborough House, Gainsborough Road,
London E11 1RS, England

and in the United States of America by
FRANK CASS & CO. LTD.
c/o Biblio Distribution Centre
81 Adams Drive, P.O. Box 327, Totowa, N.J. 07511

Copyright © 1988 Yaacov Shavit

British Library Cataloguing in Publication Data

Shavit, Yaacov
    Jabotinsky and the revisionist movement
    1925–1948.— (The Right in Zionism and
    in Israel. 1925–1985 v.1).
    1. Israel. Right-wing political movements
    I. Title   II. Series
    320.95694

ISBN 0-7146-3325-9

Library of Congress Cataloging-in-Publication Data

Shavit, Jacob.
    Jabotinsky and the revisionist movement, 1925–1948.

    Bibliography: p.
    Includes index.
    1. Revisionist Zionism—History. 2. Jabotinsky,
Vladimir, 1880–1940. I. Title.
DS150.R5S52   956.94'001   88-997
ISBN 0-7146-3325-9

Printed and bound in Great Britain by
A. Wheaton & Co. Ltd, Exeter

Contents

TO THE MEMORY OF
MY PARENTS

List of Illustrations

between pages 20 and 21

Acknowledgments

I started my research on the Zionist Right some 15 years ago, while studying at the School of History of Tel-Aviv University. I owe a deep debt of gratitude to Professor Walter Laqueur for his encouragement and guidance during the writing of my Ph.D. thesis on this subject.

Since then I have published a number of books and articles on various aspects of the history of the Right, but to the best of my knowledge the present book is the first effort by anyone to present a general and comprehensive summation of the history of the Zionist-Israeli Right. Many of the topics dealt with in this book have been subjects of public and academic discussion and controversy, which has enabled me to clarify my own ideas and verify my sources.

I owe special thanks to the Jabotinsky Institute and its staff, in particular Mr. Pesah Gani, for their unfailing helpfulness. I would also like to thank Mr Henry Nijk, both for his excellent translation from the Hebrew and for his many constructive comments. Thanks are due also to Mr I. Ben-Sinai for assisting in this translation.

The generosity of Mrs Edith Pfeiffer and Dr Heinrich Pfeiffer, the *General-Sekretär der Alexander von Humboldt Stiftung*, enabled me to complete this study under the best possible conditions a scholar could dream of during my sabbatical in Bonn.

Last but not least I would like to record that without the assistance of my friend Professor Amos Perlmutter I would not even have attempted to write this book for the English reader.

My first book on the history of the Right, which was published in 1977, was dedicated to my parents, Pnina and Yitzhak Shavit, who supported me during my years of study. This book is dedicated to their memory.

Tel-Aviv–Bonn, 1985–1987

Foreword

The intensive interest in the nature and character of the Israeli political Right began immediately after the Israeli elections of 1977, when the long-standing Labour hegemony was broken, to be replaced by the rule of a Right-wing *Likud* coalition. This of course does not mean that the Israeli Right was an unimportant, let alone negligible, phenomenon in Israeli life before its rise to power, or that no literature was written about it. Even so the transition from its long years in opposition to the ruling party made it far more important to try and understand the meaning of 'the Right' within the specific Israeli context. This in turn has given rise to a greatly increased interest in the background of the Israeli Right, and resultant efforts to try and explain its sources and origins, not in the least because of the Right's self-image, which customarily stresses its profound debt and obligation to its historical heritage.

In his speech during the early morning hours of 18 May 1977, after the initial results of the elections for the Ninth Knesset had become known, Menahem Begin, the Prime-Minister designate, said: 'Today is a turning point in the history of the Jewish people and the history of the Zionist movement, the likes of which we have not known for 46 years – since the 17th Zionist Congress of 1931, at which Vladimir [Ze'ev] Jabotinsky proposed a resolution to the effect that the aim of Zionism is the establishment of a Jewish state in our time.' With this Begin, while submitting his party's interpretation of the course of Zionist history, also presented the election results as an historic victory of the Zionist 'right wing' over the long-enduring hegemony of the 'Left', i.e. the Labour movement, whose rule had prevailed during those long years. In his view it was a resounding vindication of the Jabotinsky school of Zionism, 52 years after it had first presented itself as a political and ideological force. At the same time he presented himself as the heir and successor of Jabotinsky: the pupil had been granted the power to implement his teacher's Zionist will and vision.

From Begin's perspective the returns of the 1977 elections represented an act of historical justice: finally the in his view central force of Zionism would hold the reins of government, after for nearly fifty years having been in the hands of a minority that had kept on ruling thanks only to its political proficiency and because the political situation had played into its hands. In election after election since 1949 Begin had failed to lead his movement towards a decisive political victory, even though several times the chances had seemed nearer than ever before. According to conventional political wisdom the *Herut* movement did not even have a sporting chance of achieving power, and the specific internal socio-political conditions within the State of Israel would forever preclude it from ruling the nation. The ideology of the *Herut* movement was considered anachronistic, while its administrative and leadership abilities were assumed to be non-existent. That is why the victory of the *Likud* in the 1977 elections was indeed a surprise to the winners as much as to the losers. Only later did the necessity arise to try and analyse both the accidental and the underlying causes which had brought the long national hegemony of the Labour movement to an end, resulting in the rise to power of the Right. For many it was a dark night in the history of Zionism, whereas for others it was 'the break of a new dawn'.

On that dramatic morning of 18 May 1977, when Begin announced the victory of the *Likud* coalition which he headed, he declared the resulting change of government in Israel to be a historical turnabout – a *ma'apah*, the name by which this turning point in Israeli politics has been known ever since. In his victory speech Begin therefore spoke of both 'change' and 'continuity'. By change he meant the profound transition which had taken place following the election results; by continuity he meant that the future *Likud* government would be founded on a solid political and ideological tradition which need not be changed, but would simply have to bring its values into practice.

The shift of political power from the Left to the Right, which occurred after fifty years of Labour hegemony of the *yishuv* and – since 1948 – the Israeli political scene, was viewed by the Left as a profound political upheaval, if not an earthquake. From the point of view of the Right it meant a revolution of historical proportions and a fulfilment of a decades-old dream: at last the Right would be able to take up the ideology of Ze'ev Jabotinsky at the point where it had been left due to the outbreak of the Second World War and the leader's death in 1940, and transfer Jabotinsky's ideological principles into the world of practical politics. After long, frustrating years in the opposition, the great moment had arrived, and now the historical opportunity presented itself to demonstrate what was 'the "right" way in Zionism'.

*   *   *

The rise to power of the *Likud*, with at its centre the *Herut* movement under the leadership of Menahem Begin, aroused considerable curiosity, more than that usually provoked by the rise to power of an opposition party. The reason for this was its nationalistic and militant image, which meant that its policies would surely lead to an immediate war with the Arab nations and impose on the State of Israel a conservative, if not fascist regime. The expectations and fears were so strong because of the fact that the Right itself had proclaimed its intentions to carry through decisive changes in the domestic and foreign policy of Israel, and to effect changes in patterns of thought and behaviour, as well as in the socio-economic structure of Israeli society.

A number of questions have become the subject of political and historical debate. For instance the question whether the Israeli Right – as opposed to pre-war Revisionism – was a new phenomenon which evolved within the specific context of the Jewish society in Eretz Israel? What are the links, if any, between the pre-State Right and the party-political Right in the State of Israel? What kind of continuity can we detect in the political traditions of the Zionist-Israeli Right?

For an answer to these questions, we need first of all a more fundamental knowledge and understanding of the Zionist Right during the pre-state period. Following this, we will be able to answer the above questions, which we propose to do in the second volume of our study.

However, the general interest in the Israel Right is not only connected with current Israeli domestic or foreign (i.e. Middle Eastern) policy. The Israeli Right is a phenomenon which must be understood within the context of similar developments in the intellectual, ideological and cultural dimensions in the Middle East and the 'West' at large: the recent emergence of the neo-conservative Right in Europe and the United States, the crises of modernity and secularism in the Western and Islamic civilizations, the rise of religious (anti-secular) world views and norms.

This general curiosity, and the intensive media exposure were responsible for the close scrutiny of the political behaviour of the *Likud* government during its two terms of office (1977–1984), for one thing to see how ideological principles were being translated into political behaviour and national policy making; what kind of changes in principles would occur once they were being put into practice; how did an opposition party act once it had come to power after many years of frustration and feelings of deprivation? Would the *Likud* give rise to new social and cultural forces, or would it stimulate and encourage the emergence of such forces? Would the *Likud* ride the wave of social and sectarian dissatisfaction, and the wave of nationalistic emotions, or would it succeed in manipulating the as yet disoriented nationalistic and discriminatory sentiments into a political bedding?

Since 1977 a wide variety of literature has been devoted to the examination of the political turnabout, which, although it was at first considered a calamity, soon enough (particularly following the second, even bigger victory at the 1981 polls) came to be understood as expressing a far more fundamental structural change in Israeli political culture. A major part of this literature ascribed the victory of the *Likud* not so much to the success of the *Likud* itself or its ideology, as to the failure of the Labour movement and its weakened impact on Israeli society. Therefore, it was argued, if only the labour parties had succeeded in adjusting themselves to the circumstances and renewed themselves, or – alternatively – stuck to their historical traditions, they would not have broken up internally, thereby paving the way for a victory of the 'Right'. Other polemical articles connected the victory of the Right to longer-term deep-seated structural changes in the Israeli socio-cultural situation, particularly following the Six-Day War of June 1967, and the impact of the resulting territorial gains on all spheres of life. These historical discussions, mainly of an apologetic and argumentative nature, and often with little historical value, brought about a measure of renewed interest in the history of the Zionist Right, its origins and its ideological and cultural evolution.

Unfortunately Zionist historiography has been unable to provide a satisfactory historical background to serve as a solid basis for this kind of discussion, due to the neglect of the history of the Right as an academic field. Most of the interest has focused on the personality of Menahem Begin, the underground and opposition leader who at long last had become prime minister of Israel. The reason for this was the general expectation that Begin himself would almost single-handedly decide upon the activities of the new government and determine its personality. The impression was that the Right under Begin was a 'one-man-show', as had been the case with the Right under the leadership of Ze'ev Jabotinsky, and in consequence the party and the movement were forgotten. As a result, the political debate was bound to be limited to perceptions, prejudices and generalizations.

The present work is not intended as a study of the Israeli political scene since 1977, even though it may serve as a broad-based and necessary background for such a discussion. My interest in the history of the Zionist Right began years before it came to power. The purpose of this study is to offer an historical interpretation of the genesis and evolution of the Zionist and Israeli Right wing, both in the intellectual-ideological field and in the political field. The Zionist 'Right' is defined in this study both as a 'type' (*topos*) of modern Jewish nationalism, and as a major stream in Zionism and in Israeli political culture; a type with unique properties, embracing a unique kind of Jewish nationalism within the framework of the contemporary Jewish national movement and the Jewish-Israeli national society. In many respects it represents an intrinsic part of Zionist ideology in general, with which it has a number of basic assumptions in common. In other respects the Right offers its own version, or emphasizes and accentuates different motives in a manner different from that of the other Zionist currents.

The Zionist Right has an image of being monolithic and mono-thematic, whereas in effect its history is very stimulating and contra-dictory, and full of sharp turns and internal changes. All the variants of the Zionist Right have a common goal: Jewish sovereignty over Palestine (*Eretz Israel*) on both banks of the Jordan River — or at least the western bank between the river and the sea. But there also exist differences in their cultural world views, their ideological arguments, their image of the political and cultural content of the Jewish national society, and the nature of the legitimate political behaviour and means. Indeed the tensions between these variants have created a fascinating and vital dynamic within the history of the Zionist-Israeli Right. The history which is told in this book forms the background for an understanding of the development of the Right in our time, beginning with its formative years, but it is also an important and interesting story in itself.

*   *   *

From the chronological point of view the history of the Zionist-Israeli Right divides into two main periods: the first period (1925–1948) covers the history of the Revisionist movement headed by

Ze'ev Jabotinsky, and the development of the two underground organizations in Eretz Israel – the *Irgun Zeva'i Le'umi* (the Etzel, or IZL) and *Lohamei Herut Israel* (Lehi); the second period (1948 onwards) covers the history of the Right in the State of Israel, mainly that of the *Herut* movement headed by Menahem Begin, and its development from an isolated opposition (until 1965) into a central, and subsequently (1977) ruling party. These two periods are characterized by major changes in the historical framework and the prevailing conditions, for which reason they required a separate historical study. This volume is devoted to the first period; my forthcoming second volume will cover the second period.

In certain aspects I have enlarged upon the scope of the narrative of this volume, for the following three reasons: (1) I wanted to avoid generalizations based on partial and fragmentary knowledge and prejudice; (2) I wanted to offer the reader a fuller description of a history which is for him a *terra incognita*; and (3) because the history of Zionism, as seen from the perspective of the Right, has a different character and development than as seen from the Left, and I believe that it is interesting as well as important for the reader to be aware of this different interpretation of modern Jewish national history.

This volume is divided into four parts.

The first part portrays the 'territory of the Right'. It describes the historical scene on which the Right emerged and developed, and its political history. In this part the reader will become acquainted with the organizations which attempted to translate ideology into political action. The second part deals with the national historical philosophy of the Right, and with the two main ideological streams which constitute its philosophy: their attitudes towards Jewish history, the Land of Israel, religion, culture, and so forth. Most of the arguments and views of the Right were shaped during this period, and this part forms therefore a necessary background to the intellectual and ideological developments within the Right during the next period. In the last chapter of Part II I will try and draw a summary general profile of the Right as a collective mentality. Part Three deals with the Revisionist programme and ideology in several major fields: the political concepts and political methods, the plan for a 'Colonization Scheme', the attitude towards the 'Arab question', and the socio-economic platform. The final chapter deals with the two underground organizations from a political and ideological point of view – as a continuation and metamorphosis of the 'old Right', and the problems connected with the evolution of the

Zionist Right into an Israeli Right. Part Four will discuss the two contradictory images, namely the fascist image, as seen from the persepective of the Left, and the image of the Zionist Left, as seen through the eyes of the Right. The book concludes with a general overview of the history of the Zionist Right.

In the above-described division of the book I was faced with a considerable problem of organizing the material in such a way as to give the reader a clear picture that is systematically organized by subjects and periods, while at the same time avoiding repetition. For this reason I have tried to deal with the material synchronically as well as diachronically, and although some repetition is unavoidable, I have tried my best to eliminate it wherever possible.

Any author writing about historical subjects which form a part of an existing political and ideological reality, will find it difficult to suppress completely his personal leanings, as a result of which he may find his writings becoming an element of, and an instrument in any ongoing struggles about the particular subject. Any writer about the Zionist Right discovers that he has to deal with two prevailing, but contradictory images. The Revisionists believe that their movement has been on the right political track all along, and that – despite having spent most of their political lives in the opposition – the movement has proved to be a Zionist bellweather on countless issues. In their eyes the Revisionist movement is characterized by self-sacrifice and heroism – the quintessential and purest expression of Zionism.

Its opponents, however, regard Revisionism as a sterile, unrealistic, cranky and sloganeering movement – a movement which not only failed to contribute its share to the upbuilding of the National Home, but also was the cause of serious splits and long-drawn-out and bitter conflicts in Zionism.

I have tried my utmost not to be influenced by these two images, which hover like dark and powerful shadows at the back of the author's consciousness. As a consequence not all my descriptions and analyses may be accepted by my readers and critics, but I like to assure them that any mistaken or distorted representations are not a reflection of any specific predisposition, prejudice or interest on my part, but solely the result of my personal judgement and evaluation. In fact, this book deviates in many aspects from the accepted negative portrayal of Revisionism by its opponents, as well as the adulatory views current in the circles of Revisionist supporters. This study also differs – both in the views expressed and the details of the historical events and circumstances – from the opinions expressed in other scholarly studies. Most of the English works on the subject (with the exception of J.B. Schechtman's biography of Ze'ev Jabotinsky) are based on selective, secondary and partisan sources, which as such lead to entirely unwarranted conclusions.

This book is based on extensive primary source material, as detailed in the annotated bibliography. Substantial parts of it are based on my previously published Hebrew books and articles on the subject, so that I have not deemed it necessary to report in full detail all the original sources used. In a way, therefore, my Hebrew writings formed the bricks and mortar of this comprehensive work, which enabled me to write it in its present integrated form. This is also the reason why I did not deem it necessary to include footnotes and detailed references to the numerous sources which form the basis of the various chapters. As mentioned, the bibliography is intended to serve the interested reader as an annotated guide to the primary sources and literature on the subject.

A final remark is in place, especially for the non-Israeli reader.

The often vituperative conflicts and debates which have taken place within the Zionist movement could conceivably provide ammunition for anti-Zionist discussions. Even though it is true that the rival camps within Zionism would at times hurl the gravest and most vitriolic accusations at their opponents, the exact nature of these recriminations can easily be taken out of context by critics and opponents of Zionism, to be used as a representation of substance rather than form. Such a use might not be informed by a genuine desire to understand the special nature of Zionism and the problems with which it was confronted, but rather by a desire to discredit it. The duty of the historian is to portray things exactly as they are, but at the same time this gives him the right to caution against an improper use of historical facts.

The Revisionist proclivity for militancy and muscle-flexing, which was far more evident in Revisionism than within the other Zionist parties, was to a great extent a reaction to an objective weakness: it was an effort to compensate for the bleak and desultory existence of many of its members. Zionism between the two world wars did not operate from a position of strength. The Zionists were unable either to control events, or direct them in a direction favourable to their goals. To describe the Zionist position as powerful or influential would be a violation of the historical truth. The opposite was the case: essentially Zionism was weak and powerless.

In fact Zionism did succeed in establishing a Jewish National

Home in Eretz Israel, but it was unable to save the Jews of Europe. During the 1930s Jewish and Zionist history moved on two parallel but conflicting tracks. As the plight of European Jewry became increasingly acute, and the pressure for emigration to Eretz Israel intensified, the *yishuv* – the Jewish community in Eretz Israel – felt increasingly competent and confident of its ability to absorb a Jewish mass immigration. This willingness was however counteracted by the sharp distinction in British policy between the 'Jewish question', the solution to which was supposed to be guided by the provisions of the Mandate, and the 'Palestinian question', the answers to which were dictated by imperial policy considerations. In effect the British government decided to renege on its obligations under the Mandate charter, even within its narrower interpretation. This was the situation which confronted Zionism on the eve of World War II, without it being able to break the vicious circle.

In light of the above, we must conclude that Revisionism was a tragic movement, and Jabotinsky a tragic leader. Jabotinsky was not a Mussolini, in the same way as Ben-Gurion was not a Lenin. History did not grant either of them the power to control events and direct them in the way they desired. Revisionism was a tragic movement because it did not succeed in bridging the gap between its dreams of power, and its achievement. Revisionism fought against time, but circumstances overtook it. It is against this background that Revisionism's unsuccessful attempts to gain influence and establish the instruments for building a national society, such as an army and instruments of state, must be judged. Regardless of whether this lack of success was due to the fact that its proposed methods – given the contemporary conditions – were unrealistic and barren, or whether it should be ascribed to objective or subjective conditions which prevented Revisionism as a political movement from achieving its goals, the fact is that ultimately it came to be not only a Zionist tragedy, but a Jewish tragedy.

The question whether, and to what extent, Zionist history was special and unique greatly occupied the two rival Zionist camps, and I will revert to this discussion in the course of this study. In theory we are faced here with the Zionist variation on the ongoing discussion between the proponents of a rationalist universalist orientation, and those of the romantic-historistic historical view. I myself am of the opinion that the *Allgemeines* (general) and *Besonderes* (unique), according to the well-known categories of Leopold von Ranke, are not two separate dimensions between which there exist different patterns of contact. The unique can only be understood within a more general conceptual framework. Comparison may not be rejected, either as a historical method, or for its own sake. Even so, comparisons do not necessarily result in similarity, let alone in an overall resemblance. The 'general' and the 'unique' are not abstract models, but concrete objects under observation. Such a concrete description of the unique against a general background is what this study aims to present.

What is Right: The Zionist Right in General Perspective – Some Methodological Comments

The Meaning of 'Right' in the Zionist Israeli Context

In Jewish tradition the term 'Right' has a positive meaning of power and salvation ('Thy right hand is full of righteousness', Ps.48:11; 'The right hand of the Lord does valiantly. The right hand of the Lord is exalted,' Ps.188,15,16; etc.).

Despite this positive connotation of the term 'Right' in the Hebrew language, not a single political stream in Zionism – excepting a passing fad during the 1970s influenced by the emergence of the 'New Right' in Western Europe and the United States – has been prepared to define itself as 'rightist'. To be labelled 'rightist' according to the classification which has been customary in political culture ever since the French Revolution, has been vigorously rejected by every stream or party to which the label 'Right' has been attached. According to this same general classification the Zionist Right defined the labour parties as 'leftist', attaching to them all the negative characteristics with which the Right customary labels the Left. When applied to itself, however, the Right has strongly rejected the validity of this generalizing classification within the Jewish Zionist context, regarding it as arbitrary and stigmatizing. There are several reasons for this rejection:

1. The principal general argument is that the division into 'Right' and 'Left' customary in European societies and European political cultures applies neither to the special Jewish historical circumstances in the Diaspora, nor to those prevailing in Palestine [*Eretz Israel*]. According to this reasoning the national aims, the social structures and political patterns evolving among the Jewish people in the Diaspora and in Jewish society during

the British Mandate and – later – in the independent Jewish state, are in no way similar to the European structure and pattern, as a result of which a comparison between these two categories also follows different rules.

What direct connection, the Zionist Right argues, can there exist between the generally agreed characteristics of the European Right and the national aims of the Zionist movement? There simply is no connection! It was the Zionist Right which struggled for Jewish national self-expression through the establishment of a Jewish state in Eretz Israel. The Right was the Zionist party which undertook the large-scale immigration [*aliyah*] of Jews, rather than a selective *aliyah* based on social or ideological considerations. The Right anticipated the Holocaust by calling for the complete evacuation of European Jewry. It was the Right which established the underground movements that fought for the termination of the Mandate and the establishment of an independent Jewish state. Could any of this be said to belong in any way to the world of the European Right? How could anyone claim that the desire to create an independent Jewish state in Palestine or, for that matter, the Jewish national aspiration to establish sovereignty over the historical borders on both sides of the Jordan river (or its western bank) are manifestations of a romantic nationalist or imperialistic ideology? These, argues the Right, are the national and historical goals of the Jewish people – the foundations and the essence of its existence! Such goals cannot possibly be defined as rightist, and thus they cannot be compared to the ideologies of any of the European rightist movements. If the rule of a Jewish majority over the Arab population of Palestine is a form of colonialism – then by all means Zionism is a colonial movement!

2. According to a more fundamental (and historiosophic) argument Jewish history occupies a unique and separate place within general history, to which Western political categories cannot be applied; as a result of this it can only be discussed in specifically 'Jewish' terms. This holds true as regards Jewish history in general, as well as with regard to various political and social phenomena forming a part of its modern history. Any attempt to apply Western categories to the Jewish historical experience is artificial, misleading and wrong.

3. From the nineteenth century onwards the European Right has been considered anti-Semitic and reactionary in character, in the same way as anti-Semitism forms a dominant (although

suppressed) part of its cultural symbol system moulding its policy towards the Jews. Not a single Zionist party could therefore possibly identify with the Right, whether this be the conservative Right or the radical 'new' Right.

4. The Zionist Right considers the division into 'right' and 'left' to have an anti-national character, liable to cause sectarian strife and a rending of the national fabric through class struggles. While the classical Zionist Right looked upon itself in social matters as a 'neutral' national movement representing the 'nation as a whole', which stood above class struggles, and in which the interests of the nation, the state and the fatherland reigned supreme, it viewed the Left as a class-bound movement representing its own partisan interests only.

We need not emphasize that in this respect the Zionist Israeli Right shared the attitude shown by the European Right towards the Left.[1] The 'Left' was considered an anti-national one-class party; the 'Right', on the other hand, represented the entire Jewish nation. In the eyes of the 'Right', the 'Left' constituted an integral part of the 'international Left', in the same way as the latter regarded the 'Right' as an integral part of the 'international Right'. Both movements saw themselves as unique political phenomena, which could only be understood within the unique contexts of Jewish history and the Jewish existence in the Diaspora and the nation that was being built in Eretz Israel. At the same time, each regarded the opponent as part of a universalistic phenomenon, to be judged by universalistic criteria.

As mentioned earlier, we are faced here with an interesting historical paradox. In the eyes of the hostile critic outside the Zionist movement (and, at times, those of the radical dissident currents from within as well) Jewish nationalism as a whole is a rightist movement, due to its inherent romantic nationalist dimension. This interpretation matches the definition of, for example, Hugh Seton-Watson, who says that 'a reactionary is one who wishes to resurrect the past, and reactionary ideologies are based on visions of the past, usually more mythical than real, which are intended to inspire political action in the present.'[2] According to this definition, Zionism in general can be understood as a reactionary, 'rightist' movement, since its underlying 'romantic' idea is the actual revival of an ancient national historic past in a land from which the nation as a whole had been absent for many centuries.

Another critical approach is that there exists no real difference between 'left' and 'right', either in the Zionist movement or in Israeli society, and that any differences are those of emphasis only. Even if, theoretically, such differences could be found, they would mainly be a matter of self-image, which in practice would fade into insignificance, or even disappear. The political behaviour of the Right and the Left would in the final analysis yield the same results. According to this view one might say that what looks like the dualism of a deeply-rooted opposition — both within Zionism and within Israeli society — is a seeming contradiction only, even if it manifests itself as a political struggle. In any case, we have here two political oligarchies trying to mobilize the masses in an effort to achieve a certain political power. In their view, the saying of the Roman historian Sallust about the struggles between the patrician factions in Rome, *'Bonum publicum pro simulantes, sua quisque potentia certabant,'*[3] applies equally to the political struggles within Israeli society. Right and Left are two faces of one and the same phenomenon!

There are also those who reject the accuracy of the 'classical' division into 'right' and 'left' from an empirical rather than an ideological point of view, reasoning that in Zionism the 'Right' is not so 'right', and the Left not so 'left', since the socio-demographic foundations of both the Zionist Right and Left cannot at all be compared with those of European society. The Israeli Left, which ruled the country until 1977, possesses extensive economic assets, and its voters belong by and large to the middle classes. The Right, on the other hand, is penniless, and its supporters and voters are recruited from the lower middle classes and the urban proletariat. According to this interpretation the Left offers a socialist platform in theory, but what it has established in Israel is a pluralistic society with a unique mixture of Socialism and Capitalism: a form of socialist State Capitalism. The real, and decisive, division between Left and Right, according to this view, is not a socio-economic, but an ideological one: a division between those adhering to nationalist and activist Zionist convictions, and those embracing a minimalist Zionist viewpoint. Zionist activism and Zionist minimalism (or rationalism), according to this interpretation, represent a political attitude towards the central national political issues, and these in turn are a matter of 'Zionist faith', or 'collective psychology'.[4] According to the rightist definition a 'minimalist' is someone who is lacking in faith, and who puts party-political interests above the national interest. He is someone whose Jewish and national identity is not strong enough, due to an excessive preoccupation with internationalism or universalism. Put differently, the real division is one between 'nationalism' and 'leftism', or between 'nationalism' and 'defeatism'. As seen from the opposing side, the two contending ideologies are 'ultra-nationalist' or 'fascist', in contrast to a 'humanitarian' and 'sane' Zionism. As of 1977 the two opposing sides have crystallized into the 'dovish' Left and the 'hawkish' Right.

The problems with a definition of the Zionist Israeli Right follow therefore from the definition of topical issues, as well as from the lack of parallelism between ideological self-awareness, on the one hand, and socio-economic structure and class stratification, on the other. The political ideological struggle has tended to accentuate the gap between the two opposing parties, leading to further polarization and a schismatic gap. In the reality of daily political life, however, these differences may on certain subjects be subdued, whereas on other occasions they will appear sharp and deep.

The student of Israeli political culture (and Israeli culture in general) will find that despite this blurring of areas and the problems connected with an objective definition, those involved will nevertheless insist on distinguishing a clear and unequivocal division into 'right' and 'left', which in most cases brings about hasty and *a priori* conclusions on most issues. For large sections of the Israeli public Right and Left represent sub-cultures which produce built-in responses to the various phenomena. Right and Left represent not only contradictory ideologies, but two contradictory mentalities and two contradictory personalities. No one can deny that the chasm between the Zionist Right and Left is one of the dominant facts of life in Zionism and Israeli society, and that it is charged with ideological differences, as well as with emotions and feelings of superiority and deprivation, not to speak of the opposing interpretations of Jewish and Zionist history. The political debates within Zionism have traditionally been informed by a deep consciousness of a fateful historical struggle being enacted, under the influence of dramatic historical events, catastrophic and revolutionary historical changes, and the establishment of a Jewish national society for the first time in modern Jewish history.

The above-discussed contradictory interpretations, namely those that attempt to blur the differences between 'right' and 'left' in the Zionist Israeli context, and those that stress their real and profound differences, do in themselves give rise to some important questions. For instance, are these interpretations based on different historical, or on different ideological and political approaches? What are the contradictions between the Right and the Left: are they fundamental, or do they concern only marginal areas that fail to influence concrete political behaviour? Are we dealing with true or with imaginary self-images – merely different models of what is regarded as the reality, and which, as it were, lead a life of their own? Comparative research should be able to provide a more accurate and reasoned answer to these questions once the available historical material on the Right has been studied.

The present study is a profile of the Zionist Right; it is not intended as a comparison of the political ideology and behaviour of either the Right or the Left. Such a discussion would necessitate a detailed analysis of the historical vicissitudes of both, before we could even begin to draw analogies and parallels between the two. My concern here is with the Right in and by itself, rather than with drawing comparisons with other factors or phenomena. Neither is it my intention to judge the Right; what I want to do is describe it, in order to facilitate an understanding of its nature and characteristics.

Ideology, Weltanschauung and Political Methods and Behaviour

'Right' is not only an operative ideology, aimed at declared goals, or a political system, but a political tradition and *Weltanschauung*, which together create a solid framework of political and cultural traditions. Certain elements of this tradition of the Right can also be found in other Zionist political traditions. The territorial romantic dimension, for instance, was as strong within a central part of the Left as within the Right; the claims with regard to Jewish national sovereignty over Palestine and its historical religious legitimization were espoused among the Zionist Left no less strongly than by the Right. However, despite these and other similarities in elements, the Right is a separate political framework, due to the fact that its various elements have coalesced into one recognizable, coherent and active unit that behaves in a specific way.

It will be useful if at this stage we explain first the concepts that are being used in this study as a means of organization and interpretation. The three concepts in question are '*Weltanschauung*', 'ideology' and 'political methods'.[5]

A *Weltanschauung* is a comprehensive view of man, society and history as a totality; it is a system of symbols and values; a code of behaviour in every sphere of life. It is also a depiction of the historical past, a vision of the future. This comprehensive view

organizes reality and the image of reality in the collective consciousness and determines 'mechanistic, *a priori* responses, attitudes
and orientations towards various events and phenomena'. Certain
symbols and slogans within this system – words such as 'state',
'tradition', 'fatherland', and so forth – have a suggestive power.

This system of symbols and references does not only apply to
political issues, and it is not represented only in the shape of formal
ideology, but also manifests itself in other forms of communication
in a culture. A collective *Weltanschauung* therefore represents
a comprehensive world view of a certain public – its collective
mentality as a part of the *Zeitgeist*. Since we are talking of the
mentality of a broad, heterogeneous and anonymous public, we
have to trace all its cultural expressions, and not only its political
culture. However it must be remembered that the connections
between an attitude toward 'culture' at large and an attitude toward
'political culture' are not unequivocal.

The writings of intellectuals and men of letters who belong to a
certain tradition have two functions. In the first place they provide a
more sophisticated and methodical manifestation of the collective
(i.e. common) wisdom of the public, and as such they attempt –
mainly within societies in transition – to provide the collective
Weltanschauung with a philosophical basis. In the second place
these writings in many instances provide sources of influence for the
public world view, providing it with new and solid arguments and
answers.

Ideology represents the effort to formalize a *Weltanschauung*, or
parts of it, into a practical system in the political sphere, and to
translate arguments into active conclusions. Differences in world
view may be unimportant at the political level, and remain in the
area of personal feeling or the intellectual and political debate. Only
when translated into an active ideology and code of behaviour does
a world view have social and political meaning. Ideology is therefore
a specific political and social opinion; a well-defined, formulated,
systematic set of goals and aims (the value dimension) and the
means and methods of attaining them (the practical dimension).
Ideology and programme are not only that systematic set of goals
which seeks to formulate practical policy; they are also the intermediate link between the world view and practical policy, between
the perception of the world and reality.

Political behaviour and methods are the ways and means whereby
a group which possesses an ideology behaves within the political
system, and the manner in which it tries to achieve its goals, while

setting a normative relationship between the 'desirable' and the 'attainable', between the 'possible' and the 'impossible', between 'expectations' and 'achievements'.

The ideology and programme can be found in the formal platform of the party, in the discussions in party conferences, and so on. The *Weltanschauung*, the emotions behind politics and the repertoire of images and symbols, is to be found in newspapers, journals, books and other forms of verbal and/or written expression. An established *Weltanschauung* and ideology within an organized political framework with a firm sense of identity, belonging and continuity, will create a strong, confident and effective *political tradition*.

Such an ideological political tradition has existed within the Zionist Right for the past 60 years. This political tradition was strong enough to weather two generations of historical upheavals which changed the Jewish world and the position of the Jewish national movement inside it. The newcomers to the rightist camp during this period therefore joined a solid political tradition, and adopted its values and systems. In the course of our discussion we will deal with the question of whether the socio-cultural profile of the newcomers, or the joining of a new elite, caused a radical change in this tradition, or merely added new elements.

*   *   *

The guiding thesis of this study revolves around the three above-mentioned concepts, in an effort to expose the continual tension between *Weltanschauung*, operative ideology and political and organizational behaviour. Revisionism was a national movement, and its *Weltanschauung* was therefore built upon an active national awareness – a striving towards the achievement of full Jewish independence in historical Eretz Israel – and upon various nationalist symbols. This national awareness determined the attitude of the Right towards the different historical occurrences; the ideology and the political platform were efforts to translate this national awareness into practical policy, and the political methods were intended as the instruments for influence and shaping the political reality in the light of the ideal.

It is my view that the formal ideology of Revisionism was unable to provide a sufficient response to the active national awareness and nationalist *Weltanschauung*. This inner tension at times even existed in the world views and behaviour of individuals, first and foremost Ze'ev Jabotinsky himself: the practical solutions which he presented did not allow themselves to be translated into effective answers to the existing expectations and aspirations. As a result of this the nationalist *Weltanschauung* cast about for different solutions, and during the 1930s it developed a new operative ideology, as well as new instruments for the implementation of the solution and new types of behaviour. It often looked as if there existed a semantic resemblance between the *Weltanschauung* and the ideology, but here and there concepts and slogans such as 'political action', 'revolution', 'rebellion', and so forth, were invested with a different interpretation. Within the context of the historical process this tension between a nationalist *Weltanschauung* and ideology and programme gave rise to a great deal of internal tension, setting into motion political processes in which the *Weltanschauung* became institutionalized in activities that were neither approved, nor guided by the organs of the movement. Eventually this resulted in the establishment of new and completely independent organizations. In addition, the tensions within the movement resulted in the evolution of two different nationalist ideologies within the Right, accompanied by splits and schisms. I maintain that the creation of the new nationalist ideology and the development of the military organizations was the result of a clash between a *Weltanschauung*, which was first expressed in journalistic articles and poetry, as well as in a public attitude, and a formal and well-defined ideology that was not merely a response to historical events, but also presented itself as a real alternative and a new political avenue.

A discussion on world views and ideology rests on the assumption that the system of symbols and the deeply-rooted responses mould behavioural patterns, and that groups with different ideologies will have different aims, different expectations, and different behavioural norms. At the same time we may not forget that political behaviour, just as policy itself, is shaped by a wide variety of forces. The status of the Right within Zionism and Israeli society, its oppositional character, as well as its inner compulsions and collective personality, have greatly influenced the nature of its behaviour within the political system, quite apart from the fact that this behaviour has undergone changes in line with the evolution of the Right's status and tasks within this system [particularly its transition from political party to underground movement (1940–1948), and from opposition to ruling party (1977–1984)]. For this reason a political history cannot limit itself to a discussion of a symbol system and a formal ideology and programme, but should subject this ideology (as well as the other components) to the test of actual practice.

It is also important to remember that a political party in the context of Zionist history, the history of the Jewish community in mandatory Palestine (to a certain extent also in modern Israeli society) was forced to maintain different patterns of involvement and activity within the historical reality from those of the Right in other countries. For this reason we will find the Right (as well as the Left) deeply involved in education, in immigration activities, in the organization of military undergrounds, in economic ventures, and so on. The question remains whether these patterns of involvement and fields of activity of the Right were different from those of the Left, and to what extent these variations stemmed from their differences in character, ability, ideology and interests.

PART ONE

THE TERRITORY AND ORGANIZATION OF THE RIGHT – POLITICAL HISTORY

Introductory Remarks

The term 'movement', by which connotation certain organizational streams in Zionism are identified, has come to express the difference between the overall character of a group and a mere political organization. A 'movement' is not just a political party; it is, in the Zionist context, a socio-political organization which also deals with education and settlement, as well as with social and defence activities. A 'movement' aims at the organization of its members for the fulfilment and implementation of a variety of tasks which exceed the party-political sphere. A 'movement' comprises not only a political party and its parliamentary faction, but also youth movements, trade unions and other enterprises in fields such as, for instance, settlement, culture and education. Revisionism was unable to separate itself from this built-in pattern of the leading Zionist movements. Although Revisionism set out as a faction of a political party, it soon turned into a movement with a similar structure to that of the Labour movement. As was the case in the Labour movement, the political system of the Right also had two constituent parts: the political party and the youth movement. At the same time the overall Zionist framework dictated binding patterns of organization and activities with regard, for instance, to electoral campaigning and the struggle for representation within the Jewish representative organs. Our main interest in the political and organizational history of the Right is to see how under the prevailing conditions it became organized, which of the various organizations claimed to express its ideology, and how the tensions between *Weltanschauung*, operative ideology and the patterns of political behaviour influenced the organizational history of the Right.

I decided to start with a review of the organizational history, since our subject is not a history of ideas as such, but of ideas existing in a certain socio-political context, or – to put it differently – with the way in which existing ideas succeeded in finding a social body willing to adopt them and carry them towards their realization.

CHAPTER ONE

The Territory of the Zionist Right: Origins and Historical Background

The Scope of Geography and Time

This book covers a specific period, namely the 25 years which elapsed between 1923/25 and 1948. This quarter century should not only be seen as the road leading towards a Jewish state, or the formative period of the Israeli Right after 1948. It should also be regarded as a specific historical period in its own right. The emergence of a Right wing within the Jewish national movement was one of the major and most crucial reactions to the situation and status of the Jews between the two world wars, both in Europe and in Eretz Israel under the mandatory regime. The Right was one of the responses to the overall situation of the Jews in the modern society, evolving in an era between war and revolution; between war and the Holocaust; and between Communism and nationalism.

Geographically, these developments span a wide area. The intellectual cradle of the Zionist Right stood in pre-revolutionary Russia; its broad demographic base was located in Poland and the Baltic states, after these states regained their independence. Here, too, we find its cultural roots as a mass movement that mobilized the middle class to its ranks. The focus of its aspirations and actions was Eretz Israel, which at the time was ruled by the British mandatory regime, whereas its political and diplomatic centres were located in London, Paris, Geneva, Warsaw and various other European capitals. Its branches were scattered all the way from the shores of the Baltic to South Africa, and even Harbin in China. The emphasis of this book will by necessity be on those centres which played pivotal roles in the history of the Right, rather than on the broader periphery.

The period under discussion witnessed a number of sweeping historical events, which did much to influence the development and shaping of the Right. Throughout the book these events will be mentioned insofar as they formed a turning point, or were instrumental in determining the course of events. The Russian October Revolution, which severed the large and vibrant Russian Zionist movement from world Zionism, was regarded by the Zionist Right as the biggest threat the Jewish people and Jewish nationalism had ever faced. In contrast to many other Zionist currents, the Right never had much faith in the New World which the Revolution was supposed to herald. The Right regarded both the Revolution and Soviet Russia itself as exponents of totalitarian barbarism and active and powerful anti-Semitism. The establishment of the new national states in Eastern and Central Europe was at first also seen as a negative development, since the nationalism prevailing in these states was tainted with anti-Semitic elements. There was every reason to fear that nationalism and national étatism would look upon the Jewish minority as an alien growth that would have to be suppressed.[1]

However, following the signing of the Minority Treaties, and the consolidation of the newly-independent European states, the Revisionists came to believe that the Jewish populations and the Jewish national movement might have the best of both worlds. Not only would they enjoy equal political and national rights, as provided under the law, but they would also be able to continue cultivating the Zionist nationalist *Gegenwartarbeit*. Jabotinsky, for instance, described Latvia as an oasis of moderate nationalism, with a markedly positive attitude towards minorities. Post-1926 independent Poland under the leadership of Pilsudski was described in a similar positive vein.[2] Unfortunately the historical developments between the two world wars failed to justify this optimism, and the Zionist Right thrived despite its difficulty to reconcile its deep appreciation of the nature of Eastern and Central European nationalism – particularly because of its opposition to Communism – on the one hand, and a deep fear of its profound and aggressive anti-Semitism, on the other. For this reason the rise to power of the Nazis in Germany at the beginning of 1933, and the death of Marshal Józef Pilsudski, the Polish leader, in the summer of 1935, may be seen as turning points in the attitude of the Revisionist movement as regards its evaluation of the situation and the fate of European Jewry. 'Breaking points' might be a better description, actually, in the sense that they spelled an end to the hopes of an autonomous national existence within the framework of the new national states in Europe.

The changes in British policy in the Middle East, both in Eretz Israel and in the Arab world as a whole, were formative events as well, and they proved the main catalysts for the formulation of fundamentally different points of view, and the evolution and internalization of certain fundamentals of the *Weltanschauung* of the Right, in particular its radical nationalism and extreme attitude towards the Arabs. In the course of this book we will time and again be confronted with the formative influences of the Arab riots of 1929, the Arab revolt during the years 1936–1939, the provisions of the White Paper of May 1939 and, of course, Great Britain's policies during World War II and the Holocaust. These were dramatic and even traumatic events, which were interpreted, often with justification, as apocalyptic and catastrophic, in which capacity they helped to shape and determine the response of the Right as a whole.

The Background: the Stage is Set

In the next chapter we shall deal at length with the organizational and political history of Revisionism. It is important therefore to consider the specific political and social conditions prevailing in the arenas in which the Zionist Right operated. Of course these were not confined to the Right, since in fact the entire Zionist movement, including all its constituent parties, was subject to the very same conditions. Even so it is important to mention this crucial aspect, since ideologies do not function in a vacuum, but within the framework of the available means and possibilities.

During the mandatory period the Zionist Right did not operate within the framework of a sovereign Jewish society. Also in the Eastern European Diaspora the Right was only one of the Jewish Zionist parties competing for the attention of the Jewish public. Politically, its struggle was not aimed at taking the reins of government, but at achieving influence and representation with the existing sovereign government and its agencies, as well as achieving a position of power within the representative bodies of the Zionist movement. The instruments of this struggle were by necessity limited to propaganda, educational activity and political organization. In other words, the activities of the Zionist Right in Europe evolved within independent, non-Jewish states, and were, by their very nature, incapable of influencing either the structure, or the economic life-style of the Jewish Diaspora society in any way. The imitation of the political and organizational patterns, as well as the nationalist motives of the European national parties, insofar as it was tried, influenced the internal character of the Right and its ideology, but without the same results.[3]

The arena in mandatory Palestine was equally beset with numerous restrictions.[4] Here too the Right did not operate within an independent Jewish national society; the struggle for government inside the *yishuv* – the Jewish community – was of a fundamentally different character from the struggle for political rule within an independent state, and the tools which could be employed in this struggle were therefore severely limited. The British mandatory authorities permitted street demonstrations, public gatherings, strike action, and so forth, but any attempts to take over the government by force, or to organize a *putsch* or a public uprising, were out of the question.

Theoretically, for instance, it would have been possible to advocate a dictatorship or one-party system, but actually carrying out a *putsch* or a civil uprising was an impossibility. Similarly any efforts to force through changes in the political structure of the representative organs of the Zionist movement or of the *yishuv* had to be ruled out.

Another factor severely limiting the ability of the Right as a political party to effect far-reaching changes in the economic and social structure of the Jewish community in Palestine was the mandatory government's control of most sectors of the economy: it was the legislative and executive authority, and its policies were determined in London, rather than by the Zionist movement.

Nevertheless, both in Palestine and in Poland, the political struggles between the Right and the Left within the respective Jewish communities showed several striking similarities. The Polish government granted substantial freedom of action to the Zionist political parties operating within the independent Polish state. The mandatory government maintained a low profile as regards its involvement in the internal life of the *yishuv*.[5] This enabled the Zionist movements in both countries – despite their totally different characters – to keep up an intensive level of political activity, and to create two autonomous Jewish societies: the Jewish Zionist public in Poland, and the Jewish community in mandatory Palestine.

It should be remembered that the European Right acted within established national societies and within the framework of sovereign states, whereas the Zionist Right functioned within an autonomous voluntary communal framework. Its principal objective, which the Right shared with Zionism as a whole, was the establishment of a national Jewish society in Eretz Israel. However, the historical goal, the circumstances, and the instruments which a movement has at its disposal are no less, and possibly more, important factors than its declared ideological contents, which merely serves to create a world view and self-image, and to shape and evaluate a certain reality. The nature of the historical framework and the available instruments determine the possibilities and the restraints confronting a political movement in the fulfilment of its goals and desires.

The Intellectual Arena

The ideas of the leading personalities in the Zionist Right, some of whom have achieved greater renown than others, were not merely shaped by the *Zeitgeist*, but also by the impact of specific contemporary ideological doctrines about which they learned either from personal experience, or through others. Quite a number of the prominent figures of the Zionist Right were alumni or students of various European universities. (Professor Joseph Klausner was a graduate of Heidelberg; Ze'ev Jabotinsky had studied at Bern and Rome, and various other universities; Abba Achimeir and Israel Scheib (Eldad) were graduates from Vienna, and so forth.) Studying their writings enables us to identify their respective direct and indirect sources of inspiration and intellectual knowledge. It is far more difficult to trace the development of the *Weltanschauung* and ideology of the movement as a whole. There is no doubt that various literary minds had a seminal influence on the movement – in the first place Jabotinsky himself, who is regarded as its spiritual father, or at least as the originator of most of its ideas. Even so there is an easily discernible ideological continuity from the nationalism of the 1880s, in other words the ideas that were born during the period of the *Hibbat Zion* (Lovers of Zion) movement and the *Ha-Tehiah* ('Revival') era in modern Hebrew literature, as well as from the Zionism of Herzl and of his period, which were developed or given a new emphasis by the Revisionist movement.

The intellectual territory of the Zionist Right is highly eclectic. In it were represented influences of Western European Positivism (through Jabotinsky and Achimeir), of the Russian Slavophilic School, Polish messianic nationalism, German neo-Romanticism, and influences of Nietzsche and Spengler, as well as of other currents and sub-currents, all of which were placed in a Zionist context. The Right also reveals clear traces of the philosophies of Achad Ha'am, Berdichevski, Herzl and Nordau, in addition to which Revisionism was of course profoundly influenced by its particular interpretation of the Jewish cultural tradition. We are therefore faced with a multi-varied and contradictory world which, despite itself, succeeded in creating a specific intellectual and ideological tradition. The question which has to be examined here is therefore how this tradition came into being, and how its various elements were joined, and welded into a unified intellectual structure, which in turn was translated into a political ideology.

Is there a Revisionist Ideology?

At this point we may ask ourselves whether Revisionism possessed an ideology. This may sound a rather strange question about a movement known for its ideological dogmatism, so that we should try and provide an answer.

When the founders of *Ha-Zohar* formulated their platform during the years 1923–1925, they were thinking of an operative Zionist programme rather than creating a new type of national ideology. All the main points in their programme were of a pragmatic, operative nature. Some of them were taken from the existing repertoire of Zionist plans, which for some reason or other had never before been included in a comprehensive programme of any other political party. The term 'ideology' was regarded as belonging to the intellectual world of the 'Left'. On the other hand, when in 1923 Jabotinsky met with the nationalist youngsters who had founded *Betar*, he did not merely offer them an operative political programme consisting of a few simple points, but tried to imbue them with an activist national consciousness, a national awareness, and a national cultural ethos. He believed that the *Betar* members were not so much in need of an ideology, as of a strong historical consciousness – a *Weltanschauung*. After all, *Betar* was intended to be a *Lebenswelt*, a spiritual home for its members in the Diaspora, as well as an organized cadre for training those who were to take part in the future national and political struggle. *Betar* as a movement was regarded as more expressive of a state of mind, a collective psychology, than of an ideology. Jabotinsky portrayed the nationalist Jewish youngsters who joined the ranks of *Betar* in the idealistic and rhetorical terms customary in romantic national movements. His descriptions are reminiscent of, for instance, the lines of Mickiewicz famous 'Ode to Youth' ('Together, young friends'), a poem written

Ze'ev Jabotinsky

M. Begin

A. Stern

Joseph Klausner

A. Achimeir

M. Grossman

V.Z. Greenberg

A. Zvi Propes

in Kovno, in which he calls upon Polish youth to wake up and unite in order to build a new world. In this light it is not surprising that the meeting in Riga inspired Jabotinsky to write 'A Timely Poem', apparently intended as an anthem, an important attribute for a youth movement that needed appropriate songs for all kinds of important occasions. The colours about which he talked in this *Farben Lied* were blue, gold and white, and its symbolic national heroes were the Maccabees. It described youth as the flywheel of history, and boyhood as the motor propelling the ship towards vistas of ideals and vibrant vitality.[6]

When Jabotinsky met in Riga with the members of the Jewish student association *Ha-Hasmonai* – a meeting with far-reaching consequences, about which we will have more to say in the next chapter – he saw before him a new type of national Jew. These students did not necessarily accept the political principles which Jabotinsky expounded because they believed in their immediate realization, but mainly because they satisfied them, and matched their nationalist mood. Jabotinsky, on his part, was particularly surprised by the active and uninhibited national awareness of the Riga group. He described it as fundamentally identical to any other national[ist] student group in its immediate (Polish, Latvian or German) environment. He envisioned a new kind of nationalist 'Hebrew' Jew, a kind of Jewish gentile possessed of an overall national culture. According to Jabotinsky, these nationalistic and idealistic Jewish students were in every respect the same as the gentile nationalist students, but they did not shy away from 'the hypnotic influence of external forms and traditions', and from joining the student fraternities and orders (*Bundeswerde*). They even drank beer and fought duels! This was a conscious effort on his part to reconstruct a Jewish national existence on the model of a neighbouring nationalism. The ideal of an active, committed nationalism, untainted by any universalist and socialist ideas (the latter in view of the fear of the enemy Soviet Communist neighbour) became the focus of the efforts to mould a nationalist Jewish youth trying to create for himself a full and satisfying national world, even if – at least not in the foreseeable future – he possessed neither a homeland, nor an independent country he could call his own.

The above explains the emphasis on character building (*Bildung*) in *Betar*. This utopian moulding of both the internal and the external personalities of the Jewish nationalist youth was based on the ethos of *hadar* ('splendour', or 'glory'), an idealized code of behaviour, reflected mainly in conduct and aesthetics, which showed clear signs of having been copied bodily from the norms of the environment, and which was grafted as a 'closed system' onto the Jewish national culture and society. Jabotinsky's utopian ideas of the 'new Jew' corresponded on many points with those of Herzl. Both saw the Jew as trying to shed his ghetto garb, and simultaneously struggling against assimilation (a form of inner ghetto), in an effort to rehabilitate his image and restore his dignity, both as an individual, and as a contemporary person with a nation behind him – all this with the incorporation of archaic as well as modern and even utopian elements. Herzl himself was the perfect model of the 'new Jew'.[7]

On the face of it, the new movement that was born here expressed a mood, whereas its programme was limited in contents. However, Revisionism was not an idealistic and romantic youth movement, or a mere political faction, and for this reason it devoted endless discussions to the question of whether the movement should have a binding ideology on all kinds of issues, particularly in the social and religious cultural field. Some claimed that the movement did possess such a comprehensive and binding ideology, whereas others made a case for pluralism on any subjects that were not of a 'purely nationalist nature'. 'Revisionism', wrote J.B. Schechtman, 'is a political movement, pure and simple, which takes a purely neutral stance in religious and social matters'.[8] Jabotinsky himself, when referring to the subject of ideology, at times talked about a detailed and systematic platform outlining a distinct action programme concerning the areas of Zionist fulfilment, and at times about a 'world view', in the sense of a definition of the intrinsic roots of Jewishness in the widest sense. In the 'Idea of Betar' of 1934, in which he tried to define the general outlook of *Betar*, he commented that a collective world view could not be the outcome of theoretical deliberations and formulations of ideals; it could only emerge spontaneously from the collective experience of the nation – in other words as a response to historical challenges taking the shape of a 'national character' and a binding normative system. In this sense the aim of Jewish nationalism was to achieve for the Jewish people a national territory, a homeland of their own, in which they would be free to organize themselves as they desired, and to lead their lives without being subjected to any outside pressures or influences. Despite this, Jabotinsky did not content himself with formulating draft platforms or incidental ideas in scattered newspaper articles. Instead he made a serious effort (for instance in his articles on 'Economic Theory') to formulate a broad and comprehensive world view, to try and meet the demand for what he called a scientific theory of Zionism.

Most Revisionists never doubted, however, that Revisionism possessed a detailed and comprehensive ideology covering any and all subjects, and that its world view formed a closed system providing satisfactory answers to all questions, and as such was capable of creating a self-evident national Jewish world. More than this, most of them had no doubt as to where the questions and the answers on virtually all these subjects were to be found: in the writings of Jabotinsky. Jabotinsky's articles, in particular those written during the 1920s and 1930s, were familiar to any contemporary reader. Party meetings, political discussions and newspaper articles were all devoted to the creation of an overall ideology.

Two Faces of the Right

Two ideological and political axioms distinguished the Revisionist movement from other political movements and parties within Zionism: the principle of the absolute and unconditional territorial integrity of Eretz Israel, and the principle of an openly-proclaimed desire to establish a sovereign state on that territory by political or military means. This is not to say that other Zionist circles did not at one time or another hold similar principles, or did not act to achieve them, but merely means that Revisionism and the Zionist Right were the only Zionist school whose position was firmly rooted in these axioms, and who never deviated from them for any political reason whatsoever.

It should be stressed once more, however, that a common definition of objectives (a Jewish state in Eretz Israel), or even a common definition of the ways and means by which these are to be realized, do not necessarily require a common intellectual and cultural basis, or, for that matter, identical visions and goals. The communality of ideas which existed within the Right was achieved by means of a consensus on certain major issues, but simultaneously there existed within the Right a wide gap between two widely different world views. During the 1930s Revisionism was divided into an 'old' Revisionism and a 'new' Revisionism, which was radical and messianic.

The division I have attempted is by necessity schematic, and disregards many subtle shadings of opinion and permutations, in addition to which I have accentuated contrasts for the sake of a clearer analysis. To some extent the division runs between the 'Westernism' and 'Slavophilism' in the Russian intellectual world of the second half of the nineteenth century. Both camps were characterized by deep controversies on numerous fundamental questions, and reflected two different utopias.[9]

The division into 'Westernized' Jews and 'autarkic', or 'authentic' Jews is not only arbitrary, but erroneous. Jabotinsky indeed openly and consciously borrowed ideas from European thinkers and philosophical schools, and his thinking betrayed historical-positivist and rationalist tendencies, but at times he dressed these up for pragmatic reasons in what he called 'Jewish philosophy'. The nationalist messianic current declared itself wholly anchored in an independent and authentic set of Jewish terms of reference, free of any influences alien to the Jewish spirit. However, a division of subjects with a common European-Jewish spiritual cultural background into absolute categories of 'European ideas' versus 'Jewish ideas' is not always a real historical distinction. Even so it can easily be shown that there are not only parallelisms and similarities, but also mutual influences and borrowings between 'Jewish-autarky', and the German idealist philosophical school, Russian Idealism and Polish messianic nationalism, to mention only the most important. All of the latter also claimed autarkic values for their particular world-views. Even so this deliberate rejection of certain 'European categories' does not mean that those concerned did not avail themselves of other European categories. On the contrary, those who opposed the rationalist and liberal foundations in Jabotinsky's thinking, speaking in the name of 'Jewish culture' instead, in the final analysis applied the same categories of criticism and 'utopian' characterization as used by the romanticists and mysticists of the European conservative tradition. In my opinion the messianic Right availed itself of European categories to define and interpret the elements of the 'new Jewish history and culture'. In the second part of this book I will devote considerable space to a discussion of these two aspects of the Right from the intellectual point of view.

The East European Background

We have already mentioned how *Betar* and *Ha-Zohar* were able to gain momentum and flourish in the climate of the new national states of Eastern Europe. These states formed the intimate environment in which their national and political culture had been shaped.

The majority of the members of the party and the youth organization had been born shortly before or after the First World War, and their formative period was the period between the two wars. The contemporary, not yet communist East European world was rent by fierce struggles between 'Right' and 'Left', and the pressures caused by the opposing aspirations of a number of contending nations, peoples and minorities. The emancipated Jews of Eastern Europe wanted to integrate in the surrounding political and social cultures of their environments – but not as individuals, or as a religious community. Neither did they want to assimilate and become an integral part of their surroundings. They wanted to belong, and to be able to live within these new multi-ethnic national frameworks as a distinct national minority with full and equal civic rights. This was a new, if not revolutionary form of integration and acculturization, which shortly met with fierce opposition from the surrounding society, and within a few years would prove to have been a tragic illusion. As the nationalism of the surrounding society grew in intensity, Jews began to be pushed to the periphery, even though many continued to delude themselves that integration would after all be possible.

Poland in particular was a representative example of the new national states. 'There were as many different Polands as there were people who cared to perceive it,'[10] and the Revisionists also had their own image of Poland, its character and power. Poland was for them the archetypical country of romantic nationalism. Jabotinsky once described the *Zeitgeist* in Poland prior to 1914 as reflecting a 'romantic and tragic' atmosphere. Between the two world wars Poland became caught up in an intensive process of nation-building and state-building; Poland was a country bursting with intense national inspiration, and the Polish national and political culture was the closest and most familiar example of a 'nation' and a 'state' for the publicity efforts of the Zionist Right. The Revisionists wanted to be 'national' in the same sense, and according to the same pattern, as their Polish surroundings, and they believed that they not only had the right, but possessed the all-embracing national heritage enabling them to do so. Polish nationalism (that is the nationalism of the Polish Right) became the model for the theory, the cult, the symbols, and the national aspirations. Much of the Revisionist literature and code of behaviour is modelled on Polish history, Polish values, and the Polish ethos and national existence. During the 1930s Poland was not only considered by Revisionists as a great and valuable political and military ally of Zionism, but it also became a model of inspiration to the ideology and praxis of political terrorism, armed underground struggle and political revolution. Marshal Pilsudski would become the model of the national and military leader; Adam Mickiewicz would be the model of the national, prophetic poet (=*wieszcz*).

The above interpretation of borrowing from and imitation of the surrounding culture, could also be explained in more coincidental terms, as the similar reaction of a similar type of nationalism with 'identical' qualities, living under a similar type of conditions – in other words, as an effort to resolve the contradictions between nationalist aspirations, to establish a state within historical borders, on the one hand, and the challenge of Socialism and Communism, and the desire to assist in the on-going struggle for the building of a national society, on the other. In light of the above, it is not surprising that many have drawn attention to the similarities between Revisionism and [European] fascism, describing Revisionism as 'Jewish fascism'. This characterization and its justification will be dealt with in a separate chapter.

At this point I would like to comment briefly on an additional internal division relating to the geographic and cultural origins of the Revisionist membership. There exists a difference between the founders of the political movement, most of whom belonged to the liberal nationalist Jewish intelligentsia which had emerged in Russia at the beginning of the twentieth century (to which in a sense should be added the graduates of the Russian gymnasia throughout the czarist Empire, whose language and culture was Russian), and the second generation of the leadership and most of the rank and file, who came from a Polish geographical and cultural background and who had been educated in Hebrew and Yiddish. However, Poland – particularly prior to the First World War - was not a single cultural entity, neither in the general nor the Jewish sense (following the war it underwent an intensive process of 'Polanization'). For instance, Jewish students learned at various kinds of gymnasia, both general and Jewish (the *Tarbut* educational network), or national religious schools (*Tahkemoni*), and the same situation prevailed in pre-revolutionary Russia. There is no doubt that there were differences in mentality between the two generations, but when we see that the leaders of the Revisionist 'radical' current, namely Achimeir and Katznelson, hailed from White Russia, the same region which produced, for instance, Berl Katznelson, one of the heads of the socialist Labour movement, we see that although geographical origins were important, they were not the causal factor of the emergence of the various streams and trends. In any case, as from 1925 the majority of the rank and file were nationals of countries outside the Soviet Union of 1917, and by then most of the Russian members had emigrated to Eretz Israel or settled in Western Europe as Jewish Zionist immigrants.

The prevailing image of the Zionist Right is that of an intellectual wilderness. The Right did not receive either support or sympathy in circles of the Jewish intelligentsia, or in the circles of writers and men of letters, who were more naturally inclined towards the ideology of the Labour movement. Even so it was not a lack of talent that caused the Right to take a secondary place in the process of the creation of a Hebrew culture, but rather the conservative nature of its cultural approach. Its writers and poets (with the exception of Uri Zvi Greenberg, the greatest of the contemporary Hebrew poets) were without exception inclined towards traditional and conservative genres, such as historical novels, epic literature, nationalist poetry, and so forth, which explains why they have remained marginal figures in the modern Hebrew literature which developed both inside and outside Eretz Israel. Despite this, the intellectual and creative elite of the Right was a suprising and exciting group of people, full of intellectual ferment, and with profound and multifarious, as well as contradictory, inspirations. In historical perspective this intellectual world, which has gone mainly unnoticed by the public (and researchers), is one of the most exciting aspects of the intellectual history of Zionism.

In the second part of this book I hope to present some of the aspects of this singular intellectual and cultural world. I will leave it to the reader to judge its quality, and the validity of its claims.

CHAPTER TWO

The Zionist Right between the Two World Wars and during the Mandatory Period (1925-1948)

A. THE POLITICAL HISTORY OF REVISIONISM: FORMATION AND GROWTH (1925-1933)

The Emergence of Revisionism

Up till the year 1925 the Zionist political system lacked a right wing. The majority of Zionists embraced liberal national views. The minority, which in course of time would become the dominant political force, had a national, socialist and constructivist outlook.[1] The right wing consisted of a conservative national religious party, the *Mizrachi*, founded at the beginning of the century, as well as various groups representing the 'middle classes' in Eretz Israel. *Mizrachi* was considered a clericalist party, whereas the bourgeois circles were leaning towards liberal social values. Actually, as early as the 1920s two kinds of social orientation could be discerned within this bourgeoisie, which went by the name of 'Civilian Bloc': a conservative and a liberal-progressive tendency. The first was represented mainly by village farmers (the inhabitants of the *moshavot*) and citrus growers, whereas the second group was composed of the urban intelligentsia and professionals. This last group showed a positive and supportive attitude towards the Labour movement, whereas the first fought its growing influence, particularly in the areas of local economics and labour relations. Prior to 1925 only one attempt was made in Eretz Israel to establish a political coalition with a well-defined 'rightist' political signature. Its founders included descendants of 'veteran' *yishuv* members, such as Itamar Ben-Avi (the son of Eliezer Ben-Yehuda), and representatives of the second generation from the old-established agrarian settlements, the *moshavot*, including Alexander Aaronsohn, the brother of the noted agricultural researcher Aaron Aaronsohn. Their group, the *Benei Benyamin* ('Sons of Benjamin'), failed to become a political force, nor did it succeed in generating a practical ideology.[2] There existed no formal or effective links between the 'rightist' organizations which emerged under the particular circumstances prevailing in Eretz Israel prior to and following the British occupation – except that they represented the interests of the well-established groups in the Jewish Palestinian society and economy – and the 'conservative' or 'liberal' Eastern European Zionist public. Although these 'liberal' groups shared several principles (among which a fear of the growing strength of the Left!), a common ideology or organization was not one of them. They faced many difficulties in their efforts to formulate a general ideology and to gain political power in Eretz Israel. The leading force in the Zionist movement was the 'Liberal Zionists', but they lacked a defined ideology.

The first manifestation of a declared rightist political programme in Zionism and in the *yishuv* dates from the year 1925, but at the time this newly-emerging political Right offered, as already mentioned, merely a 'new' political approach towards solving the main problems occupying the Zionist movement in Eretz Israel. Its appearance was principally a response to the crisis in Zionist policy in Palestine after 1920. At first this new political 'Right' was regarded neither as 'conservative' nor 'radical', but rather as a Jewish bourgeois manifestation. Neither did the Revisionists – at least until 1925 – view themselves as 'Right', and even the Left did not at first ascribe to them any 'rightist' characteristics. However, once their standpoints on various issues and their attitude to the Labour movement became clear, they soon found themselves labelled as 'the Right', or even 'Zionist fascist Right'.

Thus we see how during the 1920s the political structure of the Zionist movement was brought into line with that already existing in other Western societies, and how an anti-socialist, *völkisch* 'Right', rooted in the radicalist tendencies among the Jewish lower-middle class, emerged and became incorporated in the Zionist political culture. The way this public challenge of the hegemony and dominance of the Left on the political, ideological and intellectual level by a Zionist *avant-garde* which identified, and in turn was being identified, with Zionism as a whole, contributed to the crystallization of Revisionism and helped to cultivate and reinforce the rightist image, will be explained in more detail further on in this study.

The founding fathers of Revisionism, first and foremost Ze'ev Jabotinsky himself, made no pretence at novelty or ideological originality. Their self-image was not that of founders of a revolutionary new party; on the contrary, they considered themselves as having returned to the 'Zionist foundations' which had been laid by Herzl during the period 1897–1904 – hence also the term 'revisionism'. Neither did Jabotinsky in 1925 pretend to offer any comprehensive new theory of Jewish nationalism, or even any original social viewpoint. To him Revisionism chiefly meant the advocacy of certain political standpoints and a certain form of political behaviour, within the framework of a liberal Zionist world-view. However, the new movement developed faster than expected, and quite soon it became clear that there was a need for the formulation of a national philosophy and the definition of an identity of the new movement and its specific place within the Zionist movement. This development proved the correctness of the views of Weizmann and the leaders of the Labour movement that in the process of the realization of Zionism no distinction could be made between long-term and short-term goals, between questions of form and questions of substance, between diplomacy and politics, on the one hand, and the social structure of the Jewish society in Eretz Israel, on the other, and between politics and social values.

Jabotinsky was first joined by various groups of followers because he seemed to offer a new kind of leadership and a political alternative to the policies of Chaim Weizmann, an alternative that was thought to be capable of extricating Zionism from its crisis and the depression into which it had sunk. Jabotinsky appeared to offer operative solutions that would return Zionism to the 'Golden Age' of Herzl, the Balfour Declaration and the Jewish Legion. However, the massive enlistment of new members at the beginning of the 1930s was not only the result of the clarity and decisiveness of Jabotinsky's political stance, his fierce criticism of Zionist policy in every possible area, or to his infectious optimism. The tide swelled and overflowed because he offered the Jewish public a charismatic leadership, and because he reflected in a profound, albeit oversimplified, way the national and political aspirations of a wide Jewish public, and – almost magically – touched its innermost moods. It seemed as if a new leader had appeared who, like Herzl in his own days, was able to transform amorphous ideas and moods into a leading ideology and a practical political programme. Apart from this, there appeared to exist a correlation between explicit political demands, the national philosophy from which they derived their justification, and the methods that were suggested for their realization. In other words, a new kind of Zionism had made its appearance: dynamic, vibrant, and bursting with self-confidence.

One symptom of this process was the need for an 'original' and 'revolutionary' self-image. This new image played an overriding role in the creation of the self-identity and self-awareness of the Zionist Right. Besides stressing the elements of a 'restoration' of 'classical' Zionism, in other words the need for a 'revision', the main emphasis was placed on the new 'revolutionary' aspect of the Revisionist Zionist world-view.

A historian can show that on the theoretical plane the 'Right' offered very little in the way of original ideas (the messianic Right would propose, as we will see later on, new and 'revolutionary' principles), but originality often is not an important feature of an active political ideology. Important is that the new movement made a systematic attempt to combine various principles derived from diverse sources within an organic, operative framework, which for large numbers of people became a profound faith, and from which emerged a stable and enduring political tradition.

The Semantic Problem

The right-wing political party which was founded in 1925 is generally known as the Revisionist party (or Revisionist movement), although this name is neither accurate nor satisfactory. The very fact that even the name by which the organized political and ideological Zionist Right was to be known formed the subject of controversy and confusion, is indicative of the kind of problem with which we are dealing, as well as of the different self-images which prevailed within it. The new political party, founded in Paris in 1925 by Ze'ev Jabotinsky and a group of veteran Zionist leaders called itself *Berit Ha-Zohar* –the Union of Zionist Revisionists. It was a political movement which delegated representatives to the Zionist Congress, as well as to the Elected Assembly in Eretz Israel, and which in organizational terms showed all the features of an incipient political party. Due to the fact that its programme spoke of a 'revision' of Zionist policy, in the sense of a return to the principles and policies of Herzl ('Herzlian Zionism'), it called itself also the 'Revisionist party', its ideology 'Revisionism', and its members 'Revisionists'.[3] From 1925 onwards the terms 'Revisionist policy', 'Revisionist ideology', and even 'Revisionist mentality' and 'personality' came into popular use as slogans and stereotypes (in both the positive and

negative sense), as well as becoming the 'battle-cry' of the Revisionists.

Side by side with the party as such, the years 1924–1927 saw
the establishment of the *Betar* (the acronym of *Berit Trumpeldor*)
youth organization.[4] The interrelationship between *Betar* and
Ha-Zohar will be analysed later on, but it is worth mentioning here
that not all those who joined *Betar* were also members of *Ha-Zohar*,
or even considered themselves 'Revisionists'. Due to the fact that
during the 1930s ideological and organizational tensions arose
between the party and its leaders on the one hand, and the youth
movement on the other (and in later years between the party and the
underground IZL movement), the members of *Betar* and the IZL
considered the name 'Revisionist movement' as applying only to
those who were formal members of the political party, whereas
they themselves preferred the name 'Jabotinsky's movement' (or
'Jabotinsky's disciples'), after Ze'ev Jabotinsky, the originator and
mentor of the movement, whom they regarded as their founding-
father, leader, ideological guide, and even prophet. In this way
to all practical purposes they severed the connections with the
other party officials, retaining their connection with the one and
only 'primordial father'. Another expression frequently employed
among the members was 'national movement', due to their prevailing view of the Revisionist movement as the only 'truly pure national
movement' within Zionism (in contradistinction, of course, to the
'class-oriented' Left).

From this it follows that the label Revisionism to describe the
overall intellectual, ideological and political tradition of the years
1925–1948 with which we are dealing here, is somehow inadequate.
It will be used in this study mainly for the sake of convenience. The
name covers *Ha-Zohar, Betar* and other organizations and groups
connected in various ways with the Revisionist 'centre'. The complicated relationships between the IZL, Lehi and Revisionism will
be discussed further on.

Revisionism, as a political party, continued to exist until 1949.
Following the establishment of the *'Herut ('Freedom') Movement*,
founded by the IZL (Etzel), the *Irgun Zeva'i Leumi* as an independent political party, *Ha-Zohar* activists participated in the elections
with their own list, and were soundly beaten.[5] With this the history
of *Ha-Zohar* had come to an end – but not that of Revisionism or
Jabotinsky's movement.

From Political Faction to Political Mass Movement

Let us return to the beginning.

The Revisionist movement originated during the middle of the 1920s out of a meeting between a well-known Zionist leader, Ze'ev (Vladimir) Jabotinsky and two Zionist activist circles, namely a group of veteran Zionist activists centred around the Russian-language Zionist journal *Razsvet* ('Dawn'), which at the time was published in Berlin (but in December 1924 moved to Paris), and a group of Jewish students, members of the National Student Union in the Latvian capital Riga. These activist Zionist members of the Russian intelligentsia were critical of the Zionist leadership under Chaim Weizmann and propagated an activist political stance.[6] Within a short time the group found itself at the head of a political party and a sizeable political movement, whereas the student group evolved into the nucleus of a new Zionist youth organization. Under the leadership of Jabotinsky the two organizations became a mass movement, and launched an effort to capture the Jewish Zionist public, as well as taking over the Zionist Congress and the leadership of the Jewish settlers in Eretz Israel.

It took Jabotinsky two years to change from a member of the Zionist Executive in his own right into the leader of a new political faction. In his capacity of a member of the Executive during the years 1921–23 Jabotinsky had continuously criticized Zionist policy, which according to him destroyed the existing positive foundations of the present and future cooperation between Great Britain and Zionism. It was his opinion that the Executive permitted anti-Zionist British officials to undermine the very principles upon which the Mandate was based. His criticism created a great deal of resentment, not only because of its style, but because he failed to suggest any practical ways of changing British policies. He was therefore considered guilty of gross over-simplification. The creation of the national home, his critics pointed out, would be the end of a long journey, arduous and grey, and there simply could be no dramatic shortcuts. His colleagues in the Zionist Executive regarded him as someone who was incapable of working within a framework of collective responsibility, but only on his own, or at the head of a group of fervent admirers. He did not accept the leadership of Weizmann, and after it had become clear that he could not implement official tasks the way it suited him, but that he was expected to subject them to collective decision making, he saw no other possibility but to resign. This resignation would have far-reaching consequences for the history of Zionism, for before long this 'lone wolf' in Zionist politics was to become the leader of a mass-movement.

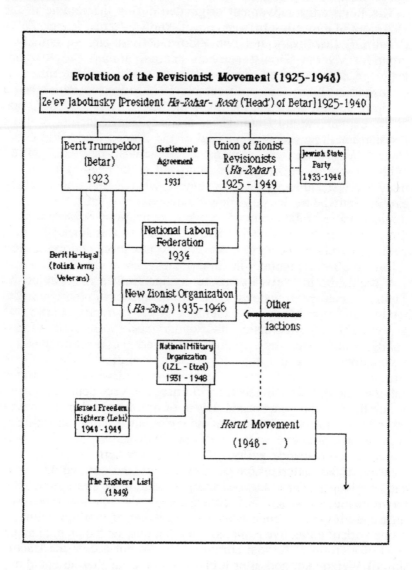

The tensions were of a personal as well as political nature, and on 8 January 1923 Jabotinsky sent a letter tendering his resignation from the Zionist Executive. In his letter he wrote that only those who fought incessantly and stubbornly for their legitimate rights would ultimately be understood, respected and accepted by the British people.[7] Jabotinsky next resorted to writing a spate of articles in the *Jewish Chronicle* and *Razsvet*, dealing with a systematic exposition of his political views. He withdrew from Zionist affairs, restricting himself for the meantime to literary activity only. Even so, despite his aesthetic reservations about political life, he was unable to stay away from it, apart from which considerable pressure was exerted on him. In 1924, on his return to Berlin from a lecture tour in the newly-established Baltic states, he already had the feeling that a legion stood behind him, that his principles were being accepted by a wide public, and that it was therefore time to roll up his sleeves and go into action. Jabotinsky chose the pages of *Razsvet* to formulate the programme for his new faction. In November 1924 he was ready to try and establish the 'true Herzlian movement', and he began rallying its supporters.

Starting as a small faction with four delegates to the 14th Zionist Congress in 1925, *Ha-Zohar* grew into a mass movement and one of the large parties in the Zionist world. From 1925 onwards *Ha-Zohar* began to play a pivotal role in the struggles within the Zionist movement and the Jewish community in Eretz Israel, leaving its mark on a variety of dramatic political and other events. In practice Jabotinsky found himself as from 1925 treading the same path that 43 years before him had been walked by Benjamin Ze'ev Herzl, the trailblazer of Zionism as an organized political mass movement. From a lone wolf on the political stage, from a journalist on current affairs, a member of the Zionist intelligentsia who wrote articles on political and cultural subjects, and initiated independent initiatives, he turned into the charismatic leader of an organized mass movement. He actually needed such a movement as an organized hinterland for his public political activities. Already in the 1920s the Zionist movement was profoundly politicized, and it had no room for a political leader relying merely on personal connections and public approval. On 4 August 1925 Jabotinsky wrote to one of his friends in Eretz Israel that Revisionism was not a mood or a collection of ideas, however correct they might be. Revisionism, he wrote, had to be an organized political movement 'with organized branches in every important location, with offices and administrative workers, as well as party funds – I will not agree to any external "action", and I will oppose any attempts at "playing a role" in Zionism and "influencing" the public. I have had enough of boisterousness *à la masse*, or "sounding the attack" while there is no army and no tents and not a single rifle barrel. For twelve months we will work in silence, and do nothing but get our forces into shape – and only when we are finished shall we enter the fray with a strength and a degree of organization such as the Jewish public has never seen before."[8]

Before long it became clear that a political movement was not merely a matter of organization, offices, resources (material necessities which Revisionism through the years did indeed try its utmost to obtain and maintain). A political mass movement in the modern sense means, among other things, the creation of a symbol system and a liturgy accompanying a collective national political culture. Leading a political mass movement of this kind required the ability to offer not only a set of theoretical political principles, but a comprehensive ideology, as well as immediate solutions to a Jewry in distress. The course of Revisionism was determined not only by its formative ideas, but by the type and kind of public from which it derived its power and in whose name it acted and spoke, as well as from the political patterns and its social and political involvement as an oppositional mass movement. The tensions between 'pure' political objectives and principles, the patterns of political involvement, the symbol system and the liturgy gradually became the principal determinant for the nature of the tensions within Revisionism as a political framework, and as such determined its image and its internal history. These tensions had existed from the movement's inception, but they were accentuated and intensified in course of time as a natural result of the expansion of the movement, and due to the historical circumstances and the Revisionist response to the changing circumstances.

The Demographic Development – A General Outline

Between the two world wars the Zionist movement received a demographic impetus, which resulted in its striking deep roots within the Jewish world. Revisionism emerged against the background of a revolutionary change of Zionism as a whole into a popular movement. Revisionism contributed in a large measure to this Zionist demographic impetus, since it addressed itself to the Jewish public at large, which had previously refused to identify with Zionism, having failed to find in it answers to its afflictions and disposition.

Some figures will illustrate this numerical growth. The principal yardstick for the growth of Revisionism is the voting strength of *Ha-Zohar* during the elections to the Zionist Congresses between 1925 and 1935. From 1935 onwards this yardstick is the number of votes for *Ha-Zach*, the 'New Zionist Organization', which had been founded in that same year, even though we should take into account that the voting criteria for *Ha-Zach* were less strict than that of the voting system used in the 'old' federation (where the right to vote had to be acquired by buying the 'Zionist *shekel*'). To these figures must be added several tens of thousands of *Betar* members who were too young to participate in the elections to the Congress (and the Elected Assembly in Palestine).

The number of votes for *Ha-Zohar* between the years 1927 and 1933 was as follows:

1927	8,446	out of a total of	123,729 votes cast
1929	18,000	out of a total of	200,000 votes cast
1931	55,848	out of a total of	233,730 votes cast
1933	99,729	out of a total of	555,113 votes cast

Some 450,000 Revisionists voted at the founding convention of *Ha-Zach* in 1935 – in addition to some 300,000 non-Revisionist voters. At the end of the 1920s approximately 10,000 members were enrolled in the ranks of *Betar*, a number that had swelled to 70,000–80,000 on the eve of the Second World War. This no doubt impressive growth within such a short period of time was mainly due to the enrolment of new members in Poland and the Baltic states (Latvia, Lithuania and Estonia), the heartland of the Revisionist movement.[9] Given the importance of Poland as the hub and the heart of Revisionism, it is appropriate that this specific Polish background be discussed in more detail, even though some of its features have been mentioned previously in our discussion of the political and cultural background of the Zionist Right.

The Demographic Growth of Revisionism in Poland

One of the major manifestations of the modernization process of Eastern European Jewry was the profound politicization of Jewish society. Zionism was only one of its expressions, and one of the factors leading to this politicization, which resulted in the emergence of a plethora of political parties (ranging from the communist Left, via the Bund, up to an orthodox party, *Agudat Israel*) and a wide range of political activities.[10] The Jews in the above-mentioned countries enjoyed considerable political freedom, both in the autonomous Jewish sphere, and within the framework of their overall national existence. This political freedom allowed the Jewish parties, including the Zionists, a very considerable freedom of action, which contributed to their expansion and enabled the use of almost all the instruments of modern politics, including propaganda, the popular press, party-political meetings and popular elections, which at times even culminated in violent encounters.

In addition to exploiting this freedom for public political activity, Revisionism enjoyed the backing of the Polish authorities, who saw in it a convenient ally for encouraging large-scale Jewish emigration from Poland. As already mentioned, Revisionism absorbed the nationalist Polish atmosphere through the schools and the public mood, and received assistance from the Polish authorities in the organization of semi-military training for *Betar* youths, as well as (from 1938 onwards) in organizing illegal immigration, the supply of arms, and the training of experienced guerilla cadres. Only in Poland was *Ha-Zohar* allowed to convene mass election meetings in the 600–700 cities and towns in which the approximately three million Polish Jews lived, to hold semi-military parades in the streets and squares, and to feel not as a persecuted national minority, but as a national movement waiting for the signal to uproot themselves from the Slavic countries and move to Eretz Israel.

Abba Achimeir described the flourishing of Revisionism in Poland as a self-evident socio-cultural phenomenon. Revisionism, he wrote, was by nature an urban type of nationalism, inasmuch as its leaders were mostly journalists and lawyers whose natural cultural environment was the city.

During the years prior to World War II, he described Jewish Warsaw as being

> full of leaders of *Ha-Zohar* and the Palestinian *Betar*. The number of *Ha-Zohar* and *Betar* functionaries returning to Poland at that time exceeded the number of functionaries of the movement emigrating to Eretz Israel . . . why did *Ha-Zohar* and *Betar* party functionaries emigrate to Warsaw? – [because of] the magic of the masses. During the 1930s and 1940s the *yishuv* lacked what is popularly called 'the masses'. The contemporary *yishuv* had a surfeit of physicians, lawyers, teachers – from kindergarten to secondary school level – shopkeepers, and above all: party activists. What was missing was 'the common man'. In Nalevki and the surrounding streets

of Warsaw there lived at that time more Jews than in the whole of Eretz Israel.[11]

The rapid growth of Revisionism in Poland and the Baltic states will be evident from the following figures: the number of *shekels* purchased, and the data on the number of voters to the Zionist Congresses for the years 1931, 1933 and 1935 in Poland and the Baltic are an unequivocal illustration of the extent of demographic growth of the Zionist movement as a whole, and the relative strength of Revisionism within the Zionist movement in particular. During the elections to the 17th Congress in 1931 283,230 votes were cast, among which 72,550 in Poland and 59,756 in the two Galician regions. The Labour bloc (The *Union of Poalei Zion* and the *Hitachdut*) received 37,789 votes in Poland and in Western and Eastern Galicia (of which 22,487 in Poland proper) and 18,513 in Eretz Israel. The Revisionists received 29,985 votes in Poland and the two Galicias (of which 20,496 in Poland) and 5,024 in Eretz Israel. During the elections for the 18th Congress in 1933 the Labour bloc received 123,913 votes in Poland and the two Galicias, of which 91,055 votes in Poland proper, in addition to 20,584 votes in Eretz Israel. The Revisionists received 74,730 votes in Poland and the two Galicias (48,871 in Poland itself), and 6,888 votes in Eretz Israel. In these decisive 1933 elections a total of 535,113 voters participated, of whom 214,398 in Poland proper, and 318,842 voters if we include the two Galicias; the total Palestinian vote amounted to 59,564. The Labour movement increased its share of the total vote from 75,801 to 226,058; more than half of the increase was gained in Poland, as was the case with the Revisionists, most of whose additional votes (more than two-thirds in fact) were obtained in Poland. The growing centrality of Poland is also apparent from the fact that, whereas at the 17th Congress Eretz Israel sent 39 delegates and Poland 33, at the 18th Congress Eretz Israel was represented with 50 delegates against Poland's 87 – or 131 delegates if the two Galicias are included.[12]

The nurturing of political hopes which lacked any substance was in fact typical of the tense atmosphere prevailing at the end of the 1930s. The expectations of a speedy national redemption received a messianic Frankist expression in the eschatological poetry of the great poet Uri Zvi Greenberg, which depicted millions of Jews crossing Poland and the Black Sea on their way to Eretz Israel in the footsteps of the messiah-saviour whose coming was surely imminent:

Whence will he come? From the Arch of Titus in Rome, or
from Nalevki's in Warsaw will his voice be heard?
And he will be as a lion arising in the *yishuv*, the Black Sea to his
right and the Baltic Sea to his left . . .
Hassidim will rush to immerse themselves, hastily donning
their Sabbath dress on an ordinary weekday. They, their
wives, their children, with quickened pace will go
to welcome him and feel his precious hand in their palm.
['He will surely come . . .', *Ha-Medina*, Warsaw, March 1938]

In 1934 a hostile critic, Nahum Sokolow, at that time President
of the Zionist Organization (during the interlude following the
removal of Chaim Weizmann from the presidency during the years
1931–1935) gave a highly sarcastic description of the – as he saw it –
phantasmagoric picture of Revisionist activity in Poland:

Among every other nation in the world this aspect is secondary
to historical vision, and central to something which exists and
stands in some organizational and essential connection with
reality, with the country in which the people live, with the
defence of the motherland, with the potential and capacity on
the battlefield and in the military campaign. While for us (the
Jews) all this is so much 'hocus-pocus'. For nobody in his
wildest imagination could conceive that this Legion could ever
rise up and fight against Britain, the Arab world, Islam ... or
anybody else. And it is this absurdity which is so attractive and
stimulating: *Credo quia absurdum* ('I believe it because it is
absurd'). And this is where the faith of fools lends a hand: this
is where the nonsensical and all-important personality cult
comes into play. Most amazing and surprising tales are being
spread about the genius-commander, about the Napoleonic
strategic talents of a man who has almost definitely never spent
a day on the battleground or known the smell of gunpowder. A
new Shabbetai Zeviism has appeared in the world, or more
accurately – a new Frankism (the later Polish form of this
delusion) in the form of the conspiracy and its attributes which
capture young hearts by means of militaristic mystery and its
superior, inferior, and ultra-superior beings, and its discipline,
which starts off in the form and dress of sport and ends in what
looks more and more like a comic army. This militarization
does not end with marches and parades and bugles and flags
and so forth, the ludicrous spectacles of show and entertain-

ment, of quixotic delusions of greatness – it is also penetrating and attacking the entire internal organization . . . .[13]

This harshly critical description, although acknowledging the plight which had caused the emergence and development of Revisionism, nevertheless places the main emphasis on the illusionary and populistic nature of the Revisionist programme. Revisionism was characterized as a mood, rather than a realistic political option; as the manifestation of an abnormal political culture arising from an abnormal reality.

Between Populism and Elitism: the Ethos of the 'Common Jew'

One dominant aspect of the situation in Poland as a result of this heterogeneous demographic growth must be mentioned here in particular. This is the tension between common populism and *avant-garde* elitism.

A political party which aims at attracting a mass following, and which sees itself as expressing the survival needs of these masses, is forced to come up with immediate solutions to the acute plight of these masses. This is exactly what Revisionism attempted to achieve by its declaration that, if only it would stand at the head of the Zionist movement, it would be able to found a Jewish state in the near future, and until such a time to secure the rights of the common man – and not only those of the so-called 'pioneers', the elite groups – to emigrate to Eretz Israel. Jabotinsky appeared as the spokesman for the Jewish plight. To back up his policy and diplomacy an organized mass movement was a necessity. But the transformation of Revisionism into a mass movement in Poland turned it by necessity into an amorphous organization. Revisionism was radical in its fundamental Zionist demands, but minimalist in the duties it imposed upon its party members. The principal obligation was to believe in Revisionist fundamentals, and to support the movement and the party. The members were not required to prepare themselves for immediate immigration to Eretz Israel, or to learn a needed profession. Neither were they required to look upon *aliyah* as a personal duty, that should be performed unconditionally as soon as the right moment presented itself.[14]

This minimalism, and the amorphous mass-movement character, caused an ambivalent reaction among the party radicals who embraced an elitist view. On the one hand they quite appreciated the point that Revisionism represented the pure and natural kind of

Zionism of the 'common Jew' (in contrast to the what they called the 'rootlessness and exaggerated intellectualism' of the socialist parties); on the other hand they observed with considerable concern the expansion of the movement and the enrolment of sizeable numbers of Jews in whom the fiery flame of nationalism and Zionist activism seemed to be entirely absent. Throughout the 1930s we find the radicals complaining bitterly about the lack of clarity and the obscurantism which enveloped the Revisionist movement due to the inclusion of thousands of what they called 'General Zionists'. The radicals contended that multitudes do not make a liberation movement: not the Jewish masses will solve the plight of the Jews; only a revolutionary militant elite can bring salvation. The tension between the two camps – the 'multitude-believers' and the elitists – was ideological as well as organizational and a matter of mentality, and it created both internal conflicts and far-reaching compromises in the political history of Revisionism, serving as a spur to many areas of Revisionist activity. The clearest example of this is that while Jabotinsky stood at the side of *Zion Sejm*, the organization of the 'parliament of the distressed', meaning a representation of the Jewish masses in Poland intended to exercise pressure on Great Britain, the 'conspiratorial cells' of the IZL in Poland developed into an elitist underground organization which aimed at conquering Eretz Israel by force.

The Growth of Revisionism in Palestine

In Eretz Israel the role of Revisionism was played out against the background of the formation of an overall modern Jewish national society. Hence the decisive importance of the history of Revisionism in Eretz Israel, despite the fact that from a demographic point of view Revisionism was not a dominant factor in the society. The rate of demographic growth in Eretz Israel was slower than that in Poland, partly due to the policy underlying the distribution of immigration certificates, which were allocated according to a party key, which mainly limited the immigration of Revisionists, in particular *Betar* members, without reference to the disproportionate growth of the latter movement. In the year 1927 *Ha-Zohar* in Eretz Israel received 2,687 votes in the elections to the Zionist Congress, whereas in the elections to the 17th Congress in 1931 the party received 5,000 votes (i.e. 10% of all the votes cast for the Congress). A more accurate yardstick for the voting strength of *Ha-Zohar* in the *yishuv* are the election returns of the Elected

Assembly, the representative organ of the Jewish settlers in mandatory Palestine. On 6 December 1925 the *Ha-Zohar* list received 2,489 votes and 15 seats out of the 201 seats in the Assembly (6.1%). In the 1931 elections *Ha-Zohar* won 10,189 votes, including the 2,121 votes of a separate Sephardi list. *Ha-Zohar* itself therefore received 8,068 votes (16.0 % of the total), and 11 seats, whereas the list of Jabotinsky's supporters from the oriental (Sephardi) community added another 5 seats, or 4.2% of the total vote. The total Revisionist share in the 1931 elections amounted therefore to 20.2%.[15]

Several factors contributed to the growing centrality of Revisionism in Eretz Israel:

1. The movement in Eretz Israel was forced to come to grips with and adapt to the reality of the special conditions prevailing in mandatory Palestine. Its involvement in the daily existence of the *yishuv* could not, therefore, remain limited to political activities alone. Eretz Israel lacked the settled Jewish masses crowded together in the centres of big cities such as Warsaw or Lodz; in Eretz Israel Revisionism had to contend with organizational problems and the absorption and acclimatization of an immigrant population. The political power of the autonomous *yishuv* was a function of the party's ability to establish organs for extending mutual social and medical assistance, employment services, job protection, and so forth. The requirements associated with this kind of organization, in other words intensive involvement with the social as well as economic aspects of daily life, confronted Revisionism in Eretz Israel with special problems, which among other things deepened the controversy between the rival movements − *Ha-Zohar* and Mapai − transplanting them from the political and ideological sphere to the area of everyday socio-economic existence, and a no-holds-barred struggle for employment opportunities.

2. From the beginning of the 1930s Revisionist immigration, for the main part the legal and illegal immigration of *Betar* members, strengthened the movement in Eretz Israel, giving rise to a militant spirit. There was a growing feeling within the movement that Revisionism found itself at the centre of historic Zionist events, and (particularly after 1930 − the year of the establishment of Mapai) that it was in Eretz Israel where the real struggle for the leadership and dominance of the Zionist movement

would be fought, and where the fate of the *yishuv* and Zionism
would be determined.

3. After 1929 the focus of the main political activities gradually
shifted to Eretz Israel. This explains the feeling of the leadership
in Eretz Israel that it stood at the centre of political developments
no less than the office of the World Executive in London.

4. The maximalists in Eretz Israel had come to the conclusion that
effective pressure on the British mandatory authorities – and
therefore on Britain – could only be applied in Eretz Israel. Since
Great Britain was concerned about its position in the Middle
East, whereas it was entirely unconcerned about the fate of the
Jews of Poland, and it would hardly be impressed by moral
actions such as the 'Petition', only rebellion, civil disobedience,
and ultimately underground activity and terror would create the
necessary pressure to influence political decisions.

5. After 1930, the year in which Mapai was established and began
its march towards hegemony in the *yishuv* and the Zionist
Organization, the 'maximalists' decided that the way to 'take
over the Congress' was not through Warsaw or Basel, but only
through Eretz Israel, which was the power centre of the Labour
movement. 'Taking over the Congress' meant undermining the
foundations on which the power of Mapai rested and, more
specifically, weakening the strength of the General Federation
of Jewish Labour, the 'Histadrut'. Gaining allies within Zionism
and in the *yishuv* necessitated an all-out struggle for the benefit
of the economic interests of the bourgeois circles, which also
meant the national Zionist interest. A struggle for the economic
interests of the Jewish middle class could only be fought in Eretz
Israel.

6. A new breed of young and influential Revisionists had come to
the fore in Eretz Israel. There is no doubt that Jabotinsky was
'first among equals', but during the early 1930s Achimeir, Yevin
and Greenberg nevertheless questioned his leadership. The
political personalities in Eretz Israel did not merit the same
admiration as Jabotinsky, but figures such as Jacob and
Avraham Weinshal, Dr. Ze'ev Von Weisl, the most flamboyant
in this group, Aryeh Altman, Eliahu Ben-Horin, Baruch Weinstein, Joseph Katzenelson, Ephraim Washitz and others constituted a rising force in the movement, which protested the
senior status of the veterans' group comprising Tiomkin, Lichtheim, Grossman, Schechtman, Zaltzman and others based in
London and Paris. The leadership group in Eretz Israel, which

was in itself not uniform in its ideas and conceptions, was during the middle thirties actively supported by the rising young leadership of *Betar* in Poland, which included among others Menachem Begin, Nathan Friedman-Yellin and Israel Scheib, who had protested the status of the veteran leadership of *Betar* under Aharon Zevi Propes and Benyamin Lubotzky. The fierce internal conflicts among the groups in Eretz Israel contributed to the weakening of the position of local Headquarters, preventing it from gaining more influence. These disputes enabled the World Executive of *Ha-Zohar* (as well as *Betar* World Headquarters) to intervene in the events in Eretz Israel and to participate in the debates between the 'moderates' (including Altman, Avniel, Rosov and Weinstein), the 'activists' (including Von Weisl, Ben-Horin and Jacob Weinshal), and the 'maximalists' (Yevin and Achimeir). The moderate faction received the backing of the World Executive, at which the activists and maximalists appealed against the authority of the centre. The split in 1933 weakened the position of the moderates in the World Executive, as well in the Central Committee in Eretz Israel.

As against this there were a number of social and organizational reasons why Revisionism – in contrast to the Labour movement – did not establish its principal social and political centre in Eretz Israel. Among these were:

1. The sheer organizational strength in 1930 of the Mapai coalition, which had been established almost a generation before the appearance of the Revisionist movement. As a result Mapai possessed considerable political influence and wielded substantial social and economic power within the *yishuv*. Upon its appearance Revisionism found itself confronted with a rival movement 25 years its senior, which in the meantime had succeeded in creating a close affinity with the leadership of the *yishuv*.

2. Revisionism in Eretz Israel lacked a homogeneous class structure; neither did it possess a plentiful and continuous stream of new immigrants whose social and economic absorption could be tackled in an organized manner. The working class was organized within a tight, centralized framework, whereas the middle class not only lacked any form of central organization, but showed neither the motivation, nor the drive to undertake steps towards greater centralization. The Left presented co-ordinated positions on political, social and economic issues; no

such integration of points of view took place within the Right.

3. Up till 1934, but to an important extent also later, the Revisionists lacked social and economic power bases within the *yishuv* society comparable to *Hevrat Ha-ovedim*, the Labour movement's economic roof organization, *Kupat Holim*, the *Histadrut* sick fund, and other branches of the General Federation of Jewish Labour.

4. In terms of organization *Ha-Zohar* in Eretz Israel suffered from a chronic structural weakness and an individualistic frame of mind within the movement, which prevented the crystallization of a collective orientation and a centralized party structure.

5. Its emphasis on the vital importance of the activities among the Jewish masses in Eastern Europe, blinded the movement to the importance of treating the development of the Jewish economy in Eretz Israel as a primary objective, compared to which political principles and objectives had to be relegated to the background.

6. The Palestinian movement was weakened by the fact that Jabotinsky lived outside Eretz Israel, following his expulsion in 1929, and that he was forbidden to return there. As a result the centre of political authority moved to wherever Jabotinsky moved.

Although Ha-Zohar in Eretz Israel did develop a specific local outlook, until 1944 – the year in which the IZL finally severed its connections with the party organs – the party enjoyed only secondary status within the World Movement.

The Centres of Policy Making and Sources of Finance

To these two demographic and social nuclei which have been discussed so far – the Eastern European centre, focused on Poland, and that in Eretz Israel – should be added several other centres which had a very different character, and which fulfilled very different functions. We are referring primarily to the political centres of *Ha-Zohar* located in Paris and London. In these two capitals the heads of the movement resided, several of whom were for extended periods cut off from the general Jewish public in Eastern Europe, and who operated as typical emigré expatriate groups occupying themselves with publishing newspapers and propaganda material, and with diplomatic activity. Here, in Paris, London and Geneva (the headquarters of the League of Nations) Revisionist diplomacy tried to translate Jewish distress and

Revisionist ideology into practical political issues, while being geographically – if not spiritually – remote from the everyday troubles of Polish Jewry, believing that Revisionist diplomacy would be powerful enough to effect a change in British policy. All this activity was very intense, resulting in countless meetings, a semblance of activity, as well as promises – none of which amounted to anything. British policy was incapable of being changed from Warsaw, Geneva, Bucharest or Rome.

Intensive contacts were maintained between the various centres, but the geographical decentralization nevertheless proved to be a weakness, since it produced differences in atmosphere and mind set, which in turn resulted in rivalries and tensions, which required Jabotinsky's authority to iron out.

Worth noting in this context is the dispersal and the geographical distances between the main centres and the territorial centres of the movement, which hampered the management of the movement's activities and the World Executive's control over the territorial centres. The heads of the movement, first and foremost Jabotinsky himself, frequently complained of the difficulties encountered in trying to handle from Europe the problems of the movement in Eretz Israel. There also was a great deal of coming and going between the main centres. When the World Executive moved to London, three out of the nine members continued to live in Paris. (Jabotinsky, Tiomkin and Trivus lived in Paris, while Grossman, Lichtheim, Machover, Schwartzman and Engel lived in London.) This is how the 'Paris group' and the 'London group' developed in the World Executive.

The Revisionist movement lacked capital or material assets, either directly or indirectly. Fund raising campaigns were not very successful, and the movement did not possess sufficient economic assets to generate the necessary working capital. Membership fees were low, and one of the few people of means who assisted *Ha-Zohar* with contributions was the Vilna-born South-African millionaire Michael Heschel. The movement in Eretz Israel was supported by a handful of property owners. Jabotinsky complained incessantly about the financial impotence of the movement, considering this the main reason for its lack of success. This shortage of liquidity prevented the movement from setting up a permanent administrative organization, and until the middle of the 1930s it was unable to establish economic enterprises or mutual aid societies in Eretz Israel which could have helped to attract new members to the movement. According to *Ha-Zohar*'s leadership in Eretz Israel, many of the movement's supporters joined the socialist *Histadrut*, to avail themselves of its medical and welfare services. Characteristically, the worker in Eretz Israel who joined the Revisionists found himself exposed to hostile attitudes. When taking into account the additional economic and social hardships he suffered, it becomes clear that his affiliation with the party could only be due to a deep attachment and ideological identification. From an organizational point of view the party was therefore somewhat of a 'skeleton party'. The number of registered members far exceeded the number of party adherents and voters. In contrast to this rather shaky and skeletal organization of a party with countless anonymous voters, *Betar* had a far more comprehensive organization with tighter internal discipline, coupled with a greater activist awareness and organic unity, facts which were to prove of great importance for the future struggle for hegemony within the movement.

The Sources of Power

So much for the factors accounting for the weakness of the movement. However, there were also factors — apart from ideological ones — which contributed to uniting the movement and its constituent parts. These were:

1. The personality of the founder and leader, Ze'ev Jabotinsky, whose authority and influence permeated the movement, in particular the members of *Betar* and the 'anonymous' voters. Quite a number voted for or joined *Ha-Zohar* because of their admiration for the personality of Jabotinsky.

2. Ideological education, mainly through publications in various languages, principally Hebrew and Yiddish, in addition to verbal indoctrination in the course of lecture tours. The movement's leaders covered the length and breadth of Poland, from city to city, and from town to town, and Revisionist literature is replete with accounts of these arduous journeys. Struggles for the control of newspapers were to a large extent due to the primary importance attached to propaganda, and the centrality of ideological identification.

3. Literature, and in particular poetry, influenced the movement and — through their role in the creation of ideology, symbols and a value system — contributed to the formation of the Revisionist sub-culture. Nationalist political poetry and literature had a particularly strong influence on the evolution and reinforcement

of the maximalist revolutionary stream in Revisionism. The poetry of Uri Zvi Greenberg probably had a more powerful ideological impact on its readers than anything ever written in modern Hebrew.

4. At no time did the movement develop a layer of 'professional' party workers with its attendant unwieldy bureaucratic apparatus, living off the party coffers or organizations with which it was ideologically connected. This undoubtedly influenced the fact that the majority of those who were active on behalf of the movement belonged to the intelligentsia or the free professions: lawyers, journalists, teachers, physicians, and so forth – people whose relative economic security gave them the required freedom of movement.

5. From the moment of its foundation Revisionism had been expanding numerically and demographically. In the course of the years many established groups as well as individuals joined its ranks. Jabotinsky at times was uneasy and worried about this growth, whereas at other times he appeared pleased, regarding it as a symbol of the singularity of the 'classless nationalism' of Revisionism. Various groups struggled for domination of the formal framework of the movement, either from inside the formal structure, or from the outside, in an attempt to influence the system and the membership as a whole. The paradox in the history of Revisionism is characterized by the profound tension between its weaker and stronger elements. Revisionism was established as a mass-movement, but its influence on the evolution of Zionist history carried the imprint of its organizational elite, in particular the the IZL and its leader, rather than that of the rank and file. As such, the plight of the Jewish masses had little or no influence on its policies.

The Formal Structure of Ha-Zohar

The formal structure of *Ha-Zohar* underwent only slight changes between 1925 and 1933. After 1935 an attempt was made to broaden the framework, and to transform *Ha-Zohar* into the central party within a new multi-party Zionist federation.

The highest forum in the Revisionist Zionist Federation was the World Council, which convened every one or two years. The World Council was composed of delegates from the various territorial branches, who were elected by the local councils. The World Council elected 15 members of the supreme council of *Ha-*

Zohar (the World Executive), whereas the territorial branches elected 25 members to the Executive. The full council elected the World Leadership (the World Executive) and the members of the various departments (the Political Department, the Budget Department, the Settlement Department, and so forth). *Ha-Zohar* was headed by a President, assisted by a Vice-President and a General Secretary. From 1925 till 1928 the World Executive was located in Paris; from there, under the presidency of Lichtheim, it moved to Berlin for a year, after which in 1929 it transferred to London under the leadership of Vice-President Grossman. The World Executive members' authority derived to a large extent from the fact that they were veterans and founding members of the party, from Jabotinsky's membership of the World Executive, and from his close connections with his veteran party colleagues, but many members of the World Council had little or no contact with the Revisionist public at large. The struggles within *Ha-Zohar*, aimed at domination of the World Council through a majority in the World Executive, were a direct result of this structure.

The World Conferences of *Ha-Zohar* (and the conventions of the World Conference of *Betar*) were held in different cities, such as Paris, Vienna (1928), Prague (1930, 1932, 1938) and Cracow (1935). The conferences were attended by delegates from all branches of the Revisionist movement (encompassing the entire Jewish world, from Warsaw to New York, and from Capetown to Shanghai). The Conferences' meetings were the forum for public confrontations, the clarification of ideological principles, and decision making on future activities. Apart from the World Conference, conventions of the local party branches and of *Betar* were held in the various countries. This political structure and the debates within the Conferences are covered extensively in Revisionist literature, with descriptions ranging from wildly enthusiastic – because of the fact that these meetings took place at all, as well as the spirited nature of the debates – to gravely critical because of the frustrating and shallow nature of some of the debates. From 1930 onwards we can find critical comments about organizational impressionism and the lack of efficiency, particularly in Eretz Israel, where the political organization played the dominant role, the absence of resources as a cause of the lack of political success, and at the same time critical comments on the burgeoning of a political and party establishment dominated by bureaucrats and vested interests. A party apparatus is the opposite of a revolutionary *avant-garde*. The *avant-garde* derives its strength from the public at large, and not from central or local organizations which fetter the *avant-garde* in the chains of a bureaucratic apparatus. It was Achimeir who derived the inspiration for this historical thesis from the Bolshevik revolution: Far better a small and united political body capable of reaching the masses, than a heterogeneous and cumbersome political body.[16] Revisionism, according to Achimeir and his supporters, had chosen the wrong path in trying to take over the Congress and the Electoral Assembly. Constitutionalism is a sign of a defeatist attitude towards national activism. It was clear to Achimeir and his colleagues that *Ha-Zohar* in Eretz Israel had to be the *avant-garde* of the movement as a whole. The Messiah will not come across a 'paper bridge': petitions to the British government and a charter, they claimed, but across a 'bridge of iron': insurrection and underground struggle. A national movement should act 'along the lines of other national liberation movements: glory, gallows and victims. And in the intervening moments of quiet – preparations for prison, gallows and victims,' wrote Achimeir.[17]

This mentality was far removed from that of Jabotinsky and his colleagues. They continued to make every effort to create a large and ramified political organization capable of performing a variety of tasks. In March 1932 Jabotinsky wrote to one of his friends that without sufficient funds *Ha-Zohar* would be ruined, and all the big plans would remain nothing but empty declarations. A party whose aspiration is to operate in parallel to the Zionist Organization, but whose hands are tied because of lack of financial support, does not deserve to exist. He never saw the movement in terms of a revolutionary organization, but as a mass-movement intended to form the underpinning of a political party and political activism.

Betar: an Avant-Garde Youth Movement and Incipient Army[18]

At this point of our treatise we come to the second branch of Revisionism, which existed side by side with the political party: the youth organization. All the Zionist youth movements, including the youth movements affiliated with the Labour movement, formed a fundamental and revitalizing element of their respective social movements. There existed, however, a different kind of relationship between youth movements such as *Ha-Noar ha-Oved* (the 'Working Youth') or the *Mahanot ha-Olim* and the Labour movement, on the one hand, and between *Betar* and *Ha-Zohar*, on the other.

The various groups which founded the earlier mentioned *Berit*

Joseph Trumpeldor of 1931 – the 'Joseph Trumpeldor Alliance' – did not plan to establish a political party, but rather a youth organization, a kind of national Boy Scouts movement, intended as an ideological training ground for the 'Jewish Legion', a training and teaching institution which would educate a new breed of nationalist Jew. It did not take long, however, before the leaders of *Betar* revealed an aspiration towards greater involvement in the political movement. This was no problem, since *Betar* members could – and in fact did – become voting members and activists of *Ha-Zohar* at the age of 18, and it was not really possible to separate the two organizations. There also existed cooperation on the organizational level; *Betar*, being the best organized and most active factor in *Ha-Zohar*, occupied itself with election propaganda and the organization of the branches, in addition to which a measure of demographic symmetry developed, as more and more former *Betar* members became active in *Ha-Zohar* and participated in its political bodies.

The necessity of some form of organized formal cooperation became more problematic, but increasingly urgent during the 1930s, when the various groups were merged into *Betar* following a resolution at the second *Ha-Zohar* Conference, which continued to consider itself the patron of the youth movement. The group of Latvian founders delegated Aharon Propes, the first member of *Betar*, to represent *Betar* in *Ha-Zohar*'s World Executive. It was decided that the organization's headquarters would be established in Warsaw, signifying a shift in the centre of gravity from Latvia, where the movement had been founded, to Poland. A newsletter, *Massuot* ['Torches'] began to appear in April 1927. The Danzig Conference, which was held from 12–16 April 1931, ended the formative period of *Betar*, and the transfer of its centre of gravity to Poland.

At the head of the movement stood the *Betar* Executive/ Commissariat, located in Warsaw, which was elected by the *Betar* World Conference. Next to the Head of *Betar*, Jabotinsky himself, there were *Betar* Headquarters and the *Betar* Headquarters' Secretariat (*Shilton*), which were situated in Paris. The organization had a paramilitary structure, consisting of territorial head- quarters, regional headquarters, local branches and battallions. *Betar* members were divided into three ranks according to age. The highest, 'adult' rank was allowed to join *Ha-Zohar*, provided that their political activity within *Ha-Zohar* was conducted in an organized fashion under the supervision of the *Betar* leadership.

The World Conference in Warsaw held on 1 January 1929 added a fourth rank, that of 'Worker', intended for *Betar* members who were undergoing training prior to their *aliyah*. *Betar* members of 18 and above who paid a membership fee (the *dinar*, the value of which in 1930 represented a value of 10 shillings) were registered members of *Ha-Zohar*. According to a census taken in 1930, 25% of the members of *Betar* were also members of *Ha-Zohar*.[19]

Ha-Zohar did its utmost to retain hegemony and control, whereas *Betar* aspired to autonomy and independence and, ultimately, hegemony within the movement. It would be difficult to depict the coordination of the two systems without their connecting and unifying factor: Jabotinsky. This was his sheer strength in the movement. At his initiative a working agreement between the two parties was reached: the 'Gentlemen's Agreement' of 19 June 1931, which granted *Betar* internal autonomy, but prevented it from undertaking independent political activities.[20]

In principle it had been decided during the first World Conference of *Betar*, which took place in Warsaw in January 1929, that '*Berit Trumpeldor* did not – and should not – constitute a part of the Revisionist movement'. In practice, however, there existed – as already mentioned – profound ideological, organizational and personal ties between the party and the Trumpeldor movement. The age gap, as well as the differences in mentality, objectives and procedures, were complementing as well as mutually fertilizing influences, in addition to which they caused deep internal tensions, which in turn were largely responsible for the internal dynamics.

The 'Gentlemen's Agreement' did not survive for long, however. The *Betar* movement, as well as the membership, kept on pressing for a change in policy and Revisionist mentality in general. Actually the Agreement turned *Betar* into a kind of ideological pressure group, which tried to take over *Ha-Zohar*. The Grossman group claimed – not without justification – that Jabotinsky was trying to overpower them by means of *Betar*, while admitting that members of *Ha-Zohar* – those who were not, and never had been, members of *Betar* – formed the minority among the active members of the movement. For this reason Grossman and his friends tried to ensure that *Betar* people should not cast their votes *en bloc*, but as voters in their own right only.

Betar was a central factor in the growing climate of confrontation and political and social polarization in Eretz Israel. Its dependence on the Jewish Agency's allocation of immigration certificates, and the in itself justified complaint about discrimination against *Betar* members in *aliyah* training camps, resulted from 1933 onwards in attempts by *Betar* to find its own immigration avenues to Eretz Israel. At the instigation of *Betar*, Raphael Rosov, who was close to private agricultural circles in Eretz Israel, tried to establish contacts with plantation owners and industrialists, in an effort to obtain certificates for so-called essential workers behind the back of the Jewish Agency. The problem became critical when *Betar* members were prevented from immigrating, despite the fact that hundreds of candidates were awaiting an opportunity to move to Eretz Israel. This situation weakened Revisionism by denying it the badly-needed demographic reinforcement.

During the 1930s three differently-oriented organizational streams evolved within *Betar* : the para-military so-called Battalions and *Kenim* ('Packs'), the 'Labour squads', who worked mainly in rural settlements in Eretz Israel, and the adult *Betar* members, who formally belonged to *Betar* or (until 1934) the *Ha-Zohar–Betar* labour organization. *Betar* placed at the disposal of Revisionism in Eretz Israel an active and efficient body of manpower that could be deployed for a variety of purposes, such as demonstrations and meetings, 'job seizures', and job protection. *Ha-Zohar* looked upon the *Betar* movement in Eretz Israel mainly as an educational and propaganda force.

Betar was by no means a monolithic body; there existed considerable differences between the *Betar* labour pioneers working in the rural settlements, the Palestinian-born youngsters, mainly city-dwellers, organized in the *Kenim* and Battalions, and the older *Betar* members who were active in *Ha-Zohar*. Ideologically *Betar* circles were strongly influenced by the maximalists in Eretz Israel, mainly through the influence of the Cadet School, which trained instructors for the *Betar* movement, and at which Achimeir was a lecturer and teacher. The involvement of *Betar* members in Revisionist party politics deepened at the initiative of Jabotinsky, as well as through pressures from the rank and file. In the years after 1933, however, *Betar* reached its first crossroads as a result of the walk-out of the Grossman group, which forced it to choose between Jabotinsky and his policies, and the maximalist conception. Propes, the veteran *Betar* commissioner in Poland, and his veteran colleagues were of the opinion that *Betar* members should not belong to any political party, and that membership of *Betar* provided sufficient belonging to last a lifetime. *Betar*, so stated Propes, was an autonomous, sovereign and totalistic movement, and its monistic character suffered from its identification with *Ha-Zohar*.

He considered the 'Gentlemen's Agreement' of 1931 as representing little more than an organizational affiliation. Jabotinsky, on the other hand, saw *Betar* as the major strategic reserve of *Ha-Zohar*: *Betar* prepared youngsters for Zionism, Revisionism and the future 'legion'. From *Betar*, Zionist youth passed directly into the party ranks. *Betar* was a training institute, and not an autonomous movement with a life of its own. Even the *Betar* chronicler agrees that there was a measure of naïveté and lack of realism in the demand for the depoliticization of *Betar*.

The issue came to a head during the *Ha-Zohar* World Conference in Poland in February 1934. At this conference Menachem Begin spoke in favour of the 'Betarization of *Ha-Zohar*' and increasing *Betar*'s influence in the party, while simultaneously warning against attempts to drive a wedge between *Betar* and *Ha-Zohar*. Other delegates, mainly those from Eretz Israel, pointed at the need to shape *Betar* along the pattern of the *Berit ha-Biryonim* (*Biryon*, or 'brigand', being the epithet of the zealots during the Jewish Revolt against the Romans). Still other *Betar* members, among them several Palestinian members from the Labour squads, saw in this kind of brigandry an omen of anarchy, since according to them *Betar* was a hierarchical movement. 'All *Betar* members are "brigands", but quiet ones', claimed one of the delegates at the Conference.

Betar intensified its involvement in *Ha-Zohar* in Poland. Members of *Betar* Headquarters, including Propes, Yunitchman, Wartman, Lerner, Klarman, Remba and Khrust were members of the National Executive of *Ha-Zohar* in Poland. In 1934 Polish *Betar* had some 40,000 members organized in 651 units, out of a total world *Betar* membership of 70,000. They were highly-charged with nationalist activism, and thousands of them were waiting for immigration certificates to Eretz Israel (in 1934 alone 3,000 members underwent immigration training courses).

This phenomenon was evident during the second World Conference of *Betar*, held in Cracow in January 1935. Once more some speakers harshly criticized the politicization of *Betar*, while others claimed that the movement was needlessly being dragged into Revisionist politics, to the point where it had begun to conduct its own politics, and was manifesting itself as a 'bloc' in the discussions within *Ha-Zohar*, instead of being an educational mass-movement and an instrument for the implementation of *Ha-Zohar*'s policies. However, the separation between education and ideological indoctrination, on the one hand, and politics on the other, proved impossible, being both out of place and out of time. Even *Betar* leaders who were in favour of 'depoliticization', voiced clear and practical political demands, while pressing for the establishment of the new Zionist Organization, out of a desire to separate themselves from the existing organization, and a complete restructuring of the movement as a whole. The chronicler of *Betar* would try to distinguish between 'national politics' and 'party politics', claiming that *Betar* was compelled through circumstances to involve itself in politics, but that this was a matter of 'national', and not party politics. The differentiation was no less naïve and arbitrary than that between political education and politics. Political education and national politics by necessity also represented party politics.

Betar was a centralized and hierarchical organization, engaged in para-military training and organizing demonstrations, on the one hand, and education in national culture, on the other. Theoretically, as envisaged by Jabotinsky, its members were destined to become soldiers of the future 'Jewish Legion' (a Jewish army as part of the British army). According to the radical militaristic conception it was this Jewish army which would conquer Eretz Israel from the British and the Arabs. Without *Betar* the Revisionist party would be no more than an ineffectual and unstable political faction. However, as with the evolution of *Ha-Zohar, Betar*'s development into a youth organization led by people who were political veterans and party workers was also fraught with a good deal of friction. Its pre-occupation with indoctrination and cultural education failed to satisfy the young leadership which had come to the fore during the 1930s, and which was looking for new channels into which to direct its activity. This radicalization did not find favour in the eyes of the veteran leadership, which was anxious about the autonomy of *Betar* and the preservation of its original 'boy scout' character, which the radicals attempted to change into a launching pad for eventual military and underground activity. By the nature of things, this development was of course also connected with a desire to shake off the control of the party (or, alternatively, take it over).

Against the background of the historical events in Europe and in Palestine during the middle of the 1930s a radicalization of *Betar* was unavoidable. The radical revolutionary ideas imported from Poland by Achimeir, Greenberg, Katznelson, as well as by the members of the *Berit ha-Biryonim* and (after 1937) the IZL , found a ready platform in the popular Yiddish (and Polish) press. One of the important consequences was the establishment by the IZL of 'secret cells' within the ranks of *Betar*, in spite of the opposition of the heads of *Betar*, as well as Jabotinsky himself. Polish *Betar* served as a cover for the evolution of the IZL under the leadership of Avraham Stern, Hillel Kook, Nathan Friedman-Yellin and their friends, who even conducted their own diplomacy through their private contacts with Polish government leaders. This state of affairs was the cause of continuous conflicts, which ended only when Menachem Begin, who was accepted by both the IZL and the members of the secret cells, was appointed Head of *Betar* in Poland. This appointment went into effect in March 1939, six months before the outbreak of World War II.

*   *   *

At this point it may be asked who in effect represented Revisionism: *Ha-Zohar* or *Betar*? Or, put differently, when we talk about Revisionism, do we mean Revisionism in the mould of *Ha-Zohar*, or Revisionism in that of *Betar*? Even at first glance the differences between the two are obvious. The question is relevant, due to the fact that from the 1940s onwards the historical tradition of 'Revisionism' had shunted aside the political party, not only in terms of political status, but also in terms of historical rights. As from this moment the political party merely represented the 'old' Revisionism, the one which was political and legalistic in character and refused to support the underground. The new tradition preferred to emphasize both the origins of the IZL and its natural place and duties as having (in the main) originated in *Betar*.

From a more recent historical perspective there is indeed a good deal of justification for relegating *Ha-Zohar* to the margins, since *Ha-Zohar* and its party political functionaries were not the dominant factors in the evolution of Revisionism in Eretz Israel. Within the context of the history of the 1920s and 1930s, however, it was *Ha-Zohar* which was most closely identified with the character, the hardships and the expectations of the contemporary Zionist Revisionist public, even though proving incapable of offering real solutions to its plight, and appearing ill-adjusted to the special conditions presented by the revolution of a Jewish national society under British mandatory rule. In the tradition of the Right Jabotinsky is much more readily remembered as *Rosh Betar* ('Head of Betar'), than as President of *Ha-Zohar*, which shows that where history and tradition are concerned, even the collective memory of a movement is selective and subject to re-interpretation.

B. THE POLITICAL HISTORY OF REVISIONISM:
REVISIONISM DURING THE 1930s – THE STRUGGLE FOR
POWER AND THE INTERNAL TENSIONS

Loyalty or Independence

The main dialogues within the Revisionist movement during the
years 1925–35 concerned the question of loyalty to the Zionist
Organization. I will dwell upon this issue because of its pivotal role
in the political history of Revisionism during the years 1925–33,
and even later, the outcome of which determined various other
problems relating to the organization, orientation and leadership of
the movement. The 'radicals' wanted to quit the Zionist Organization forthwith, but the 'moderates' opposed a split. This resulted in a
rupture of the unity of the Zionist Organization – Herzl's monumental creation. British policy in Palestine, the Arab riots of 1929,
the White Paper of 1930, the creation in 1929 of an 'enlarged' Jewish
Agency by the inclusion of non-Zionists within the Zionist leadership, the fierce struggles with Mapai (the Labour party, founded by
the merger of the two main socialist parties), as well as the dramatic
dispute about the question of the Final Aim during the Zionist
Congress of 1931 – to mention only some of the main aspects,
strengthened the position of the 'radicals'. Their view was that
Revisionism would never succeed in implementing an independent
policy as long as it remained subject to the restraints of its membership in the Zionist Organization. The increasing strength of the
'extreme' camp became apparent towards the time of the fifth
World Conference of *Ha-Zohar*, which took place in Vienna in
1932, a year before the 18th Zionist Congress. Many agreed with
Grossman that *Ha-Zohar* would win the elections in 1933, and that it
would 'throw out the garbage' in the Zionist Organization – in other
words annul the 'expansion' of the Jewish Agency and put an end to
the rule of Mapai . The 'radicals', on the other hand, did not believe
in such a prospect. The confrontation between the two camps
became unavoidable. In fact it was also a clash between different
generations in Revisionism: the moderate leaders were also the
veterans who, together with Jabotinsky, had founded *Ha-Zohar*,
although in effect they represented merely themselves, and did not
have a broad popular following.

The fulcrum of the ideological, organizational and personal

dilemma was Jabotinsky. He, too, had little faith in the Congress, but as long as the veteran and moderate faction was in charge of the movement, he could not realize his desire to quit. In principle the strengthening of the activist-maximalist wing suited him very well, because he, too, favoured independent activity. In fact, Jabotinsky was convinced that his movement would gain a sweeping victory in the forthcoming elections at the Zionist Congress, and that there was thus no need to form a coalition. The presidency would fall into his lap, not because of his success in building a new coalition, but because of his conclusive victory in the election. He believed that the Jews of Poland would hand him the victory and the presidency of the Congress. The maximalists, however, were not satisfied with abandoning the Zionist Organization and the opportunity to undertake independent diplomatic activities. They derided the value of independent political activity as proposed by Jabotinsky, which could only be implemented outside the Zionist Organization. The pressures applied by the two sides placed Jabotinsky in the uncomfortable position of having to adjudicate and try and achieve a balance between the two sides, while in fact being the one who would decide to which side of the movement the balance would swing. Jabotinsky's behaviour and reactions during this period suggest that he was sitting on the fence and hesitated to take what might prove to be a fateful decision. He feared a split in the movement and a separation from his old party colleagues. To his friend Shelomo Gafstein, one of the moderates in the Tel Aviv centre, he wrote on the eve of the elections to the 16th Congress:

> The World Conference of *Ha-Zohar* has decided unanimously that our organization will use the 16th Congress to save the Zionist Organization – if it is still possible to save it from self-destruction. The World Conference has begun, and is vigorously pursuing, its activities based on these decisions . . . *Ha-Zohar* in Eretz Israel must prepare itself unhesitatingly for the election battle for the 16th Congress.[21]

In Eretz Israel, however, strong opposition arose against this policy. The strength of the activists and maximalists had been achieved in a democratic manner, and it was clear to Jabotinsky that this increasing activist-maximalist strength would create two mutually embroiled factions within the centre in Eretz Israel. For this reason Jabotinsky made an all-out effort to prevent an internal split, without having to take sides between the two factions himself. On the one hand he too preferred a homogeneous party, even at the cost of the resignation of one group or another, over a big party riven by internal conflicts and paralyzed by a division into quarrelling factions. Thus he wrote to Grossman in December 1932.[22] At the same time Jabotinsky feared the anti-establishment mentality of the 'barefooted' (the *'Sansculottes'*), a reference to the *Berit ha-Biryonim*.

During the 17th Congress, which was held in Basle from 30 June till 15 July 1931, Jabotinsky performed a dramatic act by demonstratively tearing up his delegate card to the Congress on the dais to protest at the rejection of his proposal that the final aim of Zionism was to achieve a majority in Eretz Israel and the establishment of a Jewish state. (The nature of this proposal and the accompanying resolution will be discussed later on.) The Congress was up in arms about Weizmann's subsequent declarations to the press, which could be interpreted as if the Zionist leadership was opposed to the creation of a Jewish majority in Eretz Israel. Weizmann lost the confidence of the general public and was removed from his position as Chairman of the Zionist movement. Nahum Sokolov served in his place until 1935. The Revisionists had won a battle, but lost the campaign. The 17th Congress signalled the beginning of the lengthy hegemony of Mapai within Zionism. A disappointed Jabotinsky was unable to make up his mind whether to resign or to make another attempt at 'taking over the Congress' from within.

A temporary compromise was reached between Jabotinsky and the moderates in the leadership on 28–29 September 1931 during a meeting attended by members of the Executive from London and Paris (an event since then called the 'Calais Compromise', after the place of the meeting in the French coastal town of Calais). The compromise, which was intended to save the unity of *Ha-Zohar*, allowed the 'loyalists' to continue their membership of the Zionist Organization and to 'buy the *shekel*', but released the Revisionists from the obligatory bond of Zionist discipline. Jabotinsky had to defend the 'Caläis Compromise' against the critics, while simultaneously trying to create the impression that there existed three legitimate streams within Revisionism.[23] The 'Calais Compromise' was however unacceptable to the Zionist Organization, which considered itself the sole judge in Zionist affairs; neither was it acceptable to the 'extremist' Revisionists, who kept on pressing for a walk-out. The scene of this confrontation was the Vienna Conference, and several dozens of delegates from Eretz Israel tried to change the face of the movement. Grossman criticized the 'stagey mannerisms' of Jabotinsky, whereas the 'extremists' demanded the formulation of a new ideology for *Ha-Zohar* and a 'purging' of the ranks. The radicals from Eretz Israel, in particular Yevin, Achimeir, Katznelson and Greenberg, demanded a purge of the movement 'in the direction of London', meaning Grossman and his colleagues on the Executive. To their mind *Ha-Zohar*'s task was not to fight for a slice of the leadership of the Zionist Organization, or even to act as a loyal opposition, but to become a national liberation movement.[24]

Jabotinsky, tired and unable to decide, again cast around for a compromise. In the end the Conference approved the 'Calais Compromise' with a majority of 82 against 24, but Jabotinsky was conscious that his prestige had been damaged; 'If I cannot manage to rebuild it, I will resign,' he wrote to a friend.[25] The necessity of choosing between his old colleagues and the new, more militant generation, posed a grave problem for him, particularly since the latter had seriously criticized both his person and his political methods. Jabotinsky, however, shook off their criticism since he considered many of the statements to be little more than the rhetoric that was so fashionable at the time. He criticized them, at times bitterly and scathingly, but the other side quite openly talked of a Revisionism without the 'outmoded' Jabotinsky, and the need to liberate Jabotinsky from the restraints placed upon him by his moderate friends and a faceless party. Jabotinsky's path from 1932 onwards was characterized by a perpetual see-sawing between these two opposing worlds represented in the World Conference. The compromise which had been achieved did not fool the onlookers. One of them opined – correctly, as it was to turn out – that the 'banal hatred' which manifested itself within Revisionism as a result of its internal contradictions would sooner or later cause the movement to collapse.[26]

A Legal Putsch and Leadership Problems

The Vienna Conference refused to accept the dictatorial leadership principle which the 'radicals' from Eretz Israel and their allies had demanded to be included in the platform, nor did it declare the establishment of an independent Zionist Organization. In effect the Executive continued trying to impose its views on the majority of the movement's members, so that in the end Jabotinsky had no choice but to take a decision. At the World Executive meeting of *Ha-Zohar* in Katowitz in March 1933 Jabotinsky assumed full control and organized a plebiscite among the membership, which resulted in an overwhelming personal victory. A total of 31,724 members of *Ha-Zohar* (93.8%) voted for the decision to leave the Zionist movement and undertake independent political action, whereas only 6,066 members (6.2%) decided to remain loyal. Jabotinsky realized full well that his constitutional *putsch* was liable to substantiate the claim that *Ha-Zohar* was being led by a dictator. For this reason he went to great lengths to explain to his colleagues that he was on principle opposed to the type of leadership represented by Mussolini (a 'great man') or the Greek dictator Theodoros Pangalos ('a nonentity').[27] The 'Lodz Declaration', which announced his decision to suspend the Executive, resulted – so Jabotinsky wrote – from the fact that the members of the Executive, who represented a minority, had denied suitable representation to the majority of the movement's membership. Thus the *putsch* was an act intended to strengthen the democratic nature of the movement, rather than to establish one-man rule.

The 'Katowitz Conference' represented a significant victory for the radical opposition. Jabotinsky agreed to abandon his veteran colleagues and power brokers, in order to preserve the movement's periphery and to avoid a more serious split, but more particularly in order to retain *Betar*, as well as the Revisionists who comprised the youth movement's leadership. A schism was unavoidable: upholding the moderate veteran leadership contributed nothing to *Ha-Zohar*'s chances of coming to power, whereas its departure – at least theoretically – gave a new impetus to Revisionism. It proved what many already knew, namely that the potent factor in *Ha-Zohar* consisted not of the 'silent majority', but of the political elite, and the organized and cohesive *Betar* membership.

In this context two interesting letters should be mentioned which demonstrate the underlying tension between the political party, the youth organization and the radical group, as well as between their different structures, methods of action and political approaches.

In a letter to the *Betar* Headquarters Secretariat (*Shilton*) in Paris of 30 July 1931, written against the background of the events at the 17th Zionist Congress, and accompanied by a request that its contents be circulated to the branches of *Betar*, Jabotinsky wrote that insurmountable tensions had developed between *Ha-Zohar*'s methods as a political opposition party, and those of *Betar* as a national movement. A political party had to operate according to accepted rules within a kind of parliamentary system, and even be prepared to compromise. This did not apply to a national educational movement based on faith and fundamentalist principles. It could not be denied, Jabotinsky wrote, that political stratagems, 'despite the fact that they were a logical outcome of the situation at the Congress and *Ha-Zohar*'s undertaking towards its voters, had made a bad and harmful impression on *Betar* youth.' This was, in his opinion, merely the inevitable consequence of the basic mistake that had for some time warped *Ha-Zohar*'s methods, namely its participation in a Zionist Organization which had ceased to be Zionist. Anyone who agreed to take part in such a Congress was forced to accept tactical compromises whose practical value was doubtful, whereas there was no doubt whatsoever about their decision-making and educational value: it was in fact totally negative, dangerous and damaging, and would create confusion in the ranks of *Betar* youth who, according to their constitution, were pledged to participate in the *Ha-Zohar* movement.[28]

With this, Jabotinsky called for a deeper involvement of *Betar* members in party decisions. If *Ha-Zohar* failed to choose independence, *Betar* would be forced to leave it, whereas an independent *Ha-Zohar* would effectively represent *Betar* on the Jewish and Zionist world scene.

In a similar spirit he wrote to the World Executive of *Ha-Zohar* on 15 August 1931. He knew that the Executive was ill-disposed to the involvement of *Betar*. The leadership of *Ha-Zohar* had to understand, however, that *Betar* youth could not accept *Ha-Zohar*'s agreeing to political compromises, given the fact that its membership of the Zionist Organization compelled it to adhere to the latter's constitution and bye-laws. For this reason Jabotinsky supported a cancellation of the clause in the agreement between *Ha-Zohar* and *Betar* intended to prevent *Betar* members from operating as an independent faction within *Ha-Zohar*.[29]

The plebiscite of April 1933 gave Jabotinsky formal authority as the unquestioned leader of the Revisionist movement, in addition to his responsibilities as president of *Ha-Zohar* and head of *Betar*. However, in everyday political reality a distinction has to be made between the formal status of an organization's leader, and that leader's capacity to implement this authority. In Jabotinsky's case there were many occasions where he simply lost control.

Storm, Unity and Opposition

The murder of Dr. Chaim Arlosoroff in June 1933 and the resulting trial of the *Berit ha-Biryonim* served to unite the movement.[30] It also took a united stand against the 'Transfer Agreement' which had been signed with the German Nazi regime about the transfer of German Jewish property to Palestine,[31] the 'evacuation plan' – which will be discussed further on – and the struggle for immigration certificates for *Betar* members. Even so Jabotinsky's personal victory in 1933 was not complete. His official authority had been strengthened, but his moral and political authority were gradually being eroded. Reflecting on these developments, Jabotinsky came to the conclusion that only a charismatic leader officially invested with executive authority would be able to navigate the divided Revisionist vessel through the stormy sea of internal Zionist strife. 'You and your entire fascist generation have been right in one thing: it is forbidden to disguise leadership,' he wrote towards the end of 1933 to Shlomo Jacobi. 'If one is indeed the absolute leader of *Ha-Zohar*, it is useless to try and soften this reality by passing some of the authority to other people; formal and informal authority must be combined.'[32] Even so, Jabotinsky disliked the dictatorial leadership pattern. The Italian dictatorial model appeared to him ill-suited to the circumstances of the Revisionist (as well as of the Zionist) movement. He had no great regard for the Italian dictator – or any dictator at all: most dictators are mediocre people carried to power on a wave of hysteria, and not every dictator is a Bonaparte, he explained.[33] However, due to the structure of the Revisionist movement as a social as well as a political movement, the leader could not be assisted by an organizational apparatus; without personal admiration, and without ideological identification and attachment, Jabotinsky's authority would have been contested, no matter how much formal authority he possessed.

A new spirit and a new frame of mind had emerged within the movement, and Jabotinsky was forced to adjust himself to these. A leader is not only a person who shapes the actions and reactions of his followers; he also has to understand, interpret and respond to the aspirations of the rank and file, failing which a dangerous gap may develop between him and his followers. Jabotinsky enjoyed a long list of distinctions within the movement: he was its founder, its political leader and its foremost ideologist in all areas; a highly-talented individual and a great scholar; a lively orator and a greatly admired personality, even by those within the movement who bitterly opposed him. The authoritarian and dictatorial image of Jabotinsky does not, however, correspond with the reality. He was the man who united *Ha-Zohar* and *Betar*, and he was conscious of the need for a strong personality to mediate between the two movements. But he was equally conscious of the serious hiatus which exists in historical experience between image and reality. The status of a leader was forced upon him by the necessity to rescue Revisionism from disintegration, and to show it a new way in the face of the rebellion of Grossman and his friends, and their efforts to preserve the movement's loyalty to the Zionist Organization. At Katowitz Grossman had expressed the opinion that Revisionism would be able to exist without Jabotinsky. 'We have built an organizational structure that can virtually support itself, and the entire Executive stands behind it,'[34] he declared with an optimism not justified by the facts. Grossman in effect prepared a number of pitfalls for Jabotinsky, and the latter had to cut the Gordian knot. The idea, which was 'an unhatched egg' at the time, and which Grossman described as an 'epidemic' and a 'nightmare' of party dictatorship, was spelled out in the 'Lodz Declaration', which specified Jabotinsky's authority. In it he stated that 'as President of the World Executive of *Ha-Zohar*, I declare that from today onwards I have accepted personal responsibility for the immediate management of the *Berit* (*Ha-Zohar*) and all the affairs of the World Movement. The activities of the existing central organs will cease herewith.' All executive tasks were transferred to him; in effect he was nearly all-powerful, and without his instructions nothing could be done. But already at the founding congress of *Ha-Zach*, the 'New Zionist Organization' in Vienna at the end of 1935, his weaknesses were fully exposed. The delegates to the congress opposed the candidacies to the Executive of two veteran members, Jacobi and Shechtman, who had remained loyal to Jabotinsky; Jabotinsky himself received no more than 88 votes out of the 200 present, with two votes against, and the remainder abstaining in protest.

Leadership Patterns

This book is not a biography of Ze'ev Jabotinsky. Even so it would be impossible not to devote some space to a brief analysis of Jabotinsky's status within the movement. This status was without parallel in any other Zionist organization, to judge by the fact that Jabotinsky was the subject of hero worship even during his lifetime. There is no doubt that his personality was a key factor in the movement, and it is difficult to say whether without him it would have been established at all – and if so, whether it would have evolved as it did. This situation was one of the factors encouraging comparisons between Jabotinsky and other authoritarian and charismatic leaders who were active in the period between the two world wars. The principal difference was of course that Jabotinsky headed a party rather than a state, and that his authority was not that of a government leader. For this reason it is difficult to predict how Jabotinsky would have reacted if he had been a head of state, and what capabilities he would have shown as the leader of a political system with the responsibility for running a government.

Several times Jabotinsky did reflect on the problems of leadership in a modern society, only to discover – as already mentioned – both aesthetic and normative reservations against the collective yearning for an adulated leadership figure, such as a Duce or a Führer. The ideal leadership model from his point of view was Herzl who – so he believed – had succeeded in sweeping the masses along on the sheer strength of his personality, and through his success in giving practical expression to their basic needs. On another occasion he talked about two kinds of leadership: the leader who provided his movement with an ideological framework (intellectual leadership), and the leader who gave an impetus to his movement and imbued it with an inner fire (*pantogenetor*). With the latter type of leader it was not the ideas that counted, but only the personality.[35] There is no doubt that in the eyes of the members of the movement he (Jabotinsky) was seen as the one who generated the ideology, as well as igniting the 'inner fire'. Even those who criticized him remained his fervent admirers, and his authority has remained intact – even after his death, when everybody else is talking or prophesying in his name.

There existed a certain contradiction between the political tradition in which Jabotinsky had been reared and his self-image, on the one hand, and the psycho-cultural function which his personality fulfilled within the specific historical context of his movement, on the other. The movement needed a leader it could adore and worship, a leader who would be its omniscient guide through the complicated and frustrating historical labyrinth. Jabotinsky was at times considered not only a political leader, but a prophet and messiah. He himself by no means felt at ease with this situation. It would appear one of the ironies of the history of political Zionism that Revisionism practised the very leadership pattern that Jabotinsky considered negative, and against which he had warned the movement in its first year. In 1925 he had written an article entitled 'Fascist Zionism', aimed mainly against Weizmann, arguing that Zionism lacked great personalities in the mould of a Napoleon or Garibaldi – people who were capable of changing the course of history. At the same time, so he wrote, this kind of leadership must not become a permanent feature. The leader does not represent one absolute and eternal truth, and the effect of the charismatic fascist leadership conception is extremely harmful. Youngsters are taught that they need not burden their minds. Zionism is realized by the public at large, and not by a handful of leaders. This leadership principle causes dangerous blindness and will have disastrous results. On these grounds he advised that Zionism's internal struggles should only be conducted according to a plan that 'by its very nature should be anonymous', with no need for names or biographical details.[36]

The movement followed a diametrically opposite course from that proposed by him. It gradually became identified with 'the Name'; its programme became identified with the programme of Jabotinsky. Everyone waited for him to speak, clung to him for support, and considered him the source of the one and only absolute truth. According to Jabotinsky's own definition Revisionism had become 'fascist', and an indication of Jabotinsky's opinion on this process may be found in a private letter written in August 1927 to Mrs. Miriam Lang, the secretary of the Revisionist office in London:

> . . . I have an organic hatred of personality worship and I am repelled by it. Fascism had some good ideas, but I am simply physically unable to discuss them serenely and directly; I am repelled by the worship of the Duce as I am by any public dishonesty. When something similar happens among us, I see it as a real danger . . . . I am beginning to fear that in my constant concern not to play 'leader' for fear of [over-]influencing the movement, I keep silent when I should speak out and even insist on my opinion, like anyone else.[37]

On 30 March 1935, following the collapse, due to the opposition of the majority within the Labour movement, of the compromise agreement Ben-Gurion and himself had reached, he expressed himself in a similar vein to David Ben-Gurion. In a personal confession he wrote that most present-day youngsters did not think too deeply; that − unlike the previous generation − they were superficial and impudent; and that they had lost the power of synthesis. He placed the main responsibility for this tendency towards radicalization on Mapai, although he did not altogether absolve his own movement.[38]

The Dictatorship Principle

At this point it should be mentioned that in essence the debate about the dictatorial versus the democratic principle was not a discussion on the most desirable political regime for the Jewish society. The discussion took place within a different context. It concerned the character of the Revisionist movement itself, and was in effect a discussion on principles, revealing different frames of mind and mentalities.

The ones who openly propounded the dictatorial concept were Yevin and Achimeir, and they provided it with ideological legitimization through their view of Revisionism as a revolutionary movement under the leadership of a dictatorial leader. Jabotinsky regarded discipline inside the movement, as well as the mobilization of the nation's individuals into an activist social movement – and in fact the political essence of the nation as a whole – as a total and voluntary, and therefore not compulsory, mobilization on behalf of the State. The decisive factor was the will of the individual. If he wanted to be an anarchist, he was free to be so; if he wanted to be mobilized – he was welcome. Discipline was a value, provided it was accepted voluntarily, and not through compulsion. Discipline was the fruit of inner conviction and total identification. The radical opposition, on the other hand, posed demands for totalitarianism and authoritarianism of a formal kind.

The totalitarian concept was first, and quite freely and openly, developed by Uri Zvi Greenberg in the columns of the two Labour publications, *Kuntres* and *Davar*. As his prototype he chose the Soviet Union, ruled by an ideologically motivated regime that did not allow any deviation or dissonance. Anything that could harm the vision of Eretz Israel and lacked blood ties with the messianic vision of the soil of Eretz Israel had to be censored, 'and please don't come and bother us while we are working on the Kingdom of Israel'. The dictatorship of the proletariat, according to Greenberg, had turned into the spiritual dictatorship of the *Histadrut*. The *Histadrut* ideal of the dictatorship of Eretz Israel was not only to control the labour market, but also to control the spiritual sphere, while setting aside all 'academic debate'.[39]

Abba Achimeir, on the other hand, drew an analogy with the fascist regimes, even though his inspiration was derived from the Bolshevik revolution. He wanted to rescue the 5th World Conference in Vienna in 1932 from the 'liberal morass' into which it had sunk, and lead the movement into the era of revolutionary totalitarianism and dictatorship. His articles frightened the London Executive, as well as Jabotinsky himself, who considered them 'a stab in the back'. What Revisionism needed, acccording to Achimeir, was a leader on the 'Duce model'.[40]

Jabotinsky therefore found himself at the head of a movement in which the central forces were revolutionary firebrands who both esteemed and criticized him. He himself wrote on a number of occasions that their conduct and ideology went against the grain and were fundamentally mistaken – yet their force was as if the Angel Gabriel himself had touched their brow – in other words, they were highly talented people. He could understand if they called for his resignation from the movement, and he would do so during one of the coming years after his political system had been put to its final test.[41] Apart from this, Jabotinsky remained the charismatic leader of the majority of the members of *Ha-Zohar* and *Betar* who, even when they took a different course from him, insisted on regarding him as their guide in all aspects.

The Jewish State Party – a Political Episode

In 1933 the members of the Executive who had been defeated in the struggle against Jabotinsky left the Revisionist movement and founded an independent party, named the Jewish State Party. This party remained affiliated with the Zionist Organization, in which it became one of the smaller opposition movements representing the 'moderate Right', or – in effect – the original Revisionist platform. The party attempted to establish a parallel structure to that of the Revisionists, with first of all a youth movement intended to be a competitor to *Betar*. However, throughout the party's existence, from 1933 till 1946, its influence remained marginal. According to private testimonies Jabotinsky often longed for his old comrades, to whom he felt far closer than to the 'cultural barbarians' of the militant younger generation. If indeed he felt such longings, he kept them to himself, and they never actually surfaced in his political behaviour. In any case Jabotinsky died in 1940, and up to that time it was impossible to turn the clock back. Only in February 1946 did the *Ha-Zohar* veterans return, to be reunited with their old party comrades in a joint list for the elections to the 22nd Zionist Congress.

The New Zionist Organization (Ha-Zach) – Political Independence, and its Failure

On the face of it the split in the movement released Revisionism from its shackles and enabled it to go forward. The fog of ambiguity and confusion had been lifted, the radical newspaper *Hazit ha-Am* ('Popular Front') wrote. Certainly *Ha-Zohar* entered the 1933 elections with high hopes of emerging as the biggest party. These hopes were based on the tremendous growth which *Ha-Zohar* in Poland had experienced within a very short time. However, the Arlosoroff murder affair, as well as the intervention of Ben-Gurion and *He-Halutz*, the pioneering youth organization of the Labour movement, turned the Labour faction into the dominant group in the election. The Revisionists grew in absolute terms, but in relative terms their representation in the Zionist Congress declined. At this point even Jabotinsky realized that he had no longer anything to do in the Zionist Organization, in addition to which Mapai and its allies made strenuous efforts to expel him and isolate his movement.[42]

Thus the processes inside and outside the movement in effect worked in tandem to bring about the creation of *Ha-Zach* (the 'New Zionist Organization') in September 1935. The British government withheld its recognition from the new organization. Jabotinsky made an intense effort to win voters for the movement. Most of them were traditional religious Jews, and because of this he was prepared to moderate his public secular nationalist stand, and to recognize the important national and cultural contribution of religion in the future independent Jewish society. However, the most important task from his point of view remained to undertake diplomatic activity in the various capitals. *Ha-Zohar*'s headquarters were transferred to Warsaw, and journalistic activity was intensified by the addition of journalists from Eretz Israel (first and foremost Greenberg and Achimeir). Revisionism received the active support of the Polish authorities and made its voice heard in the League of Nations (before the Mandates Committee), as well as in Bucharest, Rome, Paris and several other European capitals. None of this resulted in any political advantage, or, for that matter, any real political success. The 'Petition campaign', in which several hundred thousand Jews signed a petition to the government in London, answered a need to involve the Jewish public at large, but from a propaganda point of view it proved to be a pathetic fiasco. In the course of four years of hard work *Ha-Zach* had provided *Ha-*

Zohar with a wider framework for its activities, but it had failed to become an alternative to the Zionist Organization. On the contrary, Weizmann and Ben-Gurion had rid themselves of a nuisance which interfered with Zionist policy making as they understood it. *Ha-Zach*'s diplomacy was unable to disrupt their policies – but the activities of the IZL in Eretz Israel were a different affair. According to Revisionist historiography the Revisionists would have needed several more years in order to become the central force in Zionism and realize the Zionist goal. History, however, did not grant the Revisionists these years of grace.

The 'Lodz Declaration' turned Jabotinsky into a leader, but Achimeir's faction disintegrated after 1933. Following its trial, the *Berit ha-Biryonim* faded out of sight, but even so Jabotinsky had lost much of his freedom of manoeuvre. On the face of it, his fight for leadership had been uncontested, but in practice he was from now on forced to listen and respond to all kinds of ideas and initiatives that were not his in the first place, and with which he found it difficult to agree, if at all. Jabotinsky's formal 'dictatorial' status and his assumption of wide-ranging political powers within the movement, creating a dictatorial image of Jabotinsky himself, and suggesting a movement which depended upon the word of a single person, resulted in a wide gap between the image and the actual situation.

Jabotinsky was of course the accepted and adored leader, the linch pin holding all the various factions and currents together, but the historical processes were stronger than him. It was not his initiative and leadership that shaped the course of the movement on major issues. Concurrent with his activities and initiatives new and more dramatic initiatives were undertaken, of which he was neither the originator, nor the guiding spirit. Sometimes he gave them his blessing; at other times he was called upon to restore order among rival personalities or factions, but he was not always the initiator and organizer of the events. Often he even found himself dragged along against his will.

Upon the outbreak of the Second World War the New Zionist Organization became an even more glaring fiction than it had been between the years 1935–1939. If prior to the war it had been merely an experiment aimed at providing a wider and more comprehensive framework for *Ha-Zohar*, it now became completely identified with *Ha-Zohar*, which had lost its large and effervescent mass following. The appearance of the IZL on the political scene, and the realization that once the war ended, the IZL leaders had no intention of retiring from politics, but would contest the leadership of the movement, caused the veteran party activists to join forces. The death of Jabotinsky in New York in August 1940 left the movement without its captain, and without anyone whose authority was able to unite the factions. The party became seriously weakened, and soon afterwards its leadership lost both their members and their influence. Several minor factions parted with Revisionism and tried to set up independent political frameworks, better suited to the new circumstances. [One of these groups, the *Benei Horin* – the 'Free Men', was headed by Abraham Weinshal, one of the leaders of *Ha-Zohar* in Eretz Israel, while the leader of another group, called *Hitna'arut* (Awakening) – and later on *Mifleget ha-Am* (People's Party) – was Dr. Benyamin Lubotzky (Eliyav), one of the leaders of *Ha-Zohar* and *Betar*.] Other party activists joined the General Zionists.

Whatever remained of the party pulled together following an internal referendum in *Ha-Zohar* in February 1946, in which some 70 per cent opted for a return to the Zionist Organization. As already mentioned the Jewish State Party and *Ha-Zohar* merged into the *Berit Ha-Zohar ha-Meuhedet* (United *Ha-Zohar* Alliance) under the leadership of Meir Grossman and Arye Altman. Understandably this choice to return to the Zionist Organization was very unpopular with the heads of the IZL, who for a long time had considered Grossman a 'deserter' from the camp, whereas his deputy, Dr. Arye Altman, was the one who had refused to give public support to the activities of the IZL. In the elections to the Zionist Congress in October 1946 a total of 205,008 votes were cast. Of these the Revisionists received 11 mandates out of 79. (The Left gained 46 delegates.)[43]

The Bourgeois Orientation: A Political Failure

The bourgeois orientation of *Ha-Zohar* formed an integral part of the movement's Zionist outlook. (Its intellectual and ideological foundations will be discussed in Chapter 9.) It was predicated upon its interpretation of the social nature of the plight of Eastern European Jewry and the important, if not vital role to be played by the private sector and private capital in building a Jewish economy in Eretz Israel, the encouragement of Jewish immigration and the foundation of a political society and Jewish demographic majority in mandatory Palestine. However, already in 1925 this outlook had an unmistakable party-political foundation, because of the hope that Revisionism would be able to attract members and supporters among the general non-Socialist, and even anti-Socialist Zionist public which elected the Congresses, the elected Assembly in Eretz Israel, as well as among the non-Socialist Zionist parties and factions and various other economic organs of the 'bourgeois' sector in Eretz Israel.

Even so *Ha-Zohar*'s bourgeois platform failed to elicit a response at the Congresses, and by and large the party found itself in the minority on virtually all issues that were raised. The qualified support of the citizens parties[44] was insufficient to turn *Ha-Zohar* into the fulcrum of a large political bloc – even before 1931, when the workers' parties had not as yet consolidated their hegemony at the Zionist Congress. No less resounding was the failure of the bourgeois orientation in Eretz Israel itself.

This failure stood in complete contrast to the expectations, notwithstanding the fact that no other non-Socialist leader invested such intensive intellectual efforts in helping the Jewish middle class to bolster its self-esteem and grant it a sense of dignity and historic mission. *Ha-Zohar* constituted itself as the protector of the economic interests of the private sector in Eretz Israel, even though it counted only a handful of capitalists, property owners and industrialists among its ranks. This paradox is the more glaring since Revisionism ranged itself unconditionally on the side of private ownership and private enterprise. On the other hand, since Mapai also operated on a reformist and pragmatic basis of cooperation with private entrepreneurs and capitalists in Eretz Israel, *Ha-Zohar*'s struggle in a sense lacked a real target. During the 1930s *Ha-Zohar* described Mapai's social policies as 'class warfare', even though during this same period they were far removed from what could be called a class struggle. However this may be, the Revisionist ideology and political propaganda directed at the ideology and praxis of Mapai's 'class struggle' elicited little response in organized economic circles in Eretz Israel. Much of the noise created by its anti-*Histadrut* and anti-Mapai propaganda was in fact aimed at the Eastern European – particularly Polish – Jewish public, even though the majority of this public, even by Revisionist estimations, belonged to the lower middle class. They were people with very little capital or discretionary purchase power, with the result that even in Poland the response to the warnings of a 'class war' in Eretz Israel – assuming that Polish Jews were at all able to judge the economic and social reality there – was lukewarm at most. Other, more logical reasons for the acceptance of the outspoken criticism of the workers' parties and the *Histadrut* by many Polish Jews were the latter's natural aversion and opposition to socialist ideology and the socialist workers' parties as such, but these reasons were therefore not so much connected with the social and political events in Eretz Israel as with their own outlook and ideology.

Summarizing, it can be said that Revisionism set out to defend the economic and class interests of those who were not in need of such protection. Its ideology and bourgeois programme expounded the Revisionist views on the aims of Zionism and the ways and means of achieving their realization, but in economic terms they did not in fact represent the interests of its voters and supporters. Politically *Ha-Zohar*'s bourgeois ideology was a failure, and its political activities neither promoted the economic interests of the private sector in Eretz Israel, nor did they contribute to forging a sizeable non-Socialist political force within the *yishuv* capable of rivalling the hegemony of the Left.

Jabotinsky and others within *Ha-Zohar* were keenly aware of the weakness and intrinsic political instability of the 'citizens' camp, but around 1925 it appeared to them as the only viable ally, particularly because of its opposition to the growing strength of the Labour movement.

At the Zionist Congress Jabotinsky accused the non-Socialist factions of harbouring platonic pro-Socialist sentiments.[45] As he put it, the workers' parties had succeeded in permeating the Zionist movement with a belief in socialist superiority and socialist missionary nationalism, causing the 'bourgeois' parties to deprecate themselves and even apologize for their 'civilian' status. The lack of unity in the non-Socialist camp was due first and foremost to an objective factor: the civilian sector did not depend upon the national budget, so that it saw no need to organize itself as a political force to try and gain control of the national funds. Industrialists, craftsmen, citrus growers, merchants and others in comparable occupations pursued their private interests, and they could be rallied only when these interests were threatened. Many in fact preferred an accommodation with the *Histadrut*, rather than fighting it. 'The Zionist middle class will pay dearly for its faint-heartedness,' Jabotinsky declared. How could he respect the middle class, when it did not respect itself and refused to defend its pre-eminent position in the *yishuv*; it was handing Mapai its hegemony on a silver platter, without heeding the tactics of the latter, who – for the time being – were hiding their true intentions, namely the foundation of a socialist society and the total liquidation of private enterprise. This argument actually contradicted another fundamental Revisionist claim, namely that private entrepreneurs depended upon the national funds to enable them to establish a firm foundation for their business enterprises. If private entrepreneurs were indeed in need of such assistance, then why did they lack the sense to organize themselves and demand what *Ha-Zohar* was prepared to claim on their behalf? Julius Brutzkus tried to provide an answer to this aggravating question. The big capitalists, he wrote, had seen fit to make their own arrangements with the *Histadrut*, in much the same way as the *Histadrut* was interested in being on good terms with these capitalists. Large private enterprises had entered into commercial partnerships with the *Histadrut* since it was to the latter's advantage to seek the support of large Jewish investors.[46] Thus an alliance had come into being between Palestinian capitalists and the workers' parties. Simultaneously the *Histadrut* had declared war on small and medium-sized capitalists, whose economic existence was already shaky. The *Histadrut* was fighting the *lumpenkapitalisten*, while concluding agreements with Jewish and Palestinian plutocrats, Jabotinsky claimed. As a result the lower middle class in Eretz Israel, which lacked financial support, was left defenceless, whereas the upper echelons of the same class played havoc with the interests of their lower-class brethren.

In this context it is interesting to read Jabotinsky's reply to a letter from Schechtman, who had complained about the latter's attack on the 'minimalism' of the workers' parties, while failing to criticize the *yishuv* bourgeoisie, which from a political point of view was no less minimalist. Jabotinsky answered that there was no one to attack at the 'Centre'; the only Jews one could criticize were citrus growers who objected to employing Jewish labour – although at times he could understand their opposition, judging how they suffered from the hostile attitude of the Left, and the losses they suffered due to their inability to withstand the pressure for Jewish labour, which – as far as they were concerned – was tantamount to paying higher wages in a market subject to cyclical swings. In bourgeois circles there were only weaklings, who lacked the will to resist.[47] It looked as if they had resigned themselves to being the whipping boys, he wrote to Achimeir, and had accepted the status of a 'cursed class', which was why they did not turn to Revisionism to rescue them from their servitude. Although this was no reason for *Ha-Zohar* to alter its programme, a change in political tactics might nevertheless be desirable. 'This does not mean that we should change our convictions, but we would of course alter our radical strategy,' Jabotinsky asserted.[48]

When the Revisionists seceded from the Zionist Organization, not a single one of the 'citizens' lists' followed them into the political wilderness. Their hopes had been pinned in particular on the 'General Zionists B'.[49] Remba accused the latter that, in their eagerness to join a coalition within the Zionist Executive, they had failed to take a sufficiently determined stand, thereby enabling Mapai 'to squeeze *Ha-Zohar* out'.[50] The General Zionists, the traditional backbone of the Zionist Organization, had agreed to become junior partners, while the middle classes, who constituted the majority of the General Zionist membership, would continue to exert themselves on behalf of the funds from which only the leftist parties would benefit, Remba claimed. Similar scornful and sarcastic sentiments were voiced in satirical feuilletons directed at the citizens' bloc, 'the faithful servant of the Left'.

The members of Betar, many of whom hailed from lower-middle-class and artisan homes, and whose organization did not receive financial support from any Zionist source, were portrayed by their rivals as representatives of the Jewish bourgeoisie and supporters of the citrus growers and industrialists in Eretz Israel. Lengthy and passionate discussions were carried on in Betar publications about the movement's social orientation. Foremost among them were anti-Socialist and pro-Socialist groups, but the anti-Socialist tendency won out. This explains why the lack of responsiveness on the part of the 'citizen bloc' and its organizations created feelings of bitterness among the members of Betar and the Revisionist workers. They depicted themselves as pioneers who hired themselves out to farmers at minimal wages, while the latter failed to reciprocate by offering them support. Here and there they even exploited them in their fights with the *Histadrut*, but at all times they 'betrayed them'.[51]

It is not surprising, therefore, that the National Labour Federation [NLF] issued a call to leave the 'bourgeois rubbish' to stew in its own juice, and instead strengthen the bonds with the workers of Eretz Israel. During the third national assembly of the NLF, held in April 1937, Dr. Benyamin Avniel called upon the Federation to initiate a struggle against the citrus growers and to cease assisting farmers who used Revisionist labour for purposes of convenience only. The assembly was deeply disturbed by the citizens' bloc support of the *Histadrut*, and the private sector's acting out of 'fear, stupidity, blindness, lack of foresight and submissiveness'. In Jabotinsky's original terminology the Jewish middle class in Eretz Israel was called a 'bourgeois' rather than a 'citizens' camp, consisting of people with civic political consciousness. The bourgeois sections of the society simply were asleep, in particular the capitalists among them. The Revisionist workers demanded that an effort be made to break the *Histadrut* monopoly of the labour market, thanks to which the Left was able to control the Jewish economy of Eretz Israel and destroy private initiative. Unfortunately, the private employers were scared to antagonize the *Histadrut*, considering it more expedient to conclude labour agreements with the latter, even if this meant excluding Revisionist workers from the labour market. The National Labour Federation asked the private sector to cooperate by allocating a certain percentage of its job availabilities to Revisionist labourers, but this demand was not accepted. Neither did the private capitalists accept the proposal to form a united front against socialist capital, all of which was concentrated in one hand. Although the private sector failed, therefore, to exploit its quantitative superiority within the Palestinian economy, there remained a number of people who refused to despair and continued to express the hope that there would ultimately be national recognition, and one day this psychological revolution among the civilian public would take place. And therefore, and only because of this hope, does the NLF labourer accept the present harsh reality and does he continue to bear his suffering.[51]

Not all the members of the Revisionist movement were equally complacent, however. In December 1937 one of the radical members, by the name of A. Perlmutter, published a vigorous protest in *Ha-Yarden* against the bourgeois orientation and those who looked for cooperation with the citizens' bloc in the *yishuv*. In this article, entitled 'The Proletarian Revisionism' (which, the editor explained, expressed the views of the author alone), Perlmutter claimed that Revisionism was not a bourgeois movement, as proved by the fact that 'the vast majority of the *Ha-Zach* and *Betar* membership consisted of poor Jews, low-income labourers and other indigent Jews. Compared to them, the real middle class members in *Ha-Zach* were few and far between.' 'Our bourgeoisie are either salon-Communists or Socialists,' he concluded his summing up of the Jewish middle class. Perlmutter did not deny, however, that *Ha-Zach* was a bourgeois movement, but according to the writer it was bourgeois in terms of its general character and orientation, rather than in its social composition. The socialists' intention to 'eliminate the bourgeoisie' had forced *Ha-Zohar* from its inception to rise to the defence of the middle class; it was true that *Ha-Zohar* had always – and rightly so – complained about the middle class being short-sighted and trying to commit suicide by its inexplicable sense of obligation towards its arch-enemy. 'Even so *Ha-Zohar* would continue to defend it, since experience showed that without a middle class, however soft and weak-kneed it was, there could be no healthy national economy, nor would it be possible to establish a Jewish state.' However, due to this attitude a bourgeois mentality had crept into Revisionism, 'and this mentality had caused the national movement to be infiltrated by other Jewish bourgeois traits, notably spinelessness, a lack of resolution, and a docile and subservient attitude to Socialism. Whereas the labour members of our NLF are gradually shaking off their socialist complex, the bourgeois minority in *Ha-Zohar* are salon-Socialists until today.'

According to Perlmutter *Ha-Zohar* presented a striking paradox: the militant element as regards the relations with the *Histadrut* was not the few bourgeois circles within the Revisionist party – which, in common with the bourgeoisie outside *Ha-Zohar*, tended towards moderation and true 'co-existence' – but, of all things, the working-class members of *Ha-Zohar* and *Betar*. We do not have to adopt the psycho-political interpretation of Perlmutter – who believed that the bourgeois circles within Revisionism (and in their wake the Revisionist party as a whole) had been infected with the inferiority complex and self-hate of the Jewish bourgeoisie, which in turn had driven them to self-abasement – to agree with his basic thesis that the roots of the conflict between Revisionism and the *Histadrut* did not lie in Revisionism's attempt to represent the class interests of the Jewish bourgeoisie in Palestine. Perlmutter's conclusion in 1937 was that a congruence should be created between the social constitution of Revisionism and the movement's political methods. It had to transform itself from a bourgeois party into a proletarian party, and 'bourgeois Revisionism' had to make way for 'proletarian Revisionism'. 'Proletarian', in the author's view, did not refer to unionized wage earners; in line with Jabotinsky, the definition of a proletarian was a lower-middle-class worker or member of the free professions who belonged to the *yishuv*, who did not form a part of the *Histadrut* society and who did not employ hired labour. According to Perlmutter one could not negate the role of the bourgeoisie in the Jewish society of Eretz Israel, and he was convinced that there existed an inverse relationship between the national economic role of the bourgeoisie and its national role in the state. The task of the *yishuv* proletariat was therefore to enter into an alliance with the bourgeoisie based on their common interests, to offer it protection against the unionized working class and extract the most favourable material conditions. Somehow the mentality of *Ha-Zohar* had to be changed. '*Ha-Zohar* must grow up and strike out on the road to wide-ranging political involvement, backed by the full weight of proletarian Revisionism.'

According to this view, the *yishuv* embodied three classes: the bourgeoisie, organized labour and the petit-bourgeoisie. The bourgeoisie and the 'proletarian' petit-bourgeoisie wings had to present a common front against the central organized working class, which alone was stronger than either of the other two. Perlmutter fails to mention which role the salaried workers who were organized in *Ha-Zohar* were intended to play in this struggle. Underlying this conception is the idea that the proletarian petit-bourgeoisie, in the absence of vested economic interests of its own, could be the middle class, around which the activities with the broadest and most promising national perspective could revolve. It was the class which, because of its extremely nebulous economic status, considered its future bound up with the national fate rather than with that of some institution or social organization. Now that the weakness of the working class and the bourgeoisie had become clear, it was the turn of the 'forgotten' class, the people who were not concerned about their private property or that of the organization to which they belonged; 'the hour had struck of the hungry masses, the unorganized poor, who lived in pressing conditions of economic hardship.'

This seems to have been one of the few manifestations during this period heralding the transition from bourgeois populism to socialist populism, but it would only be at the end of the 1940s that this transition would be realized. The *Herut* movement will be confronted, both in theory and practice, with a tension between its bourgeois populism and its appeal to the lower classes within Israeli society.

Despite its lack of success, *Ha-Zohar* did not ring down the curtain on its bourgeois orientation. In Eretz Israel the party continued to champion the interests of the middle class in the face of its economic problems. The economic crisis following the Fifth Aliyah, which persisted until the outbreak of World War II, even resulted in a revival of the bourgeois orientation. The economic weakness of the Jewish middle class in Eretz Israel was, as usual, ascribed to its lack of internal organization. Revisionism failed to correlate its analysis of the social reality, its idealistic views of this reality and the *de facto* situation. As a result it remained wedded to its bourgeois orientation long after it had become clear that it could never produce any real political gains. This situation persisted until

1965, when the Revisionists entered into a political alliance with the General Zionists, the principal Israeli Liberal party, thus ending the long freeze and breaking its long political isolation.

Political Tactics and Propaganda

The image of Revisionism as a movement employing a violent and brutal propagandistic style was to a large extent due to the influence of *Hazit ha-Am*, although this publication was by no means the only medium to express itself in such harsh and aggressive language. It should not be forgotten that the internal Zionist struggle was highly emotional and polemical in content and style, and profoundly influenced by the tense, eschatological atmosphere resulting from the fierce power struggle between the various ideologies and movements in Europe in the period between the two world wars. The Revisionist political culture was replete with dramatic symbols and metaphors, not to speak of its outspoken tendency towards demonization of its opponents. The preferred style was to describe an opponent in negative and schematic terms, loaded with pathos and rhetoric. But demonological and schematic interpretations within Zionism were not restricted to the Revisionists only. The style of communication which developed between the two sides was coarse and venomous, aimed at moral delegitimization of the opponent by denouncing him and even 'inciting' the Jewish public against him. Jabotinsky, who in the course of his political propaganda efforts at times adopted a kind of 'symbolic' language of his own, harboured certain reservations with regard to the political metaphors used by *Hazit ha-Am*. The readers do not understand symbolism, he wrote, and we should refrain from tough language, unproven accusations and hysteria. Even so, in typical Jabotinsky style, he also showed understanding of the expressions adopted by *Hazit ha-Am* after discovering 'what a dirty bunch they have to fight' in Eretz Israel. Newspaper journalism has its own rules and rhythm, he wrote, rules which are different from poetry or even those applying to personal essays.

Propaganda efforts found expression in journalism, poetry, satirical novels, and a 'yellow press', exemplified by Yevin's *Jerusalem Waits . . .* , a *roman à clef* intended 'to rip the masks' off the leaders of the *Histadrut*, and to expose their philistine cynicism.[52] Their leaders themselves no longer believed in Zionism; they were Zionists only for 'economic reasons', and they were personally and ideologically corrupt – such was the thesis of this scandal-mongering novel which Mapai did its utmost to suppress. The poetry of Uri Zvi Greenberg particularly set the tone in painting a criminal, degenerate and pathological image of the Labour movement and the leaders of 'official Zionism'.

This importance attached to propaganda can be explained by the organizational weakness, and the emotional and ideologically-motivated character of the followers of the Revisionist movement. A modern party, Kalman Katznelson wrote, was based on a leader who understood the innermost desires of the masses, on a bold and daring statement of the truth, and on great propagandistic talent capable of moving the masses. The political drawback of *Ha-Zohar* was that it lacked an organization for disseminating its truth, and for engaging in information and propaganda activities in all the available mass media. *Ha-Zohar* had no propaganda apparatus, and its propaganda efforts were erratic, spontaneous and primitive; without an effective organization Revisionism could not possibly win the battle between the impulsive, inner truth, and the [party] juggernaut with its offices and funds.[53]

The closure of *Hazit ha-Am* had left a real desire for a powerful propaganda organization, coupled with a negative attitude to the propaganda apparatus that had existed thus far. The gap between image and reality was indeed great. *Ha-Zohar* in Eretz Israel was not a strongly organized movement; its power was slight, its propaganda unstructured, its tools were weak – and despite all this it had somehow created the impression of a minority party that was able to 'seize power' by violent means. To seize power was impossible in a voluntary, non-sovereign society. A massive propaganda effort in Eretz Israel was no substitute for a political platform and socio-political power. Its oppositional standing, implacable hostility, and inability to realize the Revisionist dream were mainly responsible for creating the fierce propagandistic style likely to create the impression that the Revisionist movement intended – or in fact had the means and the strength – to achieve political hegemony by undemocratic, violent means.

Both style and contents of the propaganda messages were a sign of the times (the 1930s) and, more than to the Jews of Eretz Israel, they were addressed to the Zionist public in Poland. As already mentioned, the climate among the Jewish masses in Poland during the 1930s was rife with slogans about 'the dictatorship of the proletariat' and 'Bolshevism', on the one hand, and 'Fascism' and 'Hitlerism' on the other – slogans which sensitized and radicalized an already excitable public. This kind of propaganda therefore described the situation in Eretz Israel in terms of the situation prevailing in Spain or Poland during the same period, where a crucial power struggle for political supremacy between 'Right' and 'Left' was being fought. These apocalyptic images became an integral part of the situational picture and contemporary feeling, but at the same time were far removed from the empirical reality.

The Socio-Demographic Structure of Revisionism

To conclude this chapter it might be worthwhile to portray the social structure of Revisionism. This is no easy task, since we only have information on the structure of distinct groups, and not on the nature and stratification of the hundreds of thousands of anonymous sympathizers. There can be no doubt that Revisionism faithfully represented the socio-cultural nature of Jewish society in Eastern Europe, in particular the Zionist element in its midst. It is difficult to determine to what extent joining the Revisionists would have been feasible for all strata of the Jewish-Zionist public reached by Zionist propaganda, and whether those who joined did so because of a psychological effect, or because they belonged to a particular social class or status. Undoubtedly the influence of nationalist populist propaganda was more pronounced on the less structured and organized sectors of the public, who were searching for a means of identification and were therefore more susceptible to the magic of promises of a speedy and absolute salvation. However, since the members of the Zionist movement belonged mainly to the lower and middle strata of the Jewish middle class, it would seem that we are dealing here with a psychological rather than a sociological phenomenon: a Jewish public, part of which wanted to change its social character, and another part which had no wish to do so. There are a number of examples of members of one and the same family who parted on the issue of politics, warranting the assumption of different psychological responses and different answers to an identical situation, without the choice of the particular direction being influenced by their social background in any marked way.

Another distinction worth mentioning is that between 'fathers and sons'. The majority of *Betar* members belonged to the lower and middle strata of middle class families, and at the time of their joining *Betar* were enrolled at various secondary schools and gymnasia; some 40 per cent were clerks, salesmen and labourers (approximately 40 per cent of this latter group was 18 years or older).[54] All possessed a strong and well-developed national consciousness.

They saw themselves as a 'new breed of Jew', in contrast to their parents, whose involvement with Zionism had been limited mainly to the purchase of the *shekel* and voting for the Zionist Congress. On many other points, however, a strong resemblance existed between the members of *Betar* and the voters for *Ha-Zohar*, transcending any differences in age or mentality.

The members (and voters) of *Ha-Zohar* possessed outspoken nationalist views in which social or class considerations played no part. In this respect they resembled the Polish Jewish lower middle class as a whole, whose environment had taught them to think in national rather than in class terms. Part of the latter group's criticism against the hegemony of 'the Left' was due to a deep sense of deprivation in everything connected with Zionist emigration policy to Eretz Israel, which preferred 'pioneers' and salaried workers over people with middle-class status. The latter did not struggle for structural changes in Jewish society, and manifested no signs of rejecting the bourgeois ethos and occupations on either ideological or aesthetic grounds. In all these respects they were considered utter conformists. Worse than that, they feared and rejected the socialist ideas and the ideology of the supremacy of the working class: they refused to change their social status and socio-cultural ethos, but rather wanted to perpetuate them – both in Eretz Israel and in the Diaspora. At this point it is worth noting that in a movement whose membership included large numbers of salaried employees, practically no texts (of either a propagandistic or literary nature) in praise of manual labour can be found. As against this there exist numerous documents propagating the bourgeois ethos and bourgeois economic activity.

From a social point of view Revisionism therefore represented a conservative outlook (which also showed in its approach to cultural issues, for instance its manifest anti-modernism). In Eretz Israel, on the other hand, *Ha-Zohar* was a heterogeneous party in terms of its socio-demographic composition. Of the party's 26,000 voters in 1935 some 5,000 were employees; 3,000 belonged to the oriental community (mainly the urban proletariat), whereas the remainder consisted of the lower middle classes and professionals (both salaried and independent). All these were attracted to Revisionism because it represented a form of 'popular Zionism' which did not impose all kinds of – even theoretical – duties upon its members, certainly not to equalize one's social status with that of others.

The Revisionists rejected out of hand what in the Labour movement's 'pioneering' ideology was touted as the realization of a deep personal fulfilment. They had no intention of becoming 'pioneers', 'working the land' or, for that matter, joining a collective framework of any description; all they wanted was to live their own individualistic way of life within their own socio-economic environment. Rather than *Gesellschaft* or *Gemeinschaft*, their preferred social framework was the 'Nation', with the 'State' as its political expression. A 'State' was considered the framework which fulfilled national expectations, as well as providing the required services to its citizens. Revisionism viewed the State in the same terms as Pilsudski's Right did in Poland: a neutral framework above party influences, which imposed law and order in the socio-economic struggle to enable the organic nation to lead its own life.

The Revisionist elite consisted of an intelligentsia, a semi-intelligentsia, high school and university graduates, and members of the free professions. The leading personalities were journalists, lawyers, physicians, salaried workers and men of letters. At the beginning of the present century Weizmann described the Jewish intelligentsia as *déclassé*;[55] it would have been more correct to describe the nationalist intelligentsia as *dénationalisé*. Their national Jewish consciousness was influenced by memories of past Jewish national history, but also by (or through) the Eastern European nationalism prevailing in the period between the two World Wars. In many respects they may be said to have undergone a process of Polanization, but – as mentioned before – their purpose was not to affiliate or integrate with Polish society or, like the Poles themselves, become an inseparable part of the Polish nation. They wanted to create a Jewish national consciousness (as a Polish minority with equal rights) according to the Polish model; to be a national minority with a glorious past, with its own heroic memories, and political and territorial aspirations of its own – just like the Poles themselves. This middle class, torn between two mutually exclusive worlds – the nationalism of its surroundings and Jewish nationalism – both profoundly conflicting with other ideologies such as Communism, Bundism and Zionist Socialism, while rejecting the concept that Zionist fulfilment also demanded a change of social status, economic occupation and socio-cultural ethos, was unable to accept either the Polish 'positivist' approach, or the constructivism of the Zionist Labour movement. Their mentality was not geared to a way of life which talked in terms of the gradual 'rebuilding of a society from the bottom up'. The growing feeling during the 1930s that time was running out, served to make their opposition to the evolutionary approach even fiercer. According to their view, a society had to be built 'from the top down', by the State and its agencies in a planned and organized manner – in the same way one would undertake a national or international construction project. It is patently clear that both this outlook and this kind of approach stood in flagrant contradiction to the real possibilities during the 1920s and 1930s. However, the very gap between 'programme' and 'reality' became the force impelling the Revisionists to search for activities that would move the wheels of Zionist history.

The Revisionist movement in Poland comprised a lower class consisting of a petty bourgeoisie, and an intellectual elite, and either to join or to leave it required no commitment or sacrifice whatsoever. In Palestine recruitment and participation in the Revisionist movement and its satellite organizations were of a quite different nature. The majority of the members had come to Eretz Israel as Revisionists (members of either *Ha-Zohar* or *Betar*), and there existed a certain continuity in political identification (i.e. sons of Revisionists as a rule became Revisionists). This kind of genealogical affiliation could be found in other movements and political parties as well, but here, in Eretz Israel, the Revisionist ranks were joined by new forces, in particular members of the oriental community, who saw in Revisionism a nationalist party with a conservative and religiously traditional outlook, activist youngsters opposed to the political attitudes of the *yishuv* leadership, and other groups with real or supposed grievances against the ruling establishment. To be a Revisionist in Eretz Israel in a sense made one an outcast, and it meant exclusion from the *Histadrut* welfare system, as well as exposure to considerable social and economic pressure. The Revisionist consciousness in Eretz Israel evolved not so much against a social backdrop, as through a feeling that it had a historic mission to fulfil, on the one hand, and a feeling of being persecuted and discriminated against, on the other. The dominant *Histadrut* and Mapai-controlled society was depicted not only as ideologically and politically unsound, but as a draconian and dictatorial social system which attempted to eliminate its rivals by any means, fair or foul, or – if this did not work – through discrimination and deprivation of their rights. From the 1920s onwards this combination of an awareness of belonging to a movement which carried out the Zionist mission from a rightist perspective, on the one hand, and the acute sense of deprivation, on the other, became an active and dominant constituent of the evolution of the essence of Revisionism, and the collective experience of the Revisionists and their adherents.

C. THE POLITICAL HISTORY OF REVISIONISM:
THE EMERGENCE OF NEW ORGANIZATIONS IN THE 1930s

The Revisionist Periphery and Secondary Groups –
Berit ha-Biryonim and Berit ha-Hayal

Initially the Revisionist movement consisted of a political party and a 'youth movement', but after 1934 and 1937 these were joined by a workers' organization and a military underground movement respectively. Simultaneously a number of informal ideological and political groups existed, side by side with several peripheral organizations either affiliated with the Revisionists, or maintaining a variety of closer or incidental ideological or organizational ties with the movement.

Among these affiliated organizations was *Berit ha-Hayal al shem Ze'ev Jabotinsky* – a veteran soldiers' organization named after Jabotinsky, which was founded in the Spring of 1933 by Jewish ex-soldiers who had served in the Polish army. By 1935 the *Berit ha-Hayal* had 300 branches all over Poland, together comprising some 10,000 members. Its main ideas were borrowed from Pilsudski's Polish Legion, and after 1937 part of the membership joined the IZL and received military training with the assistance of the Polish authorities. Several of the principals at *Berit ha-Hayal* headquarters were Betar people, and they described the organization as a twin movement of Betar, which provided an organized framework for non-Betar members who wanted to join a similar, but separate organization aimed at training recruits for the future Jewish Legion. The growth of *Berit ha-Hayal* was spontaneous, and Jabotinsky regarded it as an organization of middle-class youngsters who, although they had not received a Betar education, were prepared to place themselves at the disposal of the Jewish Legion in Eretz Israel.[56] Their military training and the influence of Polish nationalism furthered the spread of the IZL's influence within *Berit ha-Hayal* after 1937. In Palestine the *Berit ha-Hayal* played only a small role, in contrast with Poland, where it played a substantial part in the internal Zionist struggles, due to its being a well-organized body of militarily experienced adults who were able to add their weight to the party political infighting. In the eyes of Mapai the organization's members were the shock troops of Revisionism in Poland, operating with the support of the regime of Pilsudski and the colonels who succeeded him, who gave them a free hand to fight the socialist Jewish parties.

A second group, founded in 1933 by religious students, was the *Berit Yeshurun*; by 1935 their number had grown to 7,000 members. *Berit Yeshurun* was associated with *Berit ha-Hasmona'im*, a religious scout movement with a Revisionist political slant. *El Al* was the name of the Revisionist student union at the institutions of higher learning in Palestine (the Haifa Technion and the Hebrew University in Jerusalem), and it in turn was affiliated with *Yavne ve-Yodefat*, the National Union of Zionist Academics, which was founded in 1934 and survived until 1936. The Revisionist Women Students Organization (*Waraf*), founded in 1935, and which had 4,000 members, had a small branch in Palestine. Other peripheral organizations emerged after 1937 from the younger members of the urban intelligentsia, which on the eve of the Second World War, and in particular after 1944, constituted a source of recruitment for the IZL.

These organizations had a formal character, whereas the group with the most impact on the ideas and traditions of the movement was the *Berit ha-Biryonim*, an informal organization which operated for some two years in Eretz Israel.[57] This was the first group with a quasi-revolutionary character which clearly manifested a radical nationalist world view, and in which this view was institutionalized. There exists a direct ideological and personal connection between the *Berit ha-Biryonim*, the IZL and Lehi, even though there is no immediate and complete genealogical continuity. In some respects *Berit ha-Biryonim* would appear to be the intermediary between the 'old' Revisionism of Jabotinsky and *Ha-Zohar*, and the ideology and practices of the IZL and Lehi.

Berit ha-Biryonim originated in a 'revolutionary Zionist' cell founded in Jerusalem under the inspiration of the ideological seminars conducted by Achimeir and a local group of 'nationalist youth'. Achimeir was possessed of a strong urge to coordinate his political activity and historical conceptions. From 1931 onwards, however, his leadership of the group left much to be desired. He was too weak a personality to be the leader of a group which believed in his kind of ideas, namely to carry out armed underground activities. Achimeir was an intellectual revolutionary rather than an underground fighter such as, for instance, Avraham Stern. Most of the activities of *Berit ha-Biryonim* were of a symbolic or demonstrative character. *Berit ha-Biryonim* and its affiliated publication, the *Hazit ha-Am*, set the tone in the propaganda struggle against Mapai

and the *Histadrut*. Most of its members were people who had left
various socialist parties, contributing to Revisionism the intense
hatred of those who had abandoned an ideal, but retained certain of
the extremist ideological elements of their former cause. The
ideological style and the thrust of their attacks were extremely
militant and aggressive, and in particular directed at the national
'minimalism' of the *Histadrut*, while completely disregarding the
'minimalism' of the members of the *yishuv* in general. Not all the
members of the *Berit* were equally satisfied with the emphasis
placed on the 'home front' – the struggle against Mapai – which they
believed to distract from the real front, namely the struggle against
the British administration. But the anti-Mapai and anti-socialist
criticism, and the polemical zeal, were so intense that neither
Achimeir, nor Yevin, Greenberg nor Katznelson were able to
restrain themselves. We are dealing here with an intellectual
hostility, the emotional dimension of which far outweighed the analytical dimension. They considered socialism a vulgar, 'diabolical'
and anti-humanistic phenomenon, and in their eyes there was no
distinction between Stalinist Communism and Mapai Socialism.

The inspiration of *Berit ha-Biryonim* was to a large extent derived
from the Second Temple Period, through the historical writings of
Klausner and the poetry of Uri Zvi Greenberg, in which the *Berit*
was compared to the *Sicarii*, armed Jewish radical zealots who
fought both the Romans and Jewish 'moderates' in the days of the
Second Temple.[58] Although the *Scroll of the Sicarii*, written by
Achimeir, purported to be a historical document rather than a
political platform, it does provide an insight into his feelings and his
ambivalent attitude to individual terrorist acts in a 'society suffering
from malaise'.[59] Achimeir no doubt preferred organized revolutionary activity over anarchism, which uses terror as its weapon. He
believed that the youth of Eretz Israel would join the Revisionists if
only the movement took a more activist stance. To this end he
conducted a propaganda campaign within *Ha-Zohar*, and although
his natural inclination tended towards dictatorial centralism, he
acted in a democratic way within the party by establishing a faction
and putting himself forward as a candidate in the elections. What
completely spoiled his chances was the trial of *Berit ha-Biryonim*
following the Arlosoroff murder trial. The serious charges laid
against him and his friends backfired against the movement as a
whole.

Achimeir described the 'London Agreement' of 1934 and the
negotiations between Ben-Gurion and Jabotinsky as a 'stab in the

back', an effort to come to terms with an arch-enemy with whom no compromise whatsoever could ever be reached. After 1934 *Ha-Zohar* in Eretz Israel took energetic steps to prevent the publication of *Hazit ha-Am*. Yevin was dismissed from *Ha-Yarden*, and in 1934 the new Executive of *Ha-Zohar* warned that if they wanted an organized leadership and a real party, they should 'take a good look at the psychology and the frame of mind of *Ha-Zohar* in Eretz Israel, understanding that if our proposals are not accepted, *Ha-Zohar* in Eretz Israel would not become an orderly organization, but would once again have to put up with the prevailing moods and sympathies as had been the case in former years.'[60] The party members sarcastically referred to Achimeir and his followers as 'Sansculottes'. The 'General Zionists', as Achimeir called the 'moderate' Revisionists, did not object to the elimination of maximalism in Eretz Israel, and the bolshevik mentality which, in their view, maximalism had introduced into liberal-bourgeois Revisionism. Achimeir said this as early as 1936, when he remarked that the idea of being 'bandits' was foreign to the majority of Betar members, notwithstanding the fact that without it Revisionism might simply lack the momentum to take off.

Jabotinsky fought against this mentality, although more in private letters than in public: a victory of the views of Achimeir and his friends would be tantamount to 'expulsion from the party', wrote Jabotinsky to Yevin in August 1932, unless they would decide to go of their own volition. *Ha-Zohar*, he wrote, was a party based on nineteenth-century democratic principles, [which aspired to] the upbuilding of Eretz Israel, the adoption of certain fundamental positions, and an 'aristocratic' (*hadar*) education towards statehood.[61] Such principles were not compatible with an underground movement, or a semi-fascist party aiming at the establishment of a dictatorial regime. Even so the struggle was mainly conducted in private, and it remained hidden from public view. However, Jabotinsky did publicly identify himself with the personal sacrifice, the courage and the ideological zeal of Achimeir and his colleagues. Their victimization and persecution by Mapai in fact prevented him from shaking them off, and compelled him to throw his full weight, and that of the party, behind them, thus effectively identifying himself with the rebels.

Between Organized Politics and 'Impressionism'

The emergence of *Berit ha-Biryonim*, with its militancy and violent

criticism, confronted *Ha-Zohar* with a critical problem, namely the
question of how much independence and initiative could be granted
to individual groups within the movement, while at the same time
preventing them from committing the movement as a whole. The
second, related, question concerned the degree of responsibility the
movement could accept for actions that were in contradiction to
its own principles and methods. Jabotinsky laid down a rule that
the party would support members who were falsely accused (as,
for instance, in the Arlosoroff case), but would refuse to accept
responsibility for 'spontaneous' actions of whatever kind. A party
was not a matter of 'mood', he declared, but of systematic principles
and an organized political approach. The derogatory description in
the Revisionist jargon for such demonstrative and emotional initiatives was 'impressionistic' – meaning that they were superficial and
erratic. The party, Jabotinsky wrote to Yevin, did not deny the
members' right to undertake independent initiatives, even where
actions were taken to which the party was opposed, or which it was
unable to undertake on its own. The only condition was that such
activities would not be undertaken in the name of the movement,
and that they would not contravene its accepted moral principles.
He knew, so he wrote, that this opinion was unacceptable to
many of the leaders of *Ha-Zohar*, who were opposed to any 'private'
initiatives.[62]

However, many of the most successful actions undertaken by
Revisionism throughout the 1930s were not initiated by the formal
and official leadership, but by groups and individuals acting on their
own. The Betar demonstration at the Wailing Wall in Jerusalem in
August 1929 was an independent initiative which took Jabotinsky
completely by surprise, and which caused serious complications.
The same can be said for the act of reprisal by Shlomo Ben-Yosef in
1937, for which the latter was executed in July 1938, making him the
first Jew to be hanged by the mandatory authorities.[63] This incident
caused a radical change in the Revisionist attitude towards Great
Britain. Many other examples of such private initiatives can be
mentioned, among which were the establishment of the Revisionist
trade union, the establishment and evolution of the IZL, the actions
of *Brit Ha-Biryonim*, the creation of the secret cells of the IZL in
Poland, and the organization of illegal immigration from Eastern
Europe – to mention only a few. All these began as 'private
initiatives', and some of them were accepted as *faits accomplis*, and
subsequently endorsed by the movement. Jabotinsky believed only
in 'moods', which according to him reflected a deep and authentic

frame of mind that was impossible to suppress and, *if* properly exploited, were of vital political value. At times he even encouraged this concept in articles dealing with the need for adventurism (in the sense of venturesome initiatives).[64] He also thought that he would be able to control them, and that they would become the driving force of his policy. In this he was wrong.

It looks as if he believed that these spontaneous moods, and their consequences, would indirectly be of political benefit to him; in other words, they would further his goals by proving to Great Britain that her policies were unacceptable to the Jewish population of Eretz Israel and to the Zionists. In the course of the 1930s it became clear to him, however, that such 'moods' had become the norm within the organizations, and had in fact become institutionalized in an ideology that was the complete antithesis of Jabotinsky's Revisionism. The organizational continuity, and the profound sense of continuity as expressed in the writings and the awareness of many (admittedly not all) of those involved, are unable to hide the fact that a number of far-reaching developments occurred during the 1930s. Some of these remained within the framework of the existing historical-political tradition, whereas others breeched this framework to create their own autonomous frameworks. 'Impressionism' and 'adventurism' won out over national and formal party politics.

Two of these organizational frameworks within Revisionism that were not the product of any initiative 'from above' warrant a more detailed discussion. Both of them were due to 'unforeseen' developments, and both of them added a new dimension to Revisionism. The first of these developments will be touched upon here only briefly, since it is connected with the 'internal aspects' of the social history of the *yishuv*. The second will be dealt with more fully, however, because it became the foremost manifestation of Revisionism in a dialectical process.

The first development concerns the founding of the Revisionist trade union; the second that of the IZL . The latter's ideology will be discussed separately, and here we will discuss only its organizational development within Revisionism.

From Trade Union to Labour Federation[65]

As early as 1925, and more strongly so in 1929, *Ha-Zohar* – a party with an essentially 'bourgeois' social orientation – began to be influenced as well as concerned by a phenomenon which was to have profound implications for its future, namely the emergence of a Revisionist working class in Eretz Israel. There were of course labourers and sons of labourers within the ranks of *Ha-Zohar* and Betar in the various European countries in which the Revisionist movement flourished, but only in Eretz Israel did the existing Revisionist working class affect the movement to any marked extent. Under the prevailing conditions in Palestine the working classes – in the cities as well as in rural settlements – were concentrated in large groups, and compelled to organize themselves in collective frameworks in their efforts to find employment, to settle down, to establish organs for mutual aid, and so forth. Immigrants from the bourgeoisie and petit bourgeoisie engaged in their own professions, and were at most organized in a particular economic industrial or trade organization, but this kind of organization was generally closed to the salaried lower- and middle-class bourgeoisie and the self-employed intelligentsia, whereas the workers were dependent upon the services of the labour exchange.

Many of the Revisionist immigrants, particularly the younger ones, did not have any profession, or had come to Palestine with the intention of finding salaried employment, which made their absorption and economic integration a serious problem. As a result, the working class became the most actively organized part of the Revisionist society in Eretz Israel. Betar in Eretz Israel depended mainly on working youngsters and students, whereas – as already mentioned – the leading segment in the political party, *Ha-Zohar*, consisted of party activists from the intelligentsia and the free professions. For this reason the Revisionist workers in Palestine were the most mature and best-organized element in the movement, with specific economic and professional interests and deeply involved in the country's day to day affairs, particularly in the area of labour relations. It is not surprising that the Revisionist labour wing was a thorn in the flesh of the Labour party in Eretz Israel, and that it was seen as the spearhead of the struggle of the bourgeoisie and *Ha-Zohar* against the *Histadrut* and the workers' parties. They realized that *Ha-Zohar* (the party) and Betar (the youth organization) were not particularly dangerous, given the fact that their strength was mainly restricted to the area of formal political activity and propaganda. Until the emergence of a Revisionist working class, the main social and professional struggles in the *yishuv* – except for a brief period of clashes between the *Histadrut* and *Ha-Po'el ha-Mizrachi* (the Religious Workers' Party) and several other, very small, organizations – had been focused on employer–employee relations.

The appearance of the Revisionist workers on the political scene, the effects of which were particularly felt after 1930, introduced a new element into the struggle: in the opinion of the labour parties this element mainly served the interests of the employers, who could use it to break the organizational power of the *Histadrut* and lower the wages of organized labour – all this in the name of the bourgeois ideology of *Ha-Zohar*. Jabotinsky himself recognized this phenomenon when commenting in a letter to Schechtman in April 1929, that the fiercest attacks on the *Histadrut* did not originate in bourgeois circles, but in those of the Revisionist workers.[66]

Except for the existence and activities of its 'labour' wing, it looks therefore as if until 1934 the Revisionist involvement in the existence of the *yishuv* was of a limited nature, consisting mainly of political street demonstrations, and political debates in the *yishuv* media and organizations. Weaker still, if not non-existent, was its practical involvement in economic and social affairs. It is ironic that the Revisionist struggle for supremacy in the private sector in Eretz Israel was partially effective only thanks to the existence of a labour wing in the Revisionist party. In practical terms, however, the Revisionist workers did not fight for the supremacy of the private sector – even though they subscribed to the Revisionist thinking about its importance and centrality – but for their own specific interests; the Revisionist worker did not enter the lists in order to become a tool in the hands of the private sector, even though it was not long before his struggle had become a part of the class struggle in Eretz Israel. Although the Revisionist worker possessed a profound ideological awareness, he was entirely lacking in class consciousness; he was the typical example of the conservative working man. He was prepared to face extreme hardships in his struggle against the *Histadrut* – hardships which left Revisionists who did not belong to the working class completely unaffected. In this respect the Revisionist workers constituted a strong ideological element, and they were acutely aware of their actions. To describe them as a 'willing tool' of the private sector in Eretz Israel would mean a complete denial of their ideological awareness and their willingness to make sacrifices for this ideology. There is no doubt that the roots of the conflict between Revisionism and the Labour movement lay in their respective ideologies and political systems, and that this root problem both fed and aggravated the problems in all other areas. Even so it was the socio-economic confrontation which in 1934 caused the political conflict to turn into a real social confrontation.

The existence of workers who refused to be members of the

Histadrut, forced the Revisionist leadership to establish a labour federation of its own, that would fulfil all the professional and economic functions of the *Histadrut*, but would not be a trade union only. There were four factors working towards a break with the *Histadrut*: (a) the Achimeir group, who saw a walk-out as a means of bringing the fight with Mapai and the *Histadrut* to a head; (b) Revisionist labourers, who wanted to free the labour market from the centralist shackles of Mapai; (c) Jabotinsky, who in 1931 had expressed the opinion that an independent Revisionist labour organization would increase the strength of *Ha-Zohar vis-à-vis* Mapai and the civilian constituency in Eretz Israel; and (d) Revisionist workers who wanted an independent organization that was not under the control of the *Histadrut* or Mapai and would be able to supply badly needed social services such as medical care, housing, and so forth.

The pressures of socio-economic reality therefore led to the establishment of an independent Revisionist labour organization, which by its very nature became an instrument in the political struggle. But for the presence of Revisionist labourers, the Revisionist movement need not have created a socio-economic entity such as the National Labour Federation, which was founded in 1934 with 4,000 members, half of whom were Revisionists and members of Betar.

However, from the moment of its inception, the Revisionist labour organization refused to accept the *Histadrut*'s rulings with regard to the labour market, so that a confrontation on socio-economic issues became unavoidable (mainly because neither the mandatory authorities nor the Zionist Organization were until the 1940s able to implement a legally based labour relations charter). From the overall Revisionist viewpoint this involvement in continuous battles about job availabilities and the nature of the labour relations system meant that the movement was being dragged into superfluous and marginal issues. Those who reasoned thus forgot that Revisionism was not only a constitutional political party engaged in diplomatic activity, but also a genuine popular social movement, which could not wilfully stand aside from all kinds of conflicts that formed an inseparable part of the creation, formation and institutionalization of a society.

The Revisionist National Labour Federation was established as a small labour union (deriving its financial support from internal Revisionist sources), which intended to provide employment, job protection and social services for its members. Apart from this it considerably weakened the monopoly of the *Histadrut* in the labour market, as a result of which it helped the employers in the private sector to reduce the wage level for Jewish workers, and maintain even lower wages for Arab workers employed by Jewish firms.

The IZL – From 'Jewish Legion' to Underground

The following paragraphs will be devoted to a brief sketch of the formal organic relationship between Revisionism and the IZL, whereas its underlying political views and methods of operation will be discussed in a separate chapter. The history of the IZL and its struggles have formed the subject of numerous treatises, many of which are available to the English reader, so that there is no need to repeat them here.[67]

The development of the *Irgun Zeva'i Le'umi* (National Military Organization, or IZL) was possibly the most dramatic development in the annals of Revisionism, and the most fundamental dialectic revolution in its history. In essence it was not only a revolution in response to a given reality, but also an issue concerning the definition of immediate political aims, and the means of achieving the accepted national political goals. However, the radical nature of the changes in approach and methods, and the very consequences of their use, made them not less revolutionary – and possibly more revolutionary and far-reaching – than the change in theoretical conceptual principles.

One of the fundamental issues for Jabotinsky had always been the establishment of regular Jewish army brigades, which would form a part of the British garrison in Eretz Israel (and the Middle East) – and in course of time might even replace it. The re-establishment of the 'Jewish Legion' which had fought in the First World War (and which had been disbanded in 1920) was a major item in the Revisionist platform, important to *Ha-Zohar* as well as Betar. The importance attached to the establishment of a regular army, i.e. a Jewish Legion, can be explained by both ideological and pragmatic reasons, but under no circumstances was this army intended to become an underground organization that would take up arms against the mandatory authorities and its agencies.

Jabotinsky believed that only a regular Jewish military force would be able to give full and formal expression to the existing mutual interests – as he conceived them – between Zionism and Great Britain, and to provide the necessary safeguards in terms of security and law and order (in the narrower as well as the wider sense) for the establishment of a Jewish national home. Jabotinsky opposed the *Haganah* (Defence), the illegal military organization established in 1920 by the *Histadrut* for self-defence purposes, which he regarded as not only an illegal, but also an ineffective militia, that would be powerless to influence the political situation. Ever since the end of the First World War his battle-cry had been to 're-establish the Brigades [*Gedudim*]!' On this subject fierce debates took place in 1921 between him and members of the Zionist Executive, who opposed the idea on pragmatic grounds ('the British are opposed to a Jewish Brigade') as well as on grounds of principle ('a Jewish Brigade will be a provocation'; 'Zionism is a moral undertaking, and cannot achieve its aims by force of arms!').[68] Jabotinsky's answer to this was that without a Jewish Brigade there would be no security in Eretz Israel, since the British would refuse to undertake the burden of imposing Zionism upon the Arabs, who also had a strong national claim on Palestine. There was a genuine need for an armed force, since there was no getting away from the fact that Arab resistance was dangerous and tangible: 'You cannot use an English Tommy Atkins to defend the Jewish settlements, or any Jewish village or [for that matter] any individual Jew,' as he put it.

The riots of 1929 only reinforced his argument. Following the riots in August of that year he wrote a series of articles under the title, 'The Defence Issue in Eretz Israel', in which he continued to drive home the reasons for his objections, both pragmatic and on principle, to the *yishuv*'s illegal *Haganah*, and his demand for regular army brigades within the framework of the Mandate. The value of self-defence, he wrote, was negligible from a military point of view, and only a regular army could operate efficiently, since 'the military' was a profession which required proficiency and knowledge in a variety of fields. A regular army operated in the open; at times its mere appearance was sufficient to have a deterrent effect. Consequently the foremost political priority of Zionism was to have regular Jewish soldiers in British uniforms![69]

It is again one of the ironies of history that actual circumstances often have further-reaching effects than principles. During the 'Arab Revolt' (1936–1939) and the Second World War it was the leaders of the Haganah who were to lay the foundations for military cooperation with Great Britain, and recognize its considerable usefulness and importance (even to the point of suppressing internal criticism, and holding back from retaliatory actions against Arabs). Even more ironic is the fact that it was Jabotinsky's movement which spawned an illegal organization that did not restrict itself to self-defence and guard duties, but initiated a system of counter-terror (first against Arabs, at a later stage also against the British). Jabotinsky considered this development fraught with danger. Within a formal framework there was a command structure and discipline, whereas in an underground organization the weapons were in the hands of individuals; in the absence of supervision this could be dangerous in places where 'nervousness is ingrained and the situation is unstable,' he wrote.

The IZL was first and foremost a product of organizational developments; only in course of time did the ideological rationale evolve, which provided it with self-awareness and new aims. From an organizational perspective the result was that Revisionism found itself irrevocably tied to an illegal underground organization, which in the year 1944 broke with party discipline, to become an independent military and political body, which – upon being disbanded – formed a new political party.

The members of the *Haganah* who left this organization in 1931 and formed the *'Haganah Bet'* organization' (which later on became the *Haganah Le'umit* ('National *Haganah'*) and eventually – by the early 1930s – the *Irgun Zeva'i Le'umi*) did so out of a sense of dissatisfaction with the apparent inability of the *Haganah* to react to the riots of 1929. Betar members who, together with other activist youths, had joined the *Haganah*, at first regarded it as a foundation for a future regular army, rather than as an underground movement. It did not take long, however, for these Betar people to become the driving force, formulating within it a nationalist revolutionary ideology and propagating, at least in their writings, the idea of a national liberation struggle. In 1933 the new organization had 300 members and established a political supervisory committee containing representatives from the various Zionist parties, including Jabotinsky, Grossman for the Jewish State Party, and delegates representing the *Mizrachi* and the 'General Zionists B' (the conservative wing of General Zionism). This committee nominated the national headquarters. By 1936 the organization numbered 2,000 members, many of whom joined the legal military frameworks being formed around that time (the Jewish Settlement Police and the Special Police).

The riots of 1936 became the turning point in the history of the IZL. The members considered the policy of *havlagah* (voluntary self-restraint) which the *yishuv* leadership practised towards Arab terrorism a political as well as a national disaster, and they began a

series of retaliatory actions.[70] In the meantime the Partition Plan
had been broached, and Avraham Tehomi, the head of the
Haganah B, who believed that the establishment of a Jewish state
was imminent, broke the agreement he had only recently signed
with Jabotinsky, and with most of his comrades and a considerable
part of the *Haganah B* membership rejoined the ranks of the
Haganah, which became the military force of the entire *yishuv*. The
Revisionist Party was left tied to the military underground organization, which continued its counter-terror activities and gradually
developed a revolutionary ideology which advocated the use of
arms (initially against Arabs only) in the political and national
struggle for Eretz Israel.

The Party and the Underground

During the second half of the 1930s the Revisionist party was led by a
Central Committee (a council of delegates) nominated by the *Ha-
Zohar* World Executive. Actually the IZL was too big for *Ha-Zohar*
to have any say in it, but it was nevertheless *Ha-Zohar* which
appointed the IZL commanders and its High Command. Both the
party and Betar in the Diaspora were well aware of the difficult
situation in which the IZL placed them, and for this reason they
rejected any formal responsibility ('Not a bridge and not a link' was
the formulation the IZL and the movement had agreed between
them), but in practice they controlled the IZL , since they were well
aware of its importance as a political tool, as a means of exercising
pressure on Great Britain, and as a lever in the struggle between the
various factors for control of the *yishuv*. In practice there existed
close cooperation between Betar and the IZL in Eretz Israel
(whereas in Poland, as the reader may remember, the IZL
developed along the lines of secret cells inside Betar), something
which caused considerable tension.

Jabotinsky's attitude towards the IZL was ambivalent, but its
existence, and the fact of its becoming an ever more vital and pivotal
factor, compelled him to reach a formal accommodation on the
relationships within the movement, particularly in view of the
frictions with regard to the question of who was responsible for the
organization of illegal immigration to Eretz Israel. This led to the
'Paris Agreement' of February 1939 (about which British Intelligence received a detailed report from its own reliable sources)
aimed at organizing the division of immigration activities, and the

relationships between the IZL and Betar in Eretz Israel and the Diaspora.[71]

The death of Jabotinsky in August 1940 and the liquidation of the IZL in Poland left the IZL in Eretz Israel as the only remaining activist force in the Revisionist movement. Up to 1944 party authority over the IZL had been substantial, which was one of the reasons for the split and breaking away of the Lehi members. Large numbers of IZL and Betar members joined the British army, in the same way as they had previously joined the auxiliary police. Jabotinsky's dream of a Jewish army within the British army as a national political factor was to be realized by others (his rivals from the Left). However, bitter disappointment with British policy resulted in the appointment of a new central command for the IZL headed by Menachem Begin. Around the end of 1943 and the beginning of 1944 the IZL severed all relations with the party and became an autonomous organization.

The party itself was torn between the desire to show solidarity with the IZL's struggle and the public criticism it suffered because of the terrorist methods it employed, and with which it was unable to identify. The most that the heads of the party were able to do was to give the IZL their moral support (many members of the party and of Betar were arrested and even exiled to Africa on the charge of belonging to an underground movement!). They preferred to see the IZL as a passing phenomenon, a product of the particular circumstances, possibly hoping that the struggle of the IZL would in the end result in a change in British policy in the Revisionist direction. These hopes were soon dashed, and for two reasons: British policy failed to undergo a change, and those in charge of the IZL refused to regard themselves as *ad hoc* combatants. They believed that when the struggle against the Mandate came to an end, they would be the legitimate and natural heirs of Jabotinsky and his tradition.

The Dynamics of Schism and Tension: Avraham (Yair) Stern and Lehi[72]

Since the IZL in Eretz Israel developed side by side with the official movement, rather than as a part of it, it did not take long for irredentist tendencies to emerge within the IZL, and its leaders began to act in open disregard of the party functionaries. IZL delegates in Poland established 'secret cells' which operated without the knowledge of the Betar leadership and the heads of the party, and in course of time also without caring in the least about the latter's outspoken opposition. The spirit of the IZL was nourished by the radicalism of Betar , and in turn encouraged it, and it was from this environment that the IZL recruited most of its supporters in Eretz Israel and in Poland during the years 1938–39.

The greatest tensions were provoked in Poland. The events in Eretz Israel, the echoes of which resounded as far as Poland, had a radicalizing effect on Polish Revisionism. The foundation of the 'secret cells' by Betar, the independent dealings of the IZL in the Polish political arena, and the establishment of autonomous IZL delegations in Geneva and New York, led to a reassessment of relations between the leaders of the IZL and those of the official movement. It was Avraham Stern who pushed the IZL in Poland towards acting on its own. Polish-born – in 1907 – Avraham (Ya'ir) Stern, who had come to Eretz Israel in 1925, had been a brilliant student at the Hebrew University of Jerusalem. His revolutionary ideas were similar to those of Achimeir, but whereas the latter was an intellectual and a platonic revolutionary, Stern was a charismatic leader. He was a combination of poet and terrorist, and profoundly influenced by the freedom fighters from the ancient Jewish past, as well as by anti-czarist terrorism in Poland and the revolutionary terrorist ethos of the P.P.S. (*Polskiej Partii Socjalistycznej Proletaryat*).[73] The Polish experience since the beginning of the century had taught Stern to distinguish between various forms of terrorism, among which were 'provocative terror', aimed at extracting political concessions, 'mass-based terror', aimed at organizing the masses with a view to exercising pressure, 'terror against authority symbols', and terror against individual functionaries of the Regime. Stern wanted put into practice the ideology of individual terror and 'armed terror' in the reality of Eretz Israel, but prior to this – as we shall see in another chapter – he designed a plan to create several Jewish army battalions on Polish soil with Polish government support, which were to be transferred by sea to Eretz Israel to take over the country in one massive military thrust.

The independent activities of Stern and his followers were a thorn in the flesh of the party heads, as well as in those of Jabotinsky himself, who considered them a danger to the unity of the party and an affront to the authority of the established political leadership. It was David Raziel, Stern's commander, his junior by three years (he was born in 1910), and ultimately his rival, who attempted to deflect the strong criticism. In several personal coded letters to Jabotinsky he described the criticism of the heads of *Ha-Zohar* and Betar as vicious slander. A letter dated 7 May 1939, addressed to Jabotinsky in Warsaw, states that Jabotinsky had been falsely informed, that he was being systematically incited by means of the wildest accusations, and that it was time that the responsible clique received its just deserts. Raziel wrote that the IZL was the sheet-anchor of the movement, and not only did not undermine him [Jabotinsky], but was 'preparing the marshal's baton for him'.[74] Several weeks earlier, on 28 March, he had written to him that the IZL would be able to defeat both the Arabs and Great Britain, and thus 'hand Jabotinsky the crown as father of the victory'.[75] It would seem, however, that Jabotinsky was influenced by the criticism, and he emphatically protested against the independent activities of Stern and his followers. It even appears that Raziel himself was unaware of some of Stern's initiatives, and it is certain that he did not agree with their trend.

On the outbreak of the Second World War, just when Jabotinsky appeared to have reverted completely to his previous political views – a renewal of the political alliance with Great Britain, preferably based on military cooperation – another blow struck. Stern and his supporters in the Polish 'secret cells' and the IZL in Eretz Israel decided that the war was no reason to waive their preparations for a fight against Britain. On the contrary – they reasoned that this was a historic opportunity for turning the screws on Great Britain. A fierce and bitter struggle ensued within the IZL. It required Jabotinsky's personal intervention, in the form of a telegram from New York, to prevent a situation in which most of the IZL members in Eretz Israel would have followed Stern and his friends, and to confirm Raziel's leadership. In the event, Jabotinsky's death in August 1940 removed the last barrier.[76]

The contrasts within the Revisionist movements were not resolved by the dramatic changes in the circumstances. They did lead to a serious weakening of the IZL, on the one hand, and the foundation of a small terrorist organization with a messianic ideology, on the other. Relations between the IZL and Lehi were extremely tense during most of their existence, and the residual animosity and hostility between the members of the two organizations would persist until their last few years, despite their common origins – or possibly even because of them.

PART TWO

THE INTELLECTUAL FOUNDATION OF THE RIGHT: BETWEEN POLITICAL NATIONALISM AND NATIONAL MESSIANISM

Introductory Remarks

The 1930s and 1940s, apart from being the formative years of the Zionist Right, proved to be a fertile period of wide-ranging intellectual and ideological ferment, during which a *Weltanschauung* was created, and successively internalized and transformed into a clearly-defined tradition. The succeeding years, by contrast, were characterized by exactly the opposite development, namely a complete absence of renewal, due to a paucity of ideas and lack of internal frictions. During the Begin era Jabotinsky became the sole spiritual mentor, even though his doctrine was customarily interpreted according to the views of only one current in Revisionism. Almost all the more serious and profound ideological and historiosophic discussions took place within the far more restricted forums on the fringes of the radical Right, and any attempts at introducing new ideas usually led to defections from the ranks and a search for new ideological and organizational identities. Thus, in contrast to the 1950s and the period thereafter, which was marked by a decidedly anti-intellectual trend, the Right represented during the years that form the subject of this discussion an effervescent and interesting intellectual 'world'.

The second part of this study is devoted to a closer look at the intellectual infrastructure (or platform) of the Right. As already mentioned in the Introduction, outsiders usually regard the Zionist Right as a homogeneous, doctrinaire and fundamentalist movement. There were those who thought that a distinction should be made between the — what they believed to be fascist or messianic — radical Revisionist stream, and the central Revisionist current, but Revisionism as a whole was judged to be a predominantly nationalist and anti-socialist movement without any shades or gradations.

The historical and historiographic literature emanating from within Revisionist circles similarly attempted to cultivate a well-defined — and obviously positive — image of Revisionism as a cohesive movement which as a matter of course comprised certain factions, undercurrents and shades of opinions, in an effort to obscure or minimize the internal conflicts. From within the rank and file of the movement it was often pointed out, however, that the Zionist Right had from the very outset possessed two faces and two souls: a liberal, legalistic, secular and 'post-emancipatory' soul, juxtaposed to a nationalist, 'organically Jewish', traditional and revolutionary soul.

Theoretically, such a division does of course suggest a polarity of views, whereas in practice there existed a dominant 'grey zone' which makes such a division far less relevant. In the next chapter we shall attempt to describe the two basic approaches of the 'Zionist Right' within its broadest connotation, as presented by its leading party theoreticians. The last chapter will try to describe the Right in terms of a composite, or collective, personality, as it acted and reacted in this 'grey zone', in terms of its world-view, its arguments and its behavioural and practical conclusions.

CHAPTER THREE

The National Philosophies of Jabotinsky, Klausner and Achimeir

Cultural Nationalism and Political Nationalism

It is customary to classify European nationalism into two types or categories: political (or civil) nationalism and cultural nationalism. Nationalism of the first type is the feeling or awareness evolving within an existing state, when that state and its regime are the operative forces shaping the partnership that is commonly referred to as the nation. Nationalism of the second type is the sense of ethnic and cultural identity and belonging that precedes the state, and which in fact attempts to realize itself through the state. This kind of nationalism involves intensive efforts towards the creation of the various aspects of a shared cultural heritage – including a national language, a national literature, a historical awareness, and so on – and only in a later stage the desire for national sovereignty within the national territory.

It is difficult to compartmentalize the modern Jewish national movement into one of the above two general categories, and this not only because the Jewish national movement evolved and took shape outside the national territory, and because as a Zionist movement it aspired towards a return to Zion (which explains its messianic nature within the context of the Jewish conceptual system). The Jewish national movement had numerous cultural foundations, in the sense that it tried to base the definition of the character of the Jewish people as a nation on the existence of a shared culture, language, historical awareness, as well as connections with a national territory (a homeland). These foundations were present in a passive sense, but failed to serve as a basis for the determination of a national identity. This explains why so many in the Zionist movement believed that cultural activity in the Diaspora, aimed at 'preparing the minds', or even 'changing values', were preconditions for the creation of a modern Jewish nation. It would seem that Jabotinsky too adopted this line of thinking, given the fact that he was an enthusiastic supporter of comprehensive Hebrew education in the Diaspora, as well as of a broad spectrum of educational and cultural activities in Eretz Israel. Officially, however, Zionism regarded Eretz Israel as the place where the Hebrew cultural revival would be realized, and the various forces which dominated the movement throughout the years believed with various degrees of doubt or conviction that this national revival would eventually culminate in an independent Jewish state. In any case, Zionism was from its inception engaged in intensive political activity to create the required conditions for the establishment of a national culture and a national society in Eretz Israel.

In this respect Revisionism was a natural offshoot of Jewish nationalism, and from an intellectual point of view it inherited the views of Achad Ha'am and Berdichevsky no less than those of Herzl. Jabotinsky and his adherents spoke of the creation of a *nation out of a people*, this nation being the restoration of the Hebrew nation of the past, but with a contemporary shape and substance. They even believed that this process of nation-building was mainly a matter of in-depth educational and cultural activity. Whereas radical, messianic Revisionism spoke in terms of *redemption*, and subsequently in terms of seizing the reins of government as a precondition for national restoration, the world-view of Jabotinsky's Revisionism was evolutionary and spoke, as we have just mentioned, of building a national society.

The three personalities who form the main subject of this chapter, Vladimir (Ze'ev) Jabotinsky, Professor Joseph Klausner and Abba Achimeir, had all received formal academic educations. They were steeped in the Western cultural tradition, and considered Hebrew culture as a part of it. All three occupied themselves with the question of how to create a positive synthesis between Judaism and 'Westernism', or – as Klausner preferred to call it – 'humanitarianism'. All three sought their way between an objectivist view of Jewish history – the search for the metritalistic factors which had shaped the nature of the Jewish people and Jewish culture – and an 'idealistic' perception which viewed the national consciousness or national genius as the determining factor in the creation of the *Volksgeist* of the Jewish people and its *Weltanschauung*.[1] Ze'ev Jabotinsky was the founding father of Revisionism, and his teachings were considered canonical and the single source of authority.

Klausner contributed Revisionism's distinctive view and image of Jewish history and the messianic underpinning of the national ideology, in particular the heroic national image of the Second Temple era. From Achimeir Revisionism inherited the idea of revolutionary politics.

The intellectual and cultural worlds of the above three personalities were not necessarily shared by the majority of the movement's members. We might even say that the historiosophic and intellectual questions which occupied them failed to touch the majority of the movement's rank and file. Fundamentally what it received from this trio was not the theoretical platform, but ready-made national assumptions and certain historical images and arguments out of which their 'world' was constructed. The philosophical foundations of these assumptions were known and understood by a limited circle only. Outside the political context we are dealing with three personalities belonging to the same generation of Russian-Jewish intellectuals who, each in his own particular way, confronted the challenge of the newly-emerging Jewish nationalism and its realization in Eretz Israel.

The first in line, in terms of his status and importance within the context of this book, is obviously Ze'ev Jabotinsky.

Jabotinsky's Intellectual Background and National Philosophy[2]

We have already mentioned how in the Revisionist consciousness Jabotinsky is considered the founding father: the originator of the idea, and the creator of an all-embracing national world-view which provided answers to virtually all relevant issues. Jabotinsky's teachings are considered a 'guide to life', and his writings a doctrine and the sole source of authority. As a result a parallel has been drawn between the intellectual world of Jabotinsky, on the one hand, and the movement bearing his name and its *Weltanschauung*, on the other. Compared to him all other personalities necessarily occupy secondary or even marginal positions.

There is an ongoing discussion about the nature of Jabotinsky's teachings, in many instances based on prejudice, selective reading, or a biased interpretation of his published works and various aspects of his personality and activities. His writings over a period of some forty years, both those of a theoretical and those of a topical, journalistic nature, reflect a variety of influences. They also reveal various changes of opinion, including those on the subject of Zionism following World War I, when the accent shifted to political issues. During his Russian period, from the moment of his conversion to Zionism in 1903, Jabotinsky was a Zionist propagandist who felt at home in Russian (and European) culture, in which capacity he took sharp issue with the opponents of Zionism, particularly those in *Bundist* and communist circles. Until 1925 he worked as a propagandist, leader and journalist without any particular political affiliation, and uncommitted to any political body. His entire life shows him as a man with an astonishing command of languages and a wide variety of interests and occupations, which has caused his rivals to suspect him of a lack of intellectual and artistic depth. In short, he was a man who projected a variety of images, and who in the course of his life appealed to various publics, including the Russian Zionist intelligentsia, the Jewish masses in Poland, and the youngsters of Betar. None of these groups, however, knew the 'whole Jabotinsky', since – for example – Yiddish speakers among his following did not read his articles in Russian (except insofar as these were translated into Yiddish or Hebrew). The same applied to those who read Hebrew, and therefore only a few knew the many faces of Jabotinsky the man, the intellectual, the artist and the politician.

Jabotinsky himself did not regard himself as a theoretician, nor as someone who could offer a systematic teaching; neither did he present his writings as a binding theory. Only twice in the course of his life did he attempt to write a systematic treatise on a particular subject. The first time was in 1912, when he was awarded a law degree on a thesis dealing with the 'Self-Rule of a National Minority';[3] the second time was in 1934, when he formulated two versions of a socio-anthropological theory entitled *The Laws of Economics* (with which I will deal in the chapter on the social ideology of the Right).[4] Nor did he pretend to be either systematic or original, to the point of justifying his attitude with the argument that the absence of a system protected one against becoming a slave of dogmas or doctrines, and that common sense was often enough.

Neither is there any basis for his followers' claim that Jabotinsky was steeped in the Jewish cultural tradition, and that it was from this source alone that he derived most of his ideas.[4] He was a stranger to vast areas of the Jewish world of thought, and nowhere does he refer to either rabbinical literary sources (such as the *Mishnah* or *Talmud*), or medieval Jewish literature. His Jewish world moved between the two poles of the Bible and the precursors of Jewish national thought. Even then he quotes the Bible only in order to dress some of his opinions on social issues in a more acceptable Jewish garb, given the fact that Betar's public was not the most appropriate audience at whom to quote, for instance, the writings of John Stuart Mill or T.H. Green. In essence Jabotinsky was no different from the contemporary nationalist and – in particular – socialist Jewish intelligentsia. The formative influences of his intellectual world were the cultural ferment in Odessa, the city of his birth, followed by Italian Liberalism and Socialism, particularly that of Antonio Labriola.[5] He did not view Marxism in the same demoniacal light as many others in his movement, but rather as a fairly useful methodology. The influence of the German *Völkerspsychologie* school of Moritz Lazarus, who in turn was influenced by Johann Frederick Herbert and Austro-Hungarian theoreticians on the issue of national identity such as Otto Bauer, Victor Adler and Rudolf Springer (= Karl Renner), is felt from the time of his stay in Vienna from the winter of 1907 till the summer of 1908.[6] In actual fact his writings reveal traces of many of the leading contemporary thinkers, including Nietzsche, Spencer, Buckle and others.

Race, Territory, National Consciousness, Objectivism and Subjectivism

During his Russian period Jabotinsky was particularly influenced by the British cultural historian Henry Thomas Buckle (1821–62). The latter's ambitious treatise *Introduction to the History of Civilization*, the only two volumes of which appeared between 1857 and 1861, was enthusiastically received in westernized intellectual circles in Russia.[7] Apart from providing the intellectual basis for the belief in the inevitable force of progress, not only to effect positive changes in human civilization, but to help it to free itself from the shackles of religion and superstition, Buckle offered Jabotinsky a rationalization of the importance of territory for shaping the national genius (even though Buckle referred more to the qualitative aspects of civilization than to the nature of the national state). Jabotinsky was particularly attracted to Buckle's positivist anthropography, which appeared to him as more rational than the organistic approaches of J. G. Herder, A. von Humboldt and others. Rather than accepting the prevailing notion that the monotheistic religious awareness of the Jewish people was shaped during their wanderings in the desert following the Exodus, Jabotinsky believed in a monotheistic (henotheistic) national consciousness which had evolved in Eretz Israel itself. Jabotinsky considered it important to stress the fundamental importance of territory (the 'ideal milieu') for the moulding of the characteristics of the ancient

Israeli nation during its formative years. For this Jabotinsky quoted Buckle's observation that the ceaseless influences of a continuous habitation of a certain geographic and climatic region created the permanent and stable fundamental properties of a nation, properties which determined its singular nature as a separate entity for all time – unless for some reason that nation was lost or assimilated. 'These natural and fundamental distinctions embedded in the race are impossible to eradicate, and are continually being nurtured by the differences in soil and climate.' They were far stronger than the mere social factors, which by their very nature were transcendent. According to this view Eretz Israel was the natural environment in which the national consciousness of the Israeli nation had been shaped, and from this it followed that only in Eretz Israel could the Jewish nation renew and revitalize its singular national characteristics. In other words:

> . . . *the true root of the nation, and the source of its distinctiveness, could only be found in Eretz Israel.* Before coming to Eretz Israel we were not a nation and we did not exist. We were born on the soil of Eretz Israel; the Hebrew nation was created out of the fragments of other peoples. In Eretz Israel we were raised, on its soil we became citizens, strengthened our faith in the one God, and breathed the air of the land; while fighting for independence and sovereignty [our minds] were fortified by its spirit and our bodies by the wheat growing on its soil . . . .
> Everything that is Hebrew in us was given to us by Eretz Israel; everything else in us is not Hebrew . . . .
> Therefore, the uninterrupted development of our Hebrew distinctiveness is possible only on the same soil and in the same natural milieu in which this distinctiveness was once born. Another climate, another flora, or different mountains will inevitably warp the body and the soul which were created by the climate, the flora and the mountains of Eretz Israel. For the body and the soul of the race are only a record of the specific combination of natural factors.[8]

The weaknesses of this objectivist national approach, based on an environmental theory, are obvious. The theory was incapable of explaining the nature of the distinctive qualitative (*sui in generis*) or environmental (*genius loci*) properties of Eretz Israel that enabled it to become the cradle of a monotheistic world-view, or, for that matter, why only the Jewish nation, among all the peoples who inhabited Eretz Israel throughout history, had developed a monotheistic faith. Neither did the theory explain why the long post-exilic sojourn of the Jews in a very different natural environment from that of Eretz Israel had not resulted in the evolution of a new distinctive character (although in one place Jabotinsky comments that local differences in the natural environment did create different Jewish typological characteristics – the oppressive atmosphere in Galicia created a different Jewish type from the clear air in Odessa!). There was no doubt a considerable measure of atavism in the claim that certain characteristics of past generations were preserved in the psycho-cultural genes of the group, and that these characteristics were capable of being renewed and revived after centuries of regression. This, of course, explained why a return to Eretz Israel was so vital for the full and complete revival of the national genius.

These patent weaknesses in his theory caused Jabotinsky to replace it by a new theory, although remnants of his previous views remained dormant in his outlook. From the lectures he attended in Italy, where he had gone to study in 1898 at the age of 17, he absorbed a concept which he would later call 'Psycho-Marxism'. According to this view it was man's creative self-awareness that elevated him from a creature struggling for his material and physical existence into a cultural being. This concept provided him with a universal explanation for the creation of human culture in general, rather than with an explanation for the evolution of peoples and nationalities with a specific national consciousness of their own. The explanation for this latter phenomenon, around which his real interests revolved, Jabotinsky found in the concept of 'race'.

Before continuing, it is important to examine carefully in precisely which meaning this word is used in the writings of Jabotinsky. It is not surprising that this meaning has at times been distorted, and interpreted as a claim for the racial superiority of the Jewish people.[9] Like many of his contemporaries, Jabotinsky borrowed the term from fashionable meta-biological and meta-historical morphological theories. 'Race' was a physiological and physiognomical concept which determined the pattern or type (*topos*) of the spiritual essence of the genes embedded in the group, and which were passed on from generation to generation by hereditary means. A race, therefore, was defined as a collection of basic characteristics (usually arranged according to certain ethnographic laws) which together created the cosmic picture, the unity of consciousness (*Besinnung*) and the perceptual system by means of symbols and images by which a given society organized its world. 'In each and every nation,' wrote Jabotinsky in 1913 in his article "Race", echoing the romantic tradition, 'there exists a genetic formative prescription which is the primary factor (*origio*) of its evolution, rather than the natural environment (in other words the objective conditions).' He continues to stress the 'individualistic' nature of the historical development of each national genius:

> We could explain this as follows: *Ceteris paribus*, in other words given the same climatic, geographic, historical, social, etcetera conditions, and assuming an equal level of personal development and personal biographies – in short, when all other conditions are the same – we will see that two individuals who vary physiologically will show different psychological reactions to the same stimulus.[10]

The essential difference between different cultures and different nations lay therefore in its inner collective psychology, which is a deterministic data whose source we cannot know. Region, language, religion and common history are not the essence of a nation, but merely descriptions of its external characteristics. Over and above these there exist collective psychological differences, differences in the collective genius and in the common consciousness, which create the national spirit (*Volksgeist*). The focus shifted therefore in Jabotinsky's mind to an idealistic view, because only through it could he explain, for instance, the phenomenon of so many different peoples and such a variety of nations living together within the czarist Empire. Only through this could he explain the eternal national distinctiveness of the Jewish people in world history in ethnocentric rather than theocentric terms (in other words without a belief in revelation or divine intervention in history). The collective consciousness is an objective and mysterious meta-historical and meta-biological fact, the *cogito ergo sum* of a nation, and as such the very soul of the national self-awareness. A nation is as it were a continuous referendum, an idea which Jabotinsky derived from Renan's widely-read work *Qu'est ce qu'une nation?* ('What is a Nation?'; 1882). But this referendum, or in other words the wish to belong to this specific group, stems first of all from one objective fact, namely the sense of belonging.

The need for a national territory now no longer resulted only from an atavistic impulse to return to the place of one's birth, but mainly from the need for a natural habitat that would enable the national group to develop freely and undisturbed, thus creating the conditions for an as authentic as possible expression of its particular genius and talents. With this viewpoint Jabotinsky in fact repeated the views of the central stream of new Jewish national thought, and he often reverted to it in ideological discussions with opponents of Jewish nationalism. This also explains his views on autonomism, Jewish national autonomy within the framework of the Eastern European multinational society, as a mere temporary solution to a tactical need – in other words, a phase in the remoulding of the national consciousness and a practical step towards preparing the return to Eretz Israel. Jewish autonomy in the Diaspora, on the other hand, in contrast to the autonomy of the other ethnic groups in Eastern Europe who were concentrated in certain regions that happened to be their natural homeland, was impossible due to the fact that the Jews were scattered over a number of regions. As a result they were always being squeezed by their immediate environment, their culture would become a dependent culture, and the surrounding heavy pressures would sooner or later cause them to mix and assimilate.[11]

Yet another elementary point vigorously underscored by Jabotinsky during his Russian period was the restoration of Jewish honour as an aesthetic as well as normative value. Nationalism, according to him, was the 'accumulation of pride and sovereign self-respect' in a rejecting and hostile cultural milieu, which would always and under all conditions remain an alien environment. Only a full and wholehearted national self-awareness and feeling, equal to the nationalism of the surrounding nations, would give the Jews the required opportunity for the expression of their own identity and sense of belonging. National territorial sovereignty was not a reactionary or anarchic form of existence, but a normal and natural form of human organization, which promoted the interests of humanity rather than acting against them. In *The Idea of Betar*, written in the year 1934, Jabotinsky restated in his own words some of the ideas he had borrowed from both Herder and Mazzini. 'Each and every nation makes its own contribution to human culture,' he wrote. A nation can fulfil its mission and task within the 'concert of nations' only as a sovereign body. The universal mission of the people of Israel could only be fulfilled through the dissemination of ideas and values within the framework of a sovereign national body. This was how the sovereign French nation had contributed to the world the principles of the Revolution, and the English nation concepts such as democracy and parliamentarianism – rather than abstract, universalistic ideas – but in both cases this had been based on the existence of French or British national bodies.[12] In an article written in 1913, entitled 'The Language of Education', Jabotinsky wrote that nationalism could not be based on natural feelings such as, for instance, 'love of country', since according to him nothing was more unstable and fleeting than patriotism or 'love of the land'.[13] At the same time, however, he was unable to hide his jealousy of the autochthonous nationals he saw around him in Eastern Europe, because of their organic ties with the soil, particularly among the peasants, which gave them a direct feeling of continuity and belonging, that required no theory or ideology to justify itself. Thus, in a story which he wrote following a short journey to Eretz Israel in 1908 as a reporter for Russian newspapers, he provides an incisive description of the difference between an ideology-based nationalism and an 'innate' self-evident sense of nationality and connectedness with one's homeland. Observing how Jewish youngsters born in Eretz Israel feel at home in their national surroundings, he writes:

> I look at them with envy. I have never known, and probably will never know, this completely organic feeling; so united and singular [is this] sense of a homeland, in which everything flows together, the past and the present, the legend and the hopes, the individual and the historical.[14]

Despite these views Jabotinsky's writings do not reveal a shred of romanticism, nor, for that matter, any descriptions of the landscape of Eretz Israel or incidents during his travels there, such as are contained in his notes on his visits to Odessa or other places where he visited or passed. Jabotinsky is totally averse to the romantic and conservative Russian slavophilic views about the eternal 'soul of the nation', as expressed in the existential rhythm of the farmer's 'return to the soil' or in folkloristic tales. As we will see further on, the national culture was an inseparable part of progress: the product of education, knowledge and science.

Religion: Its Historical Task and Future Status

Jabotinsky's views on the Jewish religion were the product of his above-described national views. These views occupied many of his supporters among the younger generation, the great majority of whom originated from traditional religious homes with a traditional world-view. They tried to prove that Jabotinsky had not always held radical secular views, but that his attitude towards religion had evolved through several phases and that, during the 1930s, he had rediscovered the value of religion in the life of the future Jewish nation.[15] In effect, however, this was more a matter of a moderation of his public stance than of a change in his private views on the subject.

During his Russian Zionist period Jabotinsky wanted to prove that Jewish existence in the Diaspora was only an external covering of the national essence. This brought him to the – entirely unoriginal – conclusion that religion served as a substitute for the physical homeland, enabling it to be turned into what Heine had called the 'portatives Vaterland' ('portable fatherland'). Religion has preserved the national memories, the historical past and the national singularity. However, once the Jewish nation returns to its land, he wrote (echoing words written many years earlier by, for instance, M.L. Lilienblum) the need for religion will disappear. Once back in Eretz Israel the people will no longer feel any need for either the theoretical or the practical commandments, as there will no longer be a specifically Jewish ghetto economy (within whose walls the Jews had lived and segregated themselves by choice rather than compulsion!). Jabotinsky by no means regarded religion either as an essential, or the sole expression of the Jewish national spirit or national psyche, but as only one of its exponents, which had assumed a central and exclusive meaning during the Exile, and which would once more become secondary following the realization of the national revival. Religion would be replaced by culture.

This simplistic representation of Jewish history, and his negative attitude towards Jewish religion, were also a direct result of his conflicts with the anti-Zionist orthodoxy of Eastern Europe and orthodox groups in the old *yishuv* in Eretz Israel. The opposition of the Jerusalem orthodoxy against the building of a modern Jewish political community in the Holy Land evoked bitter criticism on his part. According to Jabotinsky's description, the old orthodox *yishuv* suffered from cultural retardation. People like these, he wrote in a fiercely anti-clerical outburst, are the mere [biological] offspring of Adam and Eve, rather than civilized human beings, and even the advanced nations distinguish between children with beards and sidecurls and the *natio politica*.[16] More than once he warned his party's activists against entering into an alliance with the national-religious *Mizrachi* party and the views the latter tried to impose upon its partners and allies.[17]

Jabotinsky considered religion as merely one expression of the national culture which, in his view, was not centred upon the Law and the commandments, in other words on a binding normative religious system, but on the belief in the one God and the universal morality derived from it. 'There is more to Judaism than the laws of *kashrut*', he wrote. In principle he never abandoned this conviction, although political expedience caused him to moderate its public expression during the 1930s. This was not only in order to find political allies for *Ha-Zach* among the nationally-oriented religious public in Poland, but also because he felt the need to adapt himself to the prevailing mood among the membership. Despite this we will not find anywhere in his writings a single affirmative text or even comment suggesting that religion could in any way become the normative and binding system of the future Jewish state. Similarly his writings do not contain a single concrete reference as to which religious laws, if any, and in which spheres of life, would be declared binding upon its Jewish population. Even in his keynote speech at the founding convention of *Ha-Zach* in September 1935, which dealt extensively with this question, as well as during later years, he remained firm in his support of a separation of religion and state, and the non-intervention of religion in its institutions (even though he now also spoke of the lasting and positive value to society of the upholding of universal religious values). The official text of the resolution adopted at the convention of 1935 determined a need 'to implant the Sacred Laws of Judaism firmly in the future Jewish state'. This was a vague and non-committal formulation, without any reference to norms and commandments, stressing mainly the 'ethical aspects', he wrote on 14 September 1935 in an explanatory letter to his son Eri.[18] Time and again he characterized himself as an atheist who had discovered that even a humanistic legal system requires belief in a transcendental power, and that even a modern secular society at times felt the need to be suffused with a religious element, just as the secular man could believe in the existence of 'a mysterious connection between man and a divine presence'. But, he emphasized, this was his private concern.

There are those who claim that Jabotinsky's change of attitude towards religion must be ascribed to the outspoken public stand of Rabbi Kook, the Chief Rabbi of the Holy Land, on the innocence of the accused group of Revisionists in the Arlosoroff murder trial in June 1933. It is illogical, however, to connect such a fundamental change of heart with the opinion of the Chief Rabbi on this public judicial drama. In this respect, it is worth mentioning that in 1919 Jabotinsky had directed a sarcastic broadside at Rabbi Kook, describing him as 'a semi-educated autodidact with a semi-digested education'.[19] Given this attitude, it does not seem reasonable to assume that in the year 1933 this same Rabbi Kook suddenly opened for him 'the gate to the world of religion', revealing to Jabotinsky the mystical power and rapture of the religious experience. Be that as it may, it is a fact that from this moment on we find in his public statements certain expressions showing that the rationalist sceptic in him had been overcome by the 'mysterious power of tradition'. In my view Jabotinsky's change of heart is to be explained from his belief that Rabbi Kook's attitude presaged a turning point in the stand of religious Judaism towards secular Jewish nationalism, even though Jabotinsky himself did not really grasp the meaning of Rabbi Kook's messianic historical model, or the implications of his world-view. What in fact Jabotinsky discovered was the strength of the religious sentiment and the role a liturgy could play in the shaping of a 'civil religion' in a secular national society. At the same time he did not cease his vigorous opposition to any formal religious intervention in the functioning of the state and the society. This he regarded as theocracy, which he considered the worst of all regimes.

In addition, although Jabotinsky believed in the antecedence of Hebrew monotheism, he held an entirely unfundamentalist view of the Jewish historical past. According to him the Hebrew nation had been created in Eretz Israel out of a fusion of the Hebrew tribes with fragments of other nations, consisting of both autochthonous inhabitants and peoples who had entered the country in the course of sundry waves of immigration. He did not believe in the veracity of the historical Biblical accounts. Nowhere do his writings reveal a single reference to historical events such as God's covenant with Abraham (the 'Covenant of the Division'; see Gen.15.9), the Exodus, the giving of the Torah on Mount Sinai or the conquest of Eretz Israel by the Israelites.

He referred to the Bible mainly in order to find ancient Hebrew names, or for inspiration for modern social legislation. In his historical novel *Shimshon* he writes the following on the image of Moses:

> He was a leader, many of whose followers were certainly familiar with the vague tradition — a story from which without any justification whatsoever hundreds of names had been eliminated: names of teachers, rebels, commanders, scouts, all the unorganized masses of Hebrews who in the course of a hundred years or more had moulded the Jewish people into a nation. All these names had been wiped out in order to highlight one name. This hardly did justice to those involved, but those were the historical facts.

Whereas heroic national symbols from the days of the First and Second Temple played a central role in the consciousness of the movement, symbols which contributed towards shaping its attitudes towards the world and creating activist sentiments, Jabotinsky himself makes virtually no use of historical symbols or parallelisms; neither the wars of the Maccabees, the Great Revolt, the Bar-Kochba War, or any of the other struggles for an independent Jewish existence are mentioned. Since he did not envisage the Zionist fulfilment taking shape through a national war of liberation, there was no room in his world-view and his repertoire for any symbols connected with the historical wars fought by Israel or, for that matter, by any other nation. His references to Jewish history in general as an inspiration and a model for present political behaviour were a mere marginal feature of his prolific and many-sided writings throughout the years.

Nationalism and National Culture

Jabotinsky believed that only 'historical nations', in other words nations with deep historical roots that could boast a substantial contribution to human culture, deserved to be accorded cultural autonomy, let alone political sovereignty. In fact, on various occasions he wrote about ethnic groups which were attempting to become nations by cultivating a singular national culture (mainly by means of their language and literature). In this context he quoted dissimilar cases such as the United States, on the one hand, and several of the smallest and remotest national ethnic groups in the czarist Empire, or the case of Albania, on the other, to exemplify what he called 'nations during their period of state-building'. In an article written in 1913, called 'The Great Albania',[20] he fondly describes the dynamic nation-forming process in Albania as a positive model: a country without a historical past, without a culture, was turning rapidly from a mere collection of tribes into a national entity which – as he put it – would shortly have not only a literature of its own, but also a national legal and political system. In the same vein he wrote about the future evolution of the Arab national culture, although as regards the Syrians he failed for political reasons to justify their desire for immediate political independence, claiming that essentially Syria was still lacking a national culture that would enable it to become a nation. In fact, the task of French imperialism in colonial Syria, as well as in the

Maghreb countries, was to help create the required infrastructure
for a rapid cultural development:

> Under French protection Syria will become within ten years
> a model of an organized, developed state; commerce and
> industry will flourish, cities will expand, cultivation will spread,
> new roads will be built, beaches will be developed and rail-
> roads built. Security will prevail on the mountain paths, and
> the courts will mete out justice. Teachers – the magicians who
> create nations – will be found in every town and village. Then,
> indeed, will Syria be Syria, and the rest will follow by itself.[21]

I will return to this subject in the chapter on the Right's attitude to
the Arab question. Meanwhile the above shows why Jabotinsky
believed that it was the Zionist movement's task to develop an all-
embracing national culture in Eretz Israel. On this subject Jabotinsky was a clear-cut Positivist, in the same sense as the Poles
following the Polish revolt of 1863. In other words, the nation would
realize its independence not through a romantic and heroic revolt,
but through an organic creative process suffusing the entire social
and cultural fabric of the national society, supported by secular
education, cultural and scientific activities, the stimulation of
private initiative, and so forth. Culture did not mean abstract values
or literary works, but a rich and all-encompassing spectrum of
activities, including schools, libraries, evening courses, kinder-
gartens, playgrounds, scientific literature, dictionaries, maps, a
scientific terminology, and so forth.[22]

In Jabotinsky's view the ideal examples of nationality and
national culture were to be found, rather than in the glorious history
of the People of Israel (the eras of David and Solomon or the
Hasmonean kingdom), in Latvia and, from the middle of the 1920s,
in the Poland of Pilsudski. In contrast to the situation in the
Ukraine, Latvian nationalism was not based on aggressive xeno-
phobia and nationalist zeal. Latvian nationalism – he wrote –
steered a middle course, not rejecting alien influences or hating
strangers, yet refusing to absorb cultural elements that lacked
originality or might nullify its own cultural independence. It was a
positive and healthy synthesis of the two. He described Latvia as 'an
oasis' among the newly-emerged nations following the Great War.[23]
The Jewish nationalism he envisaged was to be an ideal combination
of nationalism and universalist humanism. Even so, although
Jabotinsky talked about the creation of an original Jewish culture,
he by no means thought that this new culture should be nurtured by

Jewish sources only, or in fact that it should be typically 'Jewish' at all. National sovereignty was intended to create the necessary conditions for the free and unimpeded development of an authentic national culture, in which society itself would select and adopt without any compulsion or external intervention.

His view of the nature and function of Hebrew literature in the new Hebrew culture was the complete antithesis of the literary and cultural conceptions of Uri Zvi Greenberg. While the latter spoke of messianic-style literature which fulfilled an eschatological task, Jabotinsky was thinking of writings in the Hebrew language, rather than original Hebrew literature, let alone messianic literature. On numerous occasions he pleaded the need for interesting and popular reading material, that need not be 'national' in content, provided only that it was written in the national tongue. To illustrate his point he explained that the russification of many of his contemporaries had been the result of reading Western literary translations (even of popular books) into Russian, rather than of the reading of original Russian literature.[24] He was an avid reader of romantic adventure novels in the style of Henryk Sienkiewicz and T. Mayne Reid, and even of 'penny dreadfuls'. He by no means considered such literature an assault on the 'holiness of the Hebrew tongue' or a violation of the national honour, as those with an elitist cultural approach were inclined to think. Jabotinsky saw national culture as encompassing a broad, variegated and pluralistic complex of activities, including everything from political institutions and judicial norms to everyday behaviour and fashions in dress.

Western Education and Progress

Jabotinsky's Positivism and 'Westernism' are clearly shown in his attitudes towards Rationalism, education and science. Whereas, as we will see further on, radical Revisionism from the 1930s onwards developed an outspoken anti-rationalist and anti-Western streak, which regarded Rationalism, emancipation and Western-ism as negative and even anti-Jewish values, Jabotinsky and his veteran Russian Zionist friends were unreserved and confirmed 'Westerners'. According to him, one of the main historical achieve-ments of Judaism was that it had established the foundations of Western culture in Europe. It was Judaism which had instilled in Western civilization the belief in a 'Golden Age', as well as the expectation of redemption and the historical view of history as evolution towards a higher stage of human civilization. 'The West' (i.e. Europe) represented a much higher cultural category than 'the East', nurtured as it was by values such as intellectual curiosity, criticism, freedom and science. The East stood much lower on the cultural ladder, and even represented a negative category, characterized by strife, ignorance and intellectual and cultural backwardness.[25] There are indications that Jabotinsky's failure to read the political and ideological map of Europe during the 1930s correctly was a result of his simple-minded belief in progress, and his blind adherence to the positivist faith in the redeeming power of science and technology, which would prevent humankind from sliding back into the dark ages. Like many of his nineteenth-century contemporaries, as well as Herzl before him, Jabotinsky believed in a liberal and scientific Utopia. His image of the ideal, utopian civilization was patterned on the Western liberal political and cultural model – a state in which fundamental Jewish values were as scarce and vaguely-defined as in Herzl's *Judenstaat.*

The National State and the National Territory

Jabotinsky did not see any value or virtue in a state as such, and consequently failed to attach any importance to the state as an institutional authority. His writings on social 'monism' and on the need for the involvement of the state's agencies in the process of the building of the society ('the nation') related mainly to the stages of the 'nation in the making'. In the ideal state, as envisaged by him, the authorities would have only limited tasks and responsibilities. The state, as seen by him, was merely the organizational framework for an authentic expression of national aspirations and individuality. Nowhere did he describe the state in eschatological terms as the fulfilment of messianic hopes (the 'Kingdom of Israel'), or as a meta-historic expression of Jewish identity. His model of the state described a pure liberal parliamentary system, whereas for the majority of his followers (as indeed for most Herzlians) the term 'State' was a powerful symbol representing the culmination of centuries-old hopes and expectations. Jabotinsky, on the other hand, saw in it no more than a framework for, and instrument of statehood, the realization of which would entail a slow and gradual process: the sovereign state was the end of a historic process, rather than its beginning.

An even wider gap existed between Jabotinsky's world-view and the collective national consciousness of his movement as regards the attitudes towards the historic homeland. As mentioned earlier,

Jabotinsky never showed the slightest sign of any romantic or theo-geographical attachment to the land or soil of Eretz Israel. Nowhere do we find expressions or arguments such as the 'Legacy of the Fathers' or the 'Cradle of the Nation', let alone references to such theo-political concepts as 'the Promised Land' or 'The Holy Land'. His objection to the 1937 Partition Plan for Western Palestine was not premised, as it was for most of his followers, on the idea that a division violated the organic unity of the national homeland and distorted the nature of the national redemption by an artificial and incongruous division of the national territory. His reasoning was entirely pragmatic. On the one hand he resisted the Partition Plan on the assumption that the plan would not be implemented anyway, and that therefore Zionist approval would mean a dangerous weakening of the basis of the Mandate.[26] To this he added a series of arguments of a strategic and defensive nature. However, the main thrust of his arguments concerned the fact that partition would impair the absorption capacity of the country. Time and again he amplified his strong opposition to partition with the axiomatic claim that it was the task of Zionism to settle several millions of European Jews in Eretz Israel within the space of a few decades, and that partition would seriously impair the absorption capability of the country, quite apart from which it would of course weaken the political status of Zionism in Eastern Europe. His detailed economic and settlement analyses on this subject were presented not only to British and Polish statesmen, but also to the Jewish public at large. He spoke of a population density of 100, or at a minimum 75, people per square kilometre as an optimal average. The resulting need to absorb eight to nine million Jews within the foreseeable future required both Jewish sovereignty and a settlement effort on both sides of the Jordan River.[27]

Power and Militarism

There were further sizeable gaps between Jabotinsky's concepts of power and the use of arms, on the one hand, and the interpretation by his followers and supporters (as well as critics) of the character of his 'militarism', and those of the nationalist-messianic stream within the Right, on the other. The idea of the use of force as an essential expression of the vitality of a national redemption movement was completely alien to Jabotinsky's world. The idea of force as a positive and even exalted historical or meta-historical factor, as depicted in the romantic heroic poetry written in some Revisionist circles, a poetry which extolled war, conquest and sacrifice, completely contradicted both his aesthetic and pragmatic views on militarism and military might. Neither did he consider Jewish militarism a factor that would unify the national society, apart from which he loathed the traditional military ceremonial that was so widely admired in various European countries (such as, for instance, in the cult of the *zolniez*, the Polish soldier). For this reason he did not assign soldiering and the military in general a pivotal status or role in the society or culture of the nation. He valued militarism primarily for its ritual and organizational aspects – as a method of national unification, and as a means of providing a disciplinary basis for a society which had until that time been lacking in discipline, organization and self-respect. This novel Jewish militarism seemed the antithesis of the image of the passive, persecuted and helpless Diaspora Jew. What appealed to him in the military, therefore, were the aesthetic and theatrical aspects. None of the diaries from his period of service with the Jewish Legion in Egypt and Palestine mention the hardships and suffering of military life. His opinion on the subject is very clearly expressed in his booklet on *The Question of the Defence of Eretz Israel* (Jerusalem, August 1929), in which he asserts that the finest and most important aspects of the army are 'its gala uniforms and parades, and all its official panoply . . . .' The importance of a standing army lies 'in its hierarchy, military discipline, awards and punishments'. This shows that there was a tremendous distance between his views and the heroic poetry, so fashionable during the 1930s, which spoke of 'legions ready to die on the hills of Eretz Israel, to sanctify the unity and integrity of the homeland,' and thus manifest their attitude towards Jewish history and the holiness of the soil. There is no doubt that he did not regard army life and warfare as the highest manifestations of national vitality, in contrast to the expressions which are encountered – both as an echo of European nationalism, and of the Biblical and later prophetic eschatology – in Revisionist literature from the middle of the 1930s onwards.

Between Jabotinsky and his Movement

Jabotinsky was a combination of a highly-educated, artistic Russian Jewish liberal intellectual, a populist leader and a rationalist Zionist politician. Each of these aspects is expressed in his intellectual world and his Zionist and nationalist teaching. Like Herzl, he possessed an inner world that was unknown to most of his followers. For the latter he was first and foremost a charismatic leader who expounded a simple and natural national point of view, as well as a clear and fascinating political and settlement programme. Jabotinsky spoke extensively of his 'monist' Zionist theory, focused exclusively on the establishment of a Jewish majority as a preparatory step to the establishment of a Jewish state, and which for this reason opposed a linkage of the Zionist purpose to any social goals. This monism was of a pragmatic and tactical nature, rather than an expression of any profound integrative or totalitarian nationalist views. More than that, his monism (or *had nes* — 'single banner' — in Revisionist terminology) did not imply the existence of an autarkic Jewish culture with mere nominal affiliation and contacts with other, external cultures. His penchant for unity through a ceremonial type of nationalism was more a reaction to the divisions among a scattered Diaspora Jewry, than a longing for an integrative, totalitarian national society. On the contrary, his vision was that of a minimalistic and in political terms liberal democratic state. Whatever he wrote on the need for discipline and solidarity referred to Betar, the youth movement, rather than the State and society in general.

However, as had been the case with Herzl, Jabotinsky's attraction derived not so much from his intellectual world as from his charismatic personality and oratorical ability, the programme he offered, and some of his *a priori* national principles. The national slogans which he proposed and promoted — a Jewish state on both sides of the river Jordan, mass immigration to Eretz Israel, an equal and classless society, and so forth — fell upon fertile soil because they fitted the mood of his bourgeois Jewish audience. In this respect he contributed several of the axioms of the collective *Weltanschauung* of the Right, such as the indivisibility of Eretz Israel, the public demand for a sovereign Jewish state, and the principle of a classless society.

Thus it could happen that many of Jabotinsky's programmatic principles were improperly judged on their external manifestations only, while it was these external manifestations which gave them their strength. Jabotinsky spoke of a Jewish State as a long-term objective, but popular understanding was that he demanded its immediate proclamation. He expressed his opposition to class conflicts while the National Home was being built, but this was interpreted as a plea for an integrative nationalist — in other words fascist — ideology. Jabotinsky called for a 'rebellion' against the Jewish fate, but he was understood as invoking a national war of liberation against the British Mandate. He regarded Zionism principally as a means of solving the plight of European Jewry (in Germany and the East European countries) and rehabilitating Jewish national pride and honour, whereas he was perceived as one who regarded the territorial integrity of Eretz Israel as the be-all and end-all of Jewish national interest. Jabotinsky held secular, if not radical, national views, but was considered a defender of the traditional values of religious Jewry. Whatever the case may be, it is a fact that both the programme he developed and his political methodology failed to provide answers to his proposed targets or the national *Weltanschauung*, which demanded a prompt and speedy realization of the national goals, imbuing them with an integrative/unifying national meaning. Instead they served during the 1930s to turn mood into ideology. In the political history of the Right, it was not the 'inner' Jabotinsky and his private intellectual world which were important, but the 'public' Jabotinsky, as he was perceived in his socio-political and socio-cultural roles, while his views as translated for the general public turned into *a priori* principles of the national consciousness of the Right as a whole.

Jabotinsky's views and standpoints on various issues will be featured throughout this book, as a result of his crucial and pivotal position as the man who shaped the ideology of Revisionism and guided its political activities from 1925 until his death in 1940.

Klausner: Judaism and Humanism, Nationalism and Messianism[28]

It is somewhat of a paradox that it was a personality such as Professor Joseph Gedalyah Klausner (1874–1958) who helped shape the national philosophy of the Right, and thereby served to link some of the main principles of the two kinds of 'Right'. Klausner was one of the pioneers of Hebrew science, renowned for his extensive and multifarious researches on subjects such as the history of Hebrew literature and the history of the Second Temple period. Already at the end of the nineteenth century he had been active in Jewish and Zionist activities, and in 1902 he succeeded Achad Ha'am as editor of *Ha-Shilo'ah*, the main intellectual journal of *Ha-Tehiya*, the 'Revival' movement. Although Klausner was neither a formal member of the Revisionist movement, nor was he ever elected to any of its organs, from 1930 onwards he was regarded as the foremost Zionist scholar to express open admiration of Revisionism and to support its outlook. This attitude contributed much to his isolation in intellectual and scientific circles in Palestine (Klausner had immigrated to Palestine in 1917, and eventually became professor of Hebrew Literature at the Hebrew University in Jerusalem, rather than being appointed to the Chair of the history of the Second Temple period, which had been his real ambition).

Even earlier than Jabotinsky, and in a far more fundamental manner, Klausner grappled with the basic issue confronting the theoreticians who attempted to formulate a national ideology for the new era. This issue was how to combine the evolutionary historic view which recognized the changes in the spirit of Judaism, with the meta-historical approach which posited Judaism as unique and unchanged throughout the ages – in other words: what was constant in Judaism, and what was capable of being changed? In addition, Klausner had to consider the question of the factors that had shaped the spirit of Judaism, and whether they were material or spiritual factors. Under the influence of Buckle and Renan, Klausner wrote that the spirit of Judaism had been formed through environmental influences, although he rejected the negative characteristics which Renan imputed to the spirit of Judaism (and to the 'Semitic' character in general), which – according to Renan – were the outcome of life in a monotonous desert environment. Klausner reasoned that the Children of Israel had indeed developed their monotheistic outlook and morality, as well as their idea of nationhood, in a desert environment, but this did not prevent them from possessing either poetic qualities, imagination, a capacity for scientific inquiry, or, for that matter, a sense of territorial belonging. While rejecting the fatalistic and deterministic geographical view, Klausner (in the spirit of philosophic idealism) accorded the creative spirit and the cultural genius a capacity for evolving revolutionary ideas (in particular through chosen individuals, i.e. the prophets).

Klausner regarded Judaism as a function of national awareness rather than religion, which means that his basic assumptions were ethnocentric. He believed that the Jewish people had been created as a coherent national body with a powerful built-in desire to preserve its singularity. It was this national unity that had safeguarded the existence of the Jewish people, and not the Torah, as the theocentric school of thought claimed. Proof of this lay in the fact that in matters of faith and religious law there existed within Judaism several schools and factions, and even sects. This explains his secularist view that the future existence of the Jewish people did not depend upon their continued observance of the Law and the commandments. Yet even Klausner, like Achad Ha'am before him, was forced to ask himself what was this permanent factor in the spirit of Judaism that set it apart from, for instance, Christianity? Klausner concluded that the two constant and lasting foundation stones of Judaism were nationalism (the national awareness) and its prophetically-inspired (messianic) sense of morality. Judaism was not a metaphysical abstraction, but a world-view borne by a defined national body, whereas nationality was the substratum of the changing spirit. Simultaneously this national body was not a separatist and parochial group, but one with a universal outlook occupying a place at the centre stage of world history. From the days of Ezra and Nehemiah and the prophets who had proclaimed the Return to Zion the Jewish national body had been the bearer of the morality of the prophets and the messianic idea enshrined in it. This meant that the return to Zion and the redemption of Israel formed a part of the reformation of the Universe. The return to Zion – in the past and in the future – was not merely a matter of territorial and political restoration, but part of the divine purpose: the establishment of God's kingdom on earth, a kingdom that would reflect the ideals of human morality. This was the reason why humanitarianism was intertwined in Judaism as an essential part of its way of life. There did not exist any tension or contradiction between Judaism and Universalism, or Judaism and Humanism.

What was therefore, according to Klausner, the historical mission of Zionism? Its mission was to restore the national existence of the Jewish people, and in so doing fulfil the prophetic ideal. The only relevant models were therefore the two historical periods when the Jewish people had led an independent national existence: the First and Second Jewish Commonwealths – the eras of the First and the Second Temple. During these periods the Jews enjoyed territorial sovereignty, enabling them to develop their true genius in an independent and authentic manner, and to cultivate the moral laws of the prophets and the messianic hopes (from which Christianity also sprang). This explains Klausner's preoccupation with the research of the First, and in particular, the Second Temple period.

The Jewish people's contribution to humanity was the idea of the unity of God, which brought an end to moral relativity. From this it followed that the Jewish world-view was opposed to moral relativity, and posited overriding and universal moral commandments (in contrast to the messianic view, according to which the history of the Jewish nation was impelled by singular historical and meta-historical imperatives of its own). However, so stated

Klausner after Kant, these moral imperatives were not externally imposed (heteronomic) directives, but moral directives deeply rooted in man's soul. From Lazarus he took the notion of 'God' being the model and criterion of Judaism as an ethical system. Also contrary to the national messianic stream, he did not regard the militancy of the prophets as a form of national or political militancy, but primarily as a moral confrontation with a troubled world. Political oppression was, according to him, contrary to the natural laws of justice.

Klausner's optimistic and heroic efforts to try and effect a synthesis between Judaism and universalistic humanitarianism was, as mentioned earlier, based on the concept of Judaism as the source of universal morality. Even so it was not this world-view, according to which Jewish nationalism was the medium for the implementation of universal morality, which informed the outlook of the members of the Revisionist movement who accepted Klausner's teachings. He presented a broad and authoritative heroic national-political interpretation of the history of the Jewish people in their homeland. What Klausner looked for in Zionist history were first of all manifestations of the national desire for political independence. The work that most influenced the youthful members of Betar and the Right in general was his collection of essays, *When a Nation Fights for its Freedom*, published in 1939, which up to 1951 was reprinted seven times. Klausner did not try to hide how the Arab violence in 1929 and 1936 had influenced the heroic slant of his national-historical attitude. He portrayed the struggle of the *yishuv* in terms of the defence of a national society against a fanatical and violent environment. Klausner even parallelled the *yishuv*'s struggle during the 1930s with the Jewish war against the Roman Empire. According to him the latter had been a struggle for both political and religious freedom, given the fact that national freedom was a constant, permanent and immutable value, through which other elements could evolve. Klausner therefore invested the national-historical awareness with an image of a glorious past, much the same as historiography, and the romantic historical literature in the style of Sir Walter Scott and the hero worship *à la* Thomas Carlyle had done for several European national movements. There were therefore two elements in Klausner's thinking and writing which together turned his idealistic historiography of a synthesis of Judaism and humanism into a source of historiographic and activist-nationalist inspiration, while at the same time providing the connection between the national views of Jabotinsky and the radical nationalist outlook. These were: (1) The representation of the history of the Second Temple era as a topical model for a contemporary national freedom struggle; and (2) the idea of Zionism as a messianic movement which formed an organic continuation of the national messianic idea in Jewish history.

Klausner himself never translated his language of symbols and historical parallelism into any concrete political theory. His messianic views emphasized the moral and universal elements in the national messianism and national eschatology of the Jewish people, but as we will see further on, there were others who transposed the historic parallels of the Jewish revolts and the values of national heroism into political terminology. As a consequence, the radical Right was able to give the messianic idea – for which Jabotinsky, as we have seen earlier, did not have any use – an entirely different character, namely that of a militant, messianic, nationalistic and eschatological territorialism.

Achimeir – Culture and Revolution[29]

The name of Abba Achimeir (Abba Shaul Geisinovitch; 1897–1962) has already been mentioned. His name will continue to appear as that of the first person who not only publicly contested the political thinking of Jabotinsky, but also advocated official acceptance of the idea that Zionism as a national liberation movement should also take recourse to civil resistance against the British Mandate. Achimeir was the first to introduce (at least theoretically) 'revolutionary' notions into the Revisionist movement, and as the reader will remember, he even led a small semi-conspiratorial group, the *Berit ha-Biryonim*, which engaged in demonstrative actions against the mandatory government's policies.

From where did Achimeir derive his radical ideas, which caused him to become estranged from Jabotinsky, while bringing him closer to Uri Zvi Greenberg, whose fundamentally different national philosophy turned him into a source of inspiration for messianic nationalism?

Achimeir was primarily an ambitious cultural historian and historiosopher, although as a scholar he was eclectic and pragmatic, and lacking in methodology. He was born in White Russia and at an early age was sent to study at the Herzlia Gymnasium in Tel-Aviv. Following his return to Russia in 1914 he continued his education at the universities of Liège (Belgium) and Vienna, where he received a doctorate in philosophy for his thesis on Oswald Spengler's monumental book *Der Untergang des Abendlandes* ('The Decline of the West'). Following his immigration to Palestine in 1924 he joined *Ha-Po'el ha-Za'ir* ('The Young Worker' party), but during the years 1928-29 he defected to the Right and, together with his close friend Joseph Katznelson, became a spokesman for the radical-maximalist viewpoint, and the leader of the radical opposition within *Ha-Zohar*. The accusations of his involvement in the Arlosoroff murder gained him and his ideas many supporters. He was regarded as a hero, and a victim of political libel. Following his release from prison, after having been convicted on a charge of anti-British propaganda, he went to Poland to assist in the Revisionist activities there. Eventually he gave up all political work, devoting his final years to journalism and the writing of political essays. The IZL, and in particular Lehi, were not particularly well disposed towards him, and he even failed to gain a seat in the *Knesset* as a representative of *Herut* when this party was formed after the establishment of the State. Only in recent years has his place in the history of the Right been recognized.

Achimeir was a Positivist in his historiosophic views. According to him it was senseless to ask 'from where did the Jewish people derive their singular genius', since this was an idle question which history could not answer. The real and fundamental question, in his view, concerned the nature of this genius. Since he agreed with the claim that it was the place where a nation was born that shaped its character and consciousness, and since he accepted the view that the formative years of the Jewish people were the period of their wanderings in the desert following the Exodus, he somehow had to modify the scenario as developed by Renan. According to Achimeir the desert imprinted upon the Jewish people not merely a subjective sense of extremism and superiority, but also qualities of violent and tough inflexibility. The desert was by no means an ideal environment, suitable for breeding pacifism and humanism, but a harsh and cruel milieu. The resulting innate characteristics had been passed on mainly by the tribes who occupied the Judean hills, whereas the northern tribes of Naphtali and Zevulun, which had settled in the coastal plain, had merged with the Phoenicians and had, together with these, produced the Phoenician civilization in the Mediterranean basin.

The world of Achimeir was a world of dialectic contrasts within a whole. He rejected the morphological and meta-historical division between Judaism and Hellenism (accepted by both Jews and Christians), according to which the two belonged to entirely different meta-historical and meta-cultural categories. According to him Judaism contained both a 'Greek', i.e. 'earthly', secular foundation, and a 'Jewish', i.e. spiritual, unearthly foundation. In his view, the task of the modern national movement was to reinforce the 'Hellenistic element', in other words the earthly, territorial and political dimensions, which had been weakened during the long years of Jewish exile. The historical forces which he considered 'unearthly' – in other words those which refuted, or even denied, the need for a political and territorial existence – were painted in the blackest and most extremist terms in his writings, as forces of destruction and annihilation. Titus, who destroyed the Temple, Rabbi Johanan Ben-Zakkai, who (in his academy in Yavneh) founded ex-territorial rabbinical Judaism, and the apostle Paul, who established Christianity as a universal religion (as well as Marx, in the modern era) had one thing in common, namely that all had tried to destroy the Jews as a nation. The *Talmud* was the antithesis of the spirit of the Bible, and the two of them were unable to live in harmony. Yavneh had been built on the ruins of Jerusalem, and Jerusalem could only be rebuilt and regain its status on the ruins of Yavneh. Opposite Yavneh as a spiritual centre Achimeir placed Jerusalem as the capital of a Jewish earthly kingdom. It goes without saying that the Jewish freedom fighters – the Hasmoneans, the warriors of the Great Revolt, the soldiers of Bar-Kochba – were described as sublime and revered historical heroes. They were the fighters for national (again, not religious) freedom.

In this light Achimeir could describe Communism, in its capacity of a universalist and internationalist movement, as one of the most destructive forces opposing nationalism. This also explains his admiration of Fascism as a national and cultural revival movement and, finally, his demonological portrayal of the Zionist labour movement as an organization that had surrendered to the idea of existing as a subject national group, rather than fighting for its sovereign political existence.

The view of Zionism as a form of revolution, not only in the daily lives of the Jewish people, but in their essential being – in other words revolution as a struggle for the renewal of the earthly, territorial element, rather than of the old, unearthly element – depicted the struggle within Zionism as a struggle between two souls inhabiting the same body. This brought Achimeir to the conclusion that democracy and liberalism were weak and corrupted systems unbefitting a revolutionary situation. Ironically, the most appropriate model for a total revolutionary system involving a fundamental and all-encompassing political and cultural metamorphosis was the bolshevik revolution of 1917. This was the same system which Achimeir regarded as an upsurge of anti-nationalism and internationalism, for which reason after the 1920s it was replaced in his ideology by Fascism, which – as already mentioned – he regarded as a national revival movement aimed at reviving a glorious past, and which distinguished itself by love of the fatherland, heroism, cultural originality, a sweeping, charismatic leadership guiding the people towards a great national goal, and – not in the last place – as an anti-communist movement that was the only force capable of saving the West from a new wave of Mongol barbarism in the form of militant Russian Communism.

Achimeir's personality combined a mixture of intellectual curiosity and fanaticism, of rationalism and nationalistic mysticism. His attitude to Jewish history was, as we have seen, patently non-fundamentalist, and his greatest opponent was rabbinical Judaism and its interpretation of Judaism and the Jewish essence. His writings reveal a ceaseless struggle against nineteenth-century European thinking, as well as, frequently, the fashionable contemporary scientific anti-Semitic theories. Achimeir was an admirer of Western culture – in particular British culture (not least because of the British imperialist thrust!), and he regarded Zionism as a faithful and constant ally of the civilized West against the barbarian 'East' (which included both Russian Communism and the Arab/Islamic East). Here and there Achimeir even reveals an abject anglophilia, which explains his feeling of humiliation when Great Britain, instead of considering the Jewish national movement in Palestine as her ally, treated it as a native movement (an attitude he referred to as the 'Irelandization of Eretz Israel').

On the one hand Achimeir possessed a conservative national outlook, in which respect he stood close to the conservative European romantic school, as represented by de Maistre, Bonald, Lamennais in France, Jakob Böhme, Schlegel and Schelling in Germany, and its Russian branch with Chadayev and Soloviev. The political conclusions he drew from these historiosophic and cultural viewpoints caused him to embrace such anti-democratic and anti-liberal political theories as integrative nationalism and Fascism. Like Jabotinsky, he believed the protective force of the national organism to repose in Judaism, which he regarded as a 'spirit' rather than a *codex*. His interpretation of the religious idea of the Jewish people was not that of a normative legal system, but of a 'spirit' or 'national idea', embodying collective characteristics. This kind of

Judaism, rather than representing a liberal or humanistic world-view, as was the case with Klausner, had a totalitarian character. This is what *monism* meant in the eyes of Achimeir: a totalitarian world-view in which the collective was united around a single idea and a single national goal, to be realized by the use of force. A religious community did not feel the apparent absence of freedom, since there existed complete unanimity among the members about the purpose of the idea (what Rousseau had termed 'the general will'). In the nature of this Judaism, particularly as it had been during the First and Second Temple periods, Achimeir recognized, as already mentioned, numerous 'secular' and 'earthly' funda-mentals. The Jews of the Second Temple period had been not merely a religious community, but a *nation*, who had founded a state, waged war and enlarged their borders, and so forth. In contrast to Jabotinsky and Klausner, Achimeir did not recognize the universal nature of Judaism, nor, for that matter, any kind of universal mission. For him, Judaism was a national conception pure and simple. Moses was a prophet and lawgiver for his people only, and not a prophet and lawgiver for the nations. Achimeir's conflict with rabbinical Judaism was therefore a struggle for the implemen-tation of the earlier-mentioned earthly and secular foundations of the Jewish spirit. For this same reason he completely and utterly rejected the Diaspora, since any non-territorial and non-sovereign existence was regarded as something anomalous and degenerate.

Much like Jabotinsky, Achimeir contributed to the general Revisionist world-view a simplified concept of pure and ideal nationalism. The nature of this concept is outlined in an article called Poland in Palestine published in *Ha-Mashkif* of 24 January 1941:

> The generation of the writer of these lines was educated in the lap of Russian or German culture. And it is a pity that this was the case. What Russian and German culture have in common is that they are both creations of peoples whose main concern was not the preservation of their national existence. When all is said and done, Russian culture is basically a philanthropic culture, while German culture is a culture of the individual, with all his joys and sorrows. Since both these peoples are sated in the national sense, the danger to their existence and the maintenance of their national character were of little concern to the progenitors of the Russian and German cultures. And, by absorbing the cosmopolitan ideas of the Russians and

German egotism, we [Zionists] absorbed a deadly poison. It is indeed a great error that our generation absorbed so little of nineteenth-century Polish culture. This was not the culture of all mankind, or of the individual, but rather the culture of the nation. Goethe, Dostoyevski and Tolstoy poisoned us, the sons of a people fighting for its national survival, while the superb writers and poets of Polish literature could have invigorated us.

Achimeir's historiosophic views, when placed in the political and ideological context of his writing, provide a legitimation for his attitude to Jewish nationalism as a superior moral category. From this follows his legitimization of a no-holds-barred ideological fight with dualistic manichaean structures, and the demonologizing of his ideological opponents. This is what first sowed the seeds of doubt about the general assumption that only political methods would be able to achieve the political results to which Zionism aspired. Achimeir introduced into conservative Revisionism a radical spirit suffused with an indiscriminate mixture of bolshevist and national-ist fascist elements. It is apparent that neither the Revisionist ideology nor the official Revisionist programme could satisfy him. His personal disposition, nourished by highly individualist intel-lectual resources, coalesced with the general mood of dissatisfac-tion and the vehement reaction to the events of 1929 crystallizing among growing circles of Betar and Ha-Zohar. Achimeir, a zealous intellectual who lacked organizational ability, became the leader of the hour, the symbol of the ideological pioneer and – in the end – the victim of his struggle.

Yehoshua Heschel Yevin: The Third Man in the Radical Triumvirate

In the radical group, mention should be made of Joseph Katznelson (1896–1940)[30] and the writer and editor Yehoshua Heschel Yevin (1891–1970).[31] The latter in particular was often mentioned within the context of the triumvirate Achimeir–Greenberg–Yevin. Green-berg and Yevin helped to lay the foundations for the revolutionary trend in Zionism, and reinforce its image as a revolutionary rather than a national political movement, with its principal and immediate purpose being the establishment of a Jewish state within the historical borders of Eretz Israel.

In many respects Yevin forms the clearest intellectual link

between the political nationalism in the spirit of Jabotinsky, and the messianist nationalism of a Uri Zvi Greenberg. It is also due to him that the Second Temple period and the 'Bar-Kochba ethos' were turned into active historical models. A Jewish state, he concluded, was not a goal (as, for instance, in the teachings of Jabotinsky: an instrument for rescuing Diaspora Jewry), but a value in its own right – the essence as well as culmination of the historical redemption process. Zionism was a territorial redemption movement, rather than being intended for spiritual or personal redemption. It was the Kingdom of the Israeli soil. The longing for the soil of Eretz Israel was the longing for an independent and sovereign status in the face of the entire Universe, anchored in the primordial source of the spirit of Israel.

Similarly, Yevin was the first to propagate the conceptual revolution in the nationalist ideology put forward by Greenberg, and his first apostle, crowning him poet, prophet and lawgiver. His book, *Uri Zvi Greenberg: Meshorer Mehokek* ('Uri Zvi Greenberg: Poet and Lawgiver') was published in 1938, shortly after the appearance of Greenberg's *The Book of Prosecution and Belief*. In it Yevin attempted to turn Greenberg's eschatological themes into a well-ordered system of nationalist historiosophy, and it was he who formulated the '12 Principles of the Constitution of Freedom' (a paraphrase of Maimonides' '13 Principles of the Faith'). These 12 principles were the following:

1. The transition from the Exile to Eretz Israel is not a physical move, but a move towards the concretization of the state concept on the territory of Eretz Israel. This transition requires a radical and fundamental change in the thought patterns, feelings, approach and innermost structure of the soul of the individual and the collective. Zionism is the *Hebrew Revolution*.
2. The Hebrew Revolution is a national revolution, and this requires the kind of 'healthy' and active leadership fitted to spearhead such a revolution. Socialist Zionism is the biggest obstacle to the fulfilment of this revolution, for which reason it should be fought against.
3. The adoption of the Hebrew language is not a mere change from one vernacular to another, but a manifestation of the new spiritual transformation (a conception clearly based on the classical philological view according to which language is the innate expression of the soul and the world-outlook of a people).
4. The Kingdom of Israel will be established within the natural

borders of the soil on which the Jewish nation was born. The presence there of *Ishmael* (the Arabs) and *Edom* (the British) is an alien presence. The establishment of the Kingdom of Israel means the territorial concentration of all of Diaspora Jewry — not through a process of settlement, but through the liberation of the land from foreign occupation.

5. Every nation has the right to rule over minorities living within its territorial borders.
6. From this it follows that weapons are a vital and sacred instrument.
7. A national struggle does not admit to restraint, and the holy command is 'double blood for blood; double fire for fire!'
8. Jerusalem is an eternal symbol, and as such forms the centre of the Kingdom of Israel; its liberation is a precondition for the establishment of the Kingdom of Israel.
9. Preparations for irredentist action in the eastern part of Eretz Israel [Transjordan] should constitute a central factor in the national awareness.
10. Socialism is an unholy marxist, and as such destructive theory, which is alien to Judaism and should therefore be expunged from the Jewish soul.
11. Hebrew visionary literature should guide the liberation movement and determine its goals.
12. The sense of [Jewish] dominance should be expressed through the ability to rule a non-Jewish population.

Here we reach the point at which eschatological poetry became the mentor of political messianism.

CHAPTER FOUR

National Messianism – Zionism as a Realistic Eschatology: Greenberg, Stern and Scheib

The Meaning of Messianism and Eschatology in the Jewish Context

Ever since the days of the Second Temple the messianic idea has acquired a variety of meanings and contents, and in this sense it designates different constructs regarding the human purpose in history. What we are concerned with here is historical Messianism, in other words Messianism dealing with the ultimate purpose of the history of the human race as such, rather than with a utopian cosmic eschatology, dealing with changes in the construct of our known world.[1] More specifically, we are dealing here with national Messianism, meaning the redemption of a national body, rather than with individual Messianism, which concerns individual redemption. From this point of view the term 'Messianism', within the context of the history of the Jewish people, refers to the hope of the ingathering of the Jewish exiles and the national redemption of Eretz Israel – a redemption combining elements of restoration (modelled on the Golden Era of the Kingdom of David) with futuristic utopian elements. Messianism must therefore be understood as the expectation of a redemption in the wake of the appearance of a human Messiah, a messiah of the House of David.

The messianic expectation has been a central motif in the worldview of the Jewish people throughout their history.[2] On the other hand, the several messianic movements which ended in failure (for instance the Bar-Kochba War and the Shabbetai Zvi movement), either induced religious nihilism or resulted in bitter opposition to Messianism on the part of rabbinical Judaism. Questions as to the *real* meaning of Messianism, its purposes, and the nature of the national redemption following the coming of the Messiah, have in the course of the generations become dominant and controversial theological and philosophical issues. The emergence of Zionism, which contained an unmistakable 'messianic' element in the sense that it spoke of the redemption of the Jewish people in Eretz Israel, has at times been interpreted as a messianic phenomenon, which explains the ambivalent attitudes to Zionism, quite apart from the already existing attitudes towards Messianism as an idea and a phenomenon. In this context we should remember that national redemption, as understood by the Jewish people, differed from any other struggle for national liberation, since the realization of political freedom had to be preceded by a return to Zion – in other words, Jews first had to return to their historical homeland from the countries to which they had been dispersed. During the era of Emancipation the majority of the Jews considered such a return to Zion as undesirable and unrealistic. Zacharias Frankel, the founder of the positivist-historical (Conservative) school in Judaism, wrote that the Zionist idea was intended for Jews who had so far failed to find a homeland, for instance the Jews residing in the czarist Empire – but not the Jews of Western Europe, who were already integrated into their respective societies.[3]

The attitude towards Messianism, and the relationship between modern Zionism and the messianic idea in its various manifestations, is a highly complex issue which has formed the subject of historiosophic and historical discussions almost from the earliest days of Zionism.[4] It should be stressed here that frequently, when speaking of Zionism as a messianic movement or phenomenon, the term is not used in the sense of a traditional messianic concept, but rather in the sense of rhetorical declarations regarding targets and expectations that appear hard to achieve and realize, or – alternatively – aspirations towards maximalist political or social achievements in furtherance of some kind of political or social utopia. It is not the aim of this study to enter into a detailed discussion of the nature of Messianism. Neither do I define the intellectual current that is discussed in this chapter as messianic, since I consider its objectives unrealistic and beyond the capacity or, for that matter, the actual 'needs' of Jewish nationalism. 'Political realism' is a subjective criterion that shifts with the times; something that appears unrealistic today may become realistic and achievable tomorrow. Ben-Gurion, for instance, made a distinction in the Zionist context between the 'realistic dimension' and the 'mystical dimension'. Zionist policy, he averred in 1937, has to be realistic when facing concrete political decisions, and remain mystical when dealing with the more distant future. The term 'messianic nationalism', as defined here, shows that its proponents believed that Jewish nationalism was not to be understood in 'Western' conceptual terms, but as the fulfilment of the messianic goal, in other words as a 'realistic historical' eschatology.[4] The right and proper time for its fulfilment had arrived, for the events in Jewish history were simply too momentous for them to be interpreted as ordinary historical happenings. From this follows the singular approach to Jewish history, to Judaism and to Zionism manifested by the supporters of this mode of thought. The fundamental assumptions were shaped during the 1930s, taking concrete form during the 1940s. During the 1950s they stood in the wings of the ideological arena in Israel, waiting for an opportunity to break through to centre stage. This opportunity presented itself after June 1967.[5]

The messianic trend which emerged within Revisionism was a modern but traditionalist offshoot of the traditional messianic idea. It was nihilistic in the sense that it rebelled against the authority of rabbinical Judaism, at least as long as this refused to go along with the times and adapt the *halachic* laws to the new revolutionary reality. According to this view no return to religion was needed to speed the coming of the Messiah; neither did it assume that the redeemed Israeli nation would have to observe the commandments, or believe in the Torah. Its historical conception was meta-historical and mytho-allegorical, and as such a distinct variant of European conservative nationalism with its mystical overtones that had emerged as a reaction to the French Revolution and its aftermath. Among other things it was a reaction to Modernism and to various universalistic rationalist trends, whereas the criteria of *Haskalah* and Rationalism were substituted by romantic or metaphysical concepts, such as the 'soul of the nation', its 'historic mission', and so forth.[6] The messianic Zionist Right's interest was focused mainly on the question of national political and territorial redemption, whereas other subjects which preoccupied conservative intellectual circles in Eastern and Western Europe, such as the essence of man and human society in general, involved them only to a very limited extent. Even the universal dimension in Jewish (and non-Jewish) Messianism seemed to have disappeared, leaving the redemption of the Jewish people – and the Jewish people alone – at the centre of their world. Quite possibly this could be explained as an over-reaction, resulting from the feeling of a nation under siege, or as an overcompensation for the essential weakness of the Jewish people, and their passivity and inability to play a more active role during the period in question.

The world-view of the radical Right was polarized between the sense of impending catastrophe and a belief in total redemption; these two convictions existed side by side, complementing and nourishing each other, with the focus swinging from one extreme to the other. Both the magnitude of the revolution caused by modern nationalism, and the magnitude of the revolution it wanted to bring about in Jewish history, were incapable of being interpreted in realistic historical terms, but in eschatological historical terms only. It was an eschatology which dreamed of the Golden Era of the *Pax Hebraica*, and even though possessing its own rhetorical and figurative language about divine redemption, it was an activist and 'mystic' kind of Messianism, which placed its faith in man-made redemption in near historical time, but took its inspiration from the traditional prayers about the coming of the Messiah as a sign of God's intervention in human history. It was an activist and militant kind of eschatology, which rallied the Jews to take their fate into their own hands and believed in their ability to bring about fundamental changes in their national situation — changes which would lift them out of the earthly vale of tears to the glory and might of a great Hebrew power, and from political passivity to national activism. The soon-to-be-expected Messiah was not a person, but the entire nation, or a chosen group within the nation, which portended and implemented the redemption process. This explains the tendency of the messianic stream to speak in terms of 'domination' or 'Herrenthum', rather than 'sovereignty', which was a modern, 'Western' term. 'Domination' and 'Herrenthum' expressed values superior to and exceeding mere political sovereignty, an organic synthesis of the people and their territory, a meta-historical and meta-geographic perception of the eternal link between the people and their country, comparable to the link between body and soul. Hence, also, the preference for the expression 'Kingdom' rather than 'State'. The latter signified the mere unity of its citizens under a civil political authority, whereas the former referred to the preferred framework of a unified territorial, constitutional *and* spiritual existence. A religious symbol such as the Temple, rather than being a place for religious worship, became the embodiment of the metaphysical bond between the divine presence (the *God of Israel*), the locale (*Eretz Israel*) and the nation (the *People of Israel*).

Any phenomenon or fact which seemed to prejudice the organic unity of these three members was regarded as abnormal, a fundamental flaw that should be resisted and fought by all available means.

A rational, critical understanding of the world was considered irrelevant to Jewish history and construed as 'intellectual idolatry'. 'Fate' and 'destiny' were the dynamic forces determining history. The realization of Zionism signified the fulfilment of the messianic destiny, meaning that there was no room for pragmatic economic considerations and that it could not be based upon diplomatic methods.

Ironically, Greenberg's actual historical model for the Jewish revival during the 1920s was the Bolshevik revolution, which had established a new society and created a new man out of the vortex of war, messianic and utopian visions, missionary slogans, and a zealous fervour and stubborn devotion to a purpose.

Uri Zvi Greenberg: The Emergence of a Poet as the Prophet of National-Historical Eschatology[7]

It is not surprising that the eschatological mood emerging at the turn of the 1920s, a mood that was charged with such high expectations, was first articulated by a poet with the self-awareness and self-image of a prophet. From a religious point of view this image of a poet in the role of prophet and lawgiver was nihilistic, but within the context of the contemporary national movement Greenberg's appearance and self-image played an important role. The poet was perceived as, and accorded the status of a visionary, who was able to predict the course of history, to foresee coming events, and render them in the form of exalted poetic revelations – apart from which his prophecies were seemingly validated by the actual course of events.

From the middle of the 1930s onwards Uri Zvi Greenberg's status in radical circles was that of a credible prophet who, foreseeing the imminent arrival of the Messiah and national redemption, summoned the nation to take all necessary steps to speed his coming. The appearance of Greenberg and his eschatological visions was no exceptional phenomenon within the context of European messianic and eschatological literature published at the close of the nineteenth century and in the years preceding the Great War, and neither was the intensive intellectual preoccupation with messianic phenomena characteristic of Jews only.[8] Nor were poets with the public status of prophets an unusual phenomenon. Within the context of Jewish nationalist history, however, Greenberg was *the* ideological poet, who created a non-traditional national messianic philosophy. Taking the historical messianic views of religious thinkers such as Rabbi Kalisher and Rabbi Alkalai, he turned them into the cornerstones of a topical political theology. This explains why his poetry and writings exercised such an important formative influence on the radical national mood in Eretz Israel and Poland, and why his work paved the way for turning this radical mood into an effective political ideology.

Uri Zvi Greenberg came to Hebrew literature and eschatological ideology via an involvement with modernistic European and Yiddish literature, and through an inner metaphysical perception.[9] He was profoundly affected by the Great War, in which he served as a soldier between 1915 and 1918 – until his desertion from the Austrian army. The battles, and the pogroms against Polish Jews after the war, turned his universalist apocalyptic views into a nationalist eschatological outlook.

Until 1929 – or at least until 1924, the year in which he immigrated to Eretz Israel – Uri Zvi Greenberg (who was born in East Galicia in 1896, and died in Israel in 1981) formed a part of a generation of *Weltschmerz* poets, filled with a sense of discomfort at the decadence of Western culture, as well as with a metaphysical restlessness due to the disappearance of God out of human life (*Ringen um Gott*) and a profound fear of an all-pervading emptiness (*horror vacui*). In his poetic world the European Christian civilization, particularly that of the Slavic world, represented a metaphysical and historic nightmare during the above-mentioned years. This metaphysical panic manifests itself in Greenberg's poetry in the obsessive hatred of the Christian (= *Edomite*) towards the Jew, which in turn is translated into a realistic analysis of the catastrophic conditions of East European Jewry. Uri Zvi Greenberg's poems portray the deep roots of the Jews in the 'Slavic [i.e. Polish] soil', and the murderous anti-Semitism that was liable to erupt any time now from this same soil, threatening to overwhelm and engulf the Jews.

Upon Greenberg's arrival in Palestine yet another metaphysical and political enemy became internalized in his psyche, namely *Ishmael*: the Arabs. Once in Eretz Israel, the role of the European anti-Semitic gentile was taken over in his world-view by the persecuting and murderous Jew-hating Arab. Here in Eretz Israel, however, the Jews were in their homeland, and their national pride would not allow any violence whatsoever to deflect them from the road to redemption. Greenberg arrived in Eretz Israel imbued with a prophetic missionary zeal and a profound awareness of his singularity as a modern Hebrew poet. On a number of occasions he describes himself in his poems as the messenger and harbinger of the

Messiah, and his poetry as a Divinely ordained mission in the name of Jewish history. ('The prophet will bring the Messiah. And the prophet will lead you, O nation!'; from 'A Speech to the Nation', *Ha-Yarden*, 27.5.1931). At other moments he suddenly took a modest stance, describing himself merely as 'one of the Legions':

> Napoleon, Bar Kochba is not with us,
> Nor Shabbetai Zvi after his apostasy.
> And there is no astrologer in the camp.
> . . .
> The speech of one of you in the Legions.
> *A Vision of one of the Legions, 1928*

The torchbearers of the Redemption, the national *avant-garde*, during the second half of the 1920s were the pioneers of the Third Aliyah (1919–23), whom Greenberg describes as a sacred band of pioneers who, like the Essenes, lived spartan lives in the Judean desert and sacrificed themselves on the altar of the redemption of the homeland. These pioneers were implementing God's kingdom on earth. (Incidentally, this is only one example of Greenberg's penchant for the use of Christian motifs.)

> California is not Eretz Israel, and it is not because of its
>   golden veins that we worship her soil,
> but because through her we hope to mend the flaws in our
>   souls.
> We want to establish a government there, a government of
>   justice and honesty, the Kingdom of God.
> Not a heavenly kingdom, though, that encourages idlers
>   and flatterers, nor a heavenly kingdom based on robbery
>   and injustice,
> nor a kingdom that sets nation against nation, and man
>   against his brother,
> but a kingdom of God, founded on physical work and the
>   labour of one's hand.
> *The Army of Labour, 1927*

He describes as poetry and magic the labour of the Hebrew workers in Eretz Israel, a small island wedged between the desert and the sea.

Towards the end of the 1920s, particularly after August 1929, Greenberg's attitude underwent a radical turn. He had started out as the poet of the Labour movement in Eretz Israel, the exponent of the messianic dimension within socialist nationalism, as one who regarded Zionism as a communist movement in terms of its spiritual make-up, its sense of purpose and its striving for total revolution. In 1929 he ceased his contributions to the newspapers and periodicals of the Labour movement and pitched his tent in the Revisionist camp, but at its radical end. Labour became his arch-enemy, a movement that had lost its messianic character and become a small and insignificant settlement movement entirely lacking in political perspective and messianic fervour, a movement which had betrayed the grand ideals of the Jewish historical revival. His earlier loathing for Jewish clericalism and the Jewish and Palestinian *petit bourgeoisie* was transformed into an boundless hatred of the Labour partics.

Although the target of his enmity and criticism had shifted, its point of departure remained the same. Since Greenberg perceived the return to Zion in eschatological terms, Zionism had to be a totalitarian movement in the spiritual and cultural sense, devoted to one sacred purpose only. Its driving force was not political considerations, but nationalist magic and mysticism. This eschatological movement would establish a new Jewish culture in Eretz Israel that would revitalize and refine the soul of the nation to its former purity. This explains why everything that was understood to fall within the category of 'Diaspora' and 'Diaspora values' was regarded as a profanation of this sacred spirit.

Greenberg did not regard the Fourth Aliyah, the period from 1924 till 1926, during which years large numbers of lower-middle-class immigrants arrived from Poland – mainly due to the oppressive economic legislation of the Grabski government – as a mass immigration that gave any reason for rejoicing. Neither did he see it as a flight to safety – the escape of Jews from the burning Slavic soil. Greenberg's negative attitude is explained by his view that this was no messianic immigration, but a mass immigration entirely lacking in messianic drive and motivation. This kind of Judaism without vision would import the degenerate Diasapora into the Holy Land; it was not the Zionism of the Hebrew renaissance, but a mere influx of shopkeepers, café owners, tradesmen and speculators who were liable to swamp the minority pioneering vanguard that had risked life and limb to reclaim the swamps. 'In Warsaw I lived in the Jewish Diaspora,' he wrote in 1925 (*Sadna Dar'ah*), 'and here I find myself in the Odessa of little Palestine.'

After 1929 and during the 1930s Greenberg divided the messianic crown between the Jewish masses in Poland, who were in dire need of immediate redemption, and *Betar* and the IZL, who were portrayed as the vanguard in the fight for national freedom, cast in the mould of the Zealots and the Sicarii of the Second Temple era. They were the Jewish Legions that would bring about the redemption.

Greenberg's Mytho-Historiology

In his topical literary and poetic work Greenberg in effect posited a new conceptual system based on a mystical biological approach to Judaism. The Jewish people were a metaphysical biological 'tribal' entity, complete and immutable throughout the generations. Greenberg rejected out of hand the historistic evolutionary approach of Jabotinsky, Klausner and Achimeir. In his view all the revelations in the course of the history of the Jewish people were manifestations of one and the same singular, authentic, organic and unchangeable entity. The entire Jewish history was a reproduction of a limited number of events and values serving a single purpose only: the complete restoration of the Golden Age of the nation – or more correctly – the reflection of an imaginary Golden Age in the distant past. For this reason the 'spirit of Judaism' could not be compartmentalized into essentially different elements, such as the 'spirit of the Bible', the 'spirit of the Talmud', and so forth. All of them formed an indivisible part of one organic spiritual fabric.

For this reason Greenberg regarded the emancipation of the nineteenth century and all the historic processes following in its wake as destructive processes. Prior to Emancipation the Jews had traditionally formed an organic entity; the evolution which had begun with Emancipation and ended with Communism had been destructive, causing divisions and leading to the breaking up of the nation and its meta-historical spirit and essence. This explains his occasional bursts of enthusiasm for Diaspora life which, for all its national passivity, in his eyes symbolized an authentic and organic Jewish existence. It was an enthusiasm comparable to the longing for the medieval period (or, in Russia, for the period prior to the reforms of Czar Peter the Great) in European conservative national Romanticism. Greenberg's positive attitude towards religion can be explained by his appreciation of religion as an essential expression of the creative spirit of Judaism, thanks to which the organic integrity of the Jewish people had been kept intact. His negative attitude towards Rationalism and education, on the other hand, stems from his identification with mystical conservative ideas, which regarded reason as a destructive factor and invested the visionary poet (or the prophet) with the true power to foresee the course of history, since only the visionary poet possessed the quality, not of wisdom, but of a true understanding of the inner and actual reality.

The Dual Image of the West

The foregoing explains why in most of his works Greenberg appears as extremely anti-Western. Europe was the Christian continent, the embodiment of successively the Roman warrior, the Roman Catholic Church and – more recently – anti-Semitism and the perfidious British who had entered into an alliance with the Arabs against the Jewish people. The Jewish culture to which he aspired was, as we will see further on, an autarkic Jewish culture. In many respects Greenberg remains, however, a modernist, or even futurist. He regarded the European technological civilization as a part of the *Sturm und Drang* of an emerging New World. Thus he wrote that when the Messiah came, he would not again walk barefoot on the soil of Galilee, but there would be steam and electricity at his service. Eretz Israel would not be redeemed through the settlement efforts of primitive, pioneering hermits, but by a scheme that would modernize the country in much the same way as the bolshevik revolution was pursuing the electrification – in other words modernization – of czarist Russia. At the same time Greenberg was affected by a profound pessimism, which foresaw the decline of the West, and which at times made him create for himself a primitive and romanticized picture of an ideal and harmonious East. In the main, however, his appreciation of 'the East', or at least the Arab East, was that of a backward and inferior cultural category.

In light of the above he wrote in *Doar ha-Yom* of 20 May 1930, under the headline 'The Naked Truth Before Your Eyes': 'The Jewish people are implementing a cultural colonization; their societal pattern is along "European constitutional lines"'. The Jewish nation was therefore the most deserving ally for any European power wanting to further its ambitions in the East. Only the establishment of Jewish power could ensure continued Western hegemony in the East. 'There will never be peace and quiet in the East until the National Home of the Hebrews has been established in this land,' was his unequivocal conclusion. The worst sin of the Zionist leadership under Chaim Weizmann was its renunciatory policy, which had convinced Great Britain that Zionism, through both lack of strength and lack of purpose, did not aspire to become a world power. Weizmann's inferiority complex had resulted in the Jews of Eretz Israel being looked at as 'protected Jews', rather than as a 'new political power in the land of Judah, along the shores of the Mediterranean, in the heart of the in effect dormant and desolate Arabian desert – a piece of *Hebrew Europe*.' Europe was the pinnacle of culture: it was a Faustian, dynamic civilization, in which man ruled nature rather than submitting to fatalist resignation. For this reason Zionism, too, was an essentially European or, as he put it, 'Faustian' movement.[10]

Greenberg's Theography

Whereas Jabotinsky argued the Jewish people's national rights to Eretz Israel on the basis of historical considerations, Greenberg was of the opinion that these historical ties could only be explained in theographic terms. Eretz Israel was not merely a piece of territory, but a land with a symbolical and mystical significance. The relationship of the Jewish people to Eretz Israel could not be compared to that of the various European nations to their countries. His approach to this subject was a combination of geographical mysticism, investing the land with a degree of holiness, and 'autochthonism', in other words a striving after the growth of a natural relationship, in which the soil symbolized the mother. The mystical relationship to the country is not a mystical connection extending to the soil and the land, in which sense working the soil is like a cosmic unification of the person and his land;[11] it is a meta-historical connection with a country over which full national sovereignty prevails – in other words, an ownership relation. This explains a dominant theme in Greenberg's approach to this issue, namely the 'eternity of the plough being secured by the eternity of the sword – and not the reverse': in other words, Eretz Israel will not be conquered by the Jewish people through settlement and cultivation, but by force of arms. The restoration of Israel would not be comparable to the return to Zion during the Persian era, when a number of Jews returned as a religious sect under the patronage of the Persian Empire, but to the conquest and settlement of the land under Jehoshua Bin-Nun. Greenberg turned the nationalist and idealistic Romanticism of both proto-Zionism and Zionism into a new kind of romantic heroism which aspired after complete territorial sovereignty. Heroism was not merely an aesthetic value, but a call for military conquest. Eretz Israel would become Jewish through armed conquest, and only this military occupation, comparable to the settlement and expansion of the kingdoms of David and Solomon, would bring to realization the eternal ties between the people and their land. All efforts to achieve an international consensus about Jewish independence, any reliance upon the Balfour Declaration or the Mandate charter, were a grave insult to the national will and the incontestable rights of the Jews, which were not subject to the consent of outsiders. Not politics, but theo-politics; not diplomacy, but meta-politics, not nationalism, but Messianism, were the factors which would consummate the complete Jewish historical restoration in Eretz Israel. According to this view the boundaries of Eretz Israel were not the boundaries of mandatory Palestine. The restoration would not be achieved within the restricted borders of western Eretz Israel, but within the boundaries of the territories conquered by David and Solomon.

When Achimeir talked about the Messiah as a political orator, or a soldier driving a tank, rather than as a beggar riding a donkey, he previsioned a political revolution. When Greenberg, on the other hand, spoke of the Messiah riding a battle horse, and of 'blood that will decide who is the sole ruler here', the practical consequences appeared similar, but the spiritual world-view he represented was different, since Greenberg talked in terms of the eschatology of the days of the Second Temple and afterwards, rather than in terms of a modern revolution.

Greenberg's Hebrew Cultural Conception

There existed a substantial gap between the Hebrew cultural conceptions of Jabotinsky and those of Greenberg. We have already seen that Jabotinsky was an enthusiastic supporter of a secular and pluralist national culture. According to his understanding Hebrew culture was not restricted to literary masterpieces written in the Hebrew language and in a *Hebrew spirit*, but referred to a body of Hebrew writing, including Hebrew translations of European literature. Greenberg, on the other hand, averred that national literature included only works that had grown from the native soil and expressed the unique national spirit (the *Volksgeist*), examples of which, according to Greenberg, were to be found only in Russian and Polish literature. It had to be a literature expressing the continual tension of the waiting for the Messiah, a condition almost comparable to pregnancy. It had to be a visionary literature, a literature with a message, in many ways comparable to the poetry of

Walt Whitman, or to modern expressionist poetry, or to the utopian eschatology of the later prophets (Ezekiel, Zechariah). Not 'art for art's sake', but an art totally committed to the spiritual idea. This explains his comment in his 1928 manifesto *Against the Ninety-Nine* − a reference to the Hebrew writers' community, among whom he was the sole dissident − where, writing about his poetry, he states: Literature effects magic combinations of Hebrew letters, and like X-rays it has the power to penetrate deeply into the very essence of time. It should be carried 'like the Tabernacle at the head of our rallying march'. No work written in Hebrew deserved to be called Hebrew literature if it failed to express the essential Hebrew idea of 'sovereign mastery of the Land'.

Although Greenberg was also influenced by European ideas and literature, his utopian ideal concerned a culture (as expressed primarily in literature) that was 'Jewish' without any foreign influences. Although he was not very explicit about the normative aspects of this culture, one can imagine that he intended to exercise strong ideological censorship in order to 'purify' his Hebrew culture of anything suggesting foreign elements. His purpose was to create a national Hebrew culture, in the same mould as, for instance, 'Soviet culture'. In common with earlier conservative thinkers he believed that 'the West' had a negative and harmful influence on Hebrew literature. This also explains why his normative system had to be based on Jewish religious customary law, even though the *halachah* would have to be adapted to the spirit of the times. In other words, it would have to be adjusted to the new reality of political and territorial sovereignty, but this did not mean that there would be any requirement, let alone compulsion, to relinquish the Jewish faith or the belief in the *Torah* and the commandments or, for that matter, the traditional Jewish way of life.

Messianism and Revolutionary Terrorism

Avraham Stern ('Yair'; 1902–1942), the founder of Lehi, whose influence on IZL ideology was discussed in Part One, did not consider Greenberg a decisive influence on his life, nor can his intellectual development be shown to have been influenced by Greenberg's poetry. It was mainly Dr. Israel Scheib (Eldad) who during the 1940s handed to Greenberg the prophet's mantle of the anti-British revolt, and to Stern the sceptre of those who translated historiosophy into political terminology and deeds. Even so there exists a marked similarity between Stern's poetry (written under the influence of Polish national revolutionary poetry), and the nationalist poetry of Greenberg. From the 1930s onwards Stern, too, discussed Zionism in terms of a national freedom movement that would only achieve its goals by the use of military force. Like Greenberg, he was constantly preoccupied with the nature of messianic movements in the history of Israel, and with their representation as a dynamic and vital longing for political redemption. At the same time he dealt extensively with the wars of liberation of other nations – for instance the Balkan nations, the Italians, the Irish and the Poles – both as examples and prototypes, and to see what kind of historical lessons could be drawn from them (revolutionary praxis). Achimeir, as we will remember, never wrote about messianic movements, whereas Jabotinsky failed to mention them at all. Stern, Greenberg and Yevin regarded them as a chain of activist political manifestations propelled by an inner force (rather than external pressures). The whole of Jewish history was not presented as being moved by environmental pressures – disorders, anti-Semitism, pogroms, and so forth – or as a reaction to physical hardships, but as an authentic, autonomous and immanent manifestation of a deeply-rooted and firm Jewish historical foundation: the national and messianic substratum.[12] Also the apparent need in Stern's writings to refer to the Second Temple as a historical model was similar in origin to its usage in the historical essays and other literary and journalistic efforts of the Palestinian (and Polish) Right. The main and foremost difference between Stern, on the one hand, and Achimeir, Yevin and Greenberg, on the other, was that Stern's activities did not stop at writing or propaganda. Stern was an intellectual and an artist who turned to the realm of practical politics and warfare, starting (as we have already seen, and will see further on) with attempts to translate historical eschatology, the idea of the 'realistic miracle', into military and political initiatives. In contrast to the others, Stern was a charismatic leader, who in the course of his underground exploits did not shrink from taking personal risks and making personal sacrifices, and whose life was the embodiment of literary and mytho-allegorical bravery and self-sacrifice.

Greenberg refers to the members of the underground in images recalling the Zealots and Sicarii. Stern, while adopting the same imagery, compared them also with the revolutionary terrorists, the 'nameless people' of czarist Poland, immortalized in the Lehi hymn, the literal translation of which is given below:

We are the anonymous soldiers, without uniform,
Encircled by fear and the shadow of death.
All of us have been mobilized for the rest of our lives,
and only death will release us from the ranks.
In the tears of the mothers who have lost their sons,
And in the name of the pure infants,
Our bodies are attached to the bricks like mortar,
And so we shall erect the structure of the Homeland.

'The Anonymous Soldiers'
[*Ha-Metzudah* ('The Citadel'); 1932]

The Eighteen Principles of the Revival

It would seem as if the main body of Stern's writings is a combination of national messianic philosophy and the ethos of terrorism and its methods. No less important is the fact that he did not restrict himself to oppositionist activity within *Ha-Zohar* and *Betar*. Since formally he was not a member of either the party or the youth movement, he could accentuate the novel revolutionary nature of his nationalist political views. From 1938 onwards he strove towards the organizational and political independence of the IZL, based on a radical nationalist approach. His failure to achieve this end created a rift which, as already mentioned, caused a schism within the IZL. As a result Lehi, the new underground which he had founded, became the carrier and chief exponent of the radical world-view (various elements of which also became a part of the world-view and ideology of the IZL) whose political tradition was anchored in the two types of national world-view portrayed above.

In any case, Lehi's 'Eighteen Principles of the Revival', which were publicized in the second issue of its underground organ *Ba-Machteret* ('In the Underground') were a concise formulation of the stand that has been described here, and although not all Lehi members – certainly during the late 1940s – subscribed to these principles, it is clear that Stern himself in 1941 perceived them as reflecting his own philosophy, preferring them to other versions that were suggested to him. It should be mentioned here that Stern (like David Raziel, the commander of the IZL, and numerous members of both underground organizations) was a traditionally religious individual, his way of thinking was far removed from the outspoken secular views and way of life of Jabotinsky and his circle. Stern was right in presenting the Hasmonean zealots and the Bar-Kochba war as not merely national wars of liberation, but as wars with a religious cause and significance. As he wrote: 'It is thanks to this religious extremism that the purity of the national blood was preserved.'

The Eighteen Principles of the Revival were the following:

1. *The People* – The Jews are a chosen people, the creators of the monotheistic faith, who have legislated the morality of the prophets, [they are the] bearers of world culture, outstanding in their traditions and spiritual devotion, their will to live and power of endurance, [as well as] in spiritual enlightenment and their belief in redemption.

2. *The Homeland* – The homeland [of the Jews] is Eretz Israel within the borders as defined in the Bible ('To your descendants I give this land from the river of Egypt to the great river, the Euphrates'; Genesis 15:18) – this is the land of life, in which the entire Hebrew nation will dwell in safety.

3. *The People and their Country* – The Jewish people conquered Eretz Israel by the sword. Here it became a nation, and here it must return for its national restoration. For this reason the people of Israel are the sole rightful owners of Eretz Israel. This right is absolute: it has not lapsed, and cannot lapse until the end of days.

4. *The Goal* – 1. Redemption of the land. 2. The restoration of the Kingdom. 3. The revival of the nation: the revival of the nation is impossible without the redemption of the land, and no revival of the nation is possible without the restoration of the Kingdom.

And these are the tasks of the Irgun (Organisation = Lehi) in the era of war and conquest:

5. *Education* – To educate the people to love freedom and to cultivate a zealous loyalty to their eternal patrimony. To implant the idea that the people's fate lies in their own hands. To renew the recognition that 'the sword and the Book were given together from Heaven' (Levit. R. 35:8)

6. *Unity* – To unify the entire people round the flag of the Hebrew freedom movement. To exploit the genius, status and desires of individuals – and to direct the energy, dedication and zeal of the masses towards the war of liberation.

7. *Alliances* – To form alliances with all those who are interested in the war of the *Irgun* and willing to render direct assistance.

8. *Power* – To forge the fighting force and expand it in the Home-

land and abroad, in the underground and on the barricades, and to turn it into a redemption army under a Hebrew flag, with Hebrew weapons and Hebrew commanders.

9. *War* – To fight a perpetual war with everyone who obstructs the realization of the goal.
10. *Conquest* – To liberate the Homeland from foreign control [and secure it] for an eternal possession [of the Hebrew nation].

And these are the tasks of the movement in the age of domination and redemption:

11. *Mastery* – To re-establish Jewish mastery of the land following its redemption.
12. *Righteous Government* – To establish a social régime in the spirit of Jewish morality and the justice of the prophets. Under this régime there will be no hunger or unemployment, and [people will] live together in brotherhood, dignity and respect towards all the members of the nation who are its sons, and their example will be a light unto the nations.
13. *Restoration of the Desolate [Land]* – To rebuild the ruins and revitalize the wastelands [in preparation of] the immigration of millions [and] their procreation and expansion.
14. *Rules Regarding Foreigners* – The problem of foreigners [in Eretz Israel] will be solved through a population exchange.
15. *The Ingathering of the Exiles* – All the exiles will be ingathered in the Kingdom of Israel.
16. *Government* – To [achieve the] glorification of the Hebrew nation as the foremost military, political, cultural and economic power in the East and around the shores of the Mediterranean.
17. *Restoration* – To restore the Hebrew tongue as the vernacular, to renew the historical and spiritual independence of the Jewish people. To purify the national character in the crucible of the revival.
18. *The Temple* – To build the Third Temple as a symbol of the era of the completed redemption.

The Keystones of Messianic Historiosophy

The man best equipped for the task of formulating a systematic historiosophic framework for the national messianic world-view was Dr. Israel Scheib (Eldad). Scheib was born in 1910 in East Galicia.[13] A graduate of the rabbinical seminary and the University of Vienna, he had a broad Jewish and philosophical background (he later translated the works of Nietzsche into Hebrew). He lectured at the teachers' seminary in Vilna and was among the leaders of *Betar* in Poland. Upon his arrival in Palestine in 1941 he joined Lehi, becoming one of the members of Lehi's central command, as well as (together with Nathan Yellin-Mor) the movement's ideologist. In the summer of 1943 he started publishing a series of articles entitled 'Foundation-Stones', in which he stated that 'after fifty years of Zionism, we shall have to start from the beginning by re-laying the foundations'.[14] The failure of Zionism, he wrote, stemmed from its mistaken assumptions, and therefore a complete revision had to be undertaken − yet another revision, following the appearance in 1925 of Jabotinsky's 'Revisionism'. This time the revision was not intended to introduce a new political approach, but rather to formulate a change in basic concepts and undertake a spiritual reassessment. Like his predecessors, Scheib did not believe in the existence of a 'Jewish problem' in the sense of a people looking for physical survival, but only in an 'organic group expecting the arrival of the Messiah'. Here, too, the coming of the Messiah meant the conquest of the Homeland as in the days of Joshua and David, for an eternal possession, and the fulfilment of the national spirit within the promised Scriptural boundaries. What had vouchsafed the Jewish people their eternal sovereignty over the land in the past, and would vouchsafe it in the future, was the conquest by force of arms, [to restore] the land to its sole owners. The need for a sovereign country was a natural corollary of the [existence of] the living organism. Neither was Jewish nationalism in need of justification or, for that matter, recognition by outsiders; its sovereignty was implicit in its creation, and the national struggle for liberation was not a product of circumstances, but a categorical imperative − the command to revolt, rather than to build settlements. Scheib defined the state as the product of the collective and intertwined forces of body and soul within a single geographical and organic framework, resulting in the creation of unique values.

In addition Scheib tried to formulate a systematic concept of the essence of the Jews as a chosen people by suggesting three possible interpretations which, in his opinion, possessed a common denominator:[15]

1. The *transcendental* view, which held that the Jewish people owed their existence to the force of an idea, and that the nation was a spiritual entity. The circumstances under which the idea had emerged belonged to the realm of metaphysics and were, as

such, beyond our ken. The purpose of the practical [religious] commandments was to preserve the idea (including the messianic idea) in an ordered fashion.

2. The *historical-immanent* view, according to which the Jewish people were the embodiment of the pure monotheist idea. In other words, the Jewish people had been formed around a singular idea that had been imprinted upon the people, and internalized by them, thus shaping their world-view and their place in history.

3. The *functional-psychological* view, which held that the people's consciousness had been shaped as a reaction to a historical situation, which created its unique world-view and its culture.

All three interpretations wholly rejected the historisticist-evolutionary approach to Jewish history (which only the generation born in the era of emancipation had tried to dismantle), and all three viewed the Judaic idea as an organic and invulnerable entity.

This same historiosophy formed the basis of the memorandum submitted by Lehi to the United Nations' Special Commission on Palestine (UNSCOP) in June 1947. The memorandum stated that the Jewish people were a virtually autochthonous nation in Eretz Israel, in which its eternal values had been created and its culture had been shaped, in view of which there existed a practical as well as symbolic, organic and cosmic relationship with the very nature of the country. Such an attachment, stated the memorandum, knew no parallel in the history of any other people.

Although Scheib, as already mentioned, was a fundamentalist and anti-rationalist in theory, he read Jewish literature with the eye of an exegetist, and he too preferred the Biblical period, recognizing the Bible rather than the *Talmud* as the true expression of the spirit of Judaism and the Jew. As regards the contents of the Biblical books, including the Prophets, he evinced a particular preference for everything reflecting nationalist and militant values. The return to the Bible was a return to the God of the Bible, though not in His image of a moral God, but in that of a puritanical God: a warlike, jealous God who revenged and extirpated the enemies of Israel. Since the divine promise was premised upon the commandment to honour the land, it follows that to conquer it was a moral deed and a sacred goal which justified the means.

It can be said, therefore, that Scheib and the current he represented, experienced no moral scruples, and felt no need for any moral or pragmatic justifications. Suggestions of this kind were contemptuously rejected as an apologistic streak of emancipated Jews. Since an opponent existed who interfered with the fulfilment of the divine command, to wit the Arab population of Eretz Israel, this opponent had to be viewed as an enemy, and dealt with – as we shall see in another chapter – in the same way as the Canaanites of old, meaning that they would have to be either subjected or eliminated.

Portents of the Partnership between the Right and Religious-Messianic Nationalism

This eschatological view was not accepted by all the members of Lehi, and at their public convention in February 1949 – the first since the organization had emerged from the underground – it appeared that only a minority of the members were prepared to support it.[16] Meanwhile Eldad and his adherents had created an ideological circle around the periodical *Sulam* (Ladder). The manner in which they developed their views, and the convergence and linkage of these views with the religious eschatological outlook of the school of Rabbi Abraham Isaac Kook (1865–1935), belong to an era which falls outside the scope of the present volume, but even so a few preliminary comments are pertinent here.

1. The territorial integrity of Eretz Israel – particularly that of the part west of the Jordan – was one of the central doctrines of the Right, a historical and political *a priori* demand. The territorial issue became the focal point of the rightist conception, the cement that bound its members and from which it derived its historical strength. Territorial integrity became the absolute *precondition* for the realization of all other Zionist aspirations, and the fulfilment of any of the national ideals became *conditional* upon the fulfilment of the territorial goal. This territorial (read: historical-geographical) focus of the world-view of the Right (rather than, for instance, a social ideal or utopia) is the dominant characteristic of its world-outlook and ideology, and as such holds the key to every political or ideological coalition it has entered into in the course of the years. Its nature of a nationalist Right, in other words a nationalist movement with a rightist signature, has turned the focus on the territorial issue into a categorical command and into the keystone of its consciousness (even though the Right has not been alone in this). This kind of nationalism regards the national territory as the

crucial factor of the national existence and the existence of the national state. Various Revisionist publications have preached this idea and cultivated it in a number of ways, turning it into the fountainhead of their brand of Zionism, and its ultimate goal and foremost criterion.

2. As regards the new Hebrew culture, and its attitude to Jewish religion and tradition, the Right has posited two interpretations. It should be remembered that we are dealing here with theory as well as political behaviour. The first formulation regards religious tradition as an essential component of any new Hebrew culture, in which sense secular nationalism is also a direct extension of the religious Hebrew tradition. Hence the Right's positive attitude towards the idea of turning *halachah* into one of the keystones of the normative system of the new national Jewish society. In this regard the views towards religion of the mainstream of the movement's membership differed considerably from the basic attitudes of their leader, Ze'ev Jabotinsky.

The second formulation considered Jewish culture as a spontaneous construct, a mystical and sacred creation. It was a singular and autonomous cultural creation subject to special and unique historical and moral laws that applied to it alone. Not the Age of Enlightenment was the historical ideal, but the Middle Ages, the spiritual and territorial existence of the traditional Jewish community, as represented by life in the 'Pale of Settlement'.[17] Since emancipation was considered a disruptive influence which tried to impose alien criteria upon Judaism, the Jewish tradition in its entirety, including of course *halachah*, should be embraced as the cultural model. Religion was regarded as both a culture and an existentialist manifestation. As a result the ideal became of itself transformed into the ideal of a nationalist orthodox — in effect theocratic — society, which explains why the emergence of *Gush Emunim* (the 'Bloc of the Believers') during the 1970s was seen as the realization of this nationalist ideal of a territorial, messianic and orthodox (yet modern) kind of Judaism. The Right, lacking a utopian Hebrew cultural model of its own, and having rejected — without consciously admitting this — Jabotinsky's cultural model, found itself willy-nilly chained to Jewish tradition (i.e. traditionalist views), on the one hand, and the Jewish religion, on the other. The messianism of the Right, for all its nihilist symbolism, had paradoxically caused it to become the natural ally of religious messianic nationalism.

3. The messianic stream regards Liberalism and democracy as purely Western concepts, fruits of the disintegrating modern era. Democracy is merely an attempt to 'imitate the Gentiles', not so much by integration, but by attempting to emulate them, and thus evade the authenticity of the Jewish 'race' and its culture.

The diversified democratic value system is again counter-posed by the Jewish *halachic* system. Jabotinsky's Revisionism is portrayed as bourgeois, Hegelian and alien, for regarding (in common with Zionism ever since the days of Herzl) the creation of a *State*, rather than the emergence of a *new Judaism* such as had arisen after the destruction of the First Temple, as the ultimate historical event. For lack of an alternative normative system, the secularists on the Right – such as, for instance, Achimeir – were compelled to cast around for contemporary political models of totalitarian messianism (Communism as a challenge, and Fascism as a reaction), whereas those embracing the messianic stream had no recourse but to turn to the 'original values of Judaism' as embodied in the *halachah* and *Shulchan Aruch*. As long as rabbinical Judaism was the only representative of the desired kind of Judaism within orthodoxy and in the East, the only concrete model this current managed to find was in the teachings of Rabbi Kook, and after him in the radical religious nationalism of the 1970s.

It would seem that we are faced here with a profound paradox in Zionist ideology and modern Jewish nationalism, a basic paradox characteristic of Zionism as well as the political tradition of the Right. The two ideological currents that have been described above originated from a single source and had many points in common. While this created a unified political tradition, they at the time expressed two opposite poles in Zionism as such, if not the most disparate and extreme polarities imaginable: the modern secular nationalist viewpoint, on the one hand, and messianic nationalism, on the other.

The Impact of the Holocaust

As we have seen, the anti-Western and anti-Rationalist current emerged even before the Second World War, but the war itself and the Holocaust resulted in intensifying and hardening these views. Whereas IZL publications from the period after 1944 portray the European nations, all the way from Nazi Germany to Great Britain, as accomplices in the destruction of the Jews out of deeply-rooted anti-Semitic feelings, the messianic current drew much further-reaching historiographic conclusions, according to which European civilization had at last shown its true face. This time it was not portrayed (as Jabotinsky had done) as a civilization based on Judaic principles, and any desire for an integration of Judaism and universalist humanism had completely disappeared. European humanism was merely a veneer concealing Teutonic barbarism. The absorption of the Jewish Bible – represented here as both universalist and humanist – into the European psyche had been a failure. This did not mean that European scientific and technological achievements should be eschewed, but its spiritual values, i.e. European culture, must be rejected.[18]

The Holocaust greatly reinforced the redemptionist idea. The destruction of a major part of European Jewry, followed shortly after by the Israeli War of Independence, signified as it were the closing of the circle of a historical construct based on catastrophe, on the one hand, and miraculous redemption, on the other. Reality had validated the eschatological view; it had proved its desire to complete what was missing and repair the shortcomings, and in so doing had proved this completion to be the supreme imperative of the new Jewish history. Historical eschatology therefore had a utopian vision of a new era of completion and fulfilment in the national history, the nature of which could only be described in terms of metaphysical and theological generalizations.

CHAPTER FIVE

A Collective Biography –
Attitudes and Arguments within
the Zionist and Israeli Right

The Function of 'National Sentiment'

This chapter deviates from the general framework of this book in that the profile that is sketched here summarizes not merely the period before 1948, but extends much beyond it. It would appear that, although the socio-demographic profile of the Right underwent a profound transformation in the years following the establishment of the State, its basic system of symbols and attitudes has remained unchanged – a surprising continuity in a movement that in the course of more than 60 years has been faced with so many upheavals! This is why it seems important to try and draw a general outline of the movement and its members, in the form of a 'collective profile' spanning its development over half a century, rather than consider the year 1948 as a crossroads or turning point in terms of its views and behaviour. This chapter therefore belongs to the present, first volume of this study, as much as to the second volume.

In an interesting article from 1911, called 'Lessons from Shevchenko's Jubilee' (Taras Shevchenko, 1814–1861, was the Ukrainian national poet[1]) Jabotinsky offers a brief but penetrating analysis of the crisis of Liberalism and the nature of the new Ukrainian nationalism, in which he discerned several 'natural' qualities characteristic of the 'national impulse' in its various manifestations. Among these characteristics of 'natural nationalism' Jabotinsky included the rejection of the alien, and the inability to be satisfied with abstract ideas. The middle class, he wrote, is not attracted to the Liberals, since Liberalism is an abstract ideology lacking in fervour and emotion. According to Jabotinsky the middle class was far more inclined towards national ideas and national slogans. The Right (in the Ukrainian case) owed its widespread political influence to the fact that it had succeeded in touching the nationalist nerve in the heart of the middle-class urban masses, allowing it to express, not so much the positive and creative aspects of this national sensitivity, but mainly its 'negative' aspects. 'And not a flag in the world, however radiant, and however high it is raised, will succeed in capturing the hearts of the middle class,' he wrote, 'except one: the flag of one's own national protest.'[2]

These words were in some way a portent of his own future movement. Abstract liberal ideas failed to have any impact on the average member of the Zionist Right; they appealed at most to a limited group of intellectuals within its ranks. What 'the masses', who would become the social substratum of the Right, expected – and received – from Revisionism through the intermediary of Jabotinsky and other sources of influence and inspiration – was a simple national ideology that gave them self-respect and realized their national hopes. They did not ask for a system of sophisticated philosophical principles, but for simple and 'self-evident' principles of faith. The real question is therefore not whether Jabotinsky was a leader with national-liberal or national-rightist views, but what were the foundations of the *Weltanschauung* of the public which constituted the 'Right'. What is important, therefore, is to investigate the collective biography of the Right, and to try and define and characterize the cultural composite of an anonymous public and its 'personality'. This is quite a difficult task, and every effort to sketch a collective profile is bound to be an experiment in generalization, an attempt to discover a common denominator in a relative multitude.

The Closed System of the Right

Earlier I reviewed some of the formative historical and political events in the Revisionist past, in other words some of the events and incidents which left a deep imprint on the formation of the Right as a social group with a common awareness and a common tradition, imbuing it with a sense of partnership and mutual belonging. At this point I would like to try and outline a collective image of the Right as carriers of a set of *a priori* arguments and attitudes with respect to a given series of phenomena. In other words, it is my intention to sketch a systematic complex of arguments, attitudes, images, symbols and *a priori* responses, and in so doing draw the profile of an imaginary 'body' approximately 60 years old. I believe that it is possible to isolate and typify a reasonably clear collective biography of the Right out of the collective biography of Zionism and Israeli society at large. The fact that the collective biographies of the Right and of other segments of Zionism have numerous fundamentals and elements in common, as well as the fact that the Israeli body politic contains elements which do not belong to the Right, and yet react in a similar – if not more extreme – way, does not necessarily contradict the fact that we are dealing here with a 'closed system' of values, symbols, arguments and attitudes.[3] Even more, it would seem as if the opinion of a member of the 'Right' on a specific issue enables us to determine with near certainty what his opinions on other issues will be; similarly, when he evinces an attitude towards a given phenomenon, he is almost certain to have the same attitude towards other phenomena.

Many attitude researches try to determine a continuum of attitudes across the ideological spectrum by means of specific questions to the interviewees in their sample.[4] Most of the questions asked in the course of such interviews are of a general nature, meaning that the pollsters do not attempt to clarify the exact meaning of the concepts used. As a result the answers may be either authentic or anticipatory, and because of this lack of diagnostic discrimination I consider attitude research of limited value, and its diagnostic range restricted and often superficial. The overall collective biography which I intend to present here is the product of my impressions resulting from intensive reading of a large and variegated corpus of texts written over a period of some 60 years (1925–1985), consisting of articles, novels, letters to editors, private correspondence and a wide variety of sayings and reactions.

Conservatism versus Modernism

The average 'rightist individual', be he a member of what is generally called the 'conservative Right' or the 'radical Right', has the image of being 'conservative' or reactionary in nature, as a result of which he tends to react to changes in tradition with uneasiness and fear. He also has a marked tendency towards relying upon historical traditions and adhering to customs and precedents.[5] This explains why he is hesitant and uncertain about innovations or revolutionary developments, and tends to be nervous when confronted with any phenomenon smacking of 'modernity' or 'modernism'. Even if his traditionalism is in fact revolutionary compared with past (or present) usage, he will always regard himself, or present himself, as one whose convictions are rooted in the past, whose traditions he

Collective Biography 165

intends to uphold; in other words he is a restorer rather than a revolutionary.[6]

The rightist Zionist individual tends to be much more outspoken about his profound identification with Jewish religious tradition than the majority of his leftist counterparts. On the political and cultural level he will show considerable tolerance of proposals to subject private and public behaviour (particularly in the public domain) to traditional religious norms, to the point of being prepared to legitimize such attempts. This positive inclination is not merely due to political or tactical considerations, but stems from a relatively more affirmative attitude towards the place of religion and tradition in Jewish culture. Even so his view of religion is, as we have already seen, of a more national and pragmatic nature, meaning that religion and tradition are considered dominant and essential elements of Jewish identity and Jewish existence. This also explains why he will be inclined to accept the orthodox religious definition with regard to the question of 'Who is a Jew', and support religious-sponsored legislation on a variety of issues. In everyday life this affirmative attitude towards traditional religious norms will manifest itself in a somewhat more careful observance of certain central religious tenets and liturgical practices.

This fairly pronounced national and traditionalist component notwithstanding, the Zionist Right as a whole cannot be called a reactionary or conservative social force. Its conservatism is not of a kind that reacts with hostility to technical innovations or changes in economic structure. Neither is the Right composed of, for instance, conservative farmers or craftsmen protesting against the industrial or post-industrial revolution. Neither during the mandatory *yishuv*, nor in the present Israeli society would it be easy to find elements with such an anti-modernist bent, and the Right as a whole – even among its most extreme populist sections – does not form an exception in this respect.

The Right and National Culture

Contrary to what has been said before, the Israeli Right – and in fact the Right in general – evinces a pronounced hostility towards cultural 'modernism'. Our hypothetical average rightist individual refuses to show sympathy for elitist modern tendencies in culture or art. His cultural mentality tends towards conservatism. His literary preference is for historical novels or epics of an 'elevated' cultural level reflecting what he considers to be the 'healthy national spirit', and containing narratives about the Jewish people's struggle for the preservation of their national identity and cohesion. Trendy stories about the plight of individuals as individuals, divorced from society as a whole, stories about crises of values, or expressing social criticism would be regarded as overt representations of cosmopolitanism and cultural 'permissiveness', and thus unhealthy cultural phenomena. The modern literary tendency to strike at sacred values is regarded as 'pathological' and an attempt to undermine the very foundations of the national society and culture. Any attack on sacred values such as the 'State', the 'Homeland' or religion is liable to arouse angry protests on his part. Arguments in favour of creative freedom in culture and art will be countered with the argument that Israel is a 'society under siege' and cannot therefore be compared to other, liberal, Western societies. He will argue that, as regards Israel, moral or cultural 'decadence' is a stab in the back, endangering the very soul of a nation that is fighting for its national identity and physical survival. This explains why the hypothetical rightist individual is extremely sensitive to any manifestations of criticism, and will, for instance, support censorship of the theatre and the electronic mass media, which he believes to be controlled by a minority of leftist individuals (the 'leftist Mafia'), who attempt to mould and dominate public opinion. The average rightist individual will feel a sense of alienation towards the prevailing cultural elite in Israeli society (even though he could mention an array of rightist intellectuals). This is why he is somewhat suspicious and hostile towards intellectualism and intellectuals, or even institutes of higher learning, which are viewed as hotbeds of anti-national universalism, whereas in his view the individuals and institutions involved indulge in excessive and even 'pathological' self-criticism.

At times of national crisis the rightist individual will react strongly against dissenting opinions and criticism, calling his detractors 'traitors' to the national cause, or mental or ideological defectives who are influenced by partisan interests. More often than not critics will be labelled 'Communists' (during the Mandate) or 'Leftists' (during the 1970s and 1980s). The rightist individual considers himself a loyal nationalist and patriot, whereas his enemy represents an example of organically defective Jewish or Israeli identity respectively. A substantial section of the Right actively supports the integration of nationalism and liberalism, but such a merger runs into considerable difficulties in crisis situations, when Liberalism and liberal democratic freedoms seem to clash with national aspirations. The State, *raison d'état*, and security are considered to stand above the law, which – to his view – is a mere man-made, normative system, rather than an absolute norm.

The Role of Eretz Israel

The centre of the world-view of the rightist individual is occupied by the 'historical Eretz Israel'. This should not necessarily be interpreted as an emotional or intimate sentiment towards a certain piece of 'land' or 'soil', but rather as a symbolic relationship with his country, his historical homeland, in the sense of a territorial concept and a delineated territorial reality. This historical Eretz Israel embodies his 'place in the sun', which is vital for his self-image and sovereign national existence, and which enables him to articulate his expectations and power. This sovereignty over the national territory is not subject to any preconditions: it is a natural right anchored in religious, national-historical and meta-historical values. The 'lacuna' in the world-view of the Diaspora Jew due to the lack of a country (a territory) of his own was suddenly filled through the emergence of Eretz Israel, first as a potent and dominant symbol, and eventually as a living reality. In the eyes of the rightist individual the mission, purpose and focus of Zionism is sovereignty over the historical Eretz Israel. All other aims of Zionism are subject and secondary to this one objective, and Zionism is an empty promise and flawed as long as the unconditional sovereignty over the entire historical territory remains unfulfilled. This world-view is not informed by pragmatic or realistic considerations, but is an article of faith, a dogma constituting the very core of the rightist individual's belief. He would be completely unable to visualize a situation involving the political desirability or necessity of territorial concessions, but if – theoretically – such a situation were to arise, an even partial territorial concession would be ruled out for the simple reason that this would in some way be an infringement of a 'self-evident' world, comprising a clearly-delineated territory and an immutable historically-based world-view. This explains why the rightist individual consistently opposed any and all partition proposals of Eretz Israel during the Mandate, and why eighteen years after the establishment of the State – following the Six-Day War – his conviction of the incontrovertible and eternal Jewish right of sovereignty over the western part of Eretz Israel gained added strength. In his view, anyone questioning this sovereignty controverts Jewish history and undermines one of the basic concepts of the Zionist faith. In the eyes of the rightist individual 'Eretz Israel' has become a sanctified concept, and the resurgence of the political Right after June 1967 can to a large extent be explained as resulting from a combination of apparent 'realistic' political prospects and an *a priori* and axiomatic territorial world-view.

The resurgence of various immanent social, ethnic and political forces within Israeli society prior to 1977 would not have been sufficient to carry the Right to centre stage and enable it to take over the reins of government, were it not for the profound change in the Israeli territorial situation following the Six-Day War. Israeli rule over Judea and Samaria was not interpreted by the Right as a mere political event, but as the realization of a historically predetermined event and the correction of a serious blemish in the geographical situation that unfortunately had existed since 1949. The territorial idea of the 'integrity of Eretz Israel', which at one time had been regarded as unrealistic, irredentist and an invitation to war, had been realized and become a geographical and political fact-of-life under a government headed by the *Ma'arach* – the Labour coalition.

History and Fundamentalism

The hypothetical rightist individual takes a fundamentalist view of everything connected with the early history of the Jewish people. To him the Bible is a historical record, the authenticity of whose narratives and values is beyond question. To question, let alone deny, the historicity of the Bible would be tantamount to an assault on the sacredness of the nation – specifically as regards the Jewish people's right to Eretz Israel as promised in the Bible. Subsequent expositions of Biblical law (the *Mishnah* and *Talmud*) are not regarded as normative codices, but principally as manifestations of the 'spirit of Judaism'. Similarly, the rightist individual will regard Jewish history as a singular history governed by its own, unique laws which operate outside the course of general world history. In fact, Jewish history is seen as running counter to world history, in the sense that the Jews are regarded, on the one hand, as a people subject to continuous persecution by the outside world, particularly that of Christianity and Islam, and on the other hand as a heroic political and territorially-based nation. This also explains the strong emphasis in the historical consciousness of the rightist individual on the First and Second Temple eras, during which the Jewish nation flourished politically as well as territorially. The conquest of the Promised Land by Joshua, the era of the kings, the Hasmonean period, the Jewish Revolt against the Romans and the Bar-Kochba War (as well as, later, the Holocaust and the underground war against the British) constitute prime chapters in the rightist individual's historical perspective *(Geschichtsbild)*, due to the coincidence of many of their central elements, such as Jewish settlement, territorial expansion, political sovereignty, and the fusion of religious belief and national liberation with present-day reality.

The Polarization of the Historical Response

The image of the Jewish people, as viewed in the historical perspective of the Right, swings therefore between two extremes. On the one hand the Jews are perceived as occupying a marginal position as a persecuted and isolated people, friendless outcasts who are unable to trust surrounding civilization and who, as a result, are constantly threatened with extinction, even in their own land. The opposite image perceives the Jews as standing at the centre of human history, as a people with a universal and messianic historical mission. This makes the Jews a potentially powerful nation or – to put it differently – a nation with a great potential for exercising power, which enables them to realize this mission by means of a determined effort to put their subjective aspirations into practice. The inner *Weltanschauung* of the Right therefore constantly fluctuates between two poles, an impending sense of doom, on the one hand, and an eschatological consciousness, interpreted in modern political and military terms, on the other.

The rightist individual views Communism, the Soviet Union and Socialism as an essentially like-minded bloc with an organic and endemic anti-Zionist signature. In his mind communist anti-Semitism is no different from the anti-Semitism of the European Right (including that of the Nazis), and presents as serious and dangerous a threat. Communist antagonism to the Jews, to Jewish nationalism and to the State of Israel is predetermined by its very nature. Both Communism and Socialism represent an internationalist world-view which completely contradicts the nationalist spirit. In his eyes, a Jew or Zionist embracing the socialist creed is therefore an internationalist who wants to break up the nation and distorts its inborn spirit, something which he considers an aberrant and pathological phenomenon. Islam, and the Arab and Muslim world in general, are considered fundamentally anti-Jewish and anti-Zionist civilizations and cultures, which are irreconcilable with

Jewish cultural or ideological (not to speak of political) interests and aspirations. The Arab in general is portrayed as primitive, inherently violent and warped, as well as – in particular where the Palestinian Arabs are concerned – lacking in a positive sense of national identity, in addition to which he is regarded as an almost demoniacal personality in his urge to commit violence against Jews. The Arab, with his confused identity, constitutes a political as well as existential threat, whose principal objective is to murder Jews or Israelis, merely because they exist.

The Arabs as a Real Enemy and as a Symbol

Until 1929 Arabs were a virtually unknown quantity in the world-view of the rightist personality. His encounters with Arabs as members of an existing public were too limited to enable them to occupy a dominant place in his world-view. The Arab riots of 1929 marked the onset of a profound change in this situation, and during the 1930s the image of the Arab began to take on more and more threatening, and even nightmarish, proportions.

The rightist personality's response to the Arab–Zionist conflict remained confined to a reaction to brutal and murderous Arab violence that far exceeded the bounds of legitimate political opposition. Paradoxically, however, the rightist personality well understood the intensity of Arab opposition, to the point where he believed it to be an inevitable phenomenon. This was exactly the reason for his conviction that only a national Jewish force and unflinching faith and self-assurance would succeed in overcoming the stubborn and uncompromising Arab resistance.

Gradually the 'Arab' has come to occupy an increasingly central position in the world-view of the rightist individual, which has replaced that of the gentile anti-Semite and his role in the European pogroms. Frequently the Arab replaces the cossack or the rampaging and murderous Ukrainians in Jewish historical narratives, and his character is reduced to that of a primitive whose basic instinct is to kill Jews.

The rightist personality therefore has a far more fundamental reaction to the conflict between Arabs and Jews than his counterpart of the Left. In particular the fact that his national pride is stronger and more easily aroused, makes his reaction to Arab resistance more outspoken and less restrained than is the case among the Left, and the Arab plays a more crucial role as a symbol of the eternal existential threat to the Jewish people and the Jewish state. The rightist personality will be prepared to cooperate with 'loyal' Arabs within a party-political framework, but objects to social or cultural intercourse, due to both a lack of interest and dislike, as well as a deep fear of assimilation.

In its relationship to its political environment the Right as a collective combines a pragmatic and ideological attitude (based on historical and meta-historical justifications) to the use of force. The use of force is justified as a means of realizing historical objectives, and as a reaction to the uncompromising hostility of the surroundings.

The Need for a Spiritual Father and for Heroes

For many years – in fact from its inception until the year 1984 – the Right was suffused by a consciousness of the need for a father-figure whose personality and image could personify its collective aspirations and expectations. This need was satisfied by the figures of Ze'ev Jabotinsky – both during his life and after his death in 1940 – and Menachem Begin, the latter in particular during the period 1949–84. Both were regarded as 'founding fathers', personalities of historic stature, whose ideological and moral authority was unquestioned. The leader had a dual function: internally to unite the ranks, and externally as the intermediary between the movement and 'reality' (attracting new members, canvassing votes, etc.). Every time certain groups decided to question the authority of the leadership (the last time this happened was in 1978, a crisis which resulted in the split of the *Herut* movement), or when suddenly a leader disappeared (the death of Jabotinsky in 1940; the resignation of Menachem Begin as Prime Minister in 1984 and his subsequent self-imposed seclusion) signalled a crisis for the Right. None of the other Zionist political parties ever accorded such an elevated status to the head of the movement, neither as the all-powerful leader of their institutions and party apparatus, nor as their spokesman to the outside world and the masses of their followers.

Zionist History as Viewed by the Right

The rightist personality had his own unique view of Zionist history. In his eyes only the Zionist Right embodies the positive aspects of Zionist history. The Right is the only current in the Zionist movement that has unceasingly and indefatigably exerted itself for the establishment of a Jewish state in the historical Eretz Israel, as well as for the rescue of diaspora Jewry; it is the only movement which has consistently reflected the Jewish national spirit and Jewish national interests without in any way allowing partisan or class interest to intrude. It is the movement which forcibly brought the British Mandate to an end, the movement which correctly assessed the nature of the Arab–Israeli conflict, and devised the right way to solve it from a Zionist point of view.

The above convictions, with all their dramatic and heroic aspects, all of which are deeply rooted in the *Weltanschauung* of the collective Right and have been passed on as a political tradition to successive rightist generations, are reinforced by the demonology of the Zionist Left. To the traditional, universal reasons for the Right's aversion to the Left must be added specific elements connected with the settling of accounts accruing from the Zionist past. The Left cooperated with the British Mandate, and it persecuted and boycotted the Right. During the 1930s it impeded the immigration of members of rightist movements, preventing them from receiving employment in Eretz Israel, in addition to which it attempted to emasculate the Right through organized and violent actions, particularly during the 'Season' (1944–45) and 'Saint Bartholomew's Day' (the *Altalena* incident at the end of 1948).

According to the Right's perspective the Left had developed a flourishing sub-society from which the majority of the *yishuv* population was excluded. It had established a large, essentially dictatorial and parasitic, economic and administrative infrastructure and a massive party apparatus. The Left had exploited the immigrants from Arab countries for its own economic ends, undermining their traditional values and sense of identity; it had degraded them and destroyed their pride, turning them into a disadvantaged and frustrated group. The Left possessed a rare political talent and, through all kinds of political machinations, had succeeded in creating a social and cultural elite. Traditionally the Left had shown far greater tolerance towards Arabs than towards Jews whose views happened to differ from their own.

In view of all this, the rightist individual regards the social and political hegemony of the Left as morally and ethically illegal because it is based on political manipulation and the corruption of a minority. It is illegal because it failed to oppose the division of western Eretz Israel. It is illegal and unethical because, so the Right claims, the Left acted wrongly during World War II and was passive and indifferent to the fate of the Jews of Europe; it even sabotaged efforts to rescue them.

This deeply-rooted demonology (for which, needless to say, the Left has a rather different explanation) has nourished the *Weltanschauung* of the rightist individual throughout the years, determining his attitudes towards fundamental Zionist and Israeli historical issues. Politicians will at times succeed in manipulating these feelings, but only because of the pre-existence of a deeply-rooted pattern of historical perceptions, values, symbols and responses. This pattern forms the common internalized and *a priori* world-view of the average rightist individual – a pattern which does not require a sophisticated intellectual system to be accepted in his self-evident 'closed' world.

Social Ethos and Values

The rightist individual, even if he is a wage-earner, advocates a bourgeois liberal regime. He does not favour communal and egalitarian ideals, but is – on the contrary – a fervent supporter of private initiative and social and economic diversification based on talent and private ownership. The *Weltanschauung* of the Right is opposed to glorifying manual labour on social or national grounds, but believes in the value of private initiative. Even so I believe that most of these bourgeois liberal values are not authentic, and that in the Zionist and Israeli context they represent a clear reaction to the prevailing hegemony of the Labour movement and the *Histadrut*. Hostility against capitalists and large-scale employers has been deflected into hostility towards the *Histadrut* in its role of an economic and industrial concern, employer and labour union rolled into one, which virtually controls the labour market. The fact that this labour union and its economic apparatus are managed by 'leftist' party politicians has turned the *Histadrut*, in the consciousness of the Right, into the counterpart of the prototypical capitalist in the populist literature of the European *petit-bourgeoisie*. As a consequence, there are scarcely any derogatory portrayals of Israeli capitalists or industrialists in any rightist publications. The kibbutz, in its capacity of an egalitarian closed society that is alienated from its surroundings, takes the place of the private employer in the socio-economic conflict situation, in juxtaposition to the city (and eventually the Israeli development town) as an example of a privileged and exploiting social and economic element.

Socially and politically the rightist individual manifests conservative tendencies. His social ethos is of a bourgeois and conservative nature. He will object to strikes as a means of conducting social struggles; he is against abortions, supports the death penalty and criticizes what he considers excessive democratic freedom – or even the principle of democracy as the indispensable normative basis of political rule. In the final analysis his attitude is informed by opposition to and rejection of all tendencies or indications of anything regarded as anti-nationalist or threatening to the organism of a healthy and united national society. This explains why he is less open to culture and less tolerant in his beliefs, and demonstrates considerable empathy with and tolerance of nationalist and anti-democratic ideas.

Trends and Norms

The above description does not intend to juxtapose the rightist collective personality to the collective personality of the Left. The history of the Zionist Left is similarly dotted with examples of intolerant tendencies, the establishment of closed groups aimed at excluding the 'enemy' opponent, and the perpetration of verbal and physical violence against rivals inside or outside the movement. Quite a few of the characteristics of the rightist personality can be found among the Left, but even so one has to differentiate between theoretical inclinations and a preparedness to put them into effect, between predispositions and the decision to translate one's intentions into legally binding norms. We should also distinguish between, on the one hand, inclinations and intentions, and on the other the ability to put these ideas into practice under changing political and social circumstances. Neither the Right nor the Left are monolithic entities, nor are they diametrically opposed to each other. Yet, when we combine the above-mentioned properties and inclinations with the preparedness to turn them – *willingly*, rather than because of a given political constellation – into binding norms, a clear distinction emerges between the average prototypical 'right-ist' personality and his 'leftist' counterpart. In any case we must not forget that we are dealing here with political history. When viewed from this perspective, the decisive question is not merely what is the Right's fundamental infrastructure as a collective personality with a well-defined set of attitudes, but what aims and values the Right has pursued and attempted to realize in practice within the prevailing historical reality, and what instruments it has employed to this end.

Seen from the inside, the history of a political movement is not composed of intentions and values alone, but also of unfulfilled expectations, and the perpetual tensions between expectations and achievements, as well as between objectives and instruments. Such a close-up view of political history will reveal a continuous ferment due to the existence of such tensions within a political movement; on the macro-level of political history it is a reproduction of the movement's attempts to implement at least some of its values within an ever-changing historical reality. Despite all this, we should not forget that our discussion is in many ways theoretical, since the Right up to this point has not yet been in a position to create an integrated political, social and cultural system according to its own conceptions, and that the prevailing political system has so far imposed limitations and restraints in this respect. The question of how the Zionist Right would have behaved had it been given the opportunity to act according to its particular *Weltanschauung*, and to transform it into an operative policy is obviously hypothetical, and the answer will of necessity mainly be a product of expectations, fears and images.

PART THREE

IDEOLOGY, PROGRAMME AND POLITICAL METHODS

Introductory Remarks

The third part contains five chapters, dealing with the ideology and programme of Revisionism in theory and praxis. The first chapter is concerned mainly with the Revisionist preoccupation between the years 1925 and 1939 with the establishment of a colonization regime as a precondition for a Jewish state. The second chapter discusses the most central and dramatic process in the annals of Revisionism, namely the transition from the assumption that the Zionist aims had to be achieved by political means, in cooperation with Great Britain, to the belief that they could only be realized through armed struggle against the 'alien rule' of the British – in other words, the transition from political Zionism to 'revolutionary' Zionism. This change of ideological praxis resulted from the failure of the first-mentioned method and the increasingly revolutionary mood during the 1930s and 1940s, the sources of which have been outlined before, as well as – and in particular – from the dramatic changes in world history, the history of the Jewish people and the history of Eretz Israel which occurred during these years. The third chapter deals with the attitude of the Right to the 'Arab problem', and its suggested solutions. The fourth chapter discusses the social ideology of Revisionism, in particular the evolution of its bourgeois orientation, and its prescriptions for the organization of society and the economy. The final chapter deals with a crucial period for the two underground organizations when, during the middle of the 1940s, they tried to shape their ideological image during the transition from the State in the making to the independent State of Israel.

CHAPTER SIX

The Right Way to a Jewish State: From 'Colonization Regime' to Sovereign State

The Right Time for a Jewish State

In Part Two Jabotinsky's brand of Revisionism was compared with that of the revolutionary-messianic stream. The first, as we will remember, regarded the 'State' as a necessary vehicle for the free and unimpeded expression of the nation's needs and aspirations. The second saw the 'State' as a culmination of the 'national spirit' and the fulfilment of the meta-historic destiny of the people of Israel. For this reason the messianic stream spoke of *Malchut*, a 'Kingdom', rather than a 'State'. The following chapter will describe the process which led Revisionism to consider a sovereign state as a focal and immediate Zionist objective, and how it intended to achieve this objective – the establishment of a Jewish state.

In the eyes of Revisionism a Jewish state was the 'final aim', rather than an immediate objective. It did not regard the establishment of a sovereign state as something that could or, for that matter, need be achieved in the foreseeable future, let alone through the expedient of a classical 'war of liberation'. In this respect the Revisionist approach was no less evolutionary than that of the other Zionist parties. The principal differences between their approaches were the Revisionist conviction that this 'ultimate goal' should be proclaimed *a priori*, even if its realization might have to wait some considerable time, and that existing Zionist resources were insufficient to create the required conditions for the development of the National Home as a 'state-in-the-making' – for which large-scale British assistance would be needed in the form of a 'colonization regime'. Only after the necessary conditions had been realized, first among which was a Jewish demographic majority, would it be possible to establish Jewish sovereignty. In this respect Revisionism tried to continue Herzl's idea of the 'Charter', in a form adapted to the new conditions prevailing after the First World War.

The Meaning of Post-World War I Political Zionism

Following the end of the Great War, Jabotinsky and the Zionist activists believed that the spirit of secret political alliances, as represented by statesmen such as Talleyrand or Bismarck, would have died. A new international political climate would prevail, and diplomacy would emerge from the secrecy of dimly-lit backrooms (*Hintertreppen*, or 'below-stairs diplomacy', Weizmann had mockingly called Herzl's diplomatic journeys and meetings). Neither was there any more reason to fear Ottoman reactions to a public Zionist declaration of intent. The new, post-war world diplomacy, embodied in President Wilson's '14 Points', was premised on joint public declarations and a mutuality of national interests. The correct Zionist policy would therefore be to persuade Great Britain that Zionism was a genuine moral and political force, and that it would be to Britain's benefit to enlist it as her ally in the Middle East. Jabotinsky believed that only such a policy would induce Britain to make an open declaration in support of Zionist demands, which in turn would once and for all end her problems with the Arab world. Such a declaration would create a political fact, and form a stabilizing factor, whereas all balancing efforts between Jews and Arabs, while extending merely half-hearted support to the Balfour Declaration out of fear of an Arab reaction, would be taken as a show of weakness and worsen Great Britain's situation in the Middle East. According to Jabotinsky, influential circles in Britain were looking for just such cooperation for either moral or imperialist reasons, so that it was Zionism's duty to prevent at all cost any weakening of Britain's commitment to the Balfour Declaration. Any such deviation would also weaken the British friends of Zionism and undermine their confidence and cooperation. This explains the contention that Britain's deviations from the Balfour Declaration were at least partly due to the weakness and hesitancy of official Zionist policy as conducted by Weizmann.

Zionism needed land (*Eretz Israel*), people (immigrants) and material means (i.e. capital). The acquisition of these resources in the correct proportions required political stability, internal security and a clear view of the Zionist future.[1] Zionism would be able to flourish only when the political road ahead was unobstructed, but not in the prevailing 'pettifogging' atmosphere, or with a policy of 'infiltrating' [immigrants], as in the days of *Hibbat Zion*, the 'Lovers of Zion' movement. Such policies, the Revisionists claimed during the 1920s and 1930s, would fail to meet the plight of Diaspora Jewry. Neither did they constitute a basis for political demands, or represent a historical process or ideology which, under the prevailing objective conditions of the Jews, would enable people to identify or start a national mass movement. As long as Zionism lacked the 'instruments of statehood', it would have neither people nor capital, or – for that matter – a country. British rule opened the door to the 'Great Leap Forward' in Zionist history, and woe to those who failed to grasp this opportunity and reap the copious fruits that it offered. The principal difference of opinion between Jabotinsky and Weizmann was the former's belief that it would be possible to achieve Great Britain's wholehearted cooperation with the maximalist Zionist plans, whereas Weizmann was far less optimistic and more reserved, believing that such a maximalist plan not only was completely unrealistic and would be rejected by the British, but also was a grave political error which, because it was provocative and even dangerous, could turn out to be a boomerang against the Zionist cause.

The nature of Revisionism as 'political Zionism' (as opposed to the so-called 'practical Zionism' of the Labour movement) covered three basic arguments:

1. Zionism must formally and unequivocally declare that its ultimate political goal was the establishment of a Jewish state in Eretz Israel (including Transjordan). Such a public declaration must be considered to have a crucial moral and political value in its own right – both internally (within Zionism and the Jewish world) and *vis à vis* the Arab world.
2. Zionism aspired to achieve the political and constitutional instruments that would enable it to undertake Jewish immigration and settlement activities within an overall organizational and executive framework. The Zionist movement must be responsible for managing the instruments, and must control the army, customs and Inland Revenue, and functions such as land distribution. In other words, it would have to concentrate in its hands all those functions that were lacking in the voluntary self-government of the Jewish community in Eretz Israel and the Zionist organizations. This state authority would be the Palestine government, as represented by the mandatory authorities, who would conduct an actively Zionist policy.

3. Zionism would achieve its aims only if it was actively engaged in political and diplomatic activities which emphasized both the absolute moral legitimacy of the Zionist movement and its fundamental mutuality of interests with the British Empire. The political activity, the struggle in Eretz Israel with various anti-Zionist precedents in all spheres of life, and the struggle for the establishment of the instruments of statehood would automatically force Great Britain to an in every respect positive and active interpretation of the Balfour Declaration and the Mandate charter of 1922. The Revisionists believed that they would be able to influence British policy, if only the Zionists knew how to stand up for their rights and use their influence in the right place and manner – either in London itself, or through factors which were able to influence London.

The pragmatic and functional Revisionist view of the 'State' intrinsically conflicted with the radical view – as expressed by the messianic trend – which regarded the 'State' as a value in its own right and as a fulfilment of redemptionist aspirations. The common belief in various circles was that Revisionism suggested the *immediate* establishment of the Jewish state, and even commanded the means to this end. Between this belief and the official Revisionist platform there existed a wide gap. It was not the pragmatic part of this programme that attracted the public, but principally the call for a Jewish state in Eretz Israel and the idea that its realization was within reach. Many joined the Revisionist movement because it propagated the national state as a value, a sentiment which reflected the spirit of the times, and because of their belief that only Revisionism could lead the way towards the foundation of the state, at a time when other Zionist parties either hesitated, or for various ideological reasons were even reluctant to envisage Jewish political sovereignty. This explains the profound hostility towards the very concept of this policy which, it was believed, would prevent, or at the very least inhibit, the establishment of a State. In any event the above represents a clear example of the inner conflict between policy and ideology – specifically the conflict between political thinking and *Weltanschauung* – within the Revisionist movement.

The Formulation and Evolution of the Political Platform

On 19 April 1925, one week before the founding meeting of the new party, which was held in Paris on 25 April, Jabotinsky published a programmatic article in *Razsvet*, in which he argued that the time had come for an open declaration to the effect that the purpose of the Zionist movement was the establishment of a Jewish state in Eretz Israel. He suggested that it should be expressly stated that by 'National Home' the Zionists meant a *state*. Such an open declaration, he wrote, is of both fundamental and tactical value. As regards the actual definition of the concept, however, he wrote that it could be flexible, as long as it was made clear that the minimum Zionist demand was a Jewish majority leading to self-government.[2] The majority of the participants at the meeting of the new party balked at such a maximalist definition, proposing instead a more moderate definition of Zionist aims, namely 'a country with an autonomous regime and a Jewish majority'. In the end the participants agreed on a definition taken from a speech by Sir Herbert Samuel on 2 November 1919, in which he stated that the political aim of Zionism was the establishment of 'an autonomous community backed by a permanent Jewish majority'. The platform of *Ha-Zohar* declared therefore that '*the aim of Zionism is the gradual transformation of Palestine (including Transjordan) into a Jewish commonwealth, that is into a self-governing commonwealth under the auspices of an established Jewish majority'*.[3]

Although the formal platform retained the moderate terminology, it was clear to everyone that the future intention was a sovereign Jewish state (even though envisaging the possibility that it would be included as a dominion within the British Commonwealth). Even so the sovereign state idea remained, but – as already mentioned – as the long-term goal rather than the immediate objective. In this respect Revisionism was once more in consonance with the majority opinion within Zionism, which felt that the *yishuv* was as yet not ready to establish and rule an independent state, with all that this entailed, and that some considerable time would have to pass before it would be able to establish and sustain an independent state.

At the 17th Zionist Congress, held in July 1931, the *Ha-Zohar* delegates under the leadership of Jabotinsky demanded a definition of the 'final aim' of Zionism, in retaliation to the White Paper of 1930. The minimalist declarations of Weizmann provoked a sharp Revisionist response, and the Revisionist motion submitted to the Congress read as follows:

Whereas the Balfour Declaration was offered to the Jewish people because of 'His Majesty's sympathetic view of Zionist aspirations', and whereas these aspirations are aimed at the reconstitution of the Jewish state, and whereas the preamble to the Mandate charter quotes the Balfour Declaration as recognizing the reasons for the reconstitution of the Jewish National Home in Eretz Israel, and whereas the Mandate government interprets the expression 'Jewish National Home' in a manner contradicting the aspirations of the Jewish people – the Congress herewith declares that the demand for the establishment of a National Home for the Jewish people in Eretz Israel is a publicly stated and legally binding promise, and that the promised reconstitution under the Mandate of 'the Jewish National Home in Eretz Israel' means the conversion of the entire mandatory territory in Eretz Israel on both sides of the Jordan into a Jewish state, in other words a commonwealth with a Jewish majority.[4]

This formula created an identity of meaning between the terms 'Jewish state' and 'Jewish commonwealth with a Jewish majority', but even here no date was mentioned on which mandatory Eretz Israel was to be turned into a Jewish state.

The opposition to this phrasing by the majority of the Zionist Congress reflected not merely a disagreement on principle on the part of some of the factions to the objective of a sovereign state, but, more important, the assumption that an open declaration of the 'final aim' would fail to serve the purpose, and only harm Zionist interests, both politically and strategically. Apart from generating strong counter pressures, such a declaration would be mainly rhetorical, and thus lack any practical meaning. For this reason most of the Congress delegates thought it was preferable to refrain from anything that would arouse strong reactions in the Arab world and in Great Britain, and to continue the step-by-step upbuilding and strengthening of the National Home. It would seem that the Revisionist strategy of defining a 'final aim' was only partly due to political considerations (in fact such a declaration was expected to have an energizing effect and result in enlisting its British allies behind the Zionist purpose). It was also intended to try to reconcile the earlier-mentioned national world-view, which saw the Jewish state as a more or less immediate fulfilment of the national aspirations, and the politics and settlement plank of the Revisionist programme, in which the state represented only the outcome of the second stage of the evolution of Zionism. To a certain extent the declaration of the state as a 'final aim' was therefore intended to close the gap between the national aspirations and the prevailing political thinking.

When in the summer of 1937 the subject of the partition of Palestine was raised by the Royal Commission (the Peel Commission), the Revisionists belonged to its most outspoken (although not its only) opponents.[5] The Revisionists had ideological reasons for their inability to countenance a division of Western Eretz Israel, but there were also political considerations. Jabotinsky correctly realized that imperialist circles in England were equally opposed to partition (although not for the same reasons), and he believed that the Partition Plan would be scuttled in London. It was therefore self-evident that he could not support a plan that was opposed by such influential forces in London, apart from which he had good reasons to fear that the eventual cancellation of the Partition Plan would have catastrophic results: no Jewish state would be established, but the foundations of the Mandate would be severely impaired, since support for the Partition Plan was tantamount to a Zionist declaration that it no longer believed in the mandatory government. This is why Revisionism withheld its support from a plan that might have proved to be a highly practical way of rescuing the Jewish masses in Europe.

At the same time their opposition in 1937 to the possibility of the immediate establishment of a Jewish state in only part of Eretz Israel proves once more that the Revisionist party did not consider political sovereignty as an immediate goal. Even though during the same period Revisionism began to emphasize the need for massive immigration (i.e. evacuation) of Jews from Eastern Europe, it apparently failed to consider a state, even a small one, as a sufficiently practical instrument for the rescue and absorption of Jews. Neither did it agree with the immediate establishment of a sovereign state on the condition that a decision on the ultimately desired territorial framework would be held in abeyance.

During his appearance before the Royal Commission in London in February 1937 Jabotinsky repeated the formula of a state as a long-term goal, and mass immigration to Eretz Israel as an immediate goal. His definition of a 'Jewish state' was a commonwealth or country with a reasonable degree of self-government and a Jewish majority.[6] The 'Ten-Year Plan' adopted by *Ha-Zach* in 1938, one year before the outbreak of World War II, declared that a Jewish state would be established *only* when all the preconditions of the plan had been implemented – in other words not before 1948! In his last book, *The Jewish War Front*, written just before the outbreak of

World War II and published in July 1940, Jabotinsky wrote that 'among the Jewish demands as one of the goals of the Allied war effort, is a Jewish state.' He failed to define, however, within how many years following the war's end this state would have to be proclaimed.[7] The book discussed the preparation of a 'Palestine Plan' for submission to the Peace Conference that would take place after the war (which, apparently, he believed would last a short time only). Evidently Jabotinsky hoped that the Second World War would bring about an – even more successful – repetition of the Zionist experience during the Great War, and that this time around the Zionists would receive an even firmer and more outspoken commitment for the establishment of a Jewish state.

Ha-Zohar continued this political line throughout the war. Only the emergence of the IZL and its demand in 1944 for the immediate establishment of a Jewish state caused a change in its policy, as a result of which *Ha-Zohar* too broached the subject of a Jewish state as an immediate goal, albeit a state to be founded by the British and with British assistance, and on no account by fighting Great Britain, and in opposition to its policies and intentions!

The Demand for the Immediate Establishment of a State

Outside the political field a world-view existed which was not prepared to await the fulfilment of the precondition of a demographic majority that would determine the national character of the state. Its political background, both in Eretz Israel and abroad, was shaped by the Arab revolt, the intervention since 1936 of the Arab states in the Palestinian question, and the Partition Plan of 1937, as well as the international tensions, the echoes of which reached the Middle East and affected the local situation.

The radicalization of the *Betar* youth in Poland, and of the Revisionists and affiliated circles in Eretz Israel, formed the internal Zionist background of an increasingly urgent demand for the immediate proclamation of a state. After 1937 the clash between the two concepts – the desire for the immediate implementation of national sovereignty, and the perception of a sovereign state as a second stage, to be realized following the achievement of a Jewish demographic majority – became unavoidable. At the centre of the revolutionary view demanding sovereignty stood a national self-awareness and a subjective national desire believing in the ability to achieve its immediate realization. From the moment the Partition Plan was raised, to be replaced in 1939 by the White Paper, the radicals concluded that the usefulness of the Mandate had come to an end.

The first time the suggestion to replace the gradualist Revisionist concept was formally and publicly raised was in July 1937. Its mover was the poet and politician Uriel Halperin (Yonatan Ratosh). In a series of articles and a brochure entitled *Aiming for Government: The Future Front of the Liberation Movement*,[8] published in *Ha-Zohar*'s official organ *Ha-Yarden* (and subsequently in the *Betar* and IZL publications in Poland), Halperin proposed that Revisionism demand that rule over the whole of Eretz Israel should be placed in the hands of a Zionist body recognized by the League of Nations and the United States, and that *Betar* should be considered an autonomous standing army, rather than a movement subordinate to the institutions of *Ha-Zohar*.

In so doing Halperin amplified the prevailing mood within the IZL in Eretz Israel and among its supporters in Poland, whose principal spokesman was Avraham Stern. The motion was formally introduced at the IZL convention held in Prague at the beginning of 1938 – where it was voted down. Thus even in 1938 Jabotinsky's Revisionist party did not consider that the right time had come to demand from Britain the immediate establishment of an independent Jewish state, and it continued talking about a state as a long-term and conditional aim. *Ha-Zohar* publications even printed articles unequivocally rejecting the immediate replacement of *Ha-Zohar*'s programme for a 'colonization regime' under the auspices of the mandatory government by a sovereign Jewish regime. Neither did the dramatic *Betar* conference in Warsaw at the end of 1938, which will be described in the following chapter, formulate a proposal for the immediate establishment of a sovereign Jewish state. Even the White Paper of May 1939 failed to change the declared policy (although it resulted in radicalization, and a deepening distrust of Great Britain). The struggle of Revisionism (and the IZL) was against the White Paper, and its regulations and future political intentions.

This unequivocal stand behind the step-by-step plan produced tension between the IZL and the political party and – even worse – a split within the IZL itself, when the dissenting faction headed by Avraham Stern (Ya'ir) turned the demand for the immediate establishment of a state – regardless of the means – into the central plank of its programme, and into the ideological guideline for the anti-British terror which Stern and Lehi conducted from the end of 1940 onwards.

The Structure of the Political Plan

On the basis of the above description, the political programme of Jabotinsky's Revisionism was as follows:

- Its *final aim* was a Jewish state on both sides of the river Jordan, which would make possible Jewish mass immigration (and the creation of a new Hebrew-Jewish culture);
- its *intermediate* aim, as an essential precondition for the establishment of a sovereign state, was a Jewish demographic majority on both sides of the river Jordan;
- its principal *method* was the implementation of a 'colonization regime' and the establishment of a Jewish Legion – both of which required the establishment of an actively pro-Zionist British regime in Eretz Israel.

At this point our discussion on the Revisionist programme must branch out into two different directions: *the first* discusses the nature of the colonization regime and its pattern of implementation – in other words the proposed Revisionist programme for the intermediate period, or – in Revisionist terminology – the 'period of state-building'. The *second* deals with the political methods aimed at achieving the cooperation of Great Britain in the establishment of a pro-Zionist colonization regime.

This chapter will give a concise description of the nature of the colonization regime, whereas in the next chapter we shall discuss the political methods through which this goal was to be achieved, as well as the causes of its inevitable failure.

The Nature of the Colonization Regime

During the period 1925–1940 both the Zionist Labour movement and the Revisionists were convinced of the necessity of a continuation of the British Mandate over Eretz Israel, and both assumed that the creation of a Jewish majority in Eretz Israel would be the result of a gradual process, rather than of a single dramatic or miraculous event. There is a common, but mistaken, belief that the Left was only interested in building a Jewish society and deferred the idea of a state to a more distant future, whereas the Revisionists wanted its immediate establishment. The fundamental difference between the policies of the two rival movements lay first and foremost in their judgement of the priorities and their evaluation of the desirable and the possible. This fundamental difference was spelled out by David Ben-Gurion on the fundamental and ideological, as well as on the practical level. He contrasted the Labour movement's ability to develop an autonomous Jewish society in Eretz Israel by voluntary means, to the barrenness and inaction of the Revisionists, which explained why they needed the intervention of the mandatory government. From this also followed, according to him, their different political attitudes and their different readings of the political situations and opportunities.[9]

Revisionism as a political party did not believe in short-cuts, including the precipitate establishment of a state. In this respect it did not differ from the Labour movement's attitude during the pre-World War II years. Both movements specifically spoke of a 'process'. It was the method by which this process would be realized, as well as its social contents, that was different. In the Labour movement's outlook the word 'society' was used in the qualitative sense, whereas in Revisionism it had the purely quantitative meaning of a 'demographic majority'. The Labour movement saw the 'National Home' in terms of a revolutionary Jewish society that would emerge gradually by the optimal exploitation of the opportunities provided under the Mandate, but if need be even without its active and positive assistance. Revisionism regarded the 'National Home' as a framework and instrument for the realization of a Jewish demographic majority in Eretz Israel, to be achieved gradually with the closest possible cooperation of the mandatory government, and on the understanding that this cooperation would be accompanied by facilitating political conditions, transformed into specific administrative, economic and land ownership patterns. However, none of the above was to be in any way conditional upon the creation in Eretz Israel of a new and different Jewish society with new socio-economic features, a process referred to by the Labour movement as the 'normalization of Jewish society'.

Basically, therefore, this was a discussion of methods, of ways and means, and of a future perspective, but – as Weizmann had already written in August 1913 – these methodological differences were of crucial importance for a movement, the realization of whose aims (the *Endziel*) was still so far away.[10] Neither could the discussion be restricted to the practical operational level only, since the operative assumptions sprang from, and as such were representative of, a specific world-view.

The entire Revisionist colonization plan hinged on the success of its political efforts, and on British preparedness to provide political guarantees. Hence the Revisionist contention that Zionist activities must be focused on the political arena. Jabotinsky expressed this repeatedly by calling for a 'return to the Charter',[11] meaning the creation of a broad-based mutual cooperative effort between Great Britain and Zionism.

According to the Revisionist model the 'State' and its authorities had to supply the necessary framework and instruments for creating a 'society' and an 'economy', although there was no intention that it be involved in all economic and cultural areas and social strata. In this respect Revisionism did not deviate from contemporary étatist concepts; it merely added the assumption that the realization of such a complex and difficult historical project as the establishment of a National Home could not possibly be accomplished by voluntary means. This explains why critics of Revisionism have accused the movement of regarding Zionism as a 'mechanistic process' of immigration and settlement, relying on extraneous forces (Great Britain), whereas the real Zionism was a self-induced, continuous process of creativity 'from within', powered by the people themselves. This approach, according to them, also revealed the shallowness of Revisionism, its basic lack of insight into the fundamental socio-cultural and spiritual aspects of the Zionist revolution. Against this, the Revisionists asserted that although the socialist brand of voluntarism might succeed in creating a few small model communities in Eretz Israel, it could never establish a demographic majority within a reasonable period of time.

The *Ha-Zohar* platform of 1925, which remained unchanged year after year, outlined a step-by-step action plan,[12] based on the demand for a maximalist Zionist interpretation of the Balfour Declaration on the part of Great Britain. It rejected the 1922 White Paper, by which Transjordan had been severed from the territory entrusted to Britain under the Mandate. The party insisted that the mandatory regime prepare a Jewish demographic infrastructure in all spheres of life. The following were the main points of the programme:

1. Mass immigration to Eretz Israel, as a means of solving the Jewish plight in the Diaspora and the creation of a Jewish majority in Eretz Israel.
2. The annulment of the White Paper of 1922, separating Transjordan from the area of the National Home.

3. The establishment of a British colonization regime in Eretz Israel, with as its practical corollaries: the nationalization of all available uncultivated lands in Eretz Israel (including Transjordan) for the purpose of Jewish settlement, with suitable compensation to be paid to their present owners; land grants to Jews (and Palestinian Arabs) on equal terms; a reform of the tax and excise system in Eretz Israel in order to facilitate immigrant absorption and to stimulate local industrial production.
4. The formation of a Jewish Legion as a permanent part of the British garrison in Eretz Israel.
5. The election of a British High Commissioner, and the allocation of senior appointments in the mandatory administration in consultation with the Zionist Organization.
6. The transfer of decisions about the rate of Jewish immigration to the Zionist Organization, and the removal of the mandatory limitations on Jewish immigration (*quotas*).
7. The establishment of representative institutions in Eretz Israel on the exclusive basis of the numerical ratio between Jews and Arabs, this ratio to be based on the Jewish people worldwide and the local, Palestinian-Arab population.

To the above demands, directed at the British government, Ha-Zohar added two further basic demands from the Zionist Organization, namely:

1. The raising of a national Jewish loan, guaranteed by a 'Land Fund'.
2. The election of the members of the Jewish Agency Executive by the Zionist Congress, and the expansion of the right of election to the Congress by the inclusion of the entire Jewish population of Eretz Israel, all contributors to Zionist funds, and the members of all Jewish societies engaged in the building up of Zionism. The latter condition made it clear that *Ha-Zohar* was opposed to Weizmann's proposals for the enlargement of the Jewish Agency.[13]

The quantitative issue played a pivotal role in the Revisionist programme, premised as it was on the assumption that a demographic majority would determine the character of the country. The main problem occupying the *Ha-Zohar* leadership, both in 1925 and during later years, was not necessarily that of full political sovereignty. Jabotinsky explained that in the twentieth century internal as well as external political independence are subject to constraints, but practical sovereignty was determined by a rough arithmetical equation: 'The crux of a national state is the relation between the size of its arithmetical majority and its arithmetical minority.' A Jewish demographic majority, according to Jabotinsky, will ensure that no minority will rule in Eretz Israel, but that there will be Jewish rule over a Jewish majority, which will shape the future of this country. The national character of the country will be determined by the national culture of the majority, and this national culture is not a function of disparate qualitative manifestations, but of quantitative manifestations in such areas as the national psyche, customs, language, art and literature, politics and law. Besides this, only a Jewish majority will be able to create a 'spiritual centre' in Eretz Israel. On this point, stated Jabotinsky, there are no differences of opinion between the 'minimalists' and the 'maximalists' in Zionism; everybody wants a Jewish majority, and the only differences concern the question of how this majority will be brought about.[14]

Ha-Zohar's main contention was that 'colonization' was needed to develop the economy under the aegis of the 'State'. Under the prevailing vague and unstable conditions, and given the economic realities of Eretz Israel – a country lacking in financial and natural resources – there was little possibility of private Jewish capital being directed to the country, and consequently no prospect of 'natural' economic growth. This meant that the required conditions had to be created artificially, mainly by means of the distribution of land to Jewish settlers and the protection of local industry.

This 'colonization regime' for Eretz Israel was rooted in one of the most fundamental of Zionist concepts, and as such constituted a maximalist interpretation of paragraph 6 of the Mandate Charter, which stated that the Palestine government would facilitate Jewish immigration into Palestine and the close settlement of Jews on the land by distributing uncultivated government-owned lands for settlement purposes. Jabotinsky and the Revisionists understood this declaration in only one way, namely that Britain had undertaken to extend to Zionism every possible assistance to enable the Jewish community in Eretz Israel to develop; without this assistance the realization process of Zionism would proceed too slowly – so slowly, in fact, as to provoke the danger of failure and discouragement. The Balfour Declaration was not the end of the road, but only the beginning. It was, therefore, Great Britain's duty 'to pull the Zionist chestnuts out of the fire' and to see to it that demographic and economic facts were created in Eretz Israel.

The colonization regime was a programme that, in the view of *Ha-Zohar*, embraced a broad Zionist perspective, compared to which any other scheme looked like an accommodation to footdragging and a narrow, defeatist Zionist perspective. 'The creation of a Jewish majority is the first phase, to be followed by the establishment of a Jewish state,' and in order to realize this first phase, the colonization regime was needed.

A colonization regime would turn the Zionist Organization – and the Jewish Agency – into secondary instruments; national capital and national funds would become far less important. Under the new conditions Eretz Israel would be opened up to a stream of private Jewish investment capital, because the economic arrangements in mandatory Palestine would be conducive to the attraction and absorption of private capital. This in turn would enhance the political power of the middle class.

Jewish settlement was therefore considered a political, rather than a socio-economic problem. *Ha-Zohar* contended that the Labour parties, which focused mainly on the character of the society and the ideological aspects of Jewish settlement in Eretz Israel, disregarded the accompanying negative aspects of non-government assisted settlement efforts. A colonization regime would not cause any political problems, nor constitute a provocation for the Arabs; on the contrary, it would slice through any political problems and solve them once and for all. The autonomous settlement process, on the other hand, which involved purchasing lands occupied by poor Arab tenants from rich Arab *effendis*, only caused land values to increase, thus creating inflation, aggravating the economic plight of the Palestinian Arabs, and bringing to a head the confrontation between Jews and Arabs on social and economic issues.

During the 1920s the Revisionist perspective envisaged an immigration of several tens of thousands of people a year. In his testimony before the Shaw Commission in 1929 the Revisionist representative mentioned a number of 40,000 Jewish immigrants to Eretz Israel. These could be absorbed, he claimed, only if Palestine were turned from a backward territory into an advanced agricultural and industrial country. Private Jewish capital and the limited national financial resources were insufficient to carry out urbanization, industrialization and large-scale intensive agriculture, and for this massive governmental intervention was required. Capitalism could not prosper unless favourable conditions were created, not if it had to build the infrastructure for settling a penniless multitude within a limited period of time, and certainly not when these settlers, rather than being spartan pioneers, belonged to a cultured society!

For this reason it was demanded that the mandatory government provide the following facilities for the Zionist settlement effort:

1. The necessary political conditions (among which a Jewish garrison and a favourably-inclined civil service).
2. Nationalization of the millions of dunams of fallow state lands, which were to be made available for Jewish settlement. This would obviate the need to spend precious financial resources for the purchase of private land, which not only required huge amounts of capital, but drove up land prices and created social tensions within the national communities. The availability of cheap land would make possible private agricultural settlement, without people being forced in practice to accept collective settlement arrangements.
3. Development of the infrastructure of Palestine, in order to stimulate light and heavy industries and commercial enterprises.
4. A more balanced government expenditure, replacing the present British practice of allocating most of the tax revenue to the development of the Arab sector.
5. An economic protectionist regime to prevent dumping of cheap imported merchandise, thus stimulating local economic growth.

Here it should be noted that the demand for intensive British involvement in the Jewish settlement effort in the form of a colonization regime was not to be construed as a wish for British intervention in the internal affairs of the *yishuv*. The Revisionist plan intended the colonization regime merely as a framework, and a means of laying the foundations for a systematic and modern mass settlement effort. Politically and culturally, however, the Jewish settlers were to remain completely independent and free from attempts at intervention or the imposition of any educational or cultural values.

Transjordan and the West Bank as Jewish Settlement Areas

In this context we should once more emphasize the important role assigned to Transjordan (i.e. 'the eastern part of Eretz Israel') within the Revisionist programme.

It should be understood that the Jewish claim for the inclusion of the eastern bank of the Jordan in the Mandate and — within the foreseeable future — the extension of Jewish sovereignty to this territory as well, was based on the Jewish people's national historical rights to the whole of Palestine. Such was the consensus of the entire Zionist establishment up till the White Paper of 1922, as in historical terms it remained when, in the course of political events, sovereignty over Transjordan passed out of the Jewish sphere, and Jewish historical aspirations could no longer be translated in terms of a realistic political claim. Moreover, there is no doubt that the historical and emotional attachment to the area east of the Jordan was very much weaker than that to the western part of Eretz Israel. The Revisionist establishment considered Eretz Israel on both sides of the Jordan as a single geo-historical entity, and therefore it related to Transjordan as an integral part of the Jewish homeland. Since the Revisionists' association with the territory in question, rather than being based on a direct physical link, was mainly rooted in the theoretical and symbolic sphere, they found it fairly easy to discuss Transjordan in the same emotional terms as they talked about the western part of the country. Even so there was a para-doxical difference between the Revisionist association with Trans-jordan, and that with the parts of western Eretz Israel which under the terms of the Partition Plan were to be included in a Palestinian-Arab state.

Apart from the political considerations, in other words the demand that the future Jewish state should also encompass this territory, Jabotinsky regarded the areas east of the Jordan as a necessary precondition for all future Jewish settlement. Partition of Eretz Israel was considered a historical disaster and a serious security risk, but relinquishing the areas east of the Jordan would seriously endanger the chances of saving European Jewry. It should be emphasized here that Jabotinsky never talked about Jewish settlement of the Arab-populated areas of Judea and Samaria, or about the need to 'reclaim the ancient patrimony'. On the contrary, he recognized that certain areas of western Palestine were already populated, and therefore did not come into consideration for Jewish settlement. This was precisely what made Transjordan so important in the Zionist view. The rescue of European Jewry, the establish-ment of a strong Jewish state – an ally of the West in the Middle East – and the realization of the Zionist aim were, in Jabotinsky's view, inextricably bound up with the availability of the virtually un-populated areas of Transjordan for Jewish mass settlement. He believed that this was where the majority of the expected massive wave of European immigrants would settle to establish a modern society according to Herzl's utopia.

In an article entitled 'A Precondition to the Ten-Year Plan' which appeared in April 1938 in the Yiddish newspaper *Unser Welt*, Jabotinsky wrote in very specific terms:

> The settlement of Transjordan is more important for the Jewish future than the settlement of western Eretz Israel, because Transjordan is three times as large as western Eretz Israel and is thinly populated; thus it would be impossible to evacuate the Jews from Europe and settle them in Eretz Israel without having the areas of Transjordan at our disposal. The Jewish problem can only be solved if Transjordan is included in the Jewish state.

One aspect of the Revisionist views on settlement (to be discussed in more detail in Chapter 9) that has so far received insufficient attention, is the fact that urbanization, industrialization and intensive agriculture were regarded as the basic infrastructural elements of the continued expansion of Jewish settlement in Eretz Israel. From this point of view little economic importance was attached to the areas across the Jordan, due to their lack of natural resources and their unsuitability for intensive agricultural settlement. Despite this, the Revisionists time and again emphasized the need to settle this vast area within the context of the realization of Zionism and to enable the absorption of future immigration. Thus a contradiction was created between a modern settlement effort according to the Revisionist model, and the declared need for the availability of additional large settlement areas. It would be difficult to explain this contradiction in any other way than that Transjordan was regarded as the main future land reserve of Eretz Israel, taking into account that most parts of Western Eretz Israel already had a fairly dense Arab urban and agricultural population. Leaving the various Revisionist political considerations aside, it was this argument that turned Transjordan into a vital and indispensable area in terms of the Revisionist programme.

As a result of the Partition Plan of 1937 attention, both in terms of political efforts and public emotions, shifted to the issue of the territorial integrity of western Eretz Israel. This resulted in Transjordan being pushed to the sidelines and becoming a long-term vision – a fervent desire rather than a topical political issue.

Immigration – Organized Mass Evacuation and Settlement

During the 1930s the historical perspective underwent a drastic change. The death of Marshal Pilsudski in the summer of 1935 strengthened the already active anti-Semitic forces in Polish society. Jabotinsky (and, incidentally, Ben-Gurion) believed that only the Colonels stood between popular anti-Semitism and state-supported anti-Semitism. Revisionist speakers emphasized their sense of an approaching catastrophe, and the urgent need to evacuate a million Polish Jews within a short period of time; not a flight, however, but an 'evacuation', meaning organized, large-scale emigration. This inevitably created tension between the movement's sense of doom, which in speeches was painted in the starkest possible colours, and the actual plans which it prepared to meet the approaching apocalypse.

Poland was depicted as a vast and dark ghetto, which could at any moment turn into a death-trap for Polish Jewry. The evacuation scheme, however, did not envisage the emigration of the whole of Polish Jewry, but only of that part – mainly those in the intermediate age bracket – which could contribute to the building up of the National Home. The evacuation of such a large number would ease internal pressures in Poland, whose anti-Semitism – as Jabotinsky naively believed – did not form a part of the indigenous culture, but was an inevitable result of economic competition. As soon as this pressure was released, as a result of the emigration of several hundreds of thousands of Jews, the Poles would no longer have any reason for anti-Semitism, and the equal political rights of the Jewish national minority would be ensured for years to come.[15]

The evacuation of the Polish Jews (which Jabotinsky imagined would be patterned after the evacuation of the Greeks from Anatolia following the end of the Greco-Turkish war of 1920) was not going to be a rout of refugees who, stripped of all their worldly possessions, would be cast naked on some deserted beach. Quite the contrary: the evacuation of Polish Jewry was only the first stage of the programme for the urbanization, industrialization and modernization of Eretz Israel on both sides of the Jordan. The second stage was Revisionism's Ten-Year Plan, a carefully organized, modern mass settlement scheme covering a period of a decade, which was officially adopted in 1938. The plan, containing a detailed and truly utopian description of the settlement effort, had been formulated in 1934 by Dr. S. Klinger, in a booklet entitled *The Ten-Year Plan for Palestine*, and it became the official plan of *Ha-Zach*. The plan spoke of widespread industrialization and afforestation of Eretz Israel by rational means, and with the aid of a massive injection of capital. Jabotinsky quoted it in numerous articles and speeches. The plan necessitated intensive cooperation with the Polish government (the same kind of cooperation that the Revisionists objected to when the Jewish Agency Executive negotiated with the Nazi regime about the transfer of Jewish property from Germany!) However, Jabotinsky wrote, here it was not a matter of *wywtaszczenia* (the – *de facto* – confiscation of property), as many Poles would have liked, but of a planned transfer of Jewish property from Poland. The plan also talked about securities in the form of large-scale international loans and guarantees. Only in 1940, when the war had already begun, did Jabotinsky for the first time talk of the speedy evacuation of a million Jews, and their resettlement in Eretz Israel within one year, a mass exodus that would require at least £50m. to carry out.

The 'Evacuation Plan' was the outcome of a profound sense of foreboding, but both the plan and its second phase – the Ten-Year Plan – indicated political over-optimism and naiveté. The inevitable connection made within the Revisionist world between these two – the feeling of an imminent catastrophe necessitating the evacuation of the Jews to Palestine, on the one hand, and the organization of a sophisticated, but utopian mass emigration scheme, on the other – gave Jabotinsky's call for evacuation a hollow ring. No wonder that his opponents regarded the whole scheme as a form of Shabbethaian messianism. The implementation of the evacuation plan presupposed not only the consent of the Jews concerned, and a willingness of the Polish authorities to rid themselves of as many Jews as possible, but also a recognition by the British government that the Jewish plight did not clash with its imperial and Near Eastern political interests. Apart from this, international Jewry and the Zionist movement had to be able to raise the tremendous resources necessary for such an operation (on the very eve of the outbreak of World War II). These assumptions were completely devoid of realism, and the plan stood not the slightest chance of being realized.[16] In Poland the Evacuation Plan merely resulted – as we will see in the next chapter – in the emergence of minor activist trends out of Jabotinsky's philosophy, rather than in directly assisting an orderly Jewish mass emigration based on common interests.

In the Revisionist self-image and its interpretation of Zionist historiography the 'Evacuation Plan' is regarded as a most profound and ambitious Revisionist manifestation of 'humanitarian Zionism', born out of a motivation which regarded the rescue of the Jews from a threatening holocaust as the primary historic purpose of the Zionist movement (in contrast to the workers' parties, who preferred the establishment of a Jewish model society on a selective basis).[17] It would indeed be correct to say that Revisionism, both for reasons of principle and because of its socio-demographic character and political outlook, was more aware of and sensitive to the plight of Jewry as a whole, for which reason it placed this aspect at the top of its priorities, not least in the area of political activity. Nevertheless even the Revisionists linked the plight of Diaspora Jewry with the rebuilding of the homeland, apart from which they were in any case unable to rescue those they wanted to help, either theoretically or in practice. This exposes not only the Revisionist tragedy, but the great tragedy of Zionism as a whole. The difference is that in the Revisionist consciousness this tragedy was far more acute, precisely because of the fact that Revisionism had shown a greater awareness of and sensitivity to the problem as early as the 1930s, and not only after the Holocaust had already taken place.

As a result the Revisionists could console themselves with the claim that they would have been able to save the Jews, if only they had led the Zionist movement, and that it had been their opponents who had ruined the Revisionist rescue programme out of sheer stupidity and malice. Both claims have become the subject of historical myths which, from the 1940s onwards, were cultivated by the younger Revisionist generation, and turned into additional sources of hatred of official Zionism, i.e. of Mapai and its coalition partners, adding fuel to the already bitter Revisionist accusations about the latter's behaviour during the Holocaust.

Two Alternative Political Options

The internal historical reasoning described above confronted the Revisionist Zionist outlook with a choice between two kinds of activities and lines of thought.

The first was the political and diplomatic option. The establishment of the colonization regime necessitated a struggle for domination of the Zionist movement, to enable Revisionism to rule the movement on its own terms, and to conduct a policy that would achieve the British assistance so essential for the implementation of the settlement plan. The alternative would be for Revisionism to act independently, although such a policy could never be conducted by opposing the Zionist Organization from within, but only through an independent Zionist movement. As we will shortly see, the disappointment at the failure of both policy alternatives generated a recourse to 'practical' rather than political initiatives (such as illegal immigration and the emergence of an armed underground), as well as a radical shift in political orientation and in the ways and means by which political objectives were to be achieved. From now on there would be no more diplomacy, but instead military pressure, by-passing constitutional methods and formal politics.

The second option was voluntary settlement activity, and organized involvement in economic and social activities and projects in Eretz Israel. Although the colonization regime had failed to materialize, the Jewish National Home continued to progress on the basis of voluntary settlement efforts within the leeway permitted by the mandatory authorities, and with the almost exclusive assistance of Jewish and Zionist human and economic resources. If the Revisionists had persisted in their exclusive preoccupation with their colonization regime, they would have completely excluded themselves from participation in the formation and growth process of Jewish society in Eretz Israel, effectively reducing themselves to the role of mere observers. But already the programme of 1925 dealt with many aspects of Jewish society as if the colonization regime would never reach the implementation stage. Realistic considerations forced Revisionism to become more deeply involved in all aspects of the National Home and its Jewish society. In the absence of a Zionist-minded mandatory regime, the question was, which areas of economic growth had to receive priority. Which social class would be given precedence? What was the most desirable system of labour relations? What was the preferred political system? Given the prevailing circumstances, how could the Jewish economy be developed in the optimal way?

These questions, and the Revisionist model of a Jewish society, will be discussed in Chapter 9.

CHAPTER SEVEN

From Political Zionism to Revolutionary Armed Zionism

A General Perspective

In the previous chapter it was explained how the immediate political aim of Revisionism was to create a suitable colonization framework and infrastructure, prior to the establishment of an independent Jewish state in historical Eretz Israel. We have also seen that only towards the end of World War II did it raise a formal, public demand for an immediate end to the Mandate and the simultaneous establishment of an independent Jewish state. The present chapter examines by what means the Revisionist movement intended to achieve Great Britain's eventual recognition of the Zionist aims and her purposeful and active cooperation in their realization. Once it became obvious that the political orientation was bound to fail, the resulting internal crisis within the movement led to the emergence of an armed underground and – as a logical corollary – recourse to armed underground struggle. This change in tactics – from an open political struggle to underground warfare – resulted from a radical change of objectives. Efforts to convert British officialdom in Eretz Israel into supporters of Zionism, preparatory to the establishment of a Jewish state, were superseded by the concept of a Hebrew state as the *immediate, urgent and unconditional aim* of Jewish nationalism.

The path led therefore from an open and legal political and diplomatic effort to an armed underground struggle; from cooperation with Britain as an essential precondition for the establishment of a Jewish state, to the view that Great Britain was a deadly enemy and the most persistent opponent of a Jewish state. England had become perfidious Albion; the mandatory government an alien rule. It is doubtful whether this dialectical development within the Zionist Right can be explained in terms of 'Right' and 'Left'.[1] There can be no doubt, however, that the emergence of an underground organization within the Right resulted from the centralization, concretization and actualization within it of such concepts as 'independent homeland' and 'political sovereignty'. It was a dialectical process, which led a party that had from its inception striven to conduct its policies in a legal manner, to arrive at the conclusion that its only chance of gaining political influence was through underground activity, and it is therefore not surprising that this radical turnabout manifested itself in equally radical changes in patterns of organization and behaviour. One of the reasons for this dialectical change was that Revisionism, as a movement in opposition, lacked the tools for influencing either Zionist or British policy making through formal channels. Since its attempts in this direction had suffered a crushing defeat, the activist forces in the movement saw no other way than to try and sidestep the conventional methods. Thus it could happen that, even though Jabotinsky regarded their practices merely as a way of bolstering conventional political methods by indirect means, these illegal activities were in practice from the middle of the 1930s onwards elevated to the central method of radical Revisionism. The activist nationalist *Weltanschauung*, which was already formally enshrined in its revolutionary ideology (the Revolutionary Idea), provided these new methods with an ideological, historiosophical and political foundation, thus turning them from a more or less pragmatic tactical device (the 'Pressure Theory') into the ideological ethos of armed revolt.

This does not mean, of course, that this development was entirely due to subjective ideological aspirations for political freedom which refused to take practical political circumstances into account. This conceptual development also resulted from a realistic analysis of the forces operating in the international political arena and their attitude towards Zionism. Even so, it looks as if it was the radical nationalist outlook which imbued the political analysis with its vitality and strength.

The Nature of the British Orientation

Revisionism in its totality did not regard the realization of the Zionist vision as an exclusive concern of Zionism and the Jewish people 'in confrontation with the entire world'. It profoundly desired to achieve Jewish sovereignty with the cooperation and assistance of one of the Big Powers. Until the end of the 1930s there appeared to be no other partner on the horizon except Great

Britain. It was the British, who until the middle of the 1930s had virtual hegemony in the Middle East, who had created the necessary conditions for the realization of Zionism, and who, so the Revisionists believed, would certainly continue to do so.

In 1930, against the background of the Arab riots in the previous year and the publication of the Shaw Commission report, the poet Uri Zvi Greenberg wrote a poem in which he compared Great Britain with Persia from the days of Xerxes, who had permitted the Jewish exiles to return to Judea:

> You King have cheated me. Our wounded nation called to you:
> Xerxes, King – the most powerful king in the world!
> With the prayer of freedom which was covered by the follies of the generations,
> Kindle, O King, a big torch of freedom [. . .][2]

In the poet's vision the Balfour Declaration had certain aspects in common with the historical declaration issued by Xerxes, as did the messianic expectations it aroused. The Jewish people hoped to be able to build the 'Third Temple' (the Third Jewish Commonwealth) as an independent entity that would be a confederate of Great Britain, linked in an alliance of true friendship between two sovereign states. Unfortunately Britain had revealed its true and treacherous face, disclosing the eternal hatred of the Christian world towards the Jewish nation. In 1929 Great Britain, the 'perfidious Albion' became 'Edom', a name used in ancient Jewish literature for the hostile Byzantine Christian Empire. According to the above view, British policy had revealed not only the opposing interests of Zionism and Imperial Britain, but also its profound hatred of the Israelite nation. From 1929 onwards, and even more after 1936, 'Edom' became the ally of murderous Arabia: the 'Crescent' and 'the Cross' banded together against the Children of Israel. This made the Zionist struggle against Britain mandatory, and Zionism would succeed in overcoming her, for Great Britain was a declining and disintegrating empire, whose end was in sight. Its subject peoples – in Egypt, in Eretz Israel and India – would rise up and expel her, whereas her European rival – Germany – would in the near future bomb her capital from the air.[3]

Prior to and despite the publication of this kind of eschatological poetry, the traditional Revisionist orientation had been entirely towards Great Britain, without any real substitute being considered or, for that matter, available. This uncritically reverent attitude towards Great Britain was first and foremost due to a profound admiration of the British Empire and the 'white man's burden' which it had taken upon itself. Revisionism viewed Britain as representating advanced European civilization in the backward East, and it considered Zionism as an integral part of Western civilization in the East.

Jabotinsky and his associates were convinced – or tried to convince themselves – that Great Britain's supremacy in the Middle East would endure for at least another generation. The British entrepreneurs, adventurers and colonists who had founded the Empire were regarded as heroic figures worth emulating. This positive and admiring attitude was also influenced by the high regard for the British parliamentary system, coupled with a profound belief that British policy was guided by the rules of 'fair play' and a sensitivity to considerations of morality and conscience. Jabotinsky's analysis of British political culture led to the conclusion that British policy was capable of being swayed by ceaseless diplomatic effort, due to the fact that Great Britain respected those who knew how to stand up for their rights.[4]

Despite all this, there were also frequent expressions of disappointment because of the blatantly anti-Semitic attitude of many British government officials, the prevailing pro-Arabic and Oriental romanticism in London, and the cold cynicism which dictated many of the government's considerations. But overall, belief in the positive aspects of British democratic political culture prevailed, as did the conviction that British public opinion was on the side of the Jews. This kind of warm and admiring sentiment is expressed in an interesting letter from David Raziel, the third commander of the IZL, to Arthur Giles, the Deputy Inspector-General of the Palestine Police, and head of its investigative branch in Jerusalem. In this letter, dated 29 December 1938, Raziel writes that he is a confirmed anglophile, an admirer of the British civilization and language, and that he is convinced that Zionism is the firm ally of Britain and the bastion of British interests in the Middle East. Being surrounded by Arabs on three sides, the letter states, a Jewish Palestine could not exist without British support.[5]

The attitude to the mandatory Administration in Eretz Israel was rather different. Revisionism made a sharp (and arbitrary) distinction between the government in London and the administration in Jerusalem, in the sense that it did not consider the latter a true reflection of the British Empire and its culture, but rather as an almost separate entity. Most irritating of all was the attitude of

British officialdom in Palestine itself, which was considered typical of the haughty attitude of the colonial administrator who regarded Jews as 'natives' rather than as partners with a common cultural background. Even worse was the belief that British officials in Palestine favoured the Arabs, due to their ingrained anti-semitism and feelings of superiority, and their inclination towards romanticism and the exotic.

During the 1930s, which culminated in the White Paper of May 1939, and during the succeeding years of anti-British terror (1940–44, and onwards till 1948) these feelings of hostility gradually turned into hatred. Only the veteran Revisionist leadership really knew the British; the majority of the movement only knew the British mandatory administration, the British army and the British C.I.D. in Palestine. As a result, it did not take long for Revisionist *anglophilia* in journalistic and literary writings as well as in political rhetoric, to turn into *anglophobia*. Great Britain was depicted as an exploiting, violent and brutal empire whose sole interests were oil and political influence. As already mentioned, this empire was expected to disintegrate, in the same way as powers that had oppressed other nations ever since the days of Babel and Rome had fallen apart and collapsed. In the eyes of the radicals there was absolutely no merit or advantage in British parliamentarianism and British political culture, and in this respect their views were identical to those of anti-Imperialist Marxist critics. From 1944 onwards Great Britain and her administration in Palestine were described in terms of a – to all intents and purposes – brutal nazi regime.[6]

However this may be, during the entire period from 1925 until 1944 Revisionism as a political movement had a distinctly British orientation. For this reason the fundamental question facing the Revisionists was not how to oust Great Britain from Eretz Israel, but rather how to create the optimal conditions for persuading her to *stay on* as a pro-Zionist nation prepared to act as the guardian of the Jewish state. As such a very clear distinction must be made between journalistic rhetoric and nationalist eschatological poetry, on the one hand, and political orientation and diplomacy, on the other. Our entire orientation is British, wrote Jabotinsky in December 1929, and there can be no point in talking about rebelling against Great Britain.[7] He was not the only one to think like this. Neither did the spokesmen for the radical nationalist wing, who regarded the mandatory regime as an 'alien rule', see any need during the 1930s for a revolt against Great Britain. This definition of the Mandate as a 'foreign occupation' was not based on political or legal considerations. The Mandate was a form of occupation, because it was not a Jewish regime, and thus lacked historical legitimization. In this capacity its legitimacy was restricted also in time. However, even in the short term, Joseph Katznelson, one of the radical Revisionist spokesmen, said during a heated session at the *Ha-Zohar* congress in Vienna in August 1932, that a refusal to cooperate with the mandatory government 'is out of the question for us, because our circumstances are different from those in India. We strive for cooperation.'[8]

In one of his most militant so-called 'fireside' articles, called 'The New Alef-Beit', Jabotinsky reacted to the crisis in Eretz Israel following the outbreak of the Italo-Abyssinian war and the resulting international tensions in the eastern Mediterranean basin. He wrote on the need for Jewish youth to wake up and prepare themselves for a possible war in the East – but it was clear from his article that their weapons should not be turned against Britain, but would have to be used because of the vacuum that would result when a weakened Great Britain would be forced to evacuate Palestine. At that point the fatal struggle for the national future of Eretz Israel between Jews and Arabs would be fought.

> None of us is a prophet, nor can he say whether the present condition of England is a brief sickness or the beginning of the end. One thing is clear, however, even though the future may still be shrouded in mystery – you should learn to shoot. If Great Britain remains a flourishing world power, and if she will ever learn to appreciate the role Eretz Israel plays in her world-wide interests – the only way to negotiate with her is as a nation capable of establishing peace and order in the areas that are destined for Jewish settlement. And if events should turn out otherwise, if the British chapter in our history should objectively come to an end, it will also be essential to defend ourselves in this corner of the East which is bound up with our fate.[9]

Time and again *Ha-Zohar* emphasized its pro-British orientation,[10] and as late as 1947 the party even objected to the suggestion that Great Britain should refer the issue of Eretz Israel back to the United Nations. 'Submitting the problem of Eretz Israel to the United Nations would be worse than a disaster; there is every reason to side exclusively with Britain'. In the opinion of the party leadership Britain had the required clout to impose a pro-Zionist solution in Palestine, and interference by other international parties would only harm the Zionist cause.

Political Methods: The Pressure Theory

How did the Revisionists hope to persuade Great Britain to co-operate with Zionism? In the first place by lobbying within the British political establishment and influencing public opinion. Lobbying, it was believed, would persuade Britain that Islam was not a real political power, but a myth lacking any political substance; that Arab nationalism lacked cohesion, and therefore could never be a real ally of the British Empire. From this it followed that Zionism, besides its historical and moral validity, was the only appropriate partner for the Empire. There is no doubt that Jabotinsky was still under the spell of his former surprising success during the First World War, and believed that history would repeat itself. The Zionists were going to offer to rule Eretz Israel in place of Great Britain, thereby releasing Britain – and the British tax-payer – from the burden of sending an army to Palestine. All that was necessary was to convince Britain that this was to her advantage, and this too was possible, if only Zionism refused to surrender to anti-Zionist precedents, as had been the case in the recent past. Britain would choose the party that was serious and firm in its intentions, rather than the one that showed signs of weakness and vacillation.

Jabotinsky's approach to the conduct of political activity did not necessarily involve a struggle for public opinion. According to his political views, it was not general public opinion that determined the political interests of a given state and shaped its policies, nor were they decided by a limited number of leading government personalities. The factor which determined, if not dictated, foreign policies (in the present case those of Great Britain and Poland) was a specific socio-political circle which, according to him, represented general public opinion (*natio politica*). In order to change a policy, one had to influence this group of opinion leaders and the socio-cultural milieu of which they formed the centre. Only after influencing this group would it be possible to gain the ear of the minister responsible for the particular policy. The fact that British foreign policy was of a pragmatic and empirical nature (on this point Jabotinsky fully shared Weizmann's assessment of British politics), rather than guided by ideology or doctrine, meant that it was in principle possible to sway the decisive group of British opinion leaders without forcing it to abandon any particular prior positions.[11]

Jabotinsky did not explain to which group he referred, neither do his writings reveal any definition of its internal composition or the various interests it represented. He contributed several psycho-cultural analyses about the inner workings of British politics and British foreign and colonial policy, but he hardly touched upon the nature of the differences within the ruling circle, or on the differences in orientation and interests that were openly expressed. For instance, his articles do not tell us anything about the role played by oil interests in the shaping of British policy in the Middle East. His outlook was certainly as naive as that which he imputed to his political opponents (particularly Weizmann), whom he accused of being no more than modern-style 'court Jews' sitting about ministerial antechambers. On the one hand he believed that the ruling circles would be influenced by the rightful historical and moral claims of Zionism and the hardships suffered by European Jewry (which, as we know, left them completely unmoved); on the other hand he wanted to convince them by cool and even cynical pragmatic imperialist argumentation – and all the time he was completely unaware of the contradiction between the two approaches. At any rate, despite the faith in Jabotinsky's success in Revisionist circles, it would seem as if he succeeded in convincing only a handful of the exponents of the imperialist current in London, and not necessarily the most important among them – and even then with only a modicum of success, and not for the reasons for which he would have liked to be supported.

The 1929 Riots and the 'Final Aim'

The Arab riots which broke out in August 1929 appeared to be the opening shot of the stormy 1930s. These riots, culminating in the carnage among the orthodox Jewish residents of Hebron, as well as the Shaw Commission report, the *Passfield White Paper* of early 1930 and its countervailing 'MacDonald Letter', and other by now well-known milestones in the political history of Eretz Israel influenced the development of Revisionism in several ways. In the first place they set into motion the intensive process which trans-formed the 'Arab problem' from a political problem into a national existential problem. This development will be discussed separately in the chapter dealing with the Arab problem. Earlier in this book we also saw that the riots precipitated the disintegration process of the *Haganah*, which ultimately, in 1937, led to the founding of the IZL under Revisionist hegemony. On the political-constitutional level Revisionism regarded the issue of the *White Paper* as proof of the utter failure of the current Zionist coalition under the leadership of Chaim Weizmann. In its view it was a direct and unavoidable result of the intrinsic weakness of Weizmann's policies, characterized by his surrender to the anti-Zionist administration in Eretz Israel, and an inadequate sense of the need to marshal the active support of the British government behind the Zionist case. The nationalist feelings and political disenchantment during the 1930s reached their peak at the 17th Zionist Congress held in Basel in July 1931, an event which signified the nadir of both Weizmann's leadership and Mapai's prospects of achieving hegemony over the Zionist movement. Weizmann's minimalistic declarations greatly angered the Revisionists, an anger that was shared by other factions. Weizmann's words to the effect that Zionism did not aspire towards a Jewish majority in Eretz Israel were understood as the antithesis to the Revisionist view that this was the time for Zionism to issue a public declaration of its aim to establish a Jewish majority. As mentioned earlier, the Revisionists introduced a resolution at the Congress demanding the definition and formal publication of the final aim of Zionism along these lines. Specifically they demanded from the Congress a declaration to the effect that: 'the establishment of the promised National Home in Palestine means turning all the mandatory territories on both sides of the Jordan into a Jewish State, i.e. a commonwealth with a Jewish majority'.

For a moment it looked as if Jabotinsky would be victorious, and that he would be chosen Chairman of the Zionist Congress and occupy the much-coveted seat of his arch-rival Weizmann. It has been claimed that a telegram from Eretz Israel from the leaders of the *Haganah*, warning that the election of Jabotinsky as head of the Zionist coalition might set off renewed Arab riots in Eretz Israel, resulted in the Revisionists being denied their victory at the very last moment – a victory that would have changed the history of Zionism. However, even if this telegram had the suggested dramatic impact, it is still doubtful whether Jabotinsky's election would have materialized. In any event, the Revisionist motion was rejected, Nahum Sokolow was elected President of the Zionist movement, while Chaim Arlosoroff was chosen as the head of the Political Department. In a dramatic gesture of protest Jabotinsky tore up his delegate's card. The dramatic gesture notwithstanding, *Ha-Zohar* retained its membership of the Congress and even took part in the crucial elections for the 18th Congress in the summer of 1933. In Revisionist eyes the rejection of their motion only confirmed the

prevailing minimalist attitude of Zionism and the absence of the
desire for an independent state among the opponents. The majority
of those who voted against the motion did so, however, for tactical
and political reasons. Besides considering such a step ineffective,
they believed that it might even cause harm by arousing the strong
oppositional forces to Zionism. A public proclamation of the 'Final
Aim', they believed, was not the kind of banner behind which the
Zionist movement would want to rally, but a serious obstacle that
would be extremely difficult to hurdle.

It should also be remembered that the Revisionist resolution at
the 1931 Congress did not talk in terms of the immediate establishment of a Jewish state, even though the majority of the rank and file
regarded it as an unconditional declaration of intent. The truth is
that Jabotinsky did not specify a target date, and that he remained
loyal to the evolutionary idea. Despite the potential threat posed
by the Arab riots, Jabotinsky did not consider them particularly
serious or dangerous. At the same time it would seem that he was
keenly aware of the tremendous constructive impact that the slogan
of a Jewish state would have on shaping his movement – apart from
which he hoped that public support for the final aim, i.e. a
Jewish state, would yield Revisionism a few diplomatic victories in
London and Eastern Europe. Regardless of whether Jabotinsky
was realistic or correct, or plain mistaken in his analysis of the
political impact the declaration was liable to have, these political
considerations nevertheless became one of the reasons for the
tremendous attraction which the slogan of a *Judenstaat* exercised on
the multitudes who swelled the ranks of the party in the summer
of 1931, and as such contributed significantly to the strength of
Revisionism among the Jewish public.

The Arab Revolt and the Partition Plan

The Arab riots of 1929 sowed the seeds of hostility against Britain,
apart from causing a certain discomfort about the political thinking
of Jabotinsky. Even so this sentiment affected as yet only a minority
within the Revisionist movement. The most remarkable turnabout
was the change in attitude towards the use of force as a vital and
integral part of Zionist activity in Eretz Israel. Arab violence had
touched a raw nerve, in terms of the nationalist self-consciousness
and pride of the Right, provoking the argument that Arab
nationalist demands could only be countered by equal Jewish
nationalist demands, and that they should be backed up by acts of

deterrence and retaliation. Echoes of the events in Eretz Israel reached Revisionist circles in Poland, giving rise to a radicalization process in that country. It became more and more difficult to accept Jabotinsky's until then uncontested belief in Great Britain; it was even harder to accept his legalistic political aproach. The fate of Zionism was now thought to be determined by an unavoidable frontal confrontation with the Arabs of Eretz Israel. Jabotinsky himself did not consider the Arab revolt dangerous, and even in 1936 was of the opinion that it need not cause concern. He was convinced that Britain was sufficiently strong to put down any Arab attempts to try and change her policy by force. His main worry was the impact of Arab violence on the romantics among the British political establishment.[12] However, in the course of 1937 he began to realize the political danger. The Arab revolt had resulted in the Peel Commission and the Partition Plan, and Jabotinsky now regarded the emergence of a Jewish counter force not merely as a needed response to the demands for the protection of Jewish self-respect, but in the first place as proof that the Jews were also capable of using violence as a means of underlining their political demands.

This was the decisive moment at which two worlds – the nationalist *Weltanschauung* and the political view – faced each other in direct confrontation. From the official Revisionist point of view, Jewish acts of counter-terror served two purposes. In the first place they would prove that the *yishuv* was a vigorous and strong society, and that its military potential was far greater and far more important than that of the Palestinian Arabs, so that it was worthwhile to support the Jews rather than try and pacify the Arabs at their expense. In the second place they would demonstrate that the *yishuv* was no longer prepared to tolerate the anti-Zionist mandatory policies – and that if Britain insisted on imposing them on the *yishuv*, she would have to do so by force of arms – a situation she would want to avoid at all cost.

In the activist nationalist consciousness, however, things appeared in a rather different light. Both the Arab revolt and the actions of the IZL were seen as manifestations of a national war – a war of revenge and fulfilment. A new, militant spirit had arisen. The imperative of Jewish nationalism, wrote Uri Zvi Greenberg in 1937, is to avenge: Eretz Israel will be redeemed, not by the plough or by diplomacy, but by fire and blood:

Double blood for blood
Double fire for fire!

. . .
For thus races repay their enemies
throughout the generations
and throughout the times.

And as regards the eschatological world he prophesied:

Our avenger will arise from among them . . . in the blue waters
of the Mediterranean he will wash his feet . . .

This mood was translated during the mid-1930s into three new
fundamental political assumptions. They were initially voiced
mainly at a literary historical level, rather than at the concrete
political level, and we should be careful not to confuse rhetoric and
nationalist symbolism with declared policy.[13] In a sense, therefore,
it was as yet more a literary rebellion in the sphere of symbols and
images rooted in the national past than a political programme.[14] The
three assumptions were:

1. Cooperation with Great Britain has been proved to be completely illusory. Britain is anti-Zionist to the core, and nothing
   can impel her to change her politics and impose a settlement
   favourable to the Zionists in Eretz Israel. From this it follows
   that Britain is not a friend, but a foe. Zionism must look for
   partners and allies to help it conduct its activist national struggle.
2. The war against Britain must be fought like any war of national
   liberation (against an alien occupying power), by means of
   armed open warfare, as well as underground warfare.
3. The Arabs of Eretz Israel are not strong enough to form a serious
   threat to the organized yishuv, so that it should be fairly easy to
   dissuade them from participating in the fighting in Eretz Israel.

From 1937 the call to an open anti-British rebellion and an all-out
war of liberation resounded more and more frequently in all kinds
of Revisionist literature, particularly in poetry of a heroic votive
kind and in all kinds of historical treatises reflecting the collective
Revisionist *Weltanschauung*. The eras of the Great Jewish Revolt
against the Romans and the Bar-Kochba War, as well as the wars of
liberation of other nations, particularly modern Greece, Italy,
Poland and Ireland, were continually being quoted as archetypical
events and models for inspiration and imitation.[15] But in the main it
was still the Arabs, and not the British, who were the enemies, and
against whom the arms were to be held in readiness. The radical
papers, the circles of *Brit ha-Biryonim* and the IZL disseminated

this militant heroic state of mind in Eretz Israel and Poland. One of the main supporters of this new political orientation and its attendant methods was the already mentioned Avraham Stern (*Ya'ir*), one of the leaders of the IZL (although never a member of *Betar* or *Ha-Zohar*), who – as the reader may remember – had been nurtured on the anti-Czarist militant tradition of the socialist terrorist parties in Poland, as well as the tradition of the Italian *risorgiomento*.

Jabotinsky himself absolutely refused to entertain any suggestions or even thoughts of a public change in orientation, let alone proposals to declare a rebellion against Great Britain. The most Jabotinsky was prepared to countenance was a campaign of civil disobedience and non cooperation with the mandatory government, but his suggestions (a refusal to pay taxes, and a halt to the transfer of Jewish capital) lacked any practical value.

The political result of the Arab Revolt was the Partition Plan of July 1937, eventually culminating in the White Paper of May 1939 and Great Britain's retreat from the Mandate as a basis for her rule in Palestine. Jabotinsky preferred to regard both developments, the Partition Plan and the White Paper, as unfortunate episodes in British policy, that would very soon pass and be forgotten once it had become clear that they were unworkable. He was convinced that London would shelve the Partition Plan, as it contradicted British imperial interests in the Middle East as he understood them. His opposition to the Partition Plan was based on several arguments, which can be divided into political, strategic defensive, and Zionist arguments.[16]

a. *The political argument.* As mentioned earlier, Jabotinsky was convinced that the British Government would refuse to pass the Partition Plan, since the number of its opponents far exceeded that of those who supported it. (We should mention here that many of these opponents were induced by anti-Zionist motives, rather than the other way round!) This being the case, he considered that Zionism should not choose the side of the loser, nor endanger the Mandate with any alternative plan. Zionist approval of the Partition Plan would be harmful, since it meant an *a priori* renunciation of the principle of the Mandate, which ultimately would cause Zionism to lose out on both counts: Partition and the Mandate.

b. *The strategic defensive argument.* Jabotinsky believed that a Jewish state within the boundaries of the Partition Plan would be a weak state, lacking the ability to defend itself. It would not be like Piedmont, the small state that had become the core of a unified and independent Italy, but would be subject to ceaseless Arab irredentism, that would finally bring about its destruction. Partition, he prophesied (wrongly, as it would turn out), would be the end of the line for the Jews, but not for the Arabs.[17]

c. *The Zionist argument.* In the previous chapter we saw that from 1935 onwards Jabotinsky accorded prime importance to Jewish immigration from Eastern Europe. As already mentioned, it was his view that without the areas of Western Eretz Israel, and without Transjordan a yearly immigration of at least 150,000 Jews from Eastern Europe would be impossible. Obviously the fact that the Polish and Rumanian governments had, for this same reason, expressed strong opposition to the Partition Plan only reinforced Revisionist opposition to the British plan. Otherwise the Revisionists could never have agreed to a scheme that held grave political risks, and which was censured not only in Great Britain, but in Warsaw and Bucharest as well.[18]

When Jabotinsky spoke against the Partition Plan before the members of the Royal Commission of Enquiry in February 1937 in London, and before British Members of Parliament in July of the same year, he did not base his objections on ideological or historiographic grounds, but used mainly humanitarian arguments. He described Zionism first of all as a salvage instrument for millions of Jews, with the physical plight of the Jewish masses as its motive force. His arguments were therefore of a humanitarian and pragmatic nature, and to reinforce their impact he supplemented his description of Jewish hardship with computations of the absorption possibilities and the optimal population density of Eretz Israel.[19]

The diplomatic activity against Partition turned the Revisionists into partners of a broad (not necessarily pro-Zionist) coalition of Partition opponents. Although it is not due to Revisionist opposition that the plan failed, there is no doubt that the Revisionists formed the spearhead of the struggle for public opinion. The political defeat of the Partition Plan proved to be a Pyrrhic victory for Zionism, however, since it was not replaced by an improved Mandate, but by the White Paper of May 1939, which spelled the complete bankruptcy of Zionist policy, and in turn induced rebellious sentiments and feelings of intense frustration.

Official Revisionist policy had in any case been against Partition for rational reasons. Its nationalist world view, as expounded in informal forums (for instance newspaper articles, literary works and mass meetings) decried the Partition Plan as a monstrous decree: 'Cursed be he who pronounces the word,' was the Revisionist slogan. The Partition Plan was considered extremely dangerous, since it was the first initiative which recognized the concept of Arab sovereignty over part of Eretz Israel (and as from 1939, by extension, over the whole of Eretz Israel). Needless to say that this recognition was considered tantamount to the annihilation of all Zionist aspirations. It seemed as if the Partition Plan aimed at imprisoning the Jews of Eretz Israel within another ghetto as 'protected Jews', instead of letting them develop into a modern nation. Above all, the Partition Plan was considered an affront to the territorial and historical – and meta-historical – dimensions of Jewish nationalism. Hence the emotional and extreme reactions that arose from within the Zionist Right (and even certain parts of the Left). In these reactions the Partition Plan was represented as an act of submission and treason, from whose implementation there would be no return. Jabotinsky and the political wing of Revisionism, on the one hand, and the radical Right, on the other, were therefore partners in their fierce opposition to Partition, but for opposing reasons.

Both the reactions to Arab terrorist acts aimed at underlining Arab nationalist demands, and the opposition to the Partition Plan, were therefore the two main factors which stimulated attempts at translating Jewish nationalist militancy and radicalism into a political programme. As already mentioned, it began in July 1937 with a rallying cry from the movement's rank and file for an *immediate* change in the Revisionist platform, that would elevate the demand for an independent Jewish state to the leading principle of Revisionist policy. The official leadership refused to adopt this policy, holding on to its position that a Jewish state could only be established *after* all the provisions of the Mandate had been fulfilled. The political (and military) struggle was not intended as a struggle against British rule over Eretz Israel, but against Partition and the White Paper, in order to achieve a continuation of the Mandate under unequivocally pro-Zionist conditions. The two critical years for Zionist policy – from 1937 till 1939 – particularly when seen against the background of the acute plight of Polish Jewry – made a clash between the prevailing internal *Weltanschauung* and the formal Revisionist programme inevitable. Zionism as a whole was taking a militant turn. The execution of Shlomo Ben-Yosef in Acre prison on 28 June 1938, for having thrown an incendiary device at an Arab taxi in retaliation for an attack on a Jewish car on the

Rosh-Pina to Zefat road in Upper Galilee, made him the first Jewish martyr of the political struggle for Eretz Israel. The publication of the White Paper drew a response from the IZL in the form of a number of sabotage acts against British civilian installations. The mandatory authorities reacted by proclaiming emergency regulations and the arrest of some 300 Revisionists and members of *Betar*. Jabotinsky had hoped that the agitation in Eretz Israel would persuade the government in London to abandon the White Paper, but simultaneously he took a far-reaching political decision by entering into negotiations with Eliyahu Golomb, the civil commander of the *Haganah*, about a merger within a federative framework.

These talks, which were held in London at the end of 1938 and in July 1939, achieved positive results, but it was David Ben-Gurion, the chairman of the Jewish Agency Executive, who forced them to be taken off the agenda.[20] Ben-Gurion was implacably opposed to any agreement that would grant Revisionism any independent political status inside the Zionist Organization and thereby impair what he considered to be of paramount interest, namely the absolute authority of the leadership of the *yishuv* to decide its own policies and guide its own defence interests.

Illegal Immigration and the Petition Campaign

Like the acts of counter-terror against the Arabs and the violence accompanying the opposition to the White Paper of May 1939, the Revisionist initiative to organize illegal immigration was to become a point of no return. The meagre allocation of immigration certificates to the Revisionists in the face of the growing pressure from potential immigrants produced a spontaneous backlash in the ranks of the movement. The initiators of the illegal immigration scheme were ordinary party members, who eventually received the backing of the official party representatives.[21] Only at the beginning of 1939 did Jabotinsky intervene personally between *Ha-Zohar, Betar* and the IZL to divide the responsibilities for taking illegal immigrants out of Europe and smuggling them ashore in Eretz Israel. These activities formed the focus of both organized and private Revisionist activity during 1938 and 1939, in the course of which years some 15,000 illegal immigrants were taken ashore in Eretz Israel from some 25 different illegal immigrant ships. Jabotinsky extended his moral and ideological support to the scheme, although he did not see it as a real solution, but rather as yet another way of pressing the

British government – a 'live petition', as he put it. Simultaneously, illegal immigration had to prove to the Polish and Rumanian governments that the Revisionists were prepared to go to any lengths – even if it meant breaking the British law – to get the Jews out of these countries. For the IZL and *Betar* the organization of illegal immigration became the principal method of putting their revolutionary ideas into practice, with the intention of changing the face of history, not by political and diplomatic means, but through revolutionary activity.

At the same time it is crystal clear that Jabotinsky did not regard illegal immigration as the ultimate solution. To him the real solution lay in the 'Petition Campaign', and later in the *'Zion Sejm* Scheme' – the 'Parliament of Distress'. These were attempts to turn the plight of Eastern European Jewry into a means of exerting pressure on London from the 'East' (i.e. Eastern Europe). In the course of the 'Petition Campaign' of 1934 some 600,000 signatures were collected, of which 260,000 in Poland, calling upon the British government to recognize the moral and humanitarian right (according to the provisions undertaken by Great Britain under the terms the Mandate) of the Jews to immigrate into Palestine. In the petition the signatories appealed in emotion-laden words to His Majesty to recognize the fact that there was no future for the Jews in Eastern Europe, and that their only hope of survival lay in immigration to Eretz Israel. The petition was an expression of individual suffering, as well as of national aspirations. These two initiatives proved, if anything, that Revisionism had entered a dead-end street: on the one hand it reasoned that time was pressing, and that the sword was poised above the head of Polish Jewry; at the same time it engaged upon a political and public-relations process that would have taken many years of diligent marshalling of forces and application of pressure in the right places.

The British government did not turn a hair at either the 'Petition Campaign', or the 'Parliament in Distress'. Ben-Gurion and Achimeir – representing the extremes of the political spectrum – were united in their view that Jewish mass-demonstrations in Cracow and Lodz would go unnoticed in London, and were therefore useless.[22] Even the so-called 'Alliance Policy' failed to bear fruit. Meetings with various European diplomats and statesmen to try and apply diplomatic pressure on Britain remained similarly without effect: neither Poland nor Rumania, or even the League of Nations, were able to budge imperial Britain and tempt her to get stuck in the Palestinian quagmire, just to help Poland or Rumania rid themselves of their surplus Jewish populations. Even assuming that the Revisionist argumentation was received favourably in Warsaw and Bucharest, no political coin could be struck out of it.

The Search for Allies: The Polish Orientation

What was the meaning of this 'Alliance Policy'? The crucial turning point in the Revisionist political orientation was reached in 1935 with the death of Marshal Józef Pilsudski, the leader and national hero of independent Poland. I have already described the great importance of Poland for Revisionism, both as an influential model of national culture, and as the state in which Revisionism evolved as a mass culture. During the mid-1930s it first occurred to Jabotinsky that Poland might also serve as a political ally of Zionism. Until 1926 Jabotinsky had held a fairly low opinion of Poland and Polish culture; he regarded it as an anti-Semitic country whose active hatred towards Jews – both as Jews and as members of a sizeable national minority – formed an immanent part of its culture. Pilsudski's *coup d'état* in 1926 caused Jabotinsky to change his opinion, as he explains in the following quote:

> I know all the dark sides of this country, but I also know the other side of the Polish nature; when I was 14 I knew the works of Mickiewicz by heart. And I say to you that there occurred among them in 1926 an extraordinary and unparalleled phenomenon, and that is Pilsudski. At that moment, when the Polish people were on the verge of destruction, on the brink of the same abyss into which Germany fell a few years later, at that dark hour, Pilsudski arrived with a group of his followers, quietly and without rhetoric; a man who came not out of love for the Jews, and not even for the Poles, but who loved, served and fought for one thing only: fairness. And he saved his country, set it in order and planted the seed of fairness within it. Were I a Polish Jew, I would say: My friend, Marshal Pilsudski's group, his faithful followers, are your last hope of finding honest allies. I wander all over the world, from country to country, looking for allies for our cause. And I can tell you that I do not see allies more suitable and more realistic than this group of Pilsudski's followers [. . .] and there is no doubt that Pilsudski's followers, those people who now stand at the head of the Polish republic, want to set up a plan for a just solution to the question of the Jews of Poland against the rantings of anti-Semitic demagogues.[23]

From the Polish ambassador in Britain, Rachinsky, Jabotinsky had learned in 1935 about the tremendous importance the Polish regime attached to the problem of the Jewish population surplus in Poland, and its desire to promote its emigration to other countries. At the same time he was aware of Poland's dependence upon Great Britain, not only in the international political sphere, but on the economic level (Britain was Poland's largest foreign trade partner), and Poland's consequent inability to pressure Britain on the Jewish question. Privately he was sceptical of Poland's deterrent strength, more so than he appeared to be when appearing on public platforms. In a letter dated 28 February 1939 to his friend Joseph B. Schechtman, written following the visit of the Polish Foreign Minister Jozef Beck to London, Jabotinsky wrote that Britain did indeed regard Poland as a large and important power, and that Beck was likely to exert pressure on Britain on behalf of the Zionist cause.[24] However, he cautioned, it was also clear that Poland was dependent upon Britain, and not the other way around. Therefore, Polish pressure on London, if exerted, was likely to be nonproductive if it contradicted British interests. This, in fact, proved to be the case.

Thus Jabotinsky was led up a blind alley, and towards a crushing and tragic diplomatic illusion. He received support in the corridors of power in Warsaw by presenting himself as an ardent supporter of Jewish emigration. For this purpose he was prepared to turn a blind eye to both popular and official anti-Semitism. The Polish orientation dictated many of his positions during the second half of the 1930s. One of his arguments against the Partition Plan of the summer of 1937 was his assumption that a Jewish state within the proposed partition boundaries would be unable to absorb the surplus Jewish populations of Poland and the neighbouring states, and that acceptance of Partition would thus effectively rob Zionism of the support which the governments of Poland, Rumania and other states were prepared to extend to it.

However, the Revisionists were unable to make up their minds. The implementation of the 'Evacuation Plan' required a formal agreement with the Polish government (not to mention permission of Great Britain), and such an arrangement would have to be made in public. On the other hand they were afraid of too much publicity, in case the discussions provoked British resistance and induced Britain to exert counter-pressure on Poland. For this reason the Revisionists opted for secret negotiations with various government circles with a view to obtaining assistance such as the supply of surplus arms and Polish help in organizing the illegal emigration to Palestine. Jabotinsky's political vision vainly tried to combine both internal-Polish and Jewish interests. The Revisionist activities hardly helped to ease the pressure on the Polish government from extremist anti-Semitic circles among the Polish Right, nor did they offer the Zionist movement a real political alternative to its dependence on Great Britain.[25] As it happened, the only areas in which the Polish orientation had some real value were those in which the support was partial and covert, rather than whole-hearted and open, namely military training, arms supplies and illegal immigration. Other Revisionist activists in Poland were busy exploiting or bribing their personal connections in official circles and their sympathizers among the Polish Legion veterans, often acting in opposing directions, without one group knowing anything about the activities of the other group. (This explains, for instance, how Jabotinsky could be unaware of the activities of Avraham Stern and his circle in Warsaw, or the military training courses which the Polish army conducted in the course of 1939 for groups of IZL members – some of whom came from Eretz Israel – in the Carpathian mountains.) The IZL even hoped that the Poles would assist in the preparations of a plan for a seaborne invasion of Palestine, to which we shall revert later on in this chapter.

Nahum Sokolow, whose critical attitude to Polish Revisionism has already been mentioned, strongly disapproved also of its political orientation towards Poland, which he considered severely mistaken as well as illusionary:

> A policy of friendship on the part of Poland and towards Poland is essential to us. However, the blatant admiration of Polish militaristic trends and tendencies, the attempt to exploit the Polish tradition of the Legions during the previous generation (or even the tradition of the 1840s, with Mickiewicz and all that), as well as the attempt to ingratiate ourselves in this manner, is no more than a cheap stunt, which is both morally improper and practically dangerous, an act taken from the archives of assimilation, which will lead this movement into total bankruptcy.[26]

However, the fact that the Polish Orientation represented the last chance for Revisionism, explains why the belief in Polish strength did not expire until the very last moment. Thus Jabotinsky wrote as late as 1938:

Until two months ago the world believed that there was one huge fist of steel which could destroy everything, and that no one could stop it. And then one country stood up, and not the biggest of countries either, one country, and this [act] will certainly be engraved to its credit and glory in the annals of history, and said: We shall fight back, and in so doing it finally pierced a hole in that fist.[27]

Only a month before the war, on 29 July 1939, *Omer La' am*, the IZL journal in Eretz Israel, confidently wrote that Hitler would have to take 'Poland's military strength' and its willingness to fight into account, and that Germany would therefore be prepared to make important concessions.

The final, tragic, chord of the illusionary Polish orientation sounded on 2 September 1939, only hours after the Nazis had invaded Poland. That same fatal night Jabotinsky rushed a telegram from France to the Polish President, Ignacy Moscicki. The telegram is sad testimony to the end of an illusion, and the beginning of a long dark night. In it Jabotinsky expressed his faith that the Polish army would succeed in repulsing the invader. A few days earlier he had not even believed that war was likely to break out; now that it had, he once more wrongly assessed the balance of forces:

In the name of the movement which years ago was the first to realize Poland's mission as one of the world's greatest powers and conceived the Providential connection between the renaissance of the Jewish Palestine state and the triumph of Poland, I humbly call God's blessing upon your country [. . .][28]

With this pathetic phrase about the 'providential connection' between the 'triumph of Poland' and the 'renaissance of Jewish Palestine', in which Jabotinsky confirmed once more his belief in Poland's status as a great European power, and the Revisionist movement's high expectations from the Polish state, the 'Polish Orientation' expired – and with it the tragic illusion upon which it had been based.

The Internal Confrontation over Ideology and Political Methods[29]

All these deep-seated and fundamental divisions came out in the open at the Third World Conference of *Betar*, which was held in September 1938 in Warsaw. Even earlier, on the eve of the World Conference of *Ha-Zohar* during January–February 1938 in Prague, voices had been raised advocating a basic change in policy. Menachem Begin, for instance, had on 11 February 1938 written in *Unser Welt* that Eretz Israel could not be acquired with money or diplomacy, but only through 'a demonstration of despair'. He failed, however, to offer any practical proposals, except for suggesting that *Betar* members in Poland should undergo military training. In March 1938 a group calling itself the 'Revisionist Activists', among whose members were Begin, Nathan Friedman-Yellin, Shmuel Merlin and others, issued a public declaration expounding the need for a radical change in the strategic, organizational and educational foundations of the *Betar* movement:

> We are not despairing, for we firmly believe in the sacredness and truth of the teachings of Jabotinsky, according to which the nation will arise once again, free and large, in its independent homeland. But we have to create the legions that will bring this about, and that will fight for the realization of this doctrine – and this is what our suggestions are about. As from today our thinking and our propaganda efforts should not be directed at the desperate Jews in the present Diaspora, who are afraid of any radical ideas, and whose only thought is to end their days in peace and quiet. We are looking towards a young, Jewish generation which, standing on the threshold of its adult life, is caught up in a hopeless situation without knowing what tomorrow will bring.[30]

This manifesto demanded therefore that Jabotinsky's one-sided pro-British orientation be changed into a national 'non-aligned' policy based on the principle of internationalization of the Jewish problem and the question of Eretz Israel. It stated that 'from now on a new policy of active resistance must be implemented [in Eretz Israel], employing the same methods that have resulted in the liberation of all the other oppressed peoples.'

The last World Conference of *Betar* was held in Poland from 11 to 16 September 1938, with the participation of 130 delegates from 16 countries. Hundreds of *Betar* members filled the hall of the Novoski theatre in Warsaw to listen to the debates. The atmosphere was tense, and marked by deep-seated differences of opinion and secret behind the scene meetings. The conference in a sense revealed only the tip of the iceberg, as far as the prevailing differences of opinion were concerned. Dr. Scheib described the atmosphere as a struggle between the nineteenth-century mentality (of Jabotinsky) and that of the twentieth century (of Stern and his public supporters in

Betar).[31] Joseph Schechtman, Jabotinsky's loyal biographer, who after 1936 served as the permanent representative of the *Ha-Zach* presidium in Poland, and who knew the situation from close personal observation, attempts to play down the impression of the confrontation:

> The writer would be misleading his readers if he played up in too dramatic a fashion these and similar remarks by which Jabotinsky at times expressed his misgivings about the activities of the organization [the IZL] or its slogans. These outbursts were always in private, within the limited circle of trusted friends, and they did not influence in any way his general opinion on the organization and its struggle, as was also proved during the ideological debate during the Third *Betar* World Conference which was held in Warsaw in the autumn of 1938.

Summing up the Conference, Schechtman writes: 'Of course there were differences in outlook and feeling, and it would have been unnatural if such misunderstandings and differences of opinion had not cropped up here and there'.[32]

This euphoric description does not correspond in any way with the atmosphere at the meeting and the nature of the conflicts, and as such may be considered a clear effort to obfuscate the facts. Jabotinsky never ceased, in public and in his private letters, to express himself in the sharpest possible terms against IZL activities in Poland, and he repeatedly attempted to put a halt to the independent initiatives of IZL members. Neither had his opposition weakened in the summer of 1939. He left no doubt in his statements that the IZL was risking a 'dangerous estrangement' from the accepted positions of the movement and was sliding towards an autonomous status, which it would never be granted. Following his meetings with an IZL delegation in France in August 1939, he wrote that the IZL representatives 'are beginning to understand that their policies are out of step with the times, in the same way that the policy of *Ha-Zach* is out of step.'[33]

Jabotinsky used the *Betar* convention, and the presence of the *Betar* delegates, for an impassioned and deliberate attack on the irredentist ideas that were being discussed within the IZL and certain circles within *Betar*. In his opening address he talked of 'rebellion', 'rebellious blood' and a 'drift towards rebellion', but here too he was speaking in terms of general rather than political – let alone concrete political – concepts. Even more revealing as regards his attitude were his interjections during the speech of Menachem Begin, which revealed his total disagreement with the latter's words. Begin said that Zionism was entering the third stage of its development: following the first two stages of practical Zionism and political Zionism, the moment had now arrived for militant, fighting Zionism. To this end, he stated, the movement needed a leadership which combined the qualities of a Cavour and a Garibaldi, for 'Cavour would never have achieved the liberation of Italy without Garibaldi'. Begin failed to specify, however, who would play the part of Garibaldi. Even then his words sounded moderate compared to those reflecting the mood of the members of the Polish secret cells. Begin did not mention a revolt, but merely mooted a future war of liberation and the establishment of an independent military force, presumably to be based on Polish soil. He claimed that, despite its objective weakness, it was the moral force underlying this army that would give it its vigour and strength.

Jabotinsky's heated interjections were intended to expose the hollowness of Begin's words. How were the fighters of *Betar* and the IZL going to reach Eretz Israel without British approval ('we are at the mercy of strangers') and without British support, he asked. How would a war of national liberation be conducted when the balance of power in the region was so clearly tilted in favour of the Arab armies? He also dealt with the answers to these questions during his lengthy summation speech to the convention.

In this speech Jabotinsky ridiculed Begin's words, making a sharp distinction between radical expectations and mood, and realistic possibilities, on the one hand, and between emotions and historical examples and the capacity to perform, on the other. The assumptions expressed in Begin's words, he said, are totally unwarranted, so that his conclusions are also fallacious. They should therefore be 'stamped out', and the fanciful and immature ideas that have taken hold of the movement should be swept away:

> It is true that we need the spirit of a Garibaldi, and that there is room for it in *Betar* [. . .] but if you insist on this method – you will close the door [to all other options]. An action such as that of Garibaldi is an arithmetical equation. He hoped for the Italian spirit – this was simply a speculation on his part. If he had not been successful, another would have arisen in his place and succeeded . . . but assuming that we are so heroic, against whom were we going to rise? The question of how to enter Eretz Israel had to be considered before succumbing to any

outbursts of heroic zeal. [. . .] Not a single strategist in the world would claim that, under the present circumstances, we could do what Garibaldi and De Valera have done. This is just talk. Our situation bears no resemblance to that of the Italians and the Irish, and if you think that what Mr. Begin has suggested is the only way, and you have the necessary arms – go ahead and commit suicide [. . . .] Such a burst of Hebrew heroism in Eretz Israel will achieve a lot. And what will it achieve? – it will help to arouse the critical element, namely our conscience.[34]

He once more restated his fundamental beliefs: the Balfour Declaration was a product of the historical conscience; what Zionism needed was, first of all, to establish a Jewish majority in Eretz Israel. 'What we need is something that will keep the doors of Eretz Israel open until an arithmetically sufficient number of people and matériel has been brought in. Once we have a Jewish majority, we will thank the doorkeeper and tell him that from here on we can look after ourselves.' The purpose of Jewish heroism is not to achieve political successes, but 'to educate the Gentiles – an education based on the hope, or the illusion, that there is a conscience. To say that conscience is dead, would be the counsel of despair. Such thoughts must be eradicated. Naturally everyone has a right to his opinions, but there is a limit.'

This unequivocal language also shows how Jabotinsky in fact regarded the activities of the IZL: not as the opening chapter of armed struggle against the British, but as a chapter in the education of the Jews to independence, and as proof to Great Britain that the Jews were able to defend themselves and to hit back in kind.

The differences of opinion during the convention were also apparent from the speeches of other participants. Shimshon Yunitschman spoke about the need for 'strategic settlement of the hill country', contradicting Jabotinsky by stating, 'I do not understand Begin's words as any slamming of doors. I hear in them the voices of the revolution and the approaching Hebrew revolt.' Others talked about the need for military training of *Betar* members that would create 'a type of military partisan', warning against too much romanticism and heroic-romantic phraseology, 'thereby putting all our Zionist hopes on one card'.

The revision of the fourth paragraph of the *neder*, the *Betar* pledge, into, 'I will strengthen my arm for the defence of my people and the conquest of my homeland' is not indicative of Jabotinsky's attitude to such concepts as revolt and conquest. The wording was not Jabotinsky's, but was suggested by the maximalist faction and by Begin, and the vow was little more than a piece of rhetoric. Anyway, why reject a rhetorical formula which could be interpreted as a readiness to conquer Eretz Israel in the event that it came to an armed conflict between Zionists and Arabs? The example of Garibaldi was no doubt deliberately brought up because of Jabotinsky's known identification with the personality and historical role of Garibaldi, but instead of reconciling the leader, it irritated him. The reason why in some of his writings during 1939 Jabotinsky extolled the IZL activities in Eretz Israel, was his belief that reprisals demonstrated to public opinion, and to those who formulated British policy, that the Jews possessed the military strength to strike back at Arab terror – so that nobody need fear this terror or yield to it. His praise served the Zionist cause, as well as that of Britain.

There is no doubt, therefore, that Jabotinsky rejected out of hand any comparisons between the position of the Zionist movement and that of peoples who had fought for the liberation of their countries. For this reason he regarded all historical parallelisms in the Revisionist press – whether they be comparisons with the Second Temple period or with the national wars of liberation of European peoples (Poland, Ireland, Italy) – as irrelevant and groundless.

A confirmation of the chasm between the viewpoint of Jabotinsky and that represented and expressed by Begin, can be found in Begin's exchange of letters with Shimshon Yunitschman during Begin's stay in Vilna.[35] At the beginning of 1940 Yunitschman wrote from Tel-Aviv to Vilna – the short-lived capital of newly-independent Latvia – that he, Begin, 'was at present further removed from reality than ever'. He had never believed, he continued, in 'idle talk and dreams about a revolt against England', and he objected to 'analogies with Ireland and Garibaldi'. It appears from the letter that Jabotinsky had also in the course of 1938 expressed his opposition to such comparisons in personal conversations, and that he regarded talk of revolt as no more than symbol-ridden rhetoric reflecting a state of mind rather than an actual historical opportunity.

In September 1939 Jabotinsky wrote in a confidential letter to all the movement's branches that, now that war had broken out 'there was no more room for big gestures' . . . since Eretz Israel had entered a 'close season' as far as any political and diplomatic activity was concerned.[36] The conflict between Herzlian Zionism and the mandatory government should for the time being be forgotten, he wrote to David Raziel, the commander of the IZL , on 26 September 1939, for 'such is the logic with which we have to live'.[37] All his thinking from here on was guided by the conviction that the Jewish people and the Zionist movement had to rally to the side of the Allies. He did not doubt for a moment that Nazi Germany was the enemy, and that she intended to destroy the Jewish people in the Diaspora (even though the thought of total physical destruction did not enter his mind), for the simple reason that Germany was in the grip of a racist ideology. Jabotinsky therefore believed that the entire Jewish people should be mobilized in the war against Nazism, without first asking what they would get in return – and at a later stage turn the problem of European Jewry into an international issue of the first order, to be resolved – in a Zionist vein – within the framework of the peace settlements that would be negotiated following the end of the war.[38]

The Invasion from the Sea[39]

This was not the opinion of Avraham Stern and his IZL supporters in Palestine, or of the 'secret cells' of the IZL in Poland. They believed that the cooperation with Poland would have to be of a military nature. A sizeable contingent of IZL members was being trained in guerilla warfare and political insurgence methods in the Carpathian mountains, under the supervision of Polish army officers, and the Polish army had supplied the IZL with arms from surplus stocks, part of which had been smuggled into Eretz Israel. However, what Stern and his people were planning was not to continue smuggling arms into Eretz Israel, with the purpose of strengthening the IZL and preparing it for future large-scale military actions against the Arabs. They were planning a conquest of Eretz Israel from the sea, by landing tens of thousands of armed IZL members all along the coast, who would storm British army installations and establish a Hebrew state. IZL historical mythology still regards this plan as a realistic military option, which was cancelled only because the outbreak of the war at the beginning of September 1939 disrupted the preparations for a seaborne operation. Jabotinsky himself has been honoured with the title of father of the revolt, and is considered to be the person who thought up, and even personally prepared such an invasion from the sea. It is a fact that in August 1939 the idea of such a big and dramatic gesture had crossed the mind of a bitter and frustrated Jabotinsky, but it was never more than a passing fancy. The IZL people, on the other hand, embraced the idea of a seaborne invasion as a practical possibility, and took concrete steps towards its implementation – which could not possibly have succeeded, and might have ended in tragedy. The very idea of invading Eretz Israel from the sea would appear to have been more like a hypothetical battle plan, intended as an effort to somehow try and bridge the gap between eschatological hopes and nationalistic frustrations, and the lack of practical means of extricating the Jews from the trap in which they had been caught by the tragic process of Jewish history.

The dramatic international developments were therefore not the favourable wind which should have steered the Zionist vessel into a safe harbour, as the Revisionists believed. The Second World War, which broke out at the beginning of September 1939, was the tragic end of a chapter in Revisionist history – and that of Jewry as a whole.

The Undergrounds: their Politics and Methods

(a) Lehi – The Stern Group

Up to this point we have dealt with the evolution of the nationalistic ideological views within the IZL and within Revisionism in general. The organizational development is described in a later chapter. Here we will deal therefore only with the political outlooks of the IZL and Lehi (which split from the IZL in the summer of 1940) in terms of their aims and methods, the mutual points of agreement and disagreement between the two organizations, and so forth.

Lehi, which had been founded at the end of 1940, had drawn immediate, practical conclusions based upon the radical nationalist and messianic views which had evolved within the ranks of the IZL and *Betar* towards the end of the 1930s. It did not see the Second World War as a reason for returning to regular political activity, for instance by offering Great Britain and her allies cooperation in the form of voluntary enlistment of Jews, in exchange for political promises that would be honoured after the war had been won. Stern regarded the war as an opportunity to rally a national force which would offer its services to whomever would give the most in return – and this could be Britain – or even Nazi Germany (later on the Soviet Union replaced Germany). Lehi, under Stern's leadership, had come to the conclusion that Great Britain's interests in the Middle East ruled out any prospect of a change in British policy towards Eretz Israel as a result of the World War. Apart from this they believed that conditions were not yet ripe, either for a struggle for future political gains, or for partial military cooperation. Stern believed that a total, radical change in the situation regarding Eretz Israel was required, and that the proper solution should not be found at the end, but at the beginning, or in the course of the war. In the eschatological world view of the Lehi leadership the general historical events revolved around the Jewish nation and its destiny, on the assumption that Zionism and the *yishuv* possessed considerable military power. Lehi did not regard the Jewish population of Eretz Israel as a small community of settlers that would want to seek shelter amid the raging storm of a world war, but as a military power to be reckoned with – even as a 'potential big power' in its own right. Articles in contemporary Lehi publications talked about the Jewish nation as a heroic people, even a 'master race' (in contrast to the Arabs, who were considered a nation of slaves). Lehi, an underground organization boasting no more than a few dozen members, represented itself to Great Britain as a military ally – in exchange for the immediate establishment of a Jewish state. When – as is to be expected – this proposal was turned down, Lehi declared itself the arch enemy of Great Britain. Its actual strength was sufficient only for carrying out incidental attacks on individual British soldiers and police officers who had been marked as 'representatives' or 'symbols' of British rule over Eretz Israel. But, given the nature of the events, its eschatological outlook was not to be pacified with such inconsequential and marginal actions, and this led to the attempt to establish contacts with Nazi Germany, through the intermediary of the German representative in Lebanon, which was under the control of Vichy France.

Zionist historiography and political debates in general are rife with arguments about these Lehi contacts with the Axis (Germany and her allies). One of the arguments used to try and justify the negotiations which Lehi tried to initiate through Otto von Hentzig, the Axis representative in Beirut, was that in 1941 nothing was as yet known about Nazi Germany's genocidal policy, so that there was no reason to regard Germany as a worse enemy than Great Britain. The spuriousness of this contention becomes clear from even a cursory reading of Jabotinsky's last book (written in the summer of 1940), which shows that the latter fully realized the demoniacal nature of the Nazis' anti-Semitism and racism. Not for nothing did he try to organize a boycott of German goods. Jabotinsky described the anti-Semitism of the Nazis as a bestial trait, deeply rooted in German culture, rather than as a result of objective economic or demographic circumstances (as was the case in Poland). The claim that the negotiations with the Axis representatives were intended to save the Jews of Eastern Europe is equally fallacious. Articles in Lehi publications portrayed the 'Jewish front in Europe' as a lost front, that would be impossible to save. In any case, trying to save European Jewry through cooperation with Germany and her allies would have necessitated the opening of the gates of Eretz Israel to large-scale immigration. This in turn would have required the evacuation of the British forces, and the 'liberation' of Palestine by the Axis armies! Not only the British, but also most Zionists (including the IZL) regarded this initiative to try and come to terms with Nazi Germany as a fanciful attempt at pseudo-diplomacy that stood not the slightest chance of succeeding, but – worse than that as a stab in the back and a serious act of national betrayal. All that Lehi could in effect have offered Germany as its contribution to the Nazi war effort, was to act as a fifth column and try to place obstacles in the way of the British in Palestine.

The historical irony is that around the same time that a representative of Lehi went to Beirut for negotiations with a Nazi diplomat (January 1941), David Raziel left for Habanniyah in Iraq on a mission for the British army, intended to help suppress the pro-Nazi rebellion of Rashid el-Kilani (June 1941). The Lehi representative's proposals were passed on to the German embassy in Ankara for further study. There is no doubt that the contents of the report and its style – as transmitted to Berlin – reflected the spirit in which they had been conveyed to the Nazi diplomat, and that the Lehi emissary tried to convince the former of his sincerity and serious intent by means of arguments and terminology acceptable to the German representative.

What in effect Lehi had to offer was a curious partnership between the emerging Nazi-German vision of a European New Order, and the actual nationalist aspirations of the Jewish people, as represented by Lehi. [Eine Interessengemeinschaft zwischen den Belangen einer Neuordnung Europas nach deutscher Konzeption, und den wahren nationalen Aspirationen des jüdischen Volkes, die von den N.M.O. (= *Nationale Militärische Organisation (in Palestina))* verkörpert werden . . . .] He proposed a political as well as military cooperation leading to the establishment of a Jewish state on a nationalist and totalitarian footing, that would be linked by a treaty to the German Reich. [Eine Kooperation zwischen dem neuen deutschen Land und einem völkisch–nationalen Hebräertum . . . .] The document continues by outlining the history of the IZL, as well as its character and military capability, as perceived by the Lehi representative, after which follows the proposal for co-operation with Germany against Britain, both in Palestine and abroad. The document concludes with a statement confirming that in terms of its world view and structure, the IZL had a close affinity to the European totalitarian movements. [Die N.M.O. ist Ihrer Weltanschauung und Struktur nach mit den totalitären Bewegungen Europas verwandt.][40]

The death of Stern in February 1942, at the hands of British Intelligence agents who surprised and trapped him in his hiding-place, put an end to any further attempts by Lehi to find allies outside Eretz Israel, and from that moment on it concentrated on terrorist warfare inside Eretz Israel. In November 1944, while negotiations were going on with the IZL about operational co-ordination, as well as with representatives of the *Haganah*, Lehi expanded its terrorist activity to beyond the borders of Eretz Israel by assassinating Lord Moyne, the resident British minister in the Middle East, in Cairo. The murder, on 6 November, created a political uproar, with dramatic consequences. Some claimed that it effectively wrecked a political initiative that could have produced a solution to partition after the war, and that it turned Churchill from a sympathizer into an enemy.[41] Others maintain that the negative impact of the murder should not be exaggerated, since in any case nothing would have come of the partition scheme that Churchill and Moyne were said to support (and which Lehi – if it had known about it – would have opposed as a matter of course). Historians sympathetic to Lehi, as well as Lehi veterans themselves, believe that the attack was no more than a logical expression of the revolutionary and anti-imperialist character of Lehi, which looked at the struggle of the *yishuv* within an overall Middle Eastern context.

It falls outside the scope of this book to discuss the impact of the assassination on British policy. Even so I consider it important to point out that the rationale behind Lord Moyne's murder was of a tactical nature. A verbal understanding reached between Yellin-Mor and Eliyahu Golomb, the civilian leader of the *Haganah*, committed Lehi to the cessation of all terrorist activity inside Eretz Israel. This was the reason why it chose Cairo for a spectacular act of revenge. Lehi proclamations from the year 1944 do not reveal any anti-imperialist intent (in the sense of calls for a joint struggle by, for instance, Egyptians and Jews to liberate themselves from the British imperialist yoke). The ideological rationalization of the assassination would come only later. Moyne was hated because of anti-Semitic remarks he had made, but principally he was murdered because of his contribution to the implementation of the immigration regulations of the White Paper – in other words for purely nationalistic and Zionist reasons.

The murder of Moyne produced a concerted campaign by the *Haganah*, in cooperation with British Intelligence and the British mandatory police, to try and eliminate the IZL.[42] Lehi, whose action had triggered off what would become known in Eretz Israel as 'the [Hunting] Season', left the fray and put down its arms, leaving the *Haganah* to deal some vicious blows to the IZL. Several Lehi leaders even sought – and received – asylum from the *Haganah*. Although their memoirs present countless arguments to justify their behaviour during the months between the end of 1944 and the spring of 1945, none of them show themselves unduly concerned at the punishment inflicted upon the IZL, whose presumption to be the largest and most important underground movement, coupled with Begin's arrogance as the self-appointed leader of the struggle against Great Britain, were heartily resented.

After the war, and the emergence of the Soviet Union as an international power with its own stake in Middle Eastern affairs, Lehi perceived in it a possible ally of Zionism. According to its new line of thinking, the Soviets would be interested in the expulsion of the British Empire from the East (and from Russia's southern borders). The Russians therefore would assist in the establishment of an independent state (or 'power') in Eretz Israel on both banks of the river Jordan, that would be prepared to take a neutralist stance towards the Soviets, who were believed to have neither territorial nor political aspirations in the Middle East. The numerous articles in Lehi publications of this period fulminating against British (and American) imperialism, while praising the socialist Soviet society, are a clear effort to condition the public, and persuade it to regard the Soviet Union as being favourably disposed towards the establishment of a large Jewish state.

The underground Lehi publications were of a very high intellectual standard, and – as we have seen in Chapter 4 – they made a significant contribution to the evolution of the ideology of the Right. Considerable intellectual effort was devoted to proving that Lehi was not merely a gang of pistol-toting terrorists, but an avant-garde elite, whose warfare was informed and guided by a profound nationalist philosophy and by realistic and national political considerations. At the same time it should be remembered that within the context of the situation prevailing in the 1940s, Lehi must not be judged on its ideological character, but by its practical methods, and their consequences. Lehi publications might well fill their columns with articles about the fight against British imperialism, or launch into learned political and economic analyses of the nature of this imperialism; they might make realistic-sounding assessments of the changing positions of Great Britain and the Soviet Union in the world that would emerge from the ruins of the war. Nevertheless, none of this could hide the fact that all they really did was carry out a series of terrorist and sabotage acts aimed at forcing the British to give up the Mandate over Eretz Israel. Lehi (but similarly the IZL and the *Haganah*) was unable to force Great Britain to evacuate Eretz Israel, leaving an independent Hebrew state behind; Lehi – and for that matter the IZL – were simply not strong enough to determine either the boundaries of the future Jewish state, or the outcome of a war between the *yishuv* and the Arabs. Their only influence on events, if any, would have been to make the British decide against direct intervention in the tug-of-war over Eretz Israel, and to let Jews and Arabs (the latter, however, with British support) fight it out between themselves.

To all practical purposes, therefore, Lehi was a terrorist organization until 1945, operating through acts of terror against individuals, which it tried to justify with pragmatic arguments and sophistry. From 1945 onwards, the organization expanded its activities into warfare on as large a scale as its facilities would permit, while trying to imitate the IZL, whose military activities were far wider in scope and – although directed against military and civilian targets – never intentionally harmed individual soldiers or policemen. The most spectacular action by Lehi – apart from the murder of Lord Moyne – was the assassination of the United Nations' mediator, Count Folke Bernadotte, in Jerusalem on 17 September 1948.

Earlier Lehi had been the moving force in the creation of the *Tenuat ha-Meri ha-Ivri*, the Jewish Resistance Movement, a short-lived coalition of the two underground movements and the *Haganah*, and provoked by the policies of Attlee and Bevin following the Labour Party's accession in England. This cooperation came to an abrupt end in July 1946, after the explosion that destroyed a wing of the King David Hotel, but until that moment Lehi played an important role as intermediary between the heads of the *Haganah* and the IZL command.

There existed, therefore, a wide gap between the historical, eschatological thinking of Lehi – both in its messianic form (the Israel Scheib/ Eldad group), and as regards the proponents of 'Realpolitik' (the Yellin-Mor group) – and its actual capability to influence events. Since this book does not deal with the terrorist exploits of Lehi (or the IZL), there is no need to describe here its history as an underground organization. We will therefore mainly concern ourselves with an account of the evolution of its self-awareness and ideology, and the crisis produced by its conceptual transition from thinking about a 'national home' to finding themselves in a sovereign state of their own. Whereas the IZL managed to overcome this crisis with little more than some organizational and psychological upheaval, Lehi's transition was accompanied by a great deal of ideological conflict, a falling out of personalities towards the right and the left, and the creation of two fundamentally different factions. We will revert to this subject in another chapter.

(b) The IZL: The Road to Rebellion[43]

Four years afterwards the IZL followed in the footsteps of Stern and his group – but not because it claimed to have arrived at any new insights. On the contrary: the organization's decision was represented as being a logical progression, and a continuation in the footsteps of – not *Ha-Zohar*, the political party – but Jabotinsky, the politician and philosopher! The reader is reminded of Lehi's conclusion in 1940 that the outbreak of the Second World War was a 'favourable wind' that would speed disengagement from the British orientation, and turn a merely literary revolt into political action. The IZL, on the other hand, had difficulty with such a dramatic and drastic change in orientation and behaviour.

Even though the IZL in Eretz Israel was, and remained, bigger and better organized than Lehi, the split of 1940 proved a serious blow in terms of organization, manpower and arms supplies. The result was that the IZL entered a period of indecision and haphazard activity lasting until February 1944, during which period it struck out in different – and sometimes contradictory – directions. Among these activities was the organization of underground cells, the training of para-military units, and even voluntary enlistment in the British army.

Jabotinsky did not believe that underground activity would succeed in changing the British political stance, since in his view the British political establishment was far too ponderous to be moved by terrorism (or even an Arab revolt). The only use of going to the barricades in Eretz Israel, he stated in January 1935 in Cracow, is that it arouses someone's conscience, in which sense it has a moral value, but a mere 'display of heroism', on the other hand, remains an idle threat, and is therefore useless.[44] As already mentioned,

Jabotinsky had never for a moment envisaged an armed revolt against Britain; the mere prospect was a nightmare to him, and even the White Paper of 1939 had not changed his basic views on the subject. We may remember that it was Stern and his group who had drawn the dialectic conclusions from Jabotinsky's perceptions: British policy in Eretz Israel was inflexible, and too firmly anchored in British imperialist interests; these interests were basically inimical to Zionism, and their anti-Zionist and anti-Jewish nature had become even more pronounced on the eve of World War II. From this it followed that diplomacy, or appeals to the world's conscience, would be to no avail. The only solution was to change the perspective as regards who was the enemy, and to revise the operational methods. Against the background of the situation in 1940 the appeal to Great Britain for help to promote the establishment of 'an Israeli kingdom within its wide historical boundaries' (according to the definition in communiqué No.112, dated June 1940 from IZL headquarters) was therefore mere rhetoric.

The question as to whether there existed ideological differences of opinion between Raziel and Stern is actually irrelevant. Lehi members did of course contend that such differences existed, and that they were substantial; Menachem Begin, on the other hand, tried to prove that any such disputes were unimportant. The crucial fact remains, however, that an analysis of the changes in the political situation during the early 1940s caused the two, Raziel and Stern, to arrive at fundamentally different decisions, which carried them in opposite directions: cooperation with British Intelligence by the one, and anti-British terror by the other.

Menachem Begin's attitude to these two extreme options is illustrative of the conflicts and lack of direction within the ranks of the IZL during the years 1939–1944. Begin regarded himself as a loyal disciple of Jabotinsky, which prevented him from joining the Polish secret cells of the IZL, whose activities were so upsetting to Jabotinsky. Begin's election as commander of *Betar* in March 1939 was a compromise decision. Begin was a Jabotinsky loyalist, but at the same time he was acceptable in IZL circles. He believed that he would succeed in closing the ranks, and channel *Betar*'s activities towards organizing illegal immigration and military training. He was not involved with the secret cells, and very likely he was not even aware of the majority of their activities, particularly the military training courses that were going on in the Carpathian mountains, and which were even kept secret from Jabotinsky himself. Begin did not draw any personal consequences from his uncompromising speech at the conference of November 1938, remaining content with promoting what he called 'military preparedness', in other words continuing the para-military exercises which constituted the Polish *Betar* members' way of preparing themselves for any future eventuality.

In Vilna, to which he fled just before the German Nazi army's entry into Warsaw, Begin began to have second thoughts. He no longer pinned his hopes on the British Mandate, and he considered the World War a war between Germany and Great Britain – a war in which the Jews were in no way involved! To one of his confidants, the earlier-mentioned *Betar* leader Dr. Shimshon Yunitschman of Tel-Aviv, Begin wrote a letter stating, among other things, that 'anyone reading this, will no doubt say: "The man must be crazy", but the fact that Britain was at war with the Nazis, did not necessarily make it a Jewish war, and he objected to conscription in the British army'.[45] Yunitschman duly panicked upon reading these words, and went to great length to explain to Begin that the IZL's activities in Eretz Israel were not a revolt against Great Britain, but actions of a demonstrative nature, and that the establishment of a Jewish state was unthinkable without the unconditional participation of each and every Jew in the war against Nazism.

When, towards the end of 1942, Begin arrived in Eretz Israel, in the uniform of a corporal of General Anders' Free Polish Army, he at first took a wait-and-see position. He was in no hurry. He was prepared to support voluntary enlistment in the British army, on condition that an independent Jewish battalion would be established to participate in the fighting on the Western and Eastern fronts (even including soldiers mobilized from among the Jewish refugees in Russia). In September 1942 he had a grandiose vision of a Jewish army of 250,000 soldiers, equipped with tanks, artillery and planes, to be mobilized and trained in the steppes of Soviet Russia.[46] Towards 1945 he began to despair, gradually veering to the conclusion that Stern and his followers had reached as early as 1940, namely that it was impossible to rely upon world conscience, on the Englishman's love for the Bible, and on the importance of Eretz Israel to the British empire. It is now clear, he wrote in February 1943, that British interests are opposed to the Jewish interest. At the same time he unleashed fierce criticism against the concept that had formed the cornerstone of Jabotinsky's thinking, from the days of the Jewish battalions in World War I, up till his struggle for the inclusion of Jewish battalions in the Allied forces in 1940. Begin wrote:

It has been proven that British friendship, which should have been based on these two elements, is a mere figment of the Jewish imagination, a phantom, with which an entire generation has lived, and because of which an entire generation may be lost.[47]

Until the end of 1943 the IZL was organized like a regular army, with a smaller part functioning within a conspiratorial operative framework (a structure borrowed from Pilsudski's Polish Legion). Numerous IZL members served in the British army, whereas others participated regularly in military training exercises, and even organized public military displays! Dozens of others were organized within a tight conspiratorial network, called the *Red Faction*. The contemporary commander of the IZL, Yaacov Meridor, whose authority left much to be desired, was incapable of determining the IZL's future orientation. On the one hand he continued the old line of the leaders of the political party, according to which the *yishuv* had to prepare an underground standing army, ready to confront the British at the end of the war; at the same time he trained operational units in preparation for an eventual terrorist struggle. At the beginning of 1944 Begin stepped in, and decided on the strategy that was to be followed. The underground struggle was no longer capable of forcing the British to stay in Eretz Israel as a pro-Zionist protective power; from now on it had to be aimed at getting the British to *leave* Eretz Israel, and let Jews and Arabs determine their own fate.

The 'Proclamation of the Rebellion' of February 1944 was the IZL's declaration of war against Great Britain.[48] In contrast to the '18 Principles of the Revival' formulated by Lehi at the beginning of 1941, which was an ideological document, the IZL declaration was a manifesto of a pragmatic political nature. Its formulation could as yet be called 'moderate'. The principal enemies were still the 1939 White Paper and the mandatory government, rather than Great Britain itself; the IZL was even prepared to regard Britain as a future ally, provided she evacuated Eretz Israel and permitted the *yishuv* to establish an independent state. (It should be added here that soon afterwards the IZL, too, would regard British imperialism as its most implacable foe, since it was this imperialism which stood behind the Hashemite king in Amman, and supported the Egyptian invasion of Eretz Israel in 1948!) Already in 1944, however, it was no longer sufficient to declare war on the White Paper, and neither could Britain be expected to change course and offer the Jews a state in the whole of Eretz Israel (or even its western part). The immediate motive for the start of a chain of attacks and acts of sabotage was to notify the British in no uncertain terms that, now that the period covered by the 1939 White Paper had formally ended, the *yishuv* would no longer acquiesce in the continued enforcement of its restrictions. The IZL no longer wanted the British to cooperate in the establishment of a Jewish state; it now demanded that they leave it to the Jews and Arabs of Eretz Israel to decide between themselves who would rule the country. Such was the IZL's disregard for Arab military strength, that it did not have a moment's doubt that the *yishuv* would easily win this battle, and quickly take over all of western Eretz Israel (though not the part east of the Jordan).

The 'Proclamation of the Rebellion' contained a number of clear-cut, traditional Revisionist elements, such as the first paragraph, which talked about 'the establishment of a national Hebrew army', and the second paragraph about 'the large-scale evacuation of European Jewry to Eretz Israel'. Very soon, however, even these Revisionist elements in the 'Proclamation of the Rebellion' became irrelevant. In practice it proved impossible to separate the fight against the White Paper from relations with Britain as a whole. Great Britain and British imperialism in the Middle East became the enemy, and the IZL – as particularly Begin wrote – was called upon to formulate a historiosophic and political legitimization of a situation in which a revolutionary minority undertook to act in the name of Jewish history, conducting a military struggle against Great Britain, without being beholden to any formal legal authority, but allowing history to take its course.

Herewith the principal distinction between the IZL and Lehi had in fact disappeared, so that as far as both were concerned the only disagreements left were those about ideological content, a statement of purposes, and the tactics with regard to other parts of the *yishuv*. In particular Lehi tried to accentuate the ideological differences between itself and the IZL, in an effort to confirm its self-image and prove that it was an organization with an original historical revolutionary-Zionist conception, and that its vision of the Israeli state was no different from that of the IZL and, in course of time, from that of the *Herut* movement, which emerged out of the latter. The IZL, on the other hand, tried to play down the contradictions and differences of opinion, by presenting them as mere optical illusions, the result of an unfortunate internal political development.

The declared purpose of the IZL's struggle against the British was to put an immediate – and unconditional – end to the Mandate, by opposing any form of formal political settlement that would involve agreement to a division of Western Palestine. The internal logic of the IZL strategy rested on the assumption that, unless they were forced, neither the Arabs, nor Great Britain, would ever accept a British evacuation or a partition of the country. For this reason it was pointless to wait for a change in British policy, or Arab consent to the establishment of a Jewish state. The only way to drive the British out of Eretz Israel was to hit at the interests and the prestige of the Empire, to drive home to them that Eretz Israel had lost its usefulness as a strategic base for the British army. Only an unremitting and uncompromising series of painful acts of sabotage against civilian and military targets would bring Great Britain to the conclusion that it could not stay in Eretz Israel, or impose any anti-Zionist solution. Irredentist activity would also gain the *yishuv* the support and sympathy from various circles in world public opinion, as well as appropriate political and military assistance. Without armed struggle, according to this premise, the principal driving force, and the motive for the British to leave Eretz Israel, would be absent. Illegal immigration, settlement activity and diplomacy were insufficient for this purpose: the velvet glove of diplomacy should hide an iron fist.

Behind this logic, which had a deterministic character, lay two contradictory claims. The first one was that Britain regarded Palestine as a vital base for her continued rule in the Middle East, and would therefore refuse to evacuate it of her own free will. However, a series of hard-hitting attacks by the underground would cause her to relinquish this strategic asset, since this would considerably diminish Britain's international status and power. According to the second argument, British rule in Eretz Israel was such an oppressive and tyrannical 'Nazi-style' regime, that Great Britain would not hesitate to destroy the *yishuv* – but this was exactly the reason why the only alternative was to continue with terrorist activity, without counting the risks this might entail for the *yishuv* as a whole.

From the outset the anti-British struggle possessed a dynamic of its own. Rhetoric and historiosophy only served to provide it with a legitimization, and to improve the morale of the ranks and the sympathizers – and in particular to place the underground actions conducted with various degrees of success during the last four years within an overall historical framework. IZL pamphlets became as anglophobic as those of Lehi, and the struggle became punctuated with no less violent – and at times even more brutal – clashes. Even so certain rules continued to be observed, since the British army and mandatory police were vigorously restrained by the authorities, as a result of which the Jewish civilian population was hardly affected during the entire period of the revolt.

Both Zionist and non-Zionist historiography have extensively debated the degree of influence of the actions of the IZL and Lehi on the British decision to evacuate Eretz Israel. Most of those viewing this history from the point of view of the Right are adamant (although less emphatically so during the past decade) that the actions of the two underground movements were solely responsible for the British decision in 1947 to terminate the Mandate. As this 'self-written' history would have it, all British decisions in this direction during the years 1944–1948 were the result of underground actions. The majority of scholars, on the other hand, dismiss the suggestion that the underground movements in any way influenced the British decision, or at most consider them of secondary or marginal importance within the context of the overall complex of forces and considerations. It is indeed difficult to isolate individual factors in such a complex structure, so that it is hard to say whether, without the actions of the underground, an active or dynamic factor might have been missing or removed from the overall complex of considerations, that turned the need for arriving at some clear-cut decision from a theoretical, but not urgent requirement in principle, into an immediate political necessity. In any case, if the IZL did influence any events – which is doubtful – it was only the British decision to terminate the Mandate; it would not have been able to influence either the manner in which Great Britain would evacuate Eretz Israel, the developments on the international political scene (the United Nations Partition Resolution of 29 November 1947), or the balance of power between Jews and Arabs in Eretz Israel. The British evacuation did not create the Jewish state – it merely provided an opportunity for its establishment.

The history of the confrontation between the IZL and the agencies of the *yishuv* and, after May 1948, those of the government of the newly-established state, constitutes an important chapter in the political history of the State of Israel. This is not the place, however, to relate these dramatic events. At this point we will mention only that towards the end of 1947, upon its emergence from the underground, the IZL was keenly aware that the real enemy it now had to confront was the Palestinian Arabs (who, according to the IZL, were receiving direct as well as indirect British assistance in their war against the Jews). Even so the IZL strongly deprecated the military might of the Palestinian Arabs, assuming that a rapid military move would suffice to defeat them and establish a state whose borders would reach from the Jordan river to the sea. To this end the IZL reorganized its underground infrastructure into regular army battalions (which operated within the framework of *Zeva Haganah le-Israel* – the Israel Defence Army, or *Zahal* – according to an agreement concluded in June 1948 between the Israeli government and the IZL). In light of the above, the IZL command abroad also organized shipments of military equipment, and even made plans for an expeditionary force to invade Eretz Israel from the sea.[49] According to this programme, which never left the drawing board, this invasion force was intended to join up with the IZL battalions in Israel, in order to occupy those parts of Eretz Israel which on the Partition map drawn up in 1947 had remained outside Jewish jurisdiction. The contentions that the Israeli government of David Ben-Gurion accepted Partition not only as a tactical, but as a political step, thereby committing itself in advance to the 'dismemberment' of Eretz Israel, and that in the course of the War of Independence the government did nothing to try and eradicate the Partition boundaries, have been some of the major and most persistent accusations by the veterans of the underground and spokesmen of the Right against successive Mapai-dominated government coalitions ever since 1948, and up till the war of 1967. The myth, according to which it was the underground that triggered off the war, and which determined its outcome – despite its persecution by an indulgent political leadership, which even collaborated with the British, became the guiding theme of all political manifestations of the IZL, the *de facto* heir to the Revisionist tradition in Eretz Israel.

The underground myth, together with the sense of solidarity of the 'Fighting Family', produced a new political elite, which formed the principal instrument for the foundation of the new *Herut* Movement at the dawn of the new-born Jewish state.

CHAPTER EIGHT

The Right's Attitude towards the 'Arab Problem'

The Arabs as a Political and Existential Problem[1]

One of the most profound dichotomies between the formal ideology of the Right and its collective *Weltanschauung* lies in its attitude towards what in Zionist and Israeli jargon is referred to as 'the Arab problem'. This tension results basically from the fact that the formal ideology offered a political solution of an utopian character, which proved irreconcilable with the bi-national reality in Eretz Israel. It was Jabotinsky himself who foresaw that the situation in Eretz Israel would involve a lengthy, and at times even violent national conflict, resulting from a situation which he himself defined as 'tragic'. The fact that the situation indeed proved to be tragic and violent, and the realization that the formal solutions offered by Revisionism were impractical, intensified, particularly within the Right, the feeling that this subject confronted Zionism with its most difficult and crucial dilemma. As a result, its collective *Weltanschauung*, and in its wake the ideology of several of the radical groups within the Right, took an even more extremist turn in terms of their responses and the nature of their suggested solutions. For the Right (and not merely the Right), the Arab problem became not only a critical political question, but an existential cultural problem which was to occupy a central place in its world view. Many of the fundamental characteristics of the political culture of the Zionist Right originated in, and were moulded and internalized as a result of the Arab problem and its intellectual and ideological responses to this challenge.

For this reason it is appropriate to open the discussion with a review of the attitudes of the Right towards the Arab problem (or, more precisely, its attitude towards the Arab-Palestinian nation in Eretz Israel), within the broader context of, respectively, its attitude towards 'the East', Islam, pan-Arabism and Arab nationalism.

The Images of the 'East' and Islam

In more than one way the Right rejected the 'romantic' depiction of 'the East', adhering instead to a conception of a superiority of 'the West', both as a civilization and as a culture. Although its attitude towards 'the West' underwent a change after the Holocaust, its attitude towards 'the East', or rather the Muslim East, remained unchanged. This image was entirely negative, a negativism based upon a broad range of interpretations and stereotypes. 'The East, and everything associated with this concept, is alien to me . . . even among the Eskimos in the Far North I would feel more at home.'[2] Thus wrote Jabotinsky, to stress his indifference towards the East. In his view European Romanticism and mysticism was essentially a Western reaction to its industrial civilization. The British middle class, which provided the colonial administrative apparatus of the Levant, had built up a romantic picture, that was not to be spoiled by Western progress, but preserved untouched. It was characteristic of such an attitude, he wrote, to see exoticism where in reality there was only profound backwardness and social and cultural primitivism. For this reason Jabotinsky and his circle preferred to adopt the orientalist's stereotype, which turned 'the East' into a negative *topos* of civilization and culture. He modified his criticism, however, by writing that 'the East' was not a static geographical phenomenon, but a cultural category. Thus, for instance, the Islamic East had been a culturally highly developed region in medieval days, but there was no doubt that in more recent times it had stagnated, to the point of petrifying into a static civilization that was unable to develop, let alone flourish under its own power. For this reason Jabotinsky determined that 'everything that is oriental, is doomed'. The Jews were not only an integral part of European culture: they actually were the originators of this culture. The romantic call to Go East! accompanying the national revival movement under the influence of European romantic and mystic attitudes, was therefore, in his view, a most disturbing call. The Islamic spirit must be swept from Palestine, for it is a spirit of social and cultural decay, and [characteristic of] a fatalistic psychology. It is oppressive in its poverty, its political despotism, its theocratic rule and its oppression of women. It is a civilization 'whose characteristics stand in complete antithesis to European civilization, which distinguishes itself by intellectual curiosity, free investigation, dynamism and a minimum of interference of religion in everyday life, to mention only some of its positive characteristics'.[3]

The only redeeming figure Jabotinsky saw in the modern East was that of the Turkish reformer Kemal Ataturk. Thus the Jews were not returning to the East in order to be absorbed by it, but to transplant European culture from geographical Europe to the East – to sow it into the soil of Asia. One of the biggest favours the Jew could do the East (even though Jabotinsky objected to the idea of Zionism having a cultural mission in the East, since he did not believe this would bring any political benefit), was to assist it in freeing itself from its own oriental nature. To sum up his words: 'We, the Jews, have nothing in common with the so-called East – thank God.'[4]   It should be pointed out, however, that other writings, particularly certain passages in the poetry of Uri Zvi Greenberg, reveal the influence of the German neo-romantic and mystical approach, which looks to the East as a source of spiritual inspiration against 'Western' materialism, rationalism and automatism, and therefore sees the revival of Judaism as a return to these spiritual sources of the human Urgeist. His poetry is suffused with the idea of the 'the West' as a dynamic and creative civilization, and the modern, futuristic elements in his poems are far stronger than their Eastern mystic elements. Greenberg, too, prefers concrete and steam to the Oriental nirvana. The Revisionist press, on the other hand, had no such reservations; on the contrary, the dominant line was one of praise and admiration for those who rejected the claim of 'Ex Oriente Lux', as well as for Jabotinsky, for his solid Western outlook and his utter rejection of anything showing the smallest sign of 'Orientalism'.[5]

Later rightist literary sources discuss the nature of Islamic civilization and religion in a more comprehensive and detailed manner. Many of these texts concentrate upon an examination of the meaning of Islam as a political culture. The conclusions are consistent and unequivocal: Islam is essentially and fundamentally an anti-Jewish and anti-Zionist political-religious culture; its values and norms stand in complete contradiction to the Judeo-Christian culture. Islam is tyrannical, primitive, extremist, violent, treacherous, and inhuman, in that it does not have the slightest regard for either human life or the rights of the individual. From this it follows that such an Islam is the uncompromising and eternal foe of the Jewish people and of Jewish nationalism. Islam is prepared to accept Jewry as a subordinate religious community, a millet, but not as a political power in its own right. In the eyes of all currents in Islam the very existence of a Jewish political entity is an unbearable religious provocation.[6]

The literature of the Right does not depict the history of the Jews in the Islamic countries in positive contrast to their situation in medieval Christian Europe. Neither does it describe it as a Golden Age of religious tolerance and cultural symbiosis, but rather as a long period of suppression and humiliation. The Golden Age in Spain is a legend, an invention of nineteenth-century liberal German Jews, rather than a historical reality. The literature of the Right reveals a clear effort to separate the history of the Jewish people from that of Islam, and even from the much broader category of the 'Semitic' civilization, claiming that Jews are by no means an outspoken 'Semitic nation',[7] but a 'Mediterranean' and 'European' people, or – conversely – a singular nation that does not form a part of any other 'history'.

Islamic rule of Eretz Israel is also painted in stark colours in Revisionist literature. According to its image of the past, the Muslim conquest of Eretz Israel signalled the beginning of a nomadization process, leading to the systematic destruction of the country and a complete absence of any development initiative, as a result of which Eretz Israel was turned into a wretched and exploited provincial backwater, devoid of any cultural and spiritual life. From the outset the Islamic connection with Eretz Israel was alien rather than authentic, and Islam's attitude to Eretz Israel was therefore characteristic of an exploitative and suppressive regime. Eretz Israel never was a separate political entity under Arab rule, and at no time was it a homeland for the Arabs. For this reason Judaism had no common ground with Islam; on the contrary, there existed between them a fundamental meta-historical contrast, which ruled out any co-existence on the ideological and, consequently, political level.

The Arabs as an Existential Cultural Symbol

Given this outlook, the word 'Arab' became for the Right a symbol of negative human qualities. Similar extreme manifestations of contempt for the Arab as a civilized human being could also be found in political and literary expressions outside the Right, but only among the Right did the 'Arab' take on major demonological dimensions within the framework of a political and cultural tradition. Achimeir's *Notes from Prison*,[8] written during his imprisonment in the1930s (and inspired by Dostoyevsky's *The House of the Dead*), contain a characteristic description of the Arab as a 'pan-erotic' person, whose entire life revolves around perverted sex in all its bizarre forms – a person whose word can never be relied upon, who is emotional and wayward, and in the thrall of wild and fickle fantasies. The Arab lives by deceit, all that he understands is power, and any attempts at diplomatic language are wasted on him. He fears and respects only those who show that they are superior and mightier, and the only regime he will accept is that of the strong arm. 'He who comes to the East with liberal inclinations, will in the shortest possible time find himself betrayed',[9] wrote even a moderate Revisionist party worker such as Benyamin Avniel. This explains the generally-heard discussions about the 'Arab mentality', and the need for all those who were involved in the Middle East to recognize the 'Arab personality', the character and motivations of which differed so fundamentally from the 'Western personality'.

There is no doubt that August 1929 was a turning point, the moment in which the Arab changed in the *Weltanschauung* and literature of the Right from a stubborn political rival into an existential meta-historical enemy. During the 1930s this changed view found expression in the most vitriolic terms, for instance in the poetry of Uri Zvi Greenberg, and in its wake much of the poetry and articles that appeared in the newspapers and periodicals of the Right.

In Greenberg's poetry 'the Arab' has become an existential threat, a murderer who rises up against the Jew, a 'wolf-Arab', or 'beast-Arab'. The events of 1929, followed by the Arab revolt during 1936–1939, had put an end to the naive and idealistic faith in the kinship of, and cooperation between the two ancient branches of the Semitic race. Thus Greenberg wrote:

> We believed: She was a sister of our race, the daughter of
>   Arabia
> Behold the *abbaya* . . . like the Jew's prayer shawl.
> Has she, our sister, forgotten the family tree?
> We, weary and great with wisdom, would teach her our race's
>   secret:
> The teachings of the children of Shem.
> Oh, how we erred:
> When we returned home, weary, great in wisdom, and charged
>   with energy and vigour,
> Not a racial sister speaking Arabic we found,

As yet belonging to the House of Shem . . .
Woe, we found a sister and concubine of the Edomite race
And the Crescent winking to the cross at Golgotha.
(Speech of the Son of Blood, *An Oracle about Arabia*, 1929)

From 1929 onwards the demonological image of the Arab strikes firm roots in the literature of the Right, in terms of the image of a murderous cut-throat who kills Jews for the sake of killing, not only because murder is essential to his nature, but because murder is a national duty as well as a norm. The Arab is painted as a savage emerging from the desert, from his black tents, from the dark alleys of his villages and towns, shouting, 'Let's slaughter the Jews'. He in fact replaces the Christian who killed Jews during his pogroms, from the Crusaders all the way to the days of Chmielnicki and Petlyura. The practical implication of this imagery was that Palestinian Arabs did not resort to violence and terror out of a feeling of frustration and powerlessness (a conclusion which, ironically enough, Jabotinsky's analysis would have borne out), but because terror was the 'innate expression of the culture of the savage, the morality of the desert, and the religion that justifies war by any means'. According to this representation, 'the Arabs, in their profound ignorance, are petrified like blocks of basalt in an arid wilderness. They will never learn to settle countries and build states. They will never know what it means to be beholden to an ideal or to be loyal to a flag.'[10]

Even so it is clear that Arab terrorism was not murder for murder's sake, since according to Revisionism Palestinian Arab terror had a number of well-defined political aims. The Arabs were conducting a holy war against the existence and very presence of Jews in Palestine. This was not the resistance of 'natives' against foreign settlers, but the resistance of a people with national feelings who regarded themselves as masters and sovereign owners of the land. As such it was a life-and-death struggle for them, the outcome of which could only be decided by strength. Following this same line of reasoning, the literature of the Right arrives at a paradoxical conclusion. 'We should learn from no other than the Palestinian Arabs how to fight for our homeland,' writes Dr. Israel Scheib (Eldad) in January 1938. 'Don't they deserve that we learn from them how to fight . . .?' he asks rhetorically.[11] Zionism would fail if it insisted on relating to the struggle for Eretz Israel in rational political and national terms, while the Arabs were looking at the land as something holy. This geo-political Arab attitude had to be met, in Eldad's view, with a similar stand, and – as we have seen earlier – the Arab attitude towards power had to be confronted by a Jewish conception of power which equated the Zionist settlement effort with a conquest through physical occupation.

Islam as a Non-Political Force

Above all a negative picture of Islam and the 'Islamic East' was drawn, a description which resulted from cultural rejection, while at the same time it served as the basis for a more reliable appraisal of the power of the 'Arab East.'

The Revisionist's de-romanticization of the East was a reaction to a major school in British politics, as well as against an important stream in Zionism. Its actual conclusion was that Islam was not a consolidated force that needed to be taken into account politically. Islam as a unified factor in international relations did not really exist. The myth of the Muslims of India had been created by British officials in Cairo, Baghdad and Calcutta. As a political movement, Islam was reactionary and a bogey. There is no 'Islamic world' and, as of now, it poses no danger. It has no military strength, and there is no real significance in its demographic numbers. Europe can dominate the Middle East effortlessly.[12]

Islam is a paper tiger, proclaimed Jabotinsky. This is why half a million or a million Jews in Eretz Israel can represent a European bulwark in the Middle East, exercising a strong, stable and reliable cultural and military influence. The West can be confident that 'in any conflict between the West and the East, we will always side with the West, because for a thousand years or so . . . the West has been the symbol of a humane society . . . . We are . . . the foremost and most loyal bearers of Westernism . . . in the East', wrote the radical Achimeir in 1930.[13] Hence the repeated claims in Revisionist political literature that Arab support was a 'broken reed', and that the British would jeopardize their own interests by relying on Arab assistance. Not the Arabs, but the Jews, were a strategic and military asset against 'the East' (and, eventually, against the spread of Communist influence in the Middle East). The fatal mistake of British policy was that it preferred to rely on a backward East, a feudal political elite, a society that was incapable of raising a modern army, and an unreliable regime, rather than placing its confidence in the modern Jewish national society.[14]

At a later date, during the 1940s, this line of reasoning would undergo a change, particularly in the Lehi-affiliated press. Jewish nationalism would be presented as having a missionary task, namely to free the Arabs from the bonds of social feudalism and British Imperialism, which preferred the continued existence of a backward and divided East. Accordingly, Jewish national society would no longer remain passive towards events within Arab society, but would adopt a missionary stance (an attitude which in fact had been evident in certain Zionist literature as early as the beginning of the century). Anti-imperialist Zionism would shoulder the 'Hebrewman's burden', to guide the East towards the modern nationalist era.[15]

Arab Nationalism

Revisionism regarded pan-Islamism and pan-Arabism as artificial notions which had been imported from the West, but lacked any substance in an Oriental cultural and political setting. Rejecting the picture of a uniform or unified East, and belittling its common denominators, it recognized only the national aspirations of certain Arab populations, particularly those of Syria and Egypt where, according to the Revisionists, the Arab demand for territorial nationalism might have a valid historical basis (because they were nations of a 'historical nature'). Local nationalism was all right, therefore, but not pan-Arabism – a united Arab nation. For this reason Jabotinsky preferred the continued existence of the Ottoman Empire over its disintegration into individual Arab states. 'The Arabs in the various lands,' wrote Jabotinsky, 'do not have much in common. A common language and territorial contiguity do not in themselves create national unity.' This is why he assumed that during and after the Great War the Arabs might establish several national states. 'Indeed, some kind of unity might arise in the future,' he wrote. 'But the formation of an Arab empire would be a terrible disaster for Europe.'[16]

Jabotinsky did not ignore the early signs of Arab nationalist aspirations, which were becoming manifest in North Africa, Syria and Egypt. We have already mentioned that in August 1920, in the wake of the Syrian crisis and Feisal's expulsion from Damascus by the French, Jabotinsky wrote that Syria was the most 'European' of the Eastern countries, and that the national movements in Syria were the most serious among the Arab national movements. The right of the Syrian national movement, 'just like our own right, rests . . . not on force of arms, but on the force of universal morality and justice.' The Arabs of Syria possessed 'the eternal basis of national revival', for they were 'one nation, living in its country, working its land, speaking its language, a nation healthy and vigorous in body and spirit, rich in talent and with a propensity for and an inclination towards progress and development.'[17]

But neither Syria nor Palestine was as yet (in 1920) ready for political independence. As Jabotinsky put it: 'Only one path leads to the threshold of political freedom, and it is called "culture" – it is the one and only path; there are no short-cuts.'

Thus Jabotinsky and the formal ideology of Revisionism acknowledged the authenticity of the emergence of a Syrian Arab nationalism, as in effect that of an Egyptian. But they viewed them as separate and distinctive forms of nationality, and from this perspective the Right was less inclined than the other streams of the Zionist movement to accord either Syrian or Egyptian nationalism a role in the affairs of Palestine.

At this juncture we should point out the profound inner contradiction in the Revisionist image of the Arab world: on the one hand its negation of the pan-Arabic concept of a 'unified Arab nation', and on the other the argument that the Palestinian Arabs formed an integral part of a (to them non-existing) great 'Arab nation', which was supposed to serve as the framework for the expression of their cultural and political aspirations. This explains the often-stated argument in the contemporary literature of the Right that 'the Arabs' already have many states, so that there is no fundamental justification for giving them yet another state. Yet, if there exists no 'Arab nation', but only a number of separate Arab peoples, then how can one tell a certain Arab group that it must view itself as a part of the large and unified Arab nation? The contradiction, and the resulting dilemma, become even more intractable when taking into account that the Right never recognized the legitimacy of the Hashemite regime in Transjordan, viewing the Hashemite dynasty as an alien, British transplant onto the east bank of the Jordan, occupying territory that had been severed from the Jewish national home. It therefore followed that there was no 'Transjordan nation', of which the Palestinians could form an integral part. Indeed, Jabotinsky viewed the Arabs of Palestine as a separate native, national and political factor, in other words an element not integrally related to either a general Arab, or a 'Greater Syrian' nationalism or state.

It would seem that, on this point, Jabotinsky's views were clearly at cross purposes with the general and dominant mood, as well as with the *a priori* argumentation prevailing within the movement which bears his name and which was nurtured on his ideas. In

countless lectures and the majority of the articles on the subject in
the literature of the Right, we keep on encountering the argument,
reinforced by references to the recent and historical past, that there
exists only one integral Arab nation. The memorandum presented
by Lehi to the UNSCOP commission in 1947 states that 'the Arabs of
Eretz Israel form a part of their [Arab] nation in exactly the same
way as the Hungarians residing in Rumania form a part of the
Hungarian nation, rather than of a separate people . . . .'[18] Such an
assertion was necessary to justify their determined opposition to
Arab sovereignty over Eretz Israel or any part of it, and – even more
so – to lay the groundwork for the idea of an eventual 'transfer' of
the Arab population from Palestine. After all, the fact that the
Palestinian Arabs were not a separate national entity and lacked a
genuine historical connection with the country, would considerably
facilitate their re-settlement in any other Arab state outside the
historical boundaries of Eretz Israel.

The Middle Eastern Minorities as Allies

Since the Arab or Muslim world was considered essentially anti-
Zionist, and pan-Arabism an artificial creation of British Imperialism, certain segments of the Zionist Right tended to look towards
the minority nations of the Middle East as suitable partners for
Jewish nationalism. Already during the middle of the 1930s there
were those who pointed at the Druze and Maronite minorities as
groups that stood visibly apart from the otherwise uniform Muslim
East. Both communities could look back to long historical traditions, both were being suppressed by the Shi'ite and Sunni Muslim
majority, and together with other non-Arabic states – meaning
Egypt (with its own Coptic minority), Turkey and Iran – they would
be able to restore the 'glorious era of the ancient Middle East' prior
to the Muslim conquest.[19]

Palestinians and Jews – the 'Iron Wall' and the Inevitable Conflict

In the summer of 1921, while still a member of the Zionist General
Council, Jabotinsky for the first time used the expression 'the Iron
Wall', which subsequently would form the central motif of his
attitude towards the Arab question. During a discussion in the
Zionist Executive on 12 July 1921 Jabotinsky presented a dis-
passionate and realistic analysis of the dilemma facing Zionism in
Eretz Israel. The Arabs, he stated, are unable to accept the idea that

in course of time, say during the next 20 years, the Jews might constitute a majority in Eretz Israel, and it would be unrealistic to expect that they would take such a situation lying down. 'If we were Arabs, we would not accept it either. The Arabs are as good Zionists as we are. The entire country is full of Arab memories.' As a result, he argued, the Arabs will not approve of Zionism, nor can Zionism expect to buy their approval, in any manner, shape or form. 'History has decreed that the realization of Zionism will be accompanied by fierce Arab opposition, and I see no prospect of any political compromise.' This led Jabotinsky to the unequivocal conclusion that the Zionist effort could only be brought to fruition behind 'an iron wall', to be built by the Zionists in cooperation with Britain. By 'iron wall' Jabotinsky meant the imposition – either by a show of force or, if necessary, by actual physical force – of a series of political conditions that would prevent the Arabs from interfering with the Zionist enterprise. The realization of the national goal of Zionism could not be made dependent upon Arab consent, and Zionist policy should leave no doubt whatsoever in the Arab mind that in Eretz Israel the Jews, and only the Jews, would be sovereign, and that they themselves were destined to live there as a national minority.[20]

It is clear that such a 'cruelly realistic' attitude had very little chance of being accepted as the declared policy line. Even though quite a few Zionist leaders believed that Jabotinsky had indeed presented a realistic analysis of the situation, it was virtually impossible for them to state openly that this was indeed the official Zionist forecast. Some of them opposed Jabotinsky's exposition on fundamental grounds, particularly because they believed that it was by no means axiomatic that Zionism could only be realized through force of arms. Others accepted the rationality of the analysis as such, but were of the opinion that Jabotinsky's argumentation was useless as an instrument in the political struggle, as there was not the slightest chance that Great Britain would ever use force to further the Zionist aims, or agree to suppress Arab opposition on its behalf. They maintained that anyone demanding British military and political assistance for the purpose of furthering maximalist Zionist aspirations – particularly when these were announced in advance – would merely provoke Great Britain into cancelling its support of Zionism altogether. The arguments between Jabotinsky and these leaders (which differed from the more fundamental discussion on the desirable and actual connection between Zionism and the use of force, and the very morality of Zionism once it resorted to force in order to fulfil its goals) dealt with political strategy rather than with long-term goals, however desirable.

Thus, Jabotinsky believed that the resistance of the Palestinian Arabs to Zionism was authentic, and a natural and logical consequence of 'objective' circumstances. Herewith he confronted the Zionist policy-makers with a dilemma, namely the question whether it would be at all possible to conduct a Zionist policy based on the recognition of this kind of situation, and whether there would be any chance of resolving this dilemma — in other words, to continue the Zionist effort on the clear understanding that its implementation would be accompanied by continual violent (and in Arab eyes legitimate) resistance.

Even though Jabotinsky did not have too high an opinion of the cultural level of the Palestinian Arabs, he did not belittle their profound opposition to Zionism. On the contrary, he accentuated and underlined the strength of the resistance and its natural, 'deterministic' character. In his two famous articles on the subject, 'The Iron Wall' and 'The Ethics of the Iron Wall', written in 1923,[21] Jabotinsky formulated what would become the basic assumptions of Revisionism on this question. In these articles he stated unequivocally that the Arabs of Palestine were a distinct nationality, and that they possessed an inborn national feeling and consciousness, and were not merely an inseparable part of another national entity. Neither did they lack a national identity or a consciousness of historical continuity, unity or destiny. Their national consciousness was not that of some local rabble: it was local patriotism, based on a local feeling ('nativism'). It might be primitive, but it was nevertheless strong and full of authentic emotions. This patriotism was gathering all its strength in order to prevent Palestine from being turned into Eretz Israel. It was precisely the existence of an Arab nationality in Palestine that made an 'Iron Wall' policy and morality necessary. Thus he wrote: 'Even if it were possible — which I doubt — to convince the Arabs of Baghdad and Mecca that for them Palestine is only a small and unimportant piece of land, for the Arabs of Palestine it would still be not some far-away district, but their homeland, the centre and the backbone of their independent national existence.'

When formulating his 'Ten-Year Plan' in 1938, he wrote:

An end must be put to a widely accepted, but definitely mistaken view. Many believe that in the eyes of the Arabs Transjordan is more hallowed than Western Palestine . . . .

This is a fallacy. The holy places of Islam are found only in Western Palestine, in Jerusalem and Hebron. Transjordan has no recognized position in the Islamic tradition. In the history of the Arab people, Amman or As-Salt cannot be likened to Jaffa or Acre . . . . If an Arab nationalist had to choose either of the two sides of the Jordan, on the assumption that one of them had to pass into Jewish hands, there is no doubt that he would give up Transjordan.[22]

Any native people, he added, however primitive or cultured, looks upon its country as its national home and strives to reside and remain there as the undisputed and eternal owner. Such is, and had always been, the position in all colonial countries.

As noted earlier, the riots of 1929 had set off a powerful and influential stream of thought within Revisionism, resulting in the concept of the 'Iron Wall'. For Jabotinsky, however, this idea was in so far insufficient that he did not want it to be erected under the shield of a British protectorate, but by an independent Jewish effort. The sources of the idea had of course existed before this, but the year 1929 provided the impetus for its emergence and crystallization. The Arabs of Palestine came to be viewed as people who impaired the sense of mastery and Jewish ownership of the land, and who violated its spiritual and territorial integrity. Thus, for instance, wrote Uri Zvi Greenberg in his poem 'Vision of One of the Legions' (1928):

> And in the byways of Zion lives the Canaanite, with his many
>   wives, his children and his camels.
> He extracts bread from my soil,
> Squeezes honey from my trees . . .
> Cuts down every ancient wood
> And gives it to his goat to munch . . .
> who will devour every good parcel,
> And lay waste all the land.

According to this view, the Palestinian Arabs were aliens and strangers in Eretz Israel. They resided here as a result of an Islamic conquest which had taken place many centuries ago, and their very presence desecrated the soil as well as the land, that was neither their homeland, nor a holy land to them.

As another example in the same vein the Lehi newspaper *Mivrak* ('The Telegram') wrote in 1948, in order to deny even the 'native' character of the Arabs of *Eretz Israel*:

For hundreds of years they [the Arabs] have sat in the villages of the Gilboa. Have these strangers produced bread by the sweat of their brow? Somebody created this legend . . . . They sat there, idling in their smoking huts . . . telling stories about the miracles of creation, about the prophet, the caliph and – in an entirely different vein – robbers and bandits. Sometimes they would follow a broken-down and fragile plough dragged by a pair of unwilling oxen, [a plough] that was unable to penetrate the soil . . . . This soil, soaked with the blood of heroes, the blood of Saul and Jonathan, was being eroded by the rainstorms . . . . The village headman would relate the legend of the Ka'aba, the legends of the caliphs and the Thousand and one Nights . . . repeating for the hundredth or thousandth time the names of the holy cities of Allah and of Islam: Mecca, Medina, Aden . . . . It was not of Jerusalem that they dreamt, nor of Beth-El and not of the Gilboa mountains in which they lived as total strangers.[23]

This attitude stood in sharp and outspoken contrast to both Jabotinsky's views and the official Revisionist programme, which spoke of the Arabs of Eretz Israel as a national entity deeply rooted in Palestine, and which was therefore fully eligible to recognition as a national minority. Technically this moderate outlook was at variance with the growing radicalist trend in Revisionism as embodied in Lehi (a trend that would receive renewed impetus during the 1970s under the influence of the nationalist religious Right), which regarded the Arabs as a foreign element, without any natural connections with the country, and therefore undeserving of either national rights or a national status of their own.

This evolving dichotomy in the image of the Palestinian Arabs was evident in yet another central aspect: on the one hand they were described as a weak and backward, amorphous entity, totally lacking in national awareness; as people accustomed to domination, who – therefore – might be cowed by a simple show of determination and strength. At the same time, however, they were depicted as a powerful, violent and menacing group. On the one hand they were described as people devoid of national feelings or a desire for freedom, who were therefore easy to suppress, but on the other they were considered a native population whose resistance was strong enough to endanger the very existence of the *yishuv*. The fact that their violence could prevent the Jews from realizing their national and Zionist aims explained why Zionism was engaged in a struggle of life and death with them. In other words: the Arabs were at one and the same time human dust and warlike savages. These were the two faces of the Palestinian Arab in the view of the Zionist Right.

The Constitutional Political Solution

The various points of departure led to different suggestions for a solution. Jabotinsky made it clear that the situation in Eretz Israel was fraught with tragedy, also from the Arab point of view, so that an effort should be made to ease at least the Arab tragedy. This was indeed feasible, since Zionism was ready 'to grant the Arab minority in Eretz Israel every possible right that the Jews claimed for themselves, but had never achieved in other countries'. Underlying this attitude were two kinds of arguments and factors. The first, of a fundamental ideological nature, related to the liberal tradition and the actual – but even so mainly theoretical – examples of the minority rights granted in the multi-national Central and Eastern European states. The second kind were of a political nature. In the first place it was impossible to expect the British to support Zionism without an undertaking that Zionism, on its part, would ensure the rights of the Arab minority, as in fact laid down in the Balfour Declaration and the Mandate charter. In the second place it was felt that declarations denying the national or civil rights of the Arabs might induce anti-Semitic policies in Central and Eastern Europe, and reinforce existing trends aimed at cancelling all international agreements for the protection of Jewish minorities negotiated under the peace agreements following the Great War.

Since Jabotinsky regarded the Arabs of Eretz Israel as an embryonic national society, he had no ideological difficulty in formulating a solution which recognized the Palestinian Arabs' right to national autonomy and equal civil rights. Both his conception and phrasing of the Arab minority rights were modelled on the 1906 Helsingfors (Helsinki) Programme, the Russian Zionist plan for Jewish national autonomy formulated after the revolution of 1905, and the ideas of Central and Eastern European nationalist theoreticians such as Karl Renner-Springer, George Jellinek and others.[24]

Before turning to the official Revisionist platform, some introductory comments are in order. In the first place the platform reflects a programme for a political constitution, intended to be the most explicit and accurate definition of the relationship between the majority and the minority; in this respect it has a clearly constitutional character. At the same time, however, it is utopian in that it describes a static and idealistic situation. The second aspect of this incipient constitution is that it rests on the assumption of an assured Jewish majority in Eretz Israel, as well as Jewish sovereignty over the country – meaning that the plan could be implemented only following a transitional period of violent struggles, which in the optimistic view of Jabotinsky might last till the end of the 1940s. In the third place the plan was conditional upon Arab consent, since autonomy would be impossible to implement without the participation of the receiving party. But already in 1923, in his earlier mentioned article 'The Iron Wall', Jabotinsky foresaw that 'it is impossible to dream of a voluntary agreement between us and the Arabs of Palestine, not now and not in the foreseeable future. And that is because no people is willing to relinquish its national home.'

As a result, while resisting any compromise on the territorial aims of Zionism, Jabotinsky proposed a utopian vision of an Arab minority residing within a Jewish national majority. This vision was closest to the liberal political tradition in which he himself had been raised, apart from which it could be used to break down the resistance of the ruling circles in London – for he knew full well that even the most liberal and democratic platform would be unable to buy Arab consent. In practical terms he suggested that, once all the preconditions had been fulfilled and the Arabs had yielded to reality – and not until then – the Jewish state would grant them a broad range of constitutionally guaranteed freedoms. But what was to be done until the Arabs agreed, or if they rejected these conditions? To this Jabotinsky had only one answer: I anticipate a lengthy, violent and bloody struggle (the nature, duration or implications of which he failed to consider), and Zionism will have to face up to it, and prepare itself mentally and physically.

At the same time we should not take the above-described constitutional idea too seriously, since it looks as if in the final analysis it was conceived for tactical and propaganda purposes. It appears that Jabotinsky did not intend to recognize the Arabs as an autonomous national minority living within their own autonomous framework, but as citizens with equal civic rights and a degree of 'personal autonomy'. The same would apply for all other nationalities and groups (in this respect he wrote that even 300 Armenians would qualify as a 'nation'). His basic position is best reflected in an article he wrote in January 1926 in *Razsvet*, in which he stated that the future Jewish state would have five million Jews and one million Arabs. The latter would be granted autonomy, to be partially financed by themselves. But even a state based on a bi-national constitution would in effect be a Jewish national state:

for the entire spirit of the constitution directing the lives of the citizens, with the exception of the narrow frameworks of schools, religion, family and philanthropy, the entire social regime of the state, the kind of social struggle that is fought within it, all agricultural, industrial and commercial methods – all these, as well as the very rhythm of life, will bear the fundamental imprint of the independent Jewish society.[25]

All this would be a result of the decisive suitability and superiority of Jewish society and Jewish culture compared to those of the Arabs.

The Nature of the Constitutional Plan for a Majority–Minority Society

The Helsingfors Programme called for the granting of the maximum possible autonomy to the national and ethnic minorities residing within the national society of the majority (with specific reference to czarist Russia). Not integration, therefore, but the maintenance of national distinctions in all their aspects and manifestations, and their institutionalization according to law. The Helsingfors Programme defined nationalism not only as a shared historical language and culture, but as a common destiny which found expression in all spheres of life – from the parliament to the street corner. The Helsingfors Programme, in the formulation of which Jabotinsky had played a major role, sought to gain for the Jewish national minority in Russia the right to an autonomous political and cultural expression, anchored in the laws of the state (and following the Great War in international agreements). The application of the Helsingfors Programme to Palestine would mean granting the very same rights to the Arab national minority in that country.

Within the context of this principle the distinction was born between 'nationalism' and 'sovereign nationality'. Self-determination would not have to be interpreted as sovereignty. There are bi-national and multinational states, and the fundamental question is always which nation and which nationality determines a country's national character. Jabotinsky's theoretical political solution had been formulated as early as 1912 in a learned essay entitled 'Self-rule of the National Minority'.[26] In it he made a fundamental distinction between 'nationality' and 'citizenship' – in other words between sovereign national rights and autonomous national rights. The territorial integrity of Palestine was not to be impaired, but within that integrity there was room for wide-ranging 'citizens' rights'.

We see, therefore, that Jabotinsky defined a 'national minority' as a group of citizens of a particular nationality who could not be granted political sovereignty in a specific territory. As a form of collective compensation it received a guarantee for the upholding of its rights in the face of oppressive tendencies. The national minority had a right to regional self-rule in religious and cultural matters, as well as the right to unite on a country-wide basis in associations designed to safeguard its rights in educational and legal matters and in the provision of health services, employment, internal taxation and so forth.

It should also be noted here that what Jabotinsky formulated was a legal constitutional construct. In so doing he disregarded socio-economic differences and patterns of contact. He believed that the autonomous national minority would seek to consolidate itself in legal, social, financial and economic terms. He regarded the majority and the minority in Eretz Israel as 'closed societies' with hardly a contact between them; one occupied a 'high' and the other a 'low' place, yet they co-existed in harmony *because of* their mutual separation and even complete segregation. 'The existence side by side of a national majority and a national minority does not mean integration. On the contrary, segregation is necessary, at least during the long transition period, in order to keep Arab labour out of the Jewish economy, to prevent Arabs from benefiting from imported Jewish capital, etcetera.' At the same time he understood that there was no way of keeping the *yishuv* from enriching the Arabs and fostering their development. 'From us they learn how to build modern industries, and they will easily acquire the capital from our people, for their labour is cheap. Our example will raise their national consciousness, their youth will want to imitate our *halutzim* (pioneers), our legionaries, and Trumpeldor [as the proto-type Arab national hero].'[27]

There existed, therefore, the danger that the Arabs would learn and imitate the Jews, and that some Arabs would undergo a process of acculturization within the Hebrew society, but this process would only be superficial. There was no reason to fear integration or intermingling of Jews and Arabs, because of the deep cultural gap between the two sides. Furthermore, not separateness and segregation were the basic cause of conflicts; on the contrary, conflicts were mainly a result of integration and living together.

It is evident that Jabotinsky's plan ignored some of the main arguments of his own diagnosis of the Jewish national minority situation in Poland between the two world wars. From our earlier discussion the reader may remember his claim that a large minority living in the midst of a national majority caused competition for the available sources of income and employment (as well as other frictions), compared to which cultural differences were of no importance. The clashes between the majority and the minority became an existential inevitability, so that the only realistic solution was to separate the (Jewish) minority from the Polish majority (through emigration). It would seem that once Jabotinsky reached this conclusion around the middle of the 1930s, and the call for large-scale Jewish emigration had become louder and more topical than the struggle for civil and national rights for Polish Jewry, he also became far more amenable to regarding the existing plan calling for the forced transfer of the Palestinian Arabs to the neighbouring Arab states as a concept that could be discussed openly and even publicly supported.

On the basis of this cool and dispassionate analysis of the situation Jabotinsky between 1938 and 1940 formulated a most explicit formal platform on the Arab question within the framework of the Revisionist 'Ten-Year Plan'. This plan provided for the granting of complete equality of rights to the Arabs of Eretz Israel – to the point of allowing them to hold state-owned lands. There is no reason, Jabotinsky wrote, why a national or ethnic minority should necessarily be a suppressed minority. There are sufficient historical examples of countries that have granted equal rights to their minorities (Canada, Russia, Czechoslovakia, Finland, etc.). Minority status is nothing to be happy about, but neither is it a tragedy. Zionism will see to it that the status of the Arabs will be the best that a national minority can possibly achieve through a detailed bill of rights, providing for civil equality and guaranteed Arab representation in the legislative and executive organs. Every cabinet with a Jewish prime minister will have an Arab deputy-prime minister, and vice versa! The Arab public will elect parliamentary representatives according to their proportion in the total population, and it will serve in the army. The state will delegate responsibility for all religious, educational and social services to self-elected authorities. These authorities will be elected by the Arabs themselves, and they will be empowered to raise taxes.[28] Time and again Jabotinsky stressed that this plan depicted an optimal situation, and that its implementation was dependent upon the prevailing conditions. It was impossible to compare the situation of the Arab minority in Eretz Israel with that of the Jews in Europe, since the Jews had no other national state, whereas the Arabs had a number of Arab homelands to choose from. Jabotinsky therefore expressed in moderate terms what those who opposed his views – who in effect represented the majority opinion among the Revisionists and the Zionist-Palestinian Right – were saying aloud in much more forthright and vigorous language.

The 'Transfer Plan'

The radical Right was of the opinion that no parallel could be drawn between the status of the Jewish minority in, for instance, Poland, and that of the Arabs in Eretz Israel, and *not* only because the 'Arab nation' possessed a number of other independent states. A far more important argument, as some Revisionist writings emphasized, was that the Jews of Poland had elected to be content with a minority status. They did not demand sovereignty, nor did they have any territorial aspirations. In this respect they differed from the other European national and ethnic minorities (such as the Ukrainians), who objected to forming a part of the Polish state. Neither were the Palestinian Arabs content with a minority status, regardless of any constitutional guarantees, demanding full independence instead. For these reasons it was impossible to apply the Eastern European Jewish autonomous idea to the situation in Eretz Israel. Quite apart from this, from an ideological point of view, any definition, however moderate, of the Arabs of Eretz Israel as a national minority, implied an admission of the Arab claim that Palestinian Arabs constituted a nation, and this would endanger Zionism and its claim to ownership of Eretz Israel. After all, if indeed they were a nation, they would have every right to fight for the realization of their national and political aspirations. Thus, in the same way as the Zionist solution was the integral transfer of Diaspora Jewry to Eretz Israel, the solution to the Arab problem was the evacuation of the Palestinian Arabs beyond its borders.

In the face of the determined and violent Arab resistance, and viewed against the background of the profound changes in the situation of European Jewry, Jabotinsky too became more sympathetic to the idea of a population 'transfer'. The fact that in London too, particularly from the side of the Labour party, enthusiastic voices had been raised in favour of the idea (mainly within the framework of the Partition Plan), helped Jabotinsky and his party. He devoted several articles to the lessons of the population exchange between Greece and Turkey in 1923, one moment presenting it as a brutal imposition, and the other as a positive solution that had been of considerable benefit to Greece. His records of his discussions with Israel Zangwill also reflect his uncertainty. Zangwill's proposals for a 'redistribution of races' in order to reorganize the world, and his example of the *trek* of the South African Boers, also came up in these talks.[29] True to his basic view, Jabotinsky continued to insist that it would be possible to realize the Jewish majority in Eretz Israel without harming or dispossessing the Arabs, since the historical Eretz Israel was large enough to accommodate one and a half million Arabs and five million Central and Eastern European Jews. Modern colonization methods would enable the creation of a plentiful existence for the two populations, and so there was no objective reason for the Arabs to leave Eretz Israel, unless forced to emigrate against their own will. Forced emigration, he wrote, 'is an immoral solution, quite apart from the serious doubts as to its practicability. We will not, of course, object to voluntary emigration, and should even facilitate it by extending financial and other assistance.' Jabotinsky never suggested, however, that Arab emigration from Eretz Israel should in any way be encouraged or stimulated, let alone enforced.

For this reason his successors found themselves faced with two theoretical options: the constitutional liberal option of an organized Arab minority within a sovereign Jewish state, and the transfer of these Arabs outside its borders.

The IZL and the Arab Problem

IZL publications from the years 1944–48 do not appear to have paid much attention to the Arab problem. The attitude towards the Arabs was influenced by the consensus that the Jews were dealing with a determined and violent enemy, but at the same time the IZL did not rate the military potential of the Palestinian Arabs sufficiently high for them to constitute a threat to the *yishuv*. This explains their belief that they could demand the immediate withdrawal of the British, since the *yishuv* would easily be strong enough to subdue the Palestinian Arabs and secure Jewish sovereignty over the whole country. This, too, is why they were convinced that mere deterrent action would suffice to make the Arabs take a passive stance during the 'revolt' and the ensuing hostilities between British and Jews. In return, the IZL promised the local Arabs full equality of rights in the sovereign Jewish state, and an equal share in its economic prosperity. In a manifesto addressed to 'Our Arab Neighbours', published in the daily *Herut* of 15 September 1944, the IZL tried to prove that it was fighting only the British, and not the Arabs, and that it was the British who were trying, for their own purposes, to sow discord between Arab and Jew by inciting them to make war on each other.

> This war is not directed against you. We do not regard you as our enemies.
>
> We like to see you as good neighbours. We did not come here to exterminate you, or drive you from the land on which you live. In Eretz Israel there is also place for you, and also for your sons and your grandsons, as well as for the millions of Jews who have no place to live except this country.
>
> The Jewish government will grant you full and equal rights. The Arab language and the Hebrew language will together be the official languages of the country. There will be no discrimination between Arab and Jew in the allocation of governmental or public offices. The holy places of Islam will be under the supervision of your own representatives.

In addition the Arab population was promised that the Jewish government would take measures to ensure their social, economic and cultural development.

The first platform of the *Herut* movement (in the paragraph on 'Internal Policies') stated that 'the national and religious minorities will enjoy full and equal rights in all spheres of life', as well as that 'proper representation should be granted to all minorities in the agencies of the state, on the basis of unconditional loyalty to the state', and that the state's institutions should ensure the minorities' ability to educate their children in their mother tongue, and in the spirit of their own cultural and religious traditions.[30]

Here the promises were very general, nor were the detailed suggestions in Jabotinsky's plan reiterated – apart from the fact that the *Herut* programme contains not even a hint about national autonomy (talking merely of 'cultural autonomy'). On the contrary, the utopian vision is one of integration of the Arab population within the Jewish state ('on the basis of unconditional loyalty') – in other words to turn them into 'Israeli Arabs' within the Jewish national state.

Lehi and the Arab Problem

Whereas the IZL proclamation adhered to the line of Jabotinsky, although in a significantly watered-down form, Lehi, true to its usual form, could only be satisfied with something new, and as a result found itself torn between ideological innovation and ideological opportunism. On one point, however, there is no doubt: Lehi and the IZL were in agreement that the Palestinian Arabs should accept to live in a sovereign national Jewish state extending within the boundaries of the historical Eretz Israel. Lehi publications from between 1940 and 1948 reveal different attitudes to the Palestinian Arabs, ranging all the way from negative and dismissive to warmly sympathetic, but both extremes were a direct outcome of the *a priori* assumption that these Arabs would in the end resign themselves to the establishment of a Jewish state that would guarantee their civil rights and ensure their progress. However, since Lehi did not believe in the existence of an authentic Palestinian nationalism, Lehi was convinced that a declaration assuring Arabs civil rights would assist them in their war against Britain. More than this, they believed that by presenting themselves as the spearhead of those who would rid the entire Middle East of British Imperialism, Lehi would gain the support of the Soviet Union and of the neighbouring independent Arab states.

In light of the above, it is only natural that the debate on Jabotinsky's dilemma was reopened within the ranks of the radical nationalist messianic Right – of which Lehi was the prime exponent. Since it was considered out of the question that the Palestinian Arabs would submit to Jewish sovereignty, and since this in turn would produce a long-drawn-out and bloody conflict, the only remaining alternative was a population transfer. Jabotinsky's biggest mistake, in the eyes of the radicals, was his belief that a large Arab minority with its own national aspirations would accept co-existence within a Jewish state. They saw this failure as a result of his – at least theoretical – liberal tradition, which bound him to a naive and dangerous utopia, and prevented him from drawing the correct conclusions. For this reason Lehi proposed the compulsory evacuation of the *entire* Arab population of Eretz Israel, in order to remove in one fell swoop the main obstacle to peace between the Jewish state and the Arab states from the Middle Eastern scene. Even so the 'transfer' idea was not mentioned in the platform of the *Hazit ha-Lohamim* (the 'Fighters' Front') of March 1949, and the only points on which the majority and the minority were united were their vigorous opposition to the partition of Eretz Israel, and on 'the continuation of the war as the only way to liberate the entire homeland and strike at the hostile regimes' (meaning the neighbouring Arab states). Their election platform, on the other hand, apart from the paragraph talking about 'ensuring full and equal rights for all the citizens of the country, regardless of their religious or national affiliation', also contained a declaration (para.6) to the effect that

> Lehi considers an exchange of the Arab population and the Jews of Arab countries as the best solution for the troubled relationship between the Jewish people and the Arabs.   This solution will remove the danger of a bloody conflict, it will help to establish peace between the countries in the region, and rob Imperialism of its weapon of kindling national and racial hatred.[31]

At this point we should note that the most radical Revisionist platform also contained a reference to the transfer of the Palestinian Arabs from 'all areas of the historical Eretz Israel', preferably to Mesopotamia (Iraq). From 1937 onwards the geographical perspective changed, and instead we see references to an evacuation from Western Eretz Israel, or from the 'areas of the Jewish state situated within the boundaries of the Partition Plan'. The fact that the Jewish state was forced to accept a considerably truncated area compared to that of the original National Home, greatly facilitated the acceptance of a plan for the evacuation of the Palestinian Arabs from the remaining Jewish area, thus avoiding the difficulties connected with the existence of sizeable hostile population concentrations within the narrow borders of the as yet thinly-populated Jewish state (in 1948 the Jewish population amounted to no more than 600,000). After 1967, when the idea of a population transfer was again broached – and this time not only by the radical fringe – it was made to include all the Arabs residing within the boundaries of the historical Eretz Israel, in other words the 'West Bank' Palestinians as well as the Arab citizens of the State of Israel.

The Perspective of Peace and War

Time and again Jabotinsky and his movement stressed that 'peace will prevail in Eretz Israel only when the Jews constitute the majority, and when the Arabs are convinced that this solution is necessary and inescapable'. Until such time, Zionism must act by 'totally abandoning any attempts to come to an agreement in the present.' The slightest sign of readiness to yield is the axe at the root of Zionism. To yield a part of Eretz Israel is ideologically and practically tantamount to yielding the whole of Eretz Israel. For this reason it is the task of Zionism to instil into the hearts of all Jews the unswerving conviction that Zionism has full rights to Eretz Israel – an unconditional religious and historic right, anchored in universal justice and international morality. In view of our expectation of an extended national conflict, this belief should be internalized and turned into an axiomatic conviction ingrained in the very spirit of the nation.

The radical Right drew much further-reaching conclusions, under the motto that 'war is war', and that what it was dealing with was literally a struggle of life and death. Arab resistance had to be confronted by a fighting Jewish nation, intent on achieving mastery of Eretz Israel, but not only through its settlements and the achievement of political sovereignty, but in terms of a spiritual conquest. This struggle was a logical and inevitable outcome of the prevailing relationship between the Israeli people and the Arabs of Eretz Israel, and it concerned a meta-historical struggle that could only be decided by force of arms and bloodshed.

Thus, Uri Zvi Greenberg in his *Book of Indictment and Belief* (1937) wrote:

> And I say: A land is taken by blood,
> Only what is taken with blood weds the people in a holy bond of blood.
> . . .
> Blood will decide who rules here.

Whereas Uriel Halperin (Yonatan Ratosh) wrote in the same year:

> O visionary, in heaven is God, the all-powerful,
> On earth it is fire against fire.
> The heavens are a heaven for all.
> . . .
> But the earth belongs to the conqueror.[32]

This is the moral and historic imperative of the fighting Jewish nation in the era of its struggle for liberation and national redemption.

Similarly, in a long series of articles expressing the nationalist-messianic ethos, which survived into the 1950s in such periodicals as

Sulam, Israel Scheib (Eldad) repeated the main points of the messianic historiosophy that regarded the Arabs as a foreign body – as 'Canaanites', whom Jewish morality obliges us to overcome by force of arms and expel with weapons in hand, 'like the Children of Israel campaigned in the days of Yehoshua Bin-Nun', while the remainder would not be considered a national minority but – provided they accept Jewish sovereignty – as 'proselytes', citizens with specific and very limited rights – on sufferance, in other words. 'Proselytes' were individuals who followed the Jewish people, but did not regard themselves as owners or masters of the land, although in certain areas they were deserving of civil rights. The Arabs, on the other hand, were 'Canaanites' rather than proselytes, because they considered themselves masters of the land, and the struggle against them was therefore an existential struggle. In a struggle such as this any moral considerations had to give way to the Biblical command of Exodus 23: 31–33: 'I will hand over to you the people who live in the land and you will drive them out before you. Do not make a covenant with them or with their gods. Do not let them live in your land, or they will cause you to sin against me . . . .'[33]

The Three Options and the Dialectical Development

The contradictions and tensions between the existence of a political programme and a *Weltanschauung* which produced a practical radical alternative of its own, coupled with certain utopian assumptions about the possible solution of what everybody knew would be a long-drawn-out conflict, resulted within the Zionist Right in three options:

1. The official and dominant option, extending the declared policy line of Jabotinsky, albeit in a much watered-down form. This option regarded the Palestinian Arabs as an ethnic, religious and cultural minority entitled to live as equal and fully-franchised citizens of the Jewish state; as an integral, but completely separate part of Israeli society, but on condition that none of the rights granted to these 'Israeli Arabs' would prejudice the Jewish national character of the state. In 1977 Menachem Begin would change Jabotinsky's concept of national autonomy considerably by suggesting that it should apply only to the areas of Western Eretz Israel which prior to 1967 had not formed a part of the Jewish state. Apart from this the *Herut* movement during the 1950s and 1960s spearheaded the opposition to military govern-

ment over the Arab citizens of the State of Israel, ostensibly because they considered such a military regime a form of oppression and discrimination, but in effect because they considered that it would play into the hands of Mapai.

2. The radical option, which lost force after 1947, only to re-emerge in the political arena in full strength after 1967, saw the conflict in terms of a no-holds-barred struggle. For this reason the Arabs should not be granted civil rights, and the preferred solution was a government-initiated population 'transfer'. During the 1948–49 War of Independence a population transfer had in fact taken place within the new Jewish state, and as regards these events: here was a model that could be adopted without any qualms or moral scruples whatsoever. Even though for various reasons only the most extreme groups included a population transfer in their official platforms, the idea as such achieved normative status and legitimacy as a 'by all means sensible', and possibly even 'necessary' possibility.

3. During the late 1950s a small group, consisting principally of former Lehi members, concluded that no compromise was possible between recognition of the Israeli Arabs as a national minority, and the desire to implement Jewish sovereignty over the Arab minority in every part of Eretz Israel. They decided therefore that the Partition Plan should be adopted, but this time on the basis of the recognition that the Arab-Palestinian people (outside the Israeli borders of 1947–67) are a separate national entity, eligible for political sovereignty over a territory that was also its geographical homeland. This was the 'Palestinian option'.

The Re-Emergence of the Mandatory Problems after 1967

Between 1948 and 1967 the Arab problem became an internal political issue, focused on the Israeli Arabs, whereas the issue of the Palestinian Arabs outside the state's boundaries was relegated to the sidelines and virtually forgotten. When after 1967 the Palestinian question arose once again as the most crucial issue on the Israeli national agenda, the Right found itself confronted with a radically different situation from that which it had faced during the years 1925–1947; the instruments (and backing) to facilitate the realization of the programmes it had not been able to implement during 1948 and 1949, were likewise completely different from those it had at its disposal during the Mandate. It is no wonder, therefore, that the Right did not consider judging the period from 1967 onwards in terms of redemption and national, or even messianic, fulfilment – or at least in terms of a long-awaited and non-recurring historic situation – to achieve what it regarded as the main aim of Zionism, and the foremost condition for its realization.

CHAPTER NINE

The Social Philosophy, Ideology and Programme

The Necessity of a Socio-Economic Plan

Previously we reviewed the Revisionist programme for a Colonization Regime in Eretz Israel, as a necessary precondition for the establishment of the sovereign Jewish state. This programme which, despite its ideological preferences, was mainly of a pragmatic and purposive nature, formed the central plank of the Revisionist programme. In theory it offered a practical programme for the implementation of a large-scale centralized Jewish colonization effort. However, in the Revisionist ideology and *Weltanschauung* the Colonization Regime merely played a subordinate role. It was too pragmatic and empirical, in addition to which it premised the building of the foundations of the Jewish state on massive mandatory – i.e. British – involvement, rather than regarding this scheme as an independent expression of the Jewish national will. It goes without saying that at least during the 1920s even those espousing radical views found it impossible to ignore the need for direct and indirect British assistance in the Jewish colonization of the country, but at the same time they could not possibly be expected to turn this need into a precondition, let alone an essential requirement.

As a result of the above, the Colonization Regime was relegated to the margins of the historical consciousness of the Right, in marked contrast to the pivotal importance Jabotinsky and the Executive of the Revisionist movement had attached to it throughout the 1920s and 1930s. This meant that Revisionism had to come up with a plan of its own, rooted in its particular interpretation of the national will and its understanding of the national possibilities and resources. In other words, Revisionism needed more than only a settlement plan. Settlement inevitably meant building an economy and a society, and this automatically necessitated a comprehensive socio-economic programme.

The question is, therefore, what were the principles that formed the foundation of this social programme, and what were its origins.

The social ideology of Revisionism distinguished itself by an outspoken negativist and critical orientation, rather than by its positive aspects. When Revisionism appeared on the political scene it believed itself to be confronted with a well-established socio-political system which held both politics and the economy of Eretz Israel in a stranglehold. It was not long before the Revisionists associated the failure of Zionism with the hegemony of the Left, and shifted the full weight of their opposition against the Left (a subject that will be dealt with in Chapter 11), turning it into the corner-stone of their world-view, while largely ignoring the reality of the situation in Eretz Israel and the immanent weakness of Zionism as a whole.

On the face of it, Revisionism adopted a neutral stand in terms of its social ideology. Even so there were some who already during the 1930s asserted that the movement lacked a binding social ideology, and that it was a fatal mistake on its part to get itself involved in a social struggle within the *yishuv*.[1] Others, foremost among them Jabotinsky himself, sometimes suggested that the social and economic views of Revisionism were valid only 'while a Jewish majority was being built' and that, once a sovereign state had been established, new guidelines would have to be devised. According to this view, what was correct and valid during the constructive period would not necessarily apply to a society living in a sovereign state. Thus, what would be permissible or proscribed in the area of social relations would also be different. However, this differentiation between two different periods in the realization of Zionism – even assuming that it was genuine and not intended for purposes of propaganda or image-building only – was merely theoretical. The same applied to the claim of neutrality. Revisionism was a socio-political movement which represented a variety of interests and, as such, could not avoid presenting a social platform and stating preferences. Its growing involvement in the socio-economic scene was therefore due not to opportunism or a search for allies and supporters, but to an intrinsic ideological necessity directly connected with the character of a political mass-movement.

Soon after its initial declaration of 'neutrality' in social and economic affairs, the Revisionist party proceeded to boast a fully-fledged and comprehensive social and national ideology. Here, too, Jabotinsky was presented as an original thinker, who had formulated an entire social theory anchored in Jewish sources, which could serve as a model for the Jewish society in Eretz Israel. Thus it would seem appropriate, in the same way as was done in the discussion of the national and political philosophy of Revisionism, to provide an analysis and summary of the main points of Jabotinsky's social philosophy, and the extent to which it fitted the socio-economic reality of the country, as well as an examination of the corellation between his social philosophy and the *Weltanschauung* and ideology of his movement.

Étatism and Liberalism

Following the establishment of the State, the Right shifted into a new, more populist key, representing itself as the spokesman of the underprivileged strata of Israeli society, including the working class. Such a tendency was totally lacking during the period under discussion. During this time the socio-economic views of the Revisionists hinged on two, in effect opposing, foundations, namely an étatist approach and a liberal approach. The contradiction lies, of course, in the fact that Liberalism is by its very nature opposed to large-scale state intervention in social and economic life. However, the Liberalism of Jabotinsky and, in particular, his followers, was from the outset of a restricted kind. They believed, for instance, that the Zionist Organization should have a monopoly on the management of natural resources, the railways, and so forth, since the national interest required centralized intervention and supervision. At the same time they continued to stress the supremacy of private enterprise and the private sector. The contradiction between state-directed intervention and Liberalism was solved by the expedient of presenting government institutions first and foremost as patrons of the private sector and the middle class. According to Revisionism the middle class was the pivotal segment of the Zionist movement, and the private sector the foremost agent of economic and demographic growth in Eretz Israel, in which capacity it should be granted priority status. This led to the conclusion that the authorities had to assist the middle class in a variety of ways, first of all through a regime of economic protectionism and by supporting the middle class and its interests in class-related conflicts. Before long, however, such a practical and pragmatic evaluation of the contributions of private capital to economic growth no longer sufficed, and the need arose for an ideology capable of legitimizing this attitude. Here, as in other cases, the Revisionist movement found itself caught in a dilemma. On the one hand it claimed that universal class distinctions did not apply to the prevailing conditions in Eretz Israel, but on the other they talked about private capital and the private sector as universal categories, whereas, when weighing the interests of the private sector against those of the working class, the scales were quite clearly tipped in favour of the first.

The Fourth Aliyah as a Turning Point

The year 1924 was the turning point in Jabotinsky's social outlook, during which his earlier preferences became transformed into a more systematically-developed ideological framework more attuned to the political context. Prior to this, until 1924–25, the beginning of the 'Fourth Aliyah', Jabotinsky had believed that Eretz Israel was not yet ready for the absorption of middle-class Eastern European Jews. The turn of the Jewish *Mittelstand*, he wrote, will only come once a broad-based economy has developed; the middle class is cautious and conservative by nature, and not equipped to withstand a period of economic heroics. The country was ready for the absorption of large-scale capitalistic ventures and manual workers only; not for small capital-owners, craftsmen and members of the free professions, who would expect to maintain the same living standards in Eretz Israel as they had enjoyed in the Diaspora. Before we start bringing masses of people (i.e. the Jewish 'middle class') into the country, he wrote with sober pragmatism, we should ensure that they will be able to make a living here. Organized settlement is a complicated affair; 'sometimes we should open the gates, and sometimes they should be closed – and even closing the gates means settlement.'[2] But no proletarian class, however industrious and motivated it might be, nor the private capital of Jewish entrepreneurs, was sufficient in Eretz Israel. The national capital, working hand in hand with the mandatory authorities, is the principal Zionist instrument for settlement and growth. The national capital would have to subsidize both the labour economy and the private sector. Under the prevailing circumstances in Eretz Israel it was impossible to rely upon private investments only, since in Eretz Israel the general laws of political economy do not apply. Jabotinsky mocked those who, at the 12th Zionist Congress, held in Carlsbad in September 1922, presented the 'tremendous discovery that is called private enterprise'. Eretz Israel could not sustain private investment and a private economy without national support.[3] However, even national funds alone were not sufficient:

all three elements – national capital, Jewish private capital and Jewish labour – would have to cooperate within a suitable framework created by the British mandatory government.

During the 1920s Jabotinsky showed no objection in principle to communal settlement, and he even wrote warmly appreciative articles in defence of the pioneers and the working-class settlers. Even so he preferred a private economy, which he considered more in tune with the family-oriented Jewish character, and which as such should be equally eligible for subsidies from the national capital. He evinced considerable appreciation for the working class and its historic task, but considered that in light of the conditions in Eretz Israel, the interests of investors and owners of the means of production should be given preference over those of the paid workers. The establishment of an economy and the creation of sources of employment were basic preconditions for the absorption of workers, and for this reason every effort had to be made to ensure private investments and to encourage their profitability. As regards the national capital (an in effect very limited resource), its job was to support the private sector, both directly, and indirectly by subsidizing wages. Considering wages a dominant factor in the Palestinian economy, and suspecting that the profits of Jewish employers were inadequate to pay the kind of wages able to sustain the required 'cultural' standard of living of the Jewish worker, he proposed that part of the national capital be used to support the desired standard of living by subsidies in kind, in the form of cheap electricity and water, subsidized health services, education, and so forth. Although fully appreciating the contribution of the working class to economic growth, Jabotinsky happened to think in purely theoretical terms of economic output and growth, without concerning himself overmuch with the social and human aspirations of the Labour movement to establish a just and egalitarian society in Eretz Israel. In other words, Jabotinsky was convinced that the Jewish settlement effort in Eretz Israel necessitated comprehensive planning and wide-ranging controls over every aspect of economic activity and social relations, and that at the present 'heroic' stage of the economy the social dimension would have to take a back seat.

The Fourth Aliyah produced a change of perspective within the Labour movement, which considered it a dangerous and threatening occurrence – but for Jabotinsky this new wave of immigration proved to be a godsend and a fresh opportunity.

The Fourth Aliyah was not a contributing factor to the entry of the Revisionist party in the Zionist arena. Although the Revisionist

Organization began to take shape about a year after the beginning of the Fourth Aliyah in 1924, it cannot really be considered a direct reaction to the resumption of large-scale immigration or, for that matter, its socio-demographic composition. The emergence of the Revisionist faction was, as the reader may remember, due more to disappointment with Weizmann's Zionist policies than to disappointment with the settlement policy. Even so the Fourth Aliyah proved to be the wave that carried Revisionism ashore, as well as the lever for its attempt to bring about a political revolution in Zionism. More than this immigration wave as such, however, it was the economic and moral crisis which followed closely in its wake in 1926 that served as its motive force. The fact that the crisis affected all sectors of the *yishuv* and triggered off a sharp and violent social and economic struggle about the limited national budget, automatically turned any critical and deviating viewpoint into virtually unbridgeable political rivalry.

The Fourth Aliyah, a massive immigration wave which continued from 1924 till 1926, originated mainly from Poland. The majority of the immigrants were lower-middle-class Jews, specifically merchants, craftsmen and small property owners with a capital of up to, say, £1,000.[4] To the spokesmen of the Zionist middle class it seemed as if Zionism had finally discovered its true target group – an appreciative audience rooted in the very body and soul of Diaspora Jewry, which was believed to be the solution to its objective hardships. Gone were the days of the ideologically-motivated pioneers; this was an immigration of ordinary people seeking shelter and a new life. Although Jabotinsky had thus far regarded Eretz Israel as unsuitable for the absorption of middle class Jews (except the capitalists among them), after 1925 he could no longer ignore the fact that the social demography of the Zionist movement and immigration to Eretz Israel had undergone a drastic change. Given the fact that the Fourth Aliyah met with strong criticism and hostility on the part of the Labour leadership (as well as such personalities as Chaim Weizmann and Arthur Ruppin, to mention just two) and failed to receive institutional assistance, Jabotinsky was inclined to blame the serious economic crisis in Eretz Israel on two factors: Zionist policy, which had failed to exact the proper settlement conditions from the mandatory authorities, and the prejudice of the Zionist Organization in favour of the collective and labour sectors, coupled with its lack of recognition, and resulting neglect, of the private sector. It was at this juncture that Jabotinsky stated his demand for the diversion of national funds to the support of

investors and small manufacturers, and in so doing turned himself
into an enemy of the Labour movement.

What in his eyes until 1924–1925 had been a marginal discussion
point – an internal Zionist argument about the most practical and
efficient settlement methods – now turned into a fundamental
political argument. Previously Jabotinsky had been of the opinion
that the Zionists carried too little weight in the formulation of
settlement policies in comparison with the mandatory government.
'Even if we had had ideal economic methods', he wrote in 1925, 'the
crisis would have occurred.'[5] But now, after 1925, the issues of
settlement methods and the distribution of the national capital
increasingly became the focus of bitter and stormy conflicts, in
which the Revisionists revealed themselves as the fiercest, most
aggressive and most methodical critics of the Labour movement in
Eretz Israel. The tone of the dispute was set by *Raszviet* and the
World Conferences of *Ha-Zohar* of 1925 and 1927, and to no less an
extent by the Jewish press in Poland and Palestine. In Poland, where
the Jewish *petit bourgeoisie* felt itself discriminated against by the
immigration and absorption policies of the Zionist movement, this
criticism fell on particularly fertile soil.[6] This in turn greatly promoted the crystallization of the bourgeois orientation of *Ha-Zohar*
and its attempts to provide it with an ideological rationale. The next
step was the linkage of this middle-class orientation to the existing
étatist philosophy. Other ideological preferences, which had
previously failed to gain formal expression, became the ideology of
the hour following the Revisionist discovery of a supportive *Hinterland* in Eastern Europe, and a presumed political ally among the
Jewish population of Eretz Israel. A fortuitous and timely circumstance was the introduction of the 'New Economic Policy' in the
Soviet Union.[7] This assisted him in marshalling arguments against
the Left and demonstrating the value and vitality of private enterprise – for if even the Communists were forced to admit the viability
of private initiative, how much more vigorously should Zionism
pursue this method!

The Middle-Class Orientation

It was in 1925 that Jabotinsky discovered an outcast social class,
namely the Jewish middle class in Eastern Europe and Palestine. As
a consequence he could towards the end of 1925 expound the
resulting strategy of Ha-Zohar in the following words:

There is no doubt that the pivotal social class among the Jewish people and in Zionism, both in terms of the quality of its human material and its activist potential, is the Jewish proletariat. The Jewish working class contains the 'best material in the world' – intelligent youth, who are looking for 'true simplicity'. Unfortunately this youth is infected with socialist ideology, due to which it has become bogged down in national and political Zionist minimalism. The Zionist workers are lost to Revisionism, because they are devoted to the socialist ideology. Revisionism will not find supporters among the working class public. *Ahdut ha-Avodah* has 'sold' itself to Weizmann and the Zionist Executive for financial reasons. Revisionism has to try and establish itself among the *Mittelstand*, because this is the only class whose sole ideology is Zionism.[8]

Jabotinsky's arguments were of course rather negative. His orientation towards the 'middle class', the sociological definition of which was unclear to him, was described as an orientation dictated by a 'lack of choice'. The Jewish workers and their parties, although regarded as the most superior elements, refused to accept the political ideas of the Revisionists. The only alternative therefore was to put one's faith in the Jewish middle class – not because the Jewish bourgeoisie lacked economic interests of its own, but because it was not tied to such an integrated world-view as that of the Zionist workers. What looked like a disadvantage, was in effect a big advantage, and it would enable the Jewish middle class to embrace Revisionism.

There were those who pointed out that since some groups of workers in Eretz Israel were in fact joining *Ha-Zohar*, this proved that the possibility of working-class support for Revisionism should not be overlooked. Jabotinsky remained doubtful, however. 'It was true,' he wrote to a friend, 'that certain groups of workers are joining the Revisionist ranks, but the trend is as yet unclear. What course it will take, I have no idea. Maybe you will turn out to be right, in which case I will be only too happy.'[9]

Jabotinsky, however, could not afford to wait and see who would be right. A political movement or party cannot postpone defining its identity until it knows which particular groups and circles are prepared to join it. Already during the founding conference of *Ha-Zohar* in 1925 a number of activists had voiced their demand for a clear class orientation. According to their information from Eretz Israel a social class existed there which was neglected by all but the national funds. The Zionist Organization did not concern itself, so it was said, with small manufacturers who were weighed down by the problems of the mandatory economy. The Zionist Organization only assisted the agricultural settlements, and it had failed to establish a single organ for dealing with the problems of small industrialists. Eretz Israel was in the grip of a 'Histadrut dictatorship', and thus *Ha-Zohar* would have to come to the aid of the deprived class of 'outcasts' comprising the independent employers and small manufacturers, who did not receive any financial assistance and found themselves confronted by a difficult economic situation as well as a militant labour movement. Other rationalizations were not connected with the situation in Eretz Israel, but with demographic and sociological factors in the Diaspora. The number of independent Jewish craftsmen and artisans in Eastern Europe far exceeded that of salaried workers. It was these craftsmen and artisans who suffered economic hardships, and who were being driven out of their professions by the étatist policies of the governments of Poland and the Baltic countries. The problems of the small Jewish entrepreneur also had to be seen against the background of the general position of artisans and small industrialists all over Europe ever since the end of World War I.[10] The socialist intelligentsia described them as a dying class, but statistics proved otherwise. The lower middle class was the backbone of society in general, and Jewish society in particular. This was why, in the view of the above activists, *Ha-Zohar* had to demand a more favourable orientation towards the class of small entrepreneurs on the part of the Zionist Organization. These small entrepreneurs in Eretz Israel had become an outcast class without any political clout, so that it was up to *Ha-Zohar* to defend them against the dictatorship of the *Histadrut*, which backed strikes that were especially hurtful to the smaller manufacturing establishments.

Although *Ha-Zohar*'s 'national' perspective called for the adoption of a neutral stand, it had as early as 1925 been requested to lend outspoken 'class' assistance to one particular professional social segment in Eretz Israel and the Diaspora. This proposal was not only important in principle and on an ideological level; it was also a practical suggestion to take up the cudgels on behalf of the economic interests of a specific social 'class' or sector in the *yishuv*, and to defend these interests against another set of 'class interests', namely those of the *Histadrut*.

Such a demand could mean one thing only, namely the transformation of this neutral stand into concrete political action, and a more active involvement in the everyday problems of Jewish society in Eretz Israel — problems which Jabotinsky himself had pronounced as being of completely secondary importance. This explains why this demand aroused a certain resistance among other *Ha-Zohar* activists, who feared that it could harm the 'integrated' and 'objective' image of the movement, which had to stand above the everyday bickering between the various interest groups, apart from which it could drag the movement into a direct involvement in the frictions between various professional and class interests in Eretz Israel.

Actually this predilection for the private sector and a liberal economy had been central pillars of Jabotinsky's outlook prior to 1924, but as already mentioned, the Fourth Aliyah had transformed these views into an ideologically-based political orientation. Subsidizing private capital and the readiness of the workers to accept low wages was tantamount to maintaining an 'artificial economy'. In the absence of an existing ideological constellation accepting bourgeois social values and political Liberalism, Jabotinsky's shift to a bourgeois orientation would certainly have been more difficult than it proved to be in fact; the prior existence of a favourable disposition towards the bourgeoisie no doubt facilitated the crystallization of *Ha-Zohar*'s middle-class-oriented policy.

The Image of Herzl as a Liberal

In a booklet from the year 1905, entitled *Dr. Herzl*,[11] Jabotinsky discussed the criticism of Herzl and the bourgeois-liberal character of the Jewish society described in the latter's novel *Altneuland*. Jabotinsky agreed with this bourgeois-liberal signature, and volunteered to explain the reasons which he believed had brought Herzl to this conviction. In the first place, Jabotinsky said, *Altneuland* is *not* a utopia; Herzl had not described some futuristic ideal society, but had written a realistic and practical Zionist plan of action. Thus there was no reason to complain about his foreshadowing a bourgeois rather than a socialist society. To ensure that *Altneuland* would not be a utopia, but a practical programme, Herzl had to place his socio-economic platform on a realistic footing.

Jabotinsky was of the opinion that Herzl wanted to describe a social model that could be established within a reasonable period of time. Writing at the end of the nineteenth century — the 'bourgeois century' — he portrayed a society reflecting the most progressive aspects of Western-European liberal radicalism: cooperation, nationalization of land, political equality, religious tolerance, and so forth. He did not portray the kind of utopian society of an Owen or Fourier. These progressive foundations of Liberalism had not yet been realized in European society, but this did not mean that Herzl's description contradicted either Liberalism or the bourgeois way of life. *Altneuland* was not an attempt to depict a society based on new, let alone revolutionary principles, but chiefly an improved and refined society constructed on a number of already existing foundations. Thus Herzl's reasoning was informed by political and historical realism. Besides this, Herzl had aimed his book at a mainly middle-class Jewish public, so that he had to portray a society that they would regard as 'something positive and advantageous'. Should Herzl have proposed a utopian socialist society, his following would have shrunk to a fraction of the Jewish public. *Altneuland* was a propagandistic work aimed at the Jewish bourgeoisie with the intention of winning it for the Zionist idea. Jabotinsky's analysis concluded: 'A people can only be led by leaders who represent the ideology of its predominant class.' Given the distinctive make-up of Jewish society, it was unthinkable to imagine a socialist, anti-bourgeois leadership of the Zionist movement 'that would enjoy even a modicum of stability'.

Middle-Class Politics

In 1925 Jabotinsky adapted his by now 20-year-old interpretation of Herzl's aspirations to the new Zionist reality: the working class was lost to Revisionism, but the Fourth Aliyah had introduced a new era. Revisionism now became the exponent of the plight of the Jewish middle classes which were seeking a way to reach Eretz Israel, and their plight was representative of the plight of all Eastern European Jewry. For this reason he considered that after 1924 the Zionist Organization should no longer be headed by representatives of the working class, but by people capable of a broader and more comprehensive view, people who represented the largest and most important section of the Jewish public, namely the middle classes.

Following his return from Eretz Israel in 1927, Jabotinsky appeared at the 15th Zionist Congress as the principal spokesman of the private sector in that country.[12] He reinforced his arguments by an elucidation on how he had been inspired by Lenin's New Economic Policy. At the Congress Jabotinsky proposed a 'Zionist N.E.P.' as a temporary alternative to the Colonization Regime.[13] A

Zionist N.E.P. was a plan capable of being implemented within the framework of the autonomous activities of the Zionist Organization and the *yishuv*. The crisis following the Fourth Aliyah, said Jabotinsky in his speech at the Congress, was the result of a lack of suitable conditions for the absorption of private Jewish capital in the industrial sector of Eretz Israel. Jabotinsky emphasized that Eretz Israel was unlike normal countries which could attract private venture capital; it lacked natural resources, as well as financial lending institutions and a developed consumer market. Private investors who were looking for a quick and guaranteed return on their money could not be expected in Eretz Israel. Private capital would have to be directed in an organized manner for the purpose of subsidizing socially important and economically viable enterprises. As long as the market remained small, and unstable political conditions persisted, only two factors would succeed in attracting private capital, namely:

1. A policy encouraging the influx of capital and capital owners, this capital to be channelled towards productive investments, while guaranteeing easy conditions for the private sector by a change in the labour relations system aimed at safeguarding the profitability of the enterprises.
2. A change in the policy of allocating national funds, and its direction towards the subsidization of investments in the private sector.

'Let us not belittle the role of the national capital,' Jabotinsky said, 'for there are things that private capital will not do.'[14] Its role was to create the proper financial infrastructure for facilitating the exploitation of private capital. Since Jewish capital owners and private entrepreneurs in Eretz Israel lacked sufficient means to establish industries and workshops by themselves, industry could not develop in the same way it had developed in Western countries during the Industrial Revolution, through a system of *laissez faire*. Under the prevailing conditions in Eretz Israel, *laissez faire* was a direct invitation to taking the money out of the country and leaving the private economy to wither and regress even further. The national funds should provide loan capital to the private sector. The national capital was the symbol of the solidarity of Diaspora Jewry with Eretz Israel. There was no substitute for it, but it should be used to create the proper conditions for 'increasing the productivity of the capital investments of the small and medium-sized capitalist'. Underlying this attitude was yet another assumption, namely that loans and financial assistance from the national funds made through political institutions, gave these institutions tremendous economic power and created a preferential system in the distribution of such benefits. A 'purely economic' system, on the other hand, would avoid the politicization of the national capital.[15]

The Bourgeois Ideology

It was not sufficient to evaluate the role of the middle class in the field of settlement, or to analyse the position of the Jewish middle class from a demographic or sociological point of view. Virtually all sections of *Ha-Zohar* shared a bourgeois value system, in other words an ideology that accentuated the constructive aspects of the middle class in the social, economic and cultural spheres of Jewish and human history. Similarly, almost all circles within *Betar* displayed a positive attitude towards the Jewish bourgeoisie, and corresponding sentiments in favour of the Jewish middle class were expressed at the various congresses of the Revisionist workers from 1927 onwards. An exception was Uri Zvi Greenberg, as we can see not only from his articles in *Kuntres*, but later in his scathing and bitterly pessimistic reaction to the Fourth Aliyah, which according to him resulted in an influx to Eretz Israel of peddlers and assorted masses of people devoid of spiritual values or any kind of creative historical perspective.[16] Basically, however, Greenberg stood alone in this negative opinion which, at that time, was more representative of the radical Left than of Revisionism, which he was to join not long afterwards. As such, Greenberg's reaction can be considered a passing phenomenon.

Who was this 'middle class' the Revisionist movement had in mind, and how did it define 'middle class' from a sociological and ideological point of view? Did it have a well-defined and mutually agreed opinion on what constituted the 'middle class'? The answer is that Revisionism at one and the same time used three alternative definitions of the 'middle class' as a category:

1. A definition according to political values, in which the middle class individual was not a bourgeois in the social sense, but a civic patriot who fought for national freedom and independence;
2. An economic definition, according to which the middle class represented the private sector and private enterprise, and which laid the emphasis on values such as individual responsibility, private initiative and industriousness, based on the possession of

private property and private ownership of the means of production;

3. A socio-economic definition, according to which the middle class consisted of the *petit-bourgeoisie*, in other words small independent persons and professionals who did not receive support from official bodies, who ran the risk of economic impoverishment and who lacked the inner strength to become organized, and as a result needed the encouragement and support of the authorities.

In many ways, however, these categories overlapped and their use in the Revisionist context was confused.

The ideal bourgeois type in the eyes of Jabotinsky was an entrepreneur with a civic conscience; someone who from a national point of view combined in himself qualities such as republican values, economic and industrial initiative – one who was capable of moving the wheels of industry and civilization through his industrious and innovative qualities, his brains and his capital. This was the idealized image of the French and British middle class which during the nineteenth century had spearheaded the Industrial Revolution and the struggle for political emancipation, as well as the struggle for national independence in various other countries. This republican entrepreneur was an individualist with a natural dislike for the anti-liberal and anti-democratic approach of marxist and socialist collectivism. Although not overlooking the negative aspects of the nineteenth century, such as capitalist exploitation and the cruelty and oppression of Imperialism which, in his words, had made this era 'a century of dishonour', Jabotinsky nevertheless regarded it as a quantum leap in civilization, combining material progress with cultural and aesthetic progress. It was the century of genius, a century of the cultural aristocracy of intellectual giants, rather than that of the masses and their tribunes. Jabotinsky – following Benedetto Croce, who was one of his formative influences – was convinced of the adaptability and regenerative power of the liberal-bourgeois society, as shown by his quote from the notable Austrian dramatist Franz Grillparzer, *'Ich komme aus anderen Zeiten, und hoffe in anderen zu gehen.'*[17] The rise of Marxism and Socialism, as well as that of Fascism, appeared to him merely as an intermediary phase, a diversion from the highway of liberal-democratic progress that led to dictatorship and serfdom.

Even so the above definition fails to satisfy. Who were those 'civic-minded entrepreneurs'? Generally speaking Jabotinsky lumped together all those who were not salaried employees: crafts-men, artisans, petty merchants, clerks, members of the free profes-sions, scientists, and so forth — in short everyone who was not employed in industry or agriculture and who had no socialist lean-ings. The middle class consisted of the *bourgeoisie* and the *petit-bourgeoisie*, regardless of whether those concerned were self-employed or in paid employment.[18] Not counted in the middle class were Jewish capitalists, large industrialists and other high-income earners. He referred to a specific layer in between capitalists and salaried workers, a stratum which to him constituted a class in itself and which, as such, represented the backbone and simultaneously largest segment of the social pyramid.

In all his articles on the subject Jabotinsky struggled hard to try and discover the common denominator of the various elements constituting his middle class. What similarities were there between the bourgeoisie in Eretz Israel and the Jewish *petit bourgeoisie* in the Diaspora? What did a citrus grower in Eretz Israel have in common with a workshop owner, a small farmer, a retailer, a clerk, or an engineer? A common denominator seemed apparent only when this heterogeneous sociological stratum was juxtaposed to that other stratum, the organized working class. In 1934, while searching for a social characteristic of *Berit ha-Hayal*, the Revisionist Army Veterans Organization, Jabotinsky wrote that the term 'middle class' had no clear-cut meaning. It was a broad term used to define several sections of the public who did not endorse the socialist ideology. In his opinion the difference between the working class and the bourgeoisie lay in the dynamic nature of the middle class, which contrasted to the closed and static nature of the working class. The word 'worker' signified a social status, from which people tried to escape in order to become property owners. A worker was a salaried employee without any property of his own; conversely, anyone who acquired private means stopped being a worker and became a member of the bourgeoisie. This is why the working class would die a natural death: in future every worker would have private means — in other words he would become a property owner, and as a result join the 'bourgeoisie'.

However, the distinction between people with private means and those without also proved inadequate, and thus Jabotinsky tried to add yet another criterion, namely the distinction between the existing 'middle class' and the 'incipient middle class', consisting of the second generation of the Jewish bourgeoisie which embraced the national-Zionist ideology, and was thereby transformed from an amorphous layer with sociological characteristics only, into a class with an active political outlook. Through them, the bourgeois would turn into a citizen – a republican patriot.[19]

This is how Jabotinsky attempted to bridge the contradictions which he realized existed between the political consciousness of the middle class and its economic identity. This contradiction was highly relevant to the bourgeois orientation of Revisionism, both from the point of view of ideology and values, and in political terms. This was the kind of bourgeoisie that was to become the standard bearer of national activism, in the same way as it had so often spearheaded the struggles for national liberation. Jabotinsky also distinguished between 'bourgeois' as an 'existential term', the one who, he believed, was characterized by his value system and social ethos, and the 'bourgeois' in the sense of a 'citizen'. 'Bourgeois' as a life-style referred to an economic status, whereas 'bourgeois' in the civic meaning had no economic connotations at all. The first was characterized by his philistine character; in other words he was the slave of whatever material possessions he had, and his actions were circumscribed by short-sighted personal and family interests; he was a reactionary, a minimalist, and his political views were determined by his narrow social and economic preoccupations. Gentile bourgeois people were usually anti-Semitic. The Jewish bourgeois was always a minimalist Zionist. In this respect the socio-economic bourgeoisie, *petit-bourgeoisie* and socialist workers had their bourgeois traits in common! The civic-minded bourgeois, on the other hand, was a person imbued with a political consciousness, someone with a wider perspective: a national patriot. According to Jabotinsky, it was the latter kind of bourgeoisie to whom Herzl had addressed himself in *Altneuland*.

In addition, Jabotinsky attempted to give his bourgeois ideology a more solid historical footing by basing it on a re-interpretation of Jewish history. In the first place, he claimed, the Biblical Jews had been merchants and not farmers, as the popular interpretation ever since the days of the *Haskalah* would have it; not the farmer and the village formed the backbone of Biblical society, but commerce and the city. Secondly, the emphasis among Diaspora Jewry on commerce was not a result of compulsory restrictions imposed by their Christian surroundings, but represented a free choice reflecting the intrinsic character of the Jewish people. Both assumptions were anchored in historiosophic and anthropological conceptions: the view according to which the middle class, in particular the merchant, played a decisive civilizing role, and the view that the 'bourgeois nature' exuded more 'humanity' than that of any other class.

In actual fact, when borrowing values for incorporation into his 'social utopia', Jabotinsky described Biblical society as an agrarian society, but in his historical interpretation of the Biblical era the Hebrew merchant was the harbinger of progress. This predilection for the mercantile profession was first and foremost a reaction to what he considered the total disregard for commerce and the commercial profession by the Zionist Left. Merchants, he bridled, were anything but social parasites, or a superfluous social phenomenon, which did not fulfil any productive function in world history.[20] On the contrary, merchants were the true guides to progress, its creators and disseminators. The merchant adventurer, who sailed the oceans, and the peddlar who walked the highways and byways, were disseminators of material and spiritual culture. Those who walked with their heads in the clouds, the *Luftmenschen*, the small entrepreneurs, the 'Menahem Mendels' (a petty merchant who deals in *Luftgeschäften*, from a novel by Sholem Aleichem) – all these played a civilizing role that could not be overestimated. To demand from the Jew that he 'close up shop' was tantamount to asking him to vacate an important cultural position. This did not mean that the entire *yishuv* had to be merchants, but a proportion of some 10 per cent should be maintained. Trade was an instrument of economic growth, as much as a contributor to the dissemination of human culture. The Jewish concentration on finance and commerce in the Christian environment stemmed, according to him, from a desire for national exclusiveness. These occupations were the 'distinctive Jewish national territory' in the Diaspora, the kind of business that suited the national Jewish psyche, and in order to preserve this national psyche, the Jews continued their occupations wherever they settled.

With this historical interpretation Jabotinsky attempted to imbue the Jewish middle class with a sense of pride and self-respect, and to legitimize its occupation in historical and Zionist terms. To him Jewish society in the Diaspora did not look like an 'inverted pyramid' – in the sense that it was 'incomplete' and lacked a working class – and Zionism was not a process intended to 'invert this pyramid'. He considered it the function of Zionism to help achieve a situation in which the Jewish middle class could *continue* to operate as a middle class. It was a basic ambition of people to own property, to be individualists, and display initiative. Freedom and property were complementary; individualism – not collectivism – was an inborn characteristic of human beings, and Liberalism was its philosophical expression. The profit motive was the driving force of economic initiative. According to Jabotinsky the N.E.P. in bolshevik Russia proved that it was impossible to deny the creative impulse in human nature, which aspired towards owning property; individualism and the acquisition of property were intrinsic to human nature.

This being the case, it was not the workers who 'cultivated the future', but the bourgeoisie. Future society would be a progressive bourgeois-liberal society, combining political freedom with social advancement. Private capital and private initiative would provide the required impetus for a speedy realization of the Zionist idea. The existing industry in Eretz Israel was the fruit of the initiative of 'private initiators and individualists who had come to Eretz Israel bringing with them the spirit of enterprise, and the material means to turn theory into practice'. Private enterprise in Eretz Israel was 'economic adventurism'. Small capitalists invested their capital, and through their industriousness and initiative turned this capital into an instrument of productivity and growth. Achimeir expressed this concept in his own peculiar radical way by juxtaposing the agricultural worker and farmer by the ideal of the pioneers of the Industrial Revolution, such as the weaver from Yorkshire, the steelworker from Birmingham, the sailor from Liverpool, and the fisherman from Friesland.[21]

The future of Jewish society depended on the transformation of workers into bourgeois citizens, and this was a natural and inevitable process. The future of human society hinged on the annulment of the distinction between productive and non-productive labour. In future there would not even be manual labour, for its place would be taken by brain-work. Blue-collar workers as a class would disappear. The society of the future would no longer know manual labour; it would be a 'utopian society', in which work would be a purely enjoyable and leisurely activity. Not millions of people wielding hammers would set the tone in this society, but an aristocracy of intellectuals operating a sophisticated technological apparatus.

Up to this point we have presented the theoretical political foundation of the bourgeois orientation. Another question is how the Revisionists proposed to fit it into the social and economic mechanism of the new Jewish society.[22]

Towns, Villages and Hebrew Labour

A realistic settlement plan should of course have taken account of the fact that Great Britain would fail to be forthcoming, and would refuse to implement the Revisionist-inspired colonization regime. This left the Zionist settlement effort totally dependent upon Jewish national and private capital. As already mentioned, the Revisionists believed that it was the task of the national capital to develop the infrastructure of Eretz Israel in such a way as to stimulate the importation of private capital and the development of the private sector. The Revisionist programme favoured the establishment of villages composed of private homesteads (as opposed to communal farms) based mainly on intensive agriculture, rather than field crops or plantations. However, besides this predilection for smallholder settlements and medium-sized private farms, the primary attention of the Revisionists was focused on the towns, and a population employed in workshops and factories. In other words, the Revisionists were thinking more in terms of urban development based on small-scale industrial enterprises and workshops (rather than of large monopolistic companies) to be financed and assisted by the Zionist institutions. One aspect of such assistance, as we shall see shortly, were a series of measures to ensure a climate of peaceful and stable labour relations. To this end the Zionist Organization was expected to help finance the cost of labour, by providing the difference between the (necessarily low) actual wages paid to Jewish workers, and the amount required to enable them to maintain a decent standard of living. In other words, the Revisionists expected the national capital to promote the infrastructural development of the country, as well as to subsidize wages – and thus, indirectly, employers and industrialists – on the basis of Jabotinsky's dictum that low wages were a prerequisite for the development of a flourishing economy.

As mentioned earlier, another source of subsidies should have been the mandatory government which, according to the Revisionist view, was expected to finance the entire educational and health system, in order to release the Jewish economy from this heavy financial burden.

Within the context of the above, the Revisionists had to formulate their position on one of the most vexing problems during the years under discussion, namely that of the cheap Arab labour employed in the Jewish economy. The Revisionists also supported the principle of employing Jewish labour in Jewish enterprises, but their arguments were less ideologically and emotionally charged than those of the Labour movement.

The Revisionists aimed at the complete separation of the Jewish and Arab economies, both as regards cheap Arab labour and cheap Arab merchandise. Revisionist workers also competed for jobs in the citrus groves, which meant that they were in direct competition with the Arab labourers employed there. As a political party, however, Revisionism was interested in protecting the citrus growers, particularly from what it considered the total dominance of the labour market by the *Histadrut* and its affiliated labour exchanges. Jabotinsky was well aware of the complexity and sensitivity of the problem. Overtly the Revisionists professed their support of the principle of Hebrew labour, but in practice the party inclined towards the position of the citrus growers, depicting the struggle which the *Histadrut* waged against the citrus growers as motivated by political and class interests. This explains why the Revisionists rarely joined in *Histadrut* instigated labour actions. As a result the struggle of the Revisionist workers with the *Histadrut* became less and less a matter of employment opportunities, but in every respect took on the look and substance of a political struggle.

The Revisionist image of the Jewish society in Eretz Israel according to the Revisionist programme was therefore that of an urban and industrial society, side by side with a private farm economy. The national capital was expected to assist and subsidize private entrepreneurial capital, and the task of the Zionist Organization was to create a hermetic separation between the socio-economic and the political dimensions by the creation of an objective mechanism for the management and coordination of economic activity, unaffected by either political or economic interests or considerations.

A genuine desire to ensure economic growth without social unrest and continual labour conflicts, the pursuit of narrow, partisan political interests, in a quest for potential allies and the desire to weaken the *Histadrut* and Mapai, as well as ideological naivety in believing that politics and economics could be separated, proved to be the three determining aspects of the socio-economic programme of the Revisionist party and its portrayal of the desired image of the Jewish society.

The Demand for Compulsory National Arbitration

Neither the economic prosperity of the first half of the 1930s, nor the economic crisis following upon its heels in 1936, succeeded in changing the basic outlook of *Ha-Zohar*. The stabilization and expansion of the private economy during the 1930s, and Mapai's adoption of a more pragmatic economic policy, which acknowledged the essential contribution of the private sector in the development of the Jewish economy, made little if any impact. Within the overall national context the Revisionists kept up their denunciation of the mandatory government for its refusal to adopt a pro-Zionist economic policy – and of the Zionist movement for not fighting for more equitable settlement conditions. Within the internal party-political context they continued their support of the private sector, while regarding the *Histadrut* and the trade union conflict as the fundamental ills besetting the economy. The Revisionists kept on proclaiming the necessity to protect the private sector, and for the workers to support the manufacturers and agree to wage restraint. Directly and indirectly Revisionism continued to side with the citrus growers in their labour disputes, just as they almost invariably supported the manufacturers in their union troubles. This attitude, as well as the struggle of the Revisionist labourers for the allocation of employment opportunities without the intermediary of the *Histadrut*-controlled labour exchanges, were the two leading issues in the Revisionist struggle in the socio-political arena.[23]

There is no point in repeating the demands that were made of the mandatory government. The Revisionists lacked the power to be an effective pressure group, while in effect the mandatory authorities conducted a liberal regime which allowed the Jewish economy the necessary scope for free and unimpeded development.[24] The paradox was that it was the Revisionists who demanded more intervention on the part of the mandatory government, and criticized the British for not extending direct budgetary support to the Jewish educational and health system and for not introducing legislation to put the labour relations system in order. The only Revisionist demands to have effect related to the national budget and the *Histadrut*. As mentioned earlier, wages were considered the crucial determinant for the flourishing of the Jewish economy, which according to *Ha-Zohar* explained the need to keep Jewish wages as close as possible to those of the – much cheaper – Arab workers.

Jewish labour would be subsidized with money from the national funds and Jewish philanthropic institutions operating in Eretz Israel, through a system of 'wage supplements' *in natura*. Again these proposals failed to take into account that during this period the available national funds were limited, both in absolute terms, and in relation to the private capital flow to Eretz Israel.

Assuming that Revisionism did not represent a particular social status or class, or an identifiable economic interest, but that it took a neutral and objective stance reflecting the 'general' national interest, the regulation of labour relations in Eretz Israel was indeed a burning issue. How could a situation be created in which the unavoidable clash between capital and (organized) labour would not disturb the development of the economy and cause a class war within the *yishuv*? How could a balance be struck between private capital in need of subsidies and support, and the collective–bureaucratic sector (the Labour economy), which equally required assistance and therefore fought for control of the very same resources? This pragmatic dimension in the approach of *Ha-Zohar*, coupled with the ideological position which viewed class warfare as a dangerous, if not pathological, phenomenon from a Zionist point of view, paints a dramatic picture of the social relations system within the *yishuv*. It was the firm belief within *Ha-Zohar* that strikes, which in other societies were a legitimate weapon in labour struggles, were exploited by the workers' parties in Eretz Israel as a political tool for weakening the private sector, rather than as an instrument in the fight for the amelioration of labour conditions. According to this view, all strikes in Eretz Israel were politically motivated, and therefore unjustified. Hence the need to find an effective way of preventing these strikes, which sapped the strength of the employers and helped to bolster the political power of the *Histadrut* which, given the circumstances in the country, was far more cohesive than the employers' organizations. For this reason *Ha-Zohar* believed in the need for a neutral institution that would be able to determine objectively what was a reasonable level of profits, and what kind of wages could be paid under the prevailing economic conditions. This gave rise to the demand – a demand that turned into a slogan and one of the corner-stones of Revisionist ideology – for the institution of 'compulsory national arbitration' by an apolitical economic–judicial organ. What in fact they wanted was the establishment of some kind of 'supreme economic council' which, although deriving its authority from the existing political system, would be completely independent from it. The intention was not a voluntary arbitration system, based on negotiations between the parties, but a compulsory system whose decisions would be binding on all sides in all branches of the economy. This would effectively deprive the *Histadrut* and the local labour councils of most of their influence and power.

This concept of compulsory arbitration was by no means exceptional within the socio-economic constellation of Europe between the two world wars. The idea had even been accepted by the League of Nations in Geneva, which had expressed itself in favour of conciliation and arbitration in industrial conflicts. To the Labour movement, however, its emergence within the framework of the Revisionist party ideology signalled yet another manifestation of their fascist frame of mind (as we shall see in Chapter 12), and proved that they had adopted the Italian fascist ideology and praxis. Their argument was not merely ideological, but pragmatic as well: given the circumstances in Eretz Israel, the establishment of a 'neutral' institution invested with authority was impossible, declared the Mapai spokesmen who represented the pragmatic and reformist line in the Labour movement. Neither did they believe in the integrity of the Revisionists, and the programme for compulsory arbitration was considered merely an imitation of the fascist *Carta del Lavoro* of 1927, an attempt to emasculate the power of the organized workers and place the entire economy under absolutist political control.[25] Similarly *Ha-Zohar*'s demands for neutral labour exchanges, to replace the existing exchanges, which were composed of representatives of the unions and employers, was not seen as stemming from a desire for a truly neutral method of allocating job opportunities, regardless of the political affinity of the applicant, but as yet another way of weakening organized labour (which to be effective required centralized control over the allocation mechanism of work places), and thereby strengthen the position of the employers, and in particular the citrus growers.

In any other country which, like Eretz Israel, lacked binding labour legislation, the proposal might have been regarded as an honest attempt at solving some of the most intractable problems in the area of labour relations. However, under the prevailing political conditions in the country, it could only be construed as forming an inseparable part of the party-political infighting about control of the Zionist movement as well as the Zionist 'soul'. Whichever was the case, the compulsory arbitration demand served to add fuel to the flames, and to further sensitize a relational system that was already stretched close to breaking point.

We have seen, therefore, that the keystone of the Revisionist programme was the demand for a protectionist colonization regime, intended as a protective organizational framework for the development of the private sector. Among the more important aspects of this protectionist scheme were arrangements cancelling the right to strike and substantially reducing the power of the *Histadrut* in its capacity as a labour union representing both political and economic interests. In effect this was an effort to uproot the existing politicized structure of the *yishuv* society and economy. Once again we should point out that the entire programme – both explicitly and by implication – rested on the assumption that it was the British mandatory authorities who would shoulder all responsibilities that a government is supposed to undertake on behalf of its citizens. Thus the Revisionists demanded that health and education services, which bore heavily on the Zionist organizations and the *yishuv*, should be financed entirely by the mandatory authorities (although Jewish autonomy in the implementation of the relevant policies would be fully maintained). The mandatory government was expected to establish an orderly system of labour relations and intervene in other spheres through legislative and budgetary means. The paradox is clear: the same movement which is generally regarded as a national movement concentrating all its efforts on fighting mandatory rule, based its fundamental settlement and development programme (not to speak of its national political aspirations) on wide-ranging and intensive intervention by this same mandatory government – and a non-Zionist element to boot. This paradox becomes even more striking when one realizes that the Revisionist demands did not stand the smallest chance of being accepted by the British government. It is evident, therefore, that the Revisionist settlement programme was totally divorced from reality. Acceptance of the claim that large-scale Jewish settlement would be impossible without massive British intervention, would effectively have brought Jewish settlement in Eretz Israel to a halt.

Does the Right have a Social Vision?

Socialist Zionism, besides proposing a method for the realization of Zionism, also suggested a way of changing and rebuilding the Jewish society. In other words, it offered a vision or, possibly, a utopia.[26] This kind of social-eschatological and utopian dimension was almost entirely absent in the Revisionist ideology and *Weltanschauung*. Revisionism did not revolt against the Jewish Diaspora

existence because of its economic structure; it did not regard it as
an anomaly requiring a fundamental and revolutionary structural
change in the production system. The opposition between 'old' and
'new' in Jewish history did not in the Revisionist world-view extend
to social or economic elements. Even the image of the 'new Jew'
(or 'Hebrew') was not characterized by elements of social transformation. On the contrary, Revisionism rejected the social and
humanistic vision of socialist Zionism as anachronistic, reactionary
and irrelevant. Its view of the future Jewish society to be established
in Eretz Israel therefore bore an in all respects conservative imprint.
More than that, the Revisionist world-view lacked any aspiration
towards a social vision, and neither did it attempt to envisage some
form of utopian future. The very act of outlining such a future
society seemed the kind of intellectual effort which could interfere
with, and even prevent, the realization of Zionism, and as such was
more suited to the socialist intelligentsia. The aim of Zionism as an
historic movement was not to construct a model society – at least not
at the present time – but to build a Jewish national society. On this
point there is no doubt that the Revisionists were far removed from
Herzl, who had regarded a 'perfect Jewish society' as the embodiment and ultimate goal of the universalistic mission of Zionism.

The only two personalities to envisage such a future Jewish
society and relate to its intellectual foundations, were Jabotinsky
and Klausner. During the middle of the 1930s Jabotinsky concluded
that Revisionism, and in particular *Betar*, required a more systematic and profound platform than the existing one. The fact that
socialist ideology was based on an anthropo-sociological theory and
a social vision spurred him in 1934 to draft for the first time a
rationalization of his liberal-bourgeois society.[27] His image of the
future deviated considerably from the formal Revisionist programme which, as one may recall, demanded increased state
involvement in the everyday life of society. In his vision of the
future, state intervention became a marginal issue, and in its stead
came a liberal-progressive image of a welfare state. Jabotinsky's
vision of the future society reflected the intellectual foundations of
his private world, as discussed in Part Two of this book, and as such
showed distinctive traces of his studies at Western universities and
his reading of contemporary European literature on the subject.

It is typical of Jabotinsky that he declared himself against the
current fashion of 'wholesale anti-Marxism'. His declared affinity to
Marxism was to the marxist methodology. Marxism, according to
him, was a proper and valid method of historical analysis. The

marxist method, i.e. historical dialectics, revealed in the clearest possible way the relationship between the means of production and social existence. In his view, however, Marx had erred in the analytical sphere: he had tried the right method, but used it in the wrong way to analyse reality. Marx's analysis of socio-economic reality was, in Jabotinsky's view, riddled with mistakes on a number of crucial aspects, such as – for instance – his theory of the 'surplus value' resulting from the exploitation of hired labour by private capital owners; his theory of the growing concentration of capital in the hands of individual capitalists and monopolists; his theory about the polarization and proletarization of the middle class; his theory of the division of society into capitalists and proletarians; as well as in his theory on the inability of capitalism to regulate production and the distribution of resources and capital in society.

Jabotinsky's 'psycho-Marxism'[28] rested on his identification of two basic motivating forces in human history, namely 'necessity' and 'play' (or, as he puts it in the first version of his manuscript, 'necessity' and 'enjoyment'). Necessity was the sum total of the defensive drives of the individual, whereas 'play' or 'enjoyment' represented the sum total of his aggressive drives. Necessity reflected those drives which acted to preserve the existing order, to protect the biological minimum and exploit the maximum potential of the individual.

Civilization, according to this anthropological view, was the result of the 'play motive'. The 'play' or 'enjoyment' drive urged the individual to supplement his biological minimum, consisting of the elementary necessities which keep the human species alive, in particular food, clothing, and the means of defence – in other words both the material and the spiritual 'culture'. All cultural phenomena, from the most primitive to the most sophisticated, were a result of this 'play drive'.[29]

There exists a certain similarity between this theory, the anthropological approach of Buckle,[30] and the theory of the great Dutch scholar Johan Huizinga, as expounded in the latter's well-known book *Homo Ludens* (1938), a study of the 'play' element in culture, which Huizinga developed at the beginning of the 1930s in a series of lectures in Germany. It is difficult to say whether Jabotinsky had read or studied Huizinga, who defined play as 'the sum total of activities that do not have a biological purpose, but are an expression of the life force, a free activity that is not dictated by the need for survival'. Jabotinsky went much further than Huizinga, however, in defining 'play' as the creative force of both civilization and culture. Literature, cathedrals, art, philosophy, as well as weapons, steam, the wheel and machinery in general were all products of the 'play drive', which had its origin in the *psyche*. All human manifestations not immediately related to necessity, i.e. the elementary physical need for survival, were said to fall in the category of 'play'. The thesis concluded that human efforts were in the main not aimed at safeguarding existence, but at maintaining the cultural level and helping to satisfy the next higher level of cultural advancement – enabling man to satisfy his cultural 'caprices' (*Wahlbedürfnis*). Initially the human species had acted under the force of necessity. Human history, however, was the manifestation of the 'play drive'. The motive force of history was not the question who should own the means of production that provided the basic existence, but the dialectic between necessity and the play drive, while the play drive was stronger and more dominant than the drive to satisfy the need for basic necessities. Great historic events were a consequence of the play drive, rather than of the urge to satisfy elementary material needs. The Irish revolt, for instance, had not necessarily broken out as a result of economic hardship – in fact it had been against the economic interests of the Irish, but this had not prevented them from persisting in their fight against Great Britain.[31]

The above led to yet another conclusion as regards the argument with marxist and socialist ideology. Not economic necessity and manual toil were the spurs to progress, but spiritual factors such as will power, individual initiative, talent, intelligence, education and brilliance. Manual labour was a consequence of necessity, whereas spiritual qualities were exponents of the play drive. The supremacy of the 'play' drive also accounted for democratic equality. Man responded to the restrictions society imposed upon him because of his desire to form a part of the big human family. This partnership formed an unwritten 'social contract' aimed at sustaining the social and cultural existence, thus creating a basis for the play drive to foster social and cultural progress. From this it also followed that the state had to guarantee the basic necessities of life, in order to provide the necessary scope for 'play' as a motive force. The modern state could neutralize the social and economic achievements of the merchant. In a society in which 'play' was given free rein, private property represented individual freedom and individual endeavour, which in turn found their expression in culture. Technology, industrialization and science were all a consequence of the 'play drive', and as such were intended to liberate man from the yoke of necessity and physical labour, by turning onerous labour into a relaxing pastime, and increasing the number of leisure hours. The salaried worker was not 'the man of the future'. The function of the proletarian – who was supposed to provide the elementary needs of society (and himself) – was on its way out. The future belonged to the intellectual, the inventor, the professional and the artist. The proletariat was in a crisis and was about to disappear from the stage of history – which explained why it was in such a hurry to grasp political control by force. It also explained the compulsions of the various socialist movements, although from the perspective of historical progress, Socialism and allied doctrines, such as the dictatorship of the proletariat and nationalization of the means of production were reactionary rather than progressive.[32]

Social Redemption – The Fundamentals of the Future Welfare State

Already at the beginning of the century Professor Joseph Klausner undertook to formulate a non-socialist social ideology rooted in Jewish sources.[33]

Earlier we have seen that in certain situations Klausner held a deterministic view. In the social context, however, he rejected the deterministic approach to history as expounded by Marx, Darwin or Spengler. Instead he posited the existence of a singular, immanent inner world capable of surmounting the constraints of the 'outer world'. According to him, the intrinsic psychological will was capable of overcoming external 'objective' restrictive conditions. This immanent inner foundation of Jewish history was prophecy. It was the foundation of the human-Jewish characteristic in the history of the Jewish people. Externally, prophecy showed a similarity to the views of the *Ethische National-Ökonomen* – the Ethical Economists, a concept of overall societal reform by the reformation of man within the framework of a sovereign national existence. According to this view purposive human action was the fundamental of historical dynamics, while recognizing the moral and ethical dimension in every social reform. The messianic idea in Biblical prophecy concerned the reformation of this world (rather than the next, heavenly world), the rejection of evil, and the redemption of the concrete, human world by a human redeemer on the basis of (monotheistic) religious morality.[34]

Klausner developed these notions, originating from his Odessa period, in Jerusalem, in particular in an article entitled 'Prophetic Socialism' published in 1933, the thrust of which corresponds with

Jabotinsky's ideas from the early 1930s. According to Klausner, prophecy was a combination of 'sociability' (social responsibility) and individualism. The social laws of the Bible were intended to lighten the burdens of the poor, and to enforce social equality without abolishing private property, even though the latter would have to be subjected to certain restrictions in order to prevent social polarization. The laws of *Shemittah*, the sabbatical year, *yovel*, the jubilee year, and the laws of *leket, shikhhah* and *pe'ah*, concerning compulsory provisions for the poor constituted the Biblical social legislation, to which should be added the prophetic warnings against the display of riches, waste, sexual licence, greed, and so forth, against which were placed ideal norms of social and human behaviour.

Klausner posited ten main differences between scientific socialism and social responsibility as proclaimed by the prophets.

1. Prophetic morality is based on idealism rather than on materialism.
2. Prophetic morality is based on monotheism rather than on atheism.
3. Prophetic morality regards the reform of man as a precondition for the reform of the world.
4. Prophetic morality is national rather than supra-national.
5. Prophetic morality is 'monistic' and rejects the idea of a class struggle.
6. Prophetic morality is not demagogic, and does not blame one particular social class for the ills of the world.
7. According to prophetic morality any disasters that might befall society because of its moral transgressions will be general, and not descend upon the heads of one social class only.
8. The messianic King is a 'real' human being, at one and the same time a great king and an outstanding moral individual. Political sovereignty does not corrupt morals and behaviour, but is an essential complement to both.
9. The reform of the world is bound up with the rehabilitation of the situation of the Jewish nation.
10. Prophetic morality will not be realized through violent revolutionary methods, but within the course of a lengthy evolutionary process culminating in the 'End of Days' – the future Golden Era.

Jabotinsky's social vision was similarly anchored in Biblical sources, but these were complemented by contemporary theories. The Bible served as a source of ideas and values, rather than operative suggestions. These Biblical sources proved that there was no need to search for messianic theories in 'alien' creeds (i.e. Socialism), and that a ready-made Jewish theory of social redemption existed in an authentic source: the ancient history of the Jews.

What was therefore the basic difference between Socialism and Jabotinsky's social vision? Socialism, stated Jabotinsky, is 'a concrete plan for solving social problems by legislative means'. It meant the building of an entirely new society and a new social order on the ruins of the existing old order. It was a social regime that aimed at preventing inequalities in the distribution of wealth and the resulting poverty. In a 'socialist' society equality was a stable and permanent phenomenon. A 'social society', on the other hand, functioning according to a social programme, operated on the same principles, although by different methods. It was inspired by the Biblical *yovel*, which for Jabotinsky served as an ancient parallel to the liberal-bourgeois democratic society and its mechanism for the redress of social and economic injustice. A social programme, wrote Jabotinsky, did not mean a revolutionary change of the existing social order and its mode of operation through totalitarian means. A social programme was conservative and reformist in nature, and it aimed at preserving private property, free competition in the marketplace, and so forth. It did not aspire towards the imposition of economic equality; neither did it oppose private enterprise, the profit motive or class differentials. In a liberal-progressive society there would exist differences between the classes, as well as social inequality, and its social mechanism would be aimed at minimum intervention. Its sole purpose was to extend a measure of 'social protection' which, according to Jabotinsky, meant the exact opposite of social revolution. A welfare state would be possible, because a bourgeois society would by its very nature be flexible and therefore able to produce the antibodies needed to resist a socialist revolution.

Jabotinsky was not talking about the 'orthodox' Liberalism of a Smith or Malthus, let alone the social Darwinism of Spencer; his ideas did reveal a certain spiritual affinity with Disraeli's paternalism, the radical Liberalism of Joseph Chamberlain, or the State Socialism of Bismarck and its theoretician Lujo Brentano.[35] His ideal society would be a class society rather than an egalitarian society. It was the responsibility of the state to extend a 'safety net' to the citizen, to prevent him from falling into the abyss of hardship and poverty. Society was like a boxing ring in which all those with initiative and energy, the talented and the less talented, freely contested with each other. The winners reaped their deserved reward and, in so doing, helped to shift the wheels of progress. The losers merely had to be protected against social ruination by a suitable system of social welfare legislation providing a 'minimum cultural subsistence'. The task of such legislation was not to put an end to all inequity, but to fight it wherever and whenever it appeared. 'This idea is grounded in the firm conviction that a free economy is one of the fundamentals of human existence,'[36] wrote Jabotinsky. Briefly put, his social prescription read as follows:

> The essence of the cure lies in two brief and simple rules. Firstly, every person who so desires will receive an allowance from the state to cover his minimal needs, the size of this allowance to be determined by the society, depending upon the particular country and the phase of its technical culture. Secondly, the state has the right to mobilize as many people and to requisition as much materials and equipment as it may need to ensure this minimum. That is all.[37]

The above-mentioned minimum included every basic human need, including food, shelter, education and medical care. Jabotinsky's 'five *'m's' mazon* (food), *mazor* (health care), *malbush* (clothing), *moreh* (education) and *maon* (housing) show a striking correspondence with William Beveridge's 'Five Giants' – Food, Shelter, Clothing, Education and Medicine – mentioned in his famous and revolutionary report of June 1942.[38] The Government, through the national budget, the taxes of the citizens, and the compulsory mobilization of the civilian population, would guarantee a basic minimum existence for all. Poverty would disappear, and beyond the red poverty line the bourgeois society and market economy would flourish without fear of social or economic hardship.

In another article Jabotinsky attempted to formulate a number of other, more immediately applicable principles based on examples from existing Western European social legislation. According to these the welfare state would legislate:

1. a comprehensive set of compulsory labour laws fixing working hours and working conditions;
2. progressive taxation; and
3. a national social insurance system, providing comprehensive coverage for accidents, sickness, old age pensions and so on.

This system would be implemented through a national political authority which was independent of any economic interests, and which would be charged with preventing distortions in the social system.

The so-called 'social utopia' was therefore the exact opposite of the 'socialist utopia'. The socialist utopia was unnecessary, undesirable and impossible; it ran counter to human nature, deprived society of its creative drive and initiative, and imposed compulsion and 'barracks' collectivism. Mankind was moving towards a liberal welfare state, rather than a socialist society. A bourgeois society did not mean poverty, hunger and exploitation. The opposite was the case: the bolshevik experiment in the Soviet Union had proved that it was Socialism that brought hunger and exploitation, and a regime of bondage in its wake. Poverty was not an unavoidable concomitant of private enterprise and the market economy. If anything, poverty was a sickness in the bourgeois body, curable by appropriate means. Only a liberal-bourgeois society enabled the establishment of a system of cooperative class relations with the assistance of the instruments of the state.

According to this, the bourgeoisie stood for progress, reflecting a communal, national, anti-cosmopolitan and anti-totalitarian approach based on social cooperation and compromise, which stood above class differences. Only a bourgeois society – one that was neither socialist nor capitalist – could ensure a free, harmonious, reformist and democratic multi-class society on a non-egalitarian basis, which ensured a minimum subsistence for all. Such a future society would not be capitalistic, because the days of capitalism were numbered. 'A capitalist regime has not existed for a long time', he wrote naively. 'What we see around us is a liberal bourgeois society which has circumscribed the activities of the moneyed interests, as well as those of the large industrialists. The capitalist is no less a rival of the bourgeoisie than the unionized worker.' In 1937 he wrote:

> The majority of the world population are neither capitalists or labourers. They belong to the middle class, and they have multifarious and complex interests that are subject to change. This is why they need a flexible, reformist government and social and cultural pluralism. Pluralism ensures social reform: it guarantees that people will not submit to the interests of the plutocracy and will have an open ear for the demands of the needy and the poor. Far from being wrong, the bourgeois society embodies a messianic idea; it is the bearer of a social messianism that is far superior to socialist messianism.[39]

Jabotinsky's social theory was far from coherent. This is apparent, for example, from his confusion on issues concerning social and economic terminology. Thus, in one place, he equates bourgeoisie with capitalism, where he writes:

> I am absolutely certain that the regime that is called bourgeois or capitalistic will gradually create a system of ways and means for banning poverty from the world, in other words [will prevent] the reduction of wages below the level indispensable to maintain subsistence, hygiene and self-respect; were it not for the armament budgets, this could be realized in many countries even today. In addition: even if it were true that the bourgeois regime, just like any living organism, excretes sundry poisonous substances which from time to time cause unavoidable upheavals, I believe that it will be able to withstand these upheavals without being destroyed, by absorbing them within its system; thanks to its systematic, built-in system of checks and balances it will be able to exploit the unlimited opportunities for growing sophistication implicit in the recurring, but pre-planned and carefully calculated, social revolts during which — by the way — no blood will be shed. In short, I believe not only in the stability of the bourgeois system, but also that objectively it contains within itself the seeds of a certain social ideal — an ideal in the normal sense of the word, in other words a vision that is worth dreaming of and fighting for.

In other places, however, Jasbotinsky distinguished between the bourgeoisie and capitalism, stating that the latter lacked national values and was only interested in material profits.

A progressive bourgeois society promised mankind 'scope for action' rather than being a 'pasture for the herd'. Work would be a pleasure. Political freedom and minimal subsistence would be guaranteed. A bourgeois society also had aesthetic values, instead of being merely grey and egalitarian. The struggle, adventure, challenge and romance connected with economic and intellectual initiative, and whimsy and charm of creativity — all these would be preserved, rather than being suffocated, as was the case in a socialist society.

We may remember that in his *Chapters on the Philosophy of the Bible*[40] Jabotinsky attempted to discover the roots of such concepts as 'social insurance' and 'minimum of subsistence', by drawing parallels with the Biblical laws regarding the Shabbat and *leket, shikhhah ve-pe'ah* — 'gleanings, forgotten produce and the corners of the field', which he regarded as examples of formal public intervention in labour relations and the financing of a basic subsistence level for the poor by those with material means. But these analogies merely fulfilled an intellectual need, which yielded no practical operational plan, nor – for that matter – could disguise the actual intellectual origins of Jabotinsky's social theories in contemporary European social philosophy. Jabotinsky was influenced both directly and through intermediaries. It would seem that he was influenced by the social utopia of Herzl's *Altneuland*, which proclaimed a mutualistic society based on two foundations: firstly, distribution of land and the cancellation of the monopoly on land ownership, and secondly guaranteed free competition by the abolition of industrial monopolies. 'Liberal Socialism' envisioned a society carried by independent farmers and cooperative marketing, i.e. private ownership of the means of production, but consultation in matters of buying and selling raw materials. Jabotinsky's enthusiasm for science and technology, which he considered the equivalents of progress, and which could solve any and all social and economic problems, was derived from a variety of liberal utopian schemes. It would seem, however, that one of his principal sources of inspiration was the Viennese Jewish author and utopist Josef Popper (pseud. Lynkeus).[41]

Popper, whose pen-name was that of the far-sighted mythical Argonaut helmsman, tried to portray a utopian society that would impose justice and individualistic humanism. His principal work, *Die allgemeine Nährpflicht als Lösung der sozialen Frage* ('The General Right to Subsistence as a Solution to the Social Question') outlined a programme for social reform which combined political freedom with a minimum of social compulsion, recognized the inequality of people and accentuated the moral aspect of social redemption. Popper-Lynkeus distinguished between man's basic necessities of life, and luxuries, and stated that those who were able to work were obliged to devote a certain period of time towards providing for the basic needs of society. These basic needs included a comprehensive physical minimum of subsistence, to be provided not in cash, but in kind, whereas minimum cultural requirements would be supplied in the form of financial grants. His *Nährarmee* was maintained through mobilization for a compulsory stint of service, but after his release the individual was at liberty to compete in the free market. The provision of the minimum necessities of life would be a collective effort, but the acquisition of non-essentials depended upon the individual's own efforts. In Popper's future society the national economy would consist of two parts: a collective economy, whose task it was to provide the basic needs of society, and a free political economy, or – put differently: a public service apparatus, whose workers received a salary, and a private, free economy. The absence of the struggle for survival would remove the motivation for speculation or price gouging, but insofar as there was a struggle for existence in this future society, it would be more like pleasant social intercourse than a full-blown class war. Popper viewed his vision as a synthesis of Socialism and Liberalism, without the collectivist compulsion of the first, or the anarchic individualism of the second, quite apart from which it offered far more than the 'welfare state', which guaranteed a real minimum only when a person was temporarily or permanently unemployed. This vision would be realized once states were no longer compelled to spend disproportionate percentages of their national budgets on keeping ahead in the arms race. Life would no longer depend upon a person's capacity to work; even those who did not work would be entitled to a minimum – but not more than that.

This vision (or 'constructive fantasies', as Popper-Lynkeus himself described his literary works) was simplistic and naive, and it failed to address the complex problems of the modern industrial society and its mass-production technology. All he offered was a formula for a 'minimum level of subsistence', without detailing how this minimum existence would be realized, or, for that matter, how it was to be determined. Jabotinsky himself, however, did not mean to propose a 'utopia', an accurate, detailed blueprint of a society; he merely wanted to suggest an ideal and a vision. This was Jabotinsky's weakness, that instead of proposing a realistic plan, he described a utopian 'future society' as if it were imminent and feasible.

The assumption that in the twentieth century productive and non-productive labour are inseparable,[42] and the extension of the 'work' concept to include both 'manual' and 'brain' work – with as its corollary the extension of the term 'worker' to include all kinds of human creative activity – ultimately leads to the negation of the value of physical effort in the future society. In Jabotinsky's utopian future, a borrowing from several other contemporary utopian and science-fiction scenarios, work would disappear and the ancient curse that 'man was born to toil' would be revoked.[43] Thus he could write that 'in the year 2030 manual labour will have vanished from the world, and its place will have been taken by brain work'. Manual labour, which distorts the very essence of man, will have disappeared, and man will rule nature through the machines which his brain has invented. The real work will be performed by scholars and scientists. The romantic idealization of labour will be a thing of the past. In the future society work will be sport, or a pastime for people who want to fill their leisure hours. The work will be ruled by an intellectual aristocracy. One of the most problematic traditions that Jabotinsky bequeathed to his movement is that before long it would prove to be composed primarily of workers and salaried employees!

No wonder that Ben-Gurion regarded this utopia as merely another 'pseudo-scientific way of contending with the Labour movement and its labour ideology'. The truth of the matter is that Jabotinsky's utopia was anchored in his life-long overt and covert intellectual dialogue with Marxism. The leader of the movement which in Eretz Israel numbered thousands of daily-paid workers among its adherents, during the 1930s preached a utopia that celebrated a scholarly and technological aristocracy, with the purpose of imbuing an even larger group of professionals and self-employed within the movement with a sense of importance and more optimistic orientation towards the future. Nowhere in Jabotinsky's writings or, for that matter, in any other Revisionist literature, will we find any descriptions in praise of manual labour, either on the land or in industry – not even simple songs or poems extolling the joys and value of daily labour. The same movement which in the course of the years was to become the exponent of a multitude of salaried workers, possesses virtually no texts in its cultural tradition extolling this group!

The above was therefore a minimalistic social vision, containing many elements borrowed from nineteenth-century liberal utopias. Yet it contained very little that was capable of generating enthusiasm or spurring a struggle for an improvement or change of society. Given the world-view of the majority of the members of the movement this vision simply failed to inspire. In practical terms the foremost element that the movement absorbed from Jabotinsky's writings on the subject was the slogan of the 'five *m*'s', reflecting the quintessence of the liberal-progressive view on the state's responsibility for furnishing a culturally acceptable minimum existence, but without anywhere going into details about what this minimum was supposed to consist of, or what kind of gap between 'minimum' and 'maximum' could be permitted without causing a profound and dangerous polarization of the society. As will be shown in the second part of this study, Herut's principal preoccupation during the 1950s was with the problem of how to transfer social functions from the Histadrut to the state, as well as with the contradiction between State Socialism and Liberalism, which in the view of the Right could turn into a conflict between social populism aimed at the lower levels of society, and the bourgeois orientation.

The Socio-Economic Heritage

Both the ideology and the socio-economic programme of Revisionism presented its successors, specifically the IZL, Lehi and the *Herut* movement, with a number of intractable problems. The Revisionist socio-economic theory lacked clarity and definition, besides which it contained several extraneous and even contradictory elements, so that at times it looked more like an adjunct to their national and political theory.

The Revisionist successors in the main adhered to the tradition of Jabotinsky, whom they regarded as an exponent of the 'neutral' approach, whose political vision took precedence above his social views. At the same time they presented him as a man with a social liberal vision. Rightist literature keeps on stressing the liberal side of Jabotinsky's teaching – and at times even the anarchist-liberal elements of his theory. Meanwhile the Revisionists' opponents made certain to emphasize the étatist aspects in Jabotinsky's doctrine, as well as the state-capitalist and – of course – fascist aspects of his social outlook (as we will see in Chapter 12).

The *Herut* movement adopted various elements of the Revisionist programme. The demand for the separation of the trade union department of the *Histadrut* – to avoid a conflict of interests between the part of the economy which employed workers, and the trade unions which represented employees – the establishment of neutral (rather than party-affiliated) labour exchanges, and the introduction of compulsory arbitration of labour disputes, in order to prevent strikes, were some of the principal recurrent demands. These were accompanied by demands for the liberalization of the economy and the reduction of government intervention in the economy and social life (mainly because the 'state' was considered equivalent with leftist rule).

The IZL opposed the Revisionist tradition in an effort to prove that its own liberal orientation need not necessarily lead to an anti-labour stance. The tensions between Liberalism, étatism and populism which had remained dormant during the underground era, surfaced however immediately upon the foundation of the state. Lehi faced an even more intense struggle with the Revisionist tradition. Part of its membership preferred to stick to general phraseology in a messianic vein, referring to 'a just society in the spirit of the Prophets of Israel', whereas the 'leftist' faction, as we shall shortly see, adopted marxist-socialist ideological elements and rhetoric, talking in terms of 'nationalization of the means of production', and so forth. In any case, many of the subjects which the average Revisionist had regarded as secondary priorities became focal points following the establishment of the state. The State of Israel found itself confronted with countless complex social and economic problems, which forced Revisionism to reformulate its positions and establish new patterns of conduct to ensure that it would be able to function in the new Israeli society.

The Undergrounds – The Search for a Political and Ideological Identity at the Crossroads of 1944–1948

Between Continuity and Change

The previous chapters have dealt at some length with a number of ideological developments, as reflected in the ideological literature of the underground organizations. Their contents mainly concerned the organizations' thinking on the historical and national level. Another chapter discussed the evolution of the political thinking of the Right in general, and the developments which from its point of view inevitably led to, and legitimized, the armed struggle against the British Mandate. From an historical perspective both the IZL and Lehi must indeed be viewed mainly in light of their impact on the two basic objectives the underground organizations had set themselves between 1940 and 1944: (1) to achieve the immediate termination of the British Mandate and the establishment of a Jewish state, and (2) to force the cancellation of the United Nations' Partition Plan of 29 November 1947 and the application of Jewish sovereignty to both banks of the river Jordan – or at the very least the western part of Eretz Israel. Most of the underground literature was therefore devoted to propaganda and the dissemination of the two central goals which constituted the *a priori* fundamentals of the rightist Zionist creed. Besides this, considerable space was of course devoted to the formulation and consolidation of a conceptual system aimed at legitimizing the armed struggle and its attendant methods, as well as to the break with the organized *yishuv* and, finally, to the functioning of the underground organizations as two separate and independent political and military entities. The two undergrounds presented themselves as the only ones with a correct grasp of the political situation and, consequently, the only ones who knew how to react to it in the appropriate manner. Apart from this they regarded themselves as organizations fulfilling a crucial historical mission, for which reason they judged themselves by historical, rather than party-political criteria. This explains why their propaganda was couched in terms of *Realpolitik* and phrased in a rhetorical terminology of fulfilment and redemption.

Apart from these concerns, and not forgetting their principal activity – underground military actions – both organizations were to varying degrees given to introspection about their identity and profiles. This self-analysis was required for three reasons: (1) The undergrounds constituted new political and organizational entities (as well as representing, to a considerable degree, a novel social phenomenon) which had to analyse their organizational and ideological relationship to the organization from which they had sprung, while at the same time adapting themselves to the new circumstances; (2) The underground organizations formed the target of violent criticism by the majority of the organized Jewish community in Eretz Israel, which regarded them as fascist and terrorist organizations, thus forcing them to fend off these attacks while trying to put across their 'real image' to the Jewish population; (3) Lehi, which presented itself as a 'progressive' revolutionary organization which had severed all connections with its Revisionist origins, was as a consequence forced – even more than the 'traditional' IZL – to define its ideological and social identity in all areas.

At this point we could ask ourselves whether a discussion of the undergrounds as military activist organizations does at all belong in a study on the political history of the Right. This may at first seem a strange suggestion since, from a genealogical point of view, there is no doubt that both the IZL and Lehi were direct descendants of the Zionist Right, and that after 1948 they became the cornerstones of the Israeli Right in the newly-established State of Israel. It is not this issue that is in doubt; the question is rather to what extent during the period 1940–1948, the years of the 'revolt' against the Mandate, the IZL and Lehi were exponents of the ideology of the Right: whether they were 'rightist' organizations in terms of their social structure and national objectives, and whether the aims for which they fought were in fact rightist aims. Within the Left there existed no doubt whatsoever that such was the case. The Zionist Left regarded the underground organizations as fascist, which in turn was a direct and logical consequence of the Left's portrayal of Revisionism in Eretz

Israel as Fascism. The fact that it concerned armed organizations merely served to reinforce this image, for it seemed obvious that what was being witnessed here was yet another phase in the evolution of Zionist Fascism from the overt political sphere to underground terrorism. The underground organizations were not judged on their contribution to the struggle against the Mandate or by their national objectives, but – as already mentioned – mainly as a continuation of Revisionism in a different form. As such their struggle was viewed as part and parcel of the internal ideological and political struggle for control of the Jewish community in Eretz Israel. Particularly at this point, now that sovereign statehood seemed imminent, such manifestations of an internal struggle, which ultimately were bound to affect the balance of power in the independent state, took on added importance and sensitivity.

The IZL and Lehi's propaganda expertly exploited the weak point in the web of hostile arguments by portraying the labour parties as Socialists who were out to preserve their hegemony of the *yishuv*, for which purpose they were prepared to countenance, and even support the continuation of capitalist British Imperialism in Eretz Israel. No opportunity was lost to stress the fact that in other cases, for example Poland, it had been the socialist parties which had spearheaded the national struggle for liberation from 'foreign domination' or 'foreign occupation'. The argument that a violent underground struggle against British rule constituted proof of a nationalist and fascist ideology or doctrine was called – rightly, as it happens – a distortion of history founded on misguided historical conceptions. In the IZL and Lehi's view the fact that, of all people, 'dissidents' from the Right led the armed struggle against the British Mandate, was conclusive proof that the Right was the real national movement, whereas the Left was nothing but a 'class movement'.

Organization and Social Composition

The underground struggle should therefore not be viewed in terms of 'Right' or 'rightism'. There is no doubt that the earlier described national ideas that had evolved within the Right formed the seedbed and germinating force of the underground struggle, but the nature of this struggle (terrorism and urban guerilla warfare) and its objectives were in no way representative of the political Right. Opposition to the Partition Plan was during this period by no means restricted to rightist circles only; among the Zionist Left too there were powerful groups which for a variety of reasons opposed a division of Western Eretz Israel. The organizational structures of the two undergrounds showed no typical 'rightist' or 'fascist' characteristics whatsoever. They represented new organizational developments, products of specific circumstances and requirements, rather than of a particular guiding ideology. As early as 1939–40 Lehi severed all its connections with the Revisionist mother-party, and the leadership of the small organization was put into the hands of a Central Committee consisting of no more than three members. The IZL was led by a General Headquarters, composed of ten members under the leadership of Menachem Begin, who met at frequent intervals. Communications with the public were maintained by means of underground publications and an underground radio transmitter. The two headquarters, Lehi 's Central Committee and the General Headquarters of the IZL, were self-appointed bodies and as such not responsible to anyone but themselves; they were very much the 'private domain' of their organizations' military and political leadership. In this respect the IZL and Lehi were real undergrounds, not to be compared with the *Haganah* and the Palmach, the illegal 'defence forces' of the *yishuv*, which were subject to the authority of elected civilian political leaders.

The headquarters of the two undergrounds lacked the means of enforcing decisions or imposing sanctions upon the members. Participation was of a voluntary nature. Of course there existed disciplinary rules and regulations, as well as a hierarchical command structure at all levels, but these did not differ from the hierarchical and disciplinary characteristics of other closed organizations. The IZL, the largest of the two organizations under discussion, had a para-military structure, complete with staff sections, regional headquarters and local branches. However, all activities were controlled by its General Headquarters and – with the exception of Jerusalem – no operational initiatives by local or district commanders were permitted. Both the IZL and Lehi exercised individual control over their members, and with a few exceptions no partisan actions were ever undertaken that had not been initiated by Headquarters. Any decisions by Headquarters on a suspension of hostilities or a cease fire, whether for tactical or political reasons, were strictly observed by the rank and file.

The break with the mother organization was not limited to the formal, organizational level (from 1944 onwards secret ties were maintained between the IZL and *Ha-Zohar* on a personal, informal basis). This was also reflected in the social composition of the organizations. The manpower of both the IZL and Lehi originated first and foremost from the mother movement. Numerous members of the Polish secret cells of the IZL found their way to Lehi, and the same applied to members of the *Berit ha-Biryonim* in Eretz Israel. Several leading personalities at command level had never been members of either *Ha-Zohar* or *Betar*. In fact, many of those who joined the underground organizations during the 1940s lacked any previous connection with Revisionism as such. According to available information more than half the IZL membership during the final years of its existence (1947–48) had never been associated with the Revisionist movement in any way, but had joined the movement on the strength of their identification with its political objectives and methods of operation. IZL and Lehi attracted members from widely different political and ethnic backgrounds (including a significant proportion of Oriental Jews) and different social classes. For the majority the party-political infighting meant little or nothing; nor, for that matter were they in any way familiar with the internal history of Revisionism. For them, Jabotinsky was a name and a symbol, rather than a political leader whose teachings they knew and followed. Neither did all the members continue their activities after 1948 within the framework of the *Herut* movement.

Despite all this, the IZL clearly represents a stage in the continuum between Revisionism and the *Herut* movement both from an ideological and an organizational point of view. The struggle of the IZL, its heroic image and successful exploits, on the one hand, and the heritage of hatred and hostility towards the parties of the Left (particularly the residual resentment against Mapai due to the 'Season', the period between November 1944 and the summer of 1945, when the *Haganah* tried to liquidate the IZL, and the affair with the arms' ship *Altalena*), on the other, were all elements of the history and tradition of the political culture of Revisionism, and in turn became an inseparable part of this culture.

The IZL and Revisionism

More than anyone it was Menachem Begin who consistently and intensively stressed the continuity between Revisionism and the IZL. To provide a foundation for this continuity, Begin created an artificial distinction between Jabotinsky, the man and his ideas, and *Ha-Zohar*, with its party organization and party activists. The IZL, rather than the party, was portrayed as the natural heir of the political and national ideas of Jabotinsky, while Jabotinsky himself was, as mentioned earlier, proclaimed the 'Father of the Revolt'.[1] Lehi's claims of having been the precursors and originators of the revolt, under the inspiration and guidance of Avraham Stern (or, alternatively, the poetry and historiosophy of Uri Zvi Greenberg) were firmly rejected by Begin as a serious encroachment on Jabotinsky's authority. More than any of the IZL commanders, Begin wanted to be seen as Jabotinsky's disciple and natural successor, thereby representing Jabotinsky's Revisionism and the IZL as two links in a chain. Begin similarly imposed this notion of continuity and belonging on the IZL and the *Herut* movement, internalizing it as a central element of their respective world-views. Simultaneously Begin had to try and rid himself of those elements which he considered harmful to the Revisionist legacy, particularly as regards its image of a 'bourgeois' and 'legalistic' party. The succeeding years would show that the *Herut* movement never succeeded in shaking off its image of being the continuation of Revisionism, and in many ways *Herut* may indeed be called its organic successor. In fact, from the 1950s onwards the tensions within *Herut* between the bourgeois and populist ideological trends would continue to mount.

During the 1940s the IZL consistently maintained the fiercely anti-marxist and anti-socialist line of Revisionism. For its part, socialist Zionism still represented sectorial and class-oriented trends and a politically defeatist national policy. Unlike Lehi, the IZL never appealed to the working class in order to try and establish a solid social and ideological front for its revolt; nor did it ever promise to establish an egalitarian social regime based upon the working class. For this reason it is indeed a paradox that in the course of the next few decades the IZL continued to gather strength among the lower classes of the *yishuv* and – eventually – within Israeli society as a whole. Its social and economic platform, as elucidated in various IZL publications, and eventually summarized in the 'Guidelines for the Programme of the Hebrew *Herut* Movement' of the year1948, spelled out a number of patently Revisionist principles, including equal civic rights and religious and cultural autonomy for the Arab population, recognition of the right of free association, and a state-supported welfare system intended to guarantee a minimum 'cultural standard of living'. The original socio-economic platform included several outspoken étatist principles (which, however, after a short while disappeared completely from the *Herut* programme), such as the nationalization of basic industries and public services (para. 9b), the limitation of private land holdings (para. 2e), and government support for private as well as collective and cooperative pioneering settlement efforts (para. 4e). Side by side with these étatist fundamentals the programme stressed the need for a liberal-bourgeois type of government and society as exemplified by, for example, the encouragement of private economic initiatives, the prevention of any kind of monopolies – both in the labour market and the economy in general (principally aimed at the monopoly of the *Histadrut*). Generally, the programme represented an eclectic blend of socialist egalitarian principles (para 5f: a fixed maximum size of dwelling units for all citizens of the state) and liberal-capitalist fundamentals revealing, on the hand, an adherence to the ideological tradition, and on the other an effort to adapt to the new realities – and even (but only after May 1948) an internal struggle about everything concerning the shaping of the social and political identity and profile of the movement in the newly-established State of Israel.

This subject will be dealt with in greater detail in the next volume, which will describe the transformation of the IZL from an underground movement into a political party. Here it is important to point out that, even though the IZL regarded itself as a new political entity, it at no time rejected its origins. It even went to great lengths to identify with and reinforce its links with what it considered the fundamentals and the major and dominant trends in the early political tradition, and nowhere did the IZL present itself as either revolutionary or innovative, but merely as an in every respect traditionalist party.

Lehi – Messianism and Socialism; Innovation and Opportunism[2]

The position and attitude of Lehi was fundamentally different. When, early in 1944, the IZL started its revolt against Great Britain, Lehi was forced to justify its existence as a separate organization (notwithstanding the fact that its aims were identical with those of the IZL). As a result it tried to accentuate the ideological differences with the latter organization, from which it had broken away in 1940. During the years 1940 till 1949 Lehi publications constantly repeated the fact that the organization had severed all connections with Revisionism and the IZL. On a number of occasions Lehi even supported the claims of the Left to the effect that Revisionism (and the IZL) were contaminated with bourgeois-fascist ideology, or at least 'fascist influences'. 'There exists a wide gap between them and us,' stated Yitzhak Shamir (who was to become the second *Herut* prime minister) in March 1949.[3] Lehi did not restrict itself to the claim of having initiated the armed struggle against the British, or having been the party which correctly analysed the historical and political events, thereby showing the way to other organizations – especially the IZL. It was particularly important for Lehi to demonstrate how fundamentally its socio-cultural profile differed from that of the IZL and Revisionism. Lehi's realization that power in the *yishuv* was concentrated mainly within the Labour movement and its militarily trained youth, caused it to try and shake off its fascist image and to effect a change in its social ideology, with a view to extricating itself from the discrepancy in its image from which it (as well as the IZL) suffered. As from the middle of the 1940s, when Lehi – and not Lehi alone – believed that the Soviet Union might become an ally in the struggle against Great Britain's Palestinian Mandate and its continued hegemony in the Middle East (the Mandate, in their view, being another tier of the British power structure), the organization decided to play an – altogether fictitious – trump card by embracing socialist ideology in an effort to gain the Soviet Union's attention and sympathy for Lehi and its political aspirations in Palestine and the Middle East. Lehi offered itself as a party that would establish a socialist republic along the southern frontier of the Soviet Union and which, due to the nature of its regime, would be able to serve as a useful guarantor of the Soviet Union's geo-strategic interests by securing its hinterland against the ambitions of Western Imperialism.

During the early years of the 1940s Lehi invested little intellectual effort in the development of its own social and cultural ideology. As mentioned earlier, its main efforts were directed at rationalizing its national and territorial aims and its terrorist methods of operation. Such articles with intellectual depth as were published during this period were wholly dedicated to the formulation of a national-messianic doctrine, rather than to the drafting of a social platform. In this area Lehi contented itself with generalized dissertations on 'prophetic morality' and 'prophetic justice' which in no way contradicted either the general Zionist tradition or accepted Revisionist views. Paragraph 12 of the 'Principles of the Revival', written at the beginning of 1941, talks about 'the establishment of a social regime in the spirit of Jewish morality and prophetic justice'. 'Those living under such a regime will know neither hunger nor unemployment. People will live together in solidarity, friendship and dignity, showing respect for all the members of the nation, an example and a light to the Gentiles.' These words, couched in the most general and abstract terminology, could of course hardly be called a social platform.

Gradually socialist and even marxist elements became apparent in all analyses in Lehi publications dealing with the structure and the interests of British Imperialism. These analyses, which concentrated on the prevailing economic forces (such as oil interests and other powerful pressure groups) betrayed a marked influence of thinkers such as Lenin, Hilferding and Hobhouse. Besides this Lehi stressed (also in conformity with the early Zionist tradition) the social dimension behind traditional Arab–Jewish rivalry, arguing that only the expulsion of Britain from Eretz Israel would enable the rise to power of political and social groups in the neighbouring Arab states not 'artificially' interested in a national and military struggle against the Jewish state. In other words, the expulsion of Imperialism would cause the downfall of Arab reactionary feudalism, giving 'progressive' groups a chance to take over. Following the end of World War II Lehi began to present itself not only as a movement with a positive (i.e. 'neutral') political orientation towards the Soviet Union, but as a movement which regarded Socialism as a fitting, moral and just kind of regime. Studying the discussions on this subject in Lehi publications, it will strike the reader that for many of the speakers or writers Socialism by no means represented the ideal normative social system, but served mainly as an instrument for the realization of other objectives. One of the central and recurring arguments was that the workers were the pivotal class in the *yishuv*, who stood to gain most from the abrogation of the Mandate (the Mandate meaning continued dependence upon a capitalist nation and everything this entailed in socio-economic terms). For this reason the creation of a socialist workers' republic was the only way to achieve full Jewish sovereignty in the whole of the historical Land of Israel. To realize this objective it was necessary for the state to control the means of production and to have full authority to mobilize all its available forces and resources. According to Lehi's philosophy during the 1940s, a fascist regime might indeed arise in the [future] Jewish state, not because it ruled a large Arab population (Lehi, as the reader may remember, belittled the Arabs' power of resistance), but – on the contrary – because of a partition of Western Eretz Israel into two independent – Jewish and Palestinian – states.[4]

Lehi's socialist dimension – subsequent efforts to portray it as innovative and authentic notwithstanding – therefore looks like an artificial and intrinsically spurious attempt at achieving a synthesis between nationalism and socialism. Rather than a quest for an authentic model of a just society, it was the product of a pragmatic, and even opportunist, attempt at building a convenient image that would attract allies both within the country and abroad. In the final analysis Lehi, including the members who left its ranks to join the radical dovish Left, failed to leave any ideological imprint, whereas those members who continued in the activist national-messianic tradition became the custodians of the national-messianic idea and – after 1967 – participants in the ideological and political mainstream of Israeli society.

After 1948 Lehi had nothing left to offer to the Israeli political system, except for its activist nationalist world-view, its resulting total disenchantment with the outcome of the War of Independence, and a profound unhappiness with the prevailing political constellation and culture of the new state. As previously mentioned, some of its members became the principal spokesmen for those who advocated a solution of the Arab–Israeli conflict by the establishment of a Palestinian state in part of Eretz Israel west of the Jordan.

The platform of the Fighters Party (*Mifleget ha-Lohamim*) founded by Lehi, which after extensive debate was accepted by a majority decision, spoke in messianic and socialist terminology about the overlordship of the Jewish people over the historical Eretz Israel, with as a precondition the 'establishment of a socialist regime which would own all national resources and the means of production' (without specifying, however, whether this also meant the nationalization of the private means of production, and state-controlled planning on a socialist basis). The platform also claimed a complete symmetry of interests between the working class and the masses, on the one hand, and the broad national and territorial goals of Lehi, on the other. In marked contrast to the platform of the '*Herut Movement founded by the IZL*', the platform of the Fighters List stated that the *Histadrut* was the sole framework for the unionization of salaried workers, for which reason it had to be used as a weapon in the war for political and social liberation. A minority proposal (which received 19 votes, compared with 49 votes for the majority proposal) scarcely touched upon any social aspects at all, but revealed a similar favourable attitude towards the *Histadrut*, while taking a positive view of the establishment of agricultural settlements by members of the new political movement.[5]

It would seem therefore as though Lehi deluded itself by believing that the party had a chance of surviving for any length of time. Even so the members were sceptical about the capacity of a small and isolated opposition party to influence the ruling Labour movement. For this reason the platform tried to highlight the ideological affinity and the proximity between former Lehi members and the Zionist Left (some of its paragraphs had an even more outspoken marxist signature than the platforms of the parties of the extreme Zionist Left!). Lehi believed in its power to influence the Labour movement from within through the systematic dissemination of its ideas and stressing their mutual ideological proximity on certain central issues. However, its hopes were in vain, for the party's analysis of the situation, if anything, was based more on wishful thinking than on reality. There simply existed no apparent link between the social concerns of the working class and the territorial question. The opposite was the case: both the messianic and socialist aspects of Lehi's nationalist and territorial maximalism ran counter to the basic leanings and the general mood of Israeli society, which had reconciled itself to the idea of a Jewish state in a partitioned Eretz Israel. Lehi's *Fighters' Party* disintegrated after a short existence. During the elections to the First Knesset on 25 January 1949 it received 5,309 votes(1.2% of the total vote) entitling it to one seat in the Knesset; this was its first – and last – appearance in the Israeli elections. The membership dispersed, and the activities of those who remained were during the 1950s restricted mainly to journalistic efforts in the ideological journal *Sulam* and underground activity against the constitutional Israeli government: political terror and purely ideological writing remained the only way for the most radical groups within Lehi to express their profound displeasure with the new Israeli reality.

PART FOUR

CONTRADICTORY IMAGES – RIGHT VERSUS LEFT

Introductory Remarks

The struggle between Right and Left, within the Zionist movement as well as the Jewish community in Palestine, is a prominent feature of the history of the Jewish national movement. It was by no means the only – or the most important – conflict, but there is no doubt that it had a profound impact on contemporary events, and as such contributed materially to moulding the two rival political traditions in the Jewish state. The struggle was a genuine political and ideological struggle: a struggle about the future direction of Zionism, and who would lead it. Simultaneously it must be noted that this struggle took on almost apocalyptic dimensions, with a force and a bitterness that far exceeded the bounds of ordinary political opposition or differences of opinion. The propaganda and the accompanying rhetorics created a monster which at times turned on its creators. Even so it was believed, because the prevailing political climate was conducive to its acceptance. It was in the course of this struggle that the mutual images of the Zionist Right and Left were shaped – a Labour image of bolshevist totalitarianism in the eyes of the Right, and a Revisionist image of militant and reactionary fascist nationalism in those of the Left. It is impossible to say whether Zionist history would have been different if relations between the two contending movements had been more amicable. At the same time there is no doubt that they were *metus hostilis*, and that the mutual hostility and hatred did much to promote the internal unity of the respective camps.

The following two chapters will be devoted to a description and analysis of this struggle between Right and Left, a struggle between two conflicting interpretations and two images – images that were partly the outcome of party-political propaganda, and partly authentic reflections of the consciousness of the participants.

A comprehensive study of these contradictory images and the resulting conflicts is important in order to gain an understanding, not only of the ideological and emotional background of Zionist politics during the period from 1925 to 1948, but also of the sub-structure of the existing political culture in the present State of Israel.

CHAPTER ELEVEN

The Revisionist Attitude to the Labour Movement and Socialist–Zionist Ideology

The Character of a Total Confrontation

The critical Revisionist dismissal of the Labour movement, particularly the national philosophy and political methods of the labour parties led by *Ahdut ha-Avodah* (founded in 1919) and (from 1930 onwards) Mapai, coincided with the emergence of *Ha-Zohar* and *Betar*. The criticism focused on such principles as 'constructivist Socialism' and the feasibility of a synthesis of Zionism and Socialism, as well as on the moral image of the Labour movement, and the policies and practices of the General Federation of Labour, the *Histadrut*. This negative and critical disposition played an important role in shaping the mentality of the Revisionist movement, in the same way as the Labour movement's critical and dismissive attitude towards Revisionism was highly instrumental in shaping its spiritual world-view and guiding its political behaviour with regard to Zionism and the Jewish community in Eretz Israel. The Revisionists invested considerable intellectual and emotional efforts in combating the political attitudes of the labour parties, to try and prove how negative their contribution to the Zionist enterprise was. These efforts were reflected in the tremendous amounts of publicity, consisting of articles in newspapers and magazines, books, satirical and propaganda material, cartoons and caricatures, all of them aimed at undermining the ideological and moral basis of the Labour movement, by emphasizing its inner contradictions and the 'philistinism' which the Revisionists perceived in socialist Zionism. Already in the later 1920s virtually the entire ideological foundation of Revisionist criticism of the workers' parties was in place; during the 1930s only a few new elements were added, in particular the emotional elements and the sense of an almost apocalyptical struggle, much of the inspiration for which derived from the prevailing social and political climate, the ideological and class struggles during the 1930s and the political conflicts between the European Powers. The resulting ideological and spiritual polarization prevented any attempts at a more rational and pragmatic approach to the relationship between the two movements.

This chapter reviews the underlying causes and sources of the withering Revisionist criticism of the Labour movement. The Revisionist ideology and world-view possessed a very dominant and intensely negativist side, and this too warrants a closer discussion of its origins and foundations. The ideological criticism resulted in a virtually *a priori* determined frame of reference to events, phenomena and trends, and a false – and at times distorted – image of reality. The resulting image formed a catalyst to actual reactions, with the events nearly always being re-interpreted by those concerned, or used as a means of confirmation or illustration. This being the case, we cannot restrict ourselves to a review of the principal foundations of this criticism, until we have clarified some of the events and issues which helped to evoke and intensify it.

In this context the reader should remember that when Revisionism emerged on the political scene, it already found the Left entrenched as the political vanguard, and an integral part of both the Jewish society in Eretz Israel and the Zionist movement in the Diaspora. The Left, together with its organizations and values, was identified with the organic growth of the *yishuv* and portrayed (at times with unwarranted exaggeration) not only as the leading political force, but as an all-embracing establishment covering every single aspect of the *yishuv*'s daily existence. This means that the Zionist Right, in contrast to its evolution in the Western world, did not emerge as the result of a 'capitalist crisis', or out of concern about the growing strength of the socialist and communist parties, and everything this entailed. The Zionist Right was a reaction to – and a revolt against – an existing political, social and ideological establishment whose fulcrum and power base was the Labour movement. The maligned target of European socialism or European Populism was the 'bourgeois society', whereas the intrinsic national (*völkisch*) ideology of the Zionist Right found another target: the workers' parties and socialist Zionism, which were depicted as representing at one and the same time bolshevik dictatorship and bourgeois workers' philistinism!

The Onset of the Confrontation

The moderate group within *Ha-Zohar* observed with growing uneasiness and concern how the antagonism deepened and spilled over into the areas of social and labour relations. In particular it was disturbed by the question how developments had been able to take such a turn, and why? Was this fierce hostility necessary? Would it not be possible to moderate it and lead it into more temperate channels? 'Moderate' personalities for a variety of reasons regarded the confrontation between Revisionism and *Ahdut ha-Avodah*, in particular Mapai, as anything from a useless and superfluous deviation from *Ha-Zohar*'s neutral stand on social issues, to an unwarranted intervention in the economic and labour relations of Palestinian society. Jabotinsky found himself at times compelled to justify himself to these critics by explaining that the confrontation between *Ha-Zohar* and the Left had not started in 1925 with his critical article 'Basta!' directed against the Zionist Left, but that it was a logical, intrinsic rivalry, the natural outcome of the friction between two disparate ideological and political entities, between which there existed an unbridgeable gap.[1]

Those who considered a total confrontation to be an undesirable development, and therefore preferred to restrict the basic differences of opinion to the political arena, placed the blame for the eruption of the conflict and its intensity fully on the situation which had arisen in Eretz Israel since 1924. Jabotinsky's first biographer wrote that the seeds of the confrontation between Revisionism and the workers' parties had already been sown around the time of the British occupation of Palestine, and that the conflict erupted during the years of the Fourth Aliyah. Following his third visit to Eretz Israel in 1926 Jabotinsky wrote that he had discovered that the golden seeds which the socialist pioneers had sown in the fields of Eretz Israel had failed to bear fruit. In 1926, at the height of the economic and moral depression in Eretz Israel, Jabotinsky's analysis of prevailing conditions led him to the conclusion that the financial and settlement activities of the Zionist movement would from now on have to be focused on the middle class. This conclusion roused the ire of the workers' parties which, in addition to going through a deep economic crisis and struggling with problems of unemployment and lack of finance, found themselves attacked on all fronts by the Right at the Zionist Congress.[2] The danger of a new and fresh political force aligning itself with the workers' opponents forced the two workers' parties, *Ahdut ha-Avodah* and *Hapo'el ha-Za'ir*, into the forefront of socialist opposition to Revisionism.[3] *Ahdut ha-Avodah*, which was in opposition to Weizmann, now joined forces with him out of fear that Jabotinsky's strength might increase. If only Jabotinsky had proposed a settlement platform that did not reject the class struggle and preferred the workers' interests over settlement on the land and immigration, wrote the above-mentioned biographer, the leftist camp would have gone along with him. However, as soon as the workers perceived that Jabotinsky and his friends were unalterably opposed to a class war, demanding instead that the middle class receive preference in the settlement effort, they realized that if ever Revisionism became the ruling power, this would mean the end of the preferential position the workers had secured within the Zionist Organization, as well as of their increasing dominance over the *yishuv*, and the ongoing class war.

What finally turned the scales was a combination of circumstances. If *Ha-Zohar* had been an unambitious new party merely representing narrow partisan interests, it would have posed no danger to the workers' parties, and a confrontation might have been avoided. If the party had restricted its approach to political Zionist activism, without adding a middle class-oriented settlement ideology, the clash could have been averted. The combination of political activism and bourgeois Zionist orientation, however, produced an organic rivalry with the workers' parties that made it impossible to confine the confrontation to the platform of the Zionist Congress. Jabotinsky himself attempted to explain the hostility as resulting from *Ahdut ha-Avodah*'s blunted Zionist activism and its dependence on national capital, which had forced it into a coalition with Weizmann. According to him, 'national romanticism' and the activist stance of the workers had been sacrificed on the altar of the day-to-day economic needs of the working class and its supporters. 'Tel-Aviv was controlled by a Labour dictatorship which lived off the money supplied by the *Keren ha-Yesod*,' he wrote.[4]

The year 1924 was the year when Jabotinsky developed his social orientation to match his political views. The Fourth Aliyah changed his Zionist perspective, and revitalized and reinforced opinions which had already been formed prior to the Great War. The lower-middle-class immigration from Poland seemed to him the start of a new chapter, and a turning-point in the history of the Jewish immigration and settlement effort in Eretz Israel. The era of the hegemony of selective pioneering was coming to an end, and a new era of unrestricted middle-class immigration was beginning. Given the severity of the times, and the serious financial and moral crisis that the workers' parties were passing through, it is not surprising that the strengthening of middle-class Zionist forces seemed a daunting prospect, and Jabotinsky a dangerous opponent – the more so since the atmosphere at the Congresses of 1925 and 1927 was also barely sympathetic, and even outright hostile, to the pioneering settlement effort.

The Fourth Aliyah, which brought large numbers of middle class Jews, changed the social class structure of the *yishuv*. In answer to this new situation Jabotinsky developed his 'bourgeois orientation'. In his view the first objective of the Zionist Organization should now be to assist the absorption of the Fourth Aliyah. 'Why the enthusiasm for these communist collective settlements, that have swallowed enormous amounts of capital?' asked one senior Revisionist official. 'Has the Zionist Executive never heard about the experiments of Owen, Saint Simon and Lenin? The Zionist economy is totally inefficient, and it has squandered a huge amount of Jewish capital to the tune of £2,000,000.'[5] *Ha-Zohar*'s demand for a halt to the financial support of the workers' parties out of public funds at a time of terrible financial hardship, was tantamount to a declaration of war. Here was a suggestion to divert the already inadequate national capital, part of which was specifically destined for the support of the workers' economy, to extending credits to private entrepreneurs in Eretz Israel. In light of the situation prevailing in mandatory Palestine after 1925, the above 'balanced' proposal meant that, following a period during which the working class had received preferential treatment, the middle class would now be given priority. This was no longer a clash between a political and a 'practical' approach. *Ha-Zohar*'s point of departure was also practical Zionism, but a Zionism to be implemented and pioneered by the thousands of small independent middle-class and lower-middle-class entrepreneurs who were arriving with the Fourth Aliyah, and not by either hired workers, or by the collective sector organized within the framework of the *Histadrut*. This aggressive bourgeois orientation was taken as a declaration of war on the Zionist Left, not merely in terms of its political power, but on its world-view, Zionist accomplishments and all its other interests in the widest sense of the word. The reason for this, paradoxically, was not so much that the Zionist Left represented clearly-defined economic interests or pressure groups, but rather that it had emerged out of a movement with political aspirations that plainly appeared to have turned economic hardship and the existence of economic interests into a political lever.

1929–1939 – The Image of the Labour Movement as Traitors of the National Cause

As a rule Jabotinsky was not overmuch preoccupied with criticizing the national philosophy of the Palestinian Labour movement. To his mind its main weakness was not so much its national outlook, as its attempt to combine national and political objectives with social (or, as he believed, class-related) objectives. His main criticism was directed at the political methods of the workers' parties which, he believed, in the main formed a common front with Chaim Weizmann. Fundamentally he stuck to his opinion that Zionism stood no chance of realizing its aims without the implementation of a government-supported colonization regime in close cooperation with Great Britain. In any case he believed that in order to achieve this objective, the offensive had to be undertaken in London. Jabotinsky accused the Labour movement and Weizmann of political subversion, and of inability to grasp the fact that popular activism was the cornerstone of Zionist political activity. Time and again he stated his conviction that the final aim of Zionist politics was to gain the necessary *political conditions.* Time and again he voiced his opinion that the workers' parties, by their concentration on building the economy and their own independent rural settlements, were in effect opting for the abandonment of the fight for political terms through political pressure, satisfying themselves with the development of a labour economy. The Labour movement in Eretz Israel and its affiliated parties were therefore blamed for agreeing to Weizmann's evolutionary political methods and, in so doing, bringing about the failure of Zionism. Against the political approach and tactics of Weizmann and his ally, Mapai, Jabotinsky placed his own political method.

In actual fact, Jabotinsky did not accuse the workers' parties of political minimalism, which he considered an 'organic' characteristic of the Labour movement. As already mentioned, he blamed the socio-economic model underlying the evolution of the workers' parties, which required public funds for managing a private economy, which in turn brought about their complete dependence upon Weizmann.

This issue, as well as the Arab riots of 1929 and the White Paper of

1930, proved to be the turning-points. The Jewish Agency, Weizmann and the workers' parties were accused of having lost sight of the national vision, of appeasing the Arabs and jeopardizing the security of the *yishuv*. The expression *'Sanballatim'*, after Sanballat, the Biblical Samarian leader who had actively opposed the efforts of the Jews to return from Babylon to Jerusalem in order to rebuild its Temple, became a frequently-used pejorative in contemporary Revisionist literature. Uri Zvi Greenberg's poetry, and at a later stage Achimeir's articles, accused the heads of the Jewish Agency and the leadership of Mapai of responsibility for the massacre of Jews. Criticism of political tactics turned into accusations of 'moral turpitude', which had inspired these political tactics.

> Who breached the wall of the homeland?
> Who opened the gate to the Arab wolf?
> Ah, I know the Jewish hand,
> The filthy hand that opened the gate:
> The hand that takes the people's money, saved for redemption;
> The hand that turns the truth inside out . . . .
> You are guilty of the blood shed in Zion,
> As guilty as the murderous Arab and Edomite . . . .
> *The Speech of the Son of Blood*, 1929

The criticism became more and more widespread and fierce, and clashes in the areas of labour relations and the competition for immigration certificates, in addition to the political struggle, contributed to intensifying the tensions between the two camps. Even though the MacDonald letter in effect cancelled the White Paper of 1930, setting the door ajar for a fast and intensive development of the National Home, throughout the 1930s the Revisionists continued to suspect Mapai and Weizmann of being willing to sacrifice the Jewish State, and even the creation of a Jewish majority in Eretz Israel. The basic accusation was that of appeasement of the Arabs and, from 1937 onwards, a suspicion of preparedness to terminate the Mandate and agreeing to a partition of Western Eretz Israel.

Two almost simultaneous and closely connected political events further deepened and intensified the hatred towards the workers' parties, namely the Arab revolt during the years 1936-1939 and the policy of *havlagah* (voluntary 'self-restraint'), which the leaders of the *yishuv* and the *Haganah* had decided to impose upon themselves, and the Partition Plan of the Royal Commission under Lord Peel (the 'Peel Commission').

The *yishuv* leadership had decided upon a policy of restraint, in other words purposeful self-discipline and self-control, towards organized acts of Arab terror which had started in April 1936. It did not believe that Jewish counter-terror, particularly indiscriminate acts of terror prompted by a desire for revenge, would deter the Palestinian Arabs, and thus would have any real effect. Apart from this, the *yishuv* had formally adopted a policy to try and cooperate with Britain in maintaining law and order, so that it could scarcely afford to be found engaging in counter-terrorist activities. Heated discussions erupted within the *yishuv* at this time about various practical points relating to defence and security, as well as morality and points of principle, for instance about the question of whether it was allowed to use force, and under what circumstances, and to what extent? As far as the Revisionists were concerned, the policy of self-restraint fell outside the scope of pragmatic political con-siderations (and even if it did not, it was – to their mind – fundamen-tally misguided anyway). Nothing demonstrated better the intrinsic indecisiveness of the Mapai-controlled leadership of the *yishuv*. The Jewish Agency and the heads of Mapai were accused of 'the terrible crime of sacrificing the *yishuv*' and, in so doing, 'creating a Jewish ghetto in Eretz Israel in which, while frightened Jews are trying to squeeze in, murderous Arab [bands] are able to infiltrate unchecked and murder to their hearts' content'. According to this version the Jewish Agency and Mapai, by lacking the moral courage to use force and to react with force, had jeopardized the lives and security of the Jews. Their national convictions were simply unequal to the task of a national struggle, which had turned into a violent battle of life and death, and they were unable to draw the elemen-tary and vital conclusion that violence and force could only be met with violence and force, and terror with even stronger counter-terror. The succession of violent incidents during the years 1936– 1939 intensified the conviction within the Right that it was engaged in a no-holds-barred struggle with the Arabs, and that only the Right possessed the inner strength and conviction, untrammelled by either moral doubt, hesitation or ideological inhibitions, to take recourse to armed force. The policy of restraint was considered an abomination, a clear and shocking sign of national treason and historical defeatism.[6] Revisionist publications during those years were replete with articles, poems, readers' letters, and so forth, decrying the 'criminal abandonment of the *yishuv*', both politically and in terms of its physical survival. Such a policy, wrote the author Y.H. Yevin, was an open betrayal of the confidence of the people; it was DECEIT, of the kind for which leaders in every responsible nation would be court-marshalled .... The declarations of self-restraint only granted *carte blanche* and immunity to the murderers: 'You can kill, in the full confidence that the Jews won't touch you.' It was like the *Gleichschaltung* of the Nazis – the *yishuv* was being led like sheep to the slaughter, just like the Jews in the Diaspora, without anybody caring or trying to stop them. It was tantamount to a declaration that Jewish blood was cheap; those who spilled it would not be prosecuted . . . it was like losing a battle before even having entered the war; it was like justifying a verdict, and admitting defeat without even trying to defend oneself .... The Jewish leadership bore a heavy burden of guilt for its crime and its responsibility for all the Jewish blood that had been shed, for the shame it had brought over us, for jeopardizing our lives and our property, and for the coercive legislation to which they [the Jews] are now being subjected as a result of being abandoned . . . .[7]

The Partition Plan which the Royal Commission proposed in July 1937 triggered off a bitter controversy within Zionism, subsequently often referred to as the 'Partition controversy'. The strongest opposition came from the Revisionist camp, as a result of both ideological and emotional considerations. The territorial integrity of the historical Land of Israel under Jewish sovereignty was a political dogma, and one of the keystones of the Revisionist belief, which played a central role in the world-view of the Right. As such the agreement to partition by the Jewish Agency and the majority within Mapai was interpreted as nothing short of high-treason. In fact, the Revisionists asserted that a Zionist leadership which could support a proposal for the division of Western Eretz Israel had forfeited any claim to political legitimacy. The decision to partition Eretz Israel did not fall within the category of compromises on border disputes; it was a matter of partitioning the Homeland, and as such a betrayal of Jewish history and a denial of one of the central pillars of the Jewish world-outlook, namely the unconditional and unbreakable Jewish bond with the whole of the historical Eretz Israel. Apart from this, the partitioning of Eretz Israel would effectively imprison the *yishuv* within a narrow territorial ghetto, giving the Jewish population the status of 'protected Jews', such as existed in the Middle Ages.

While Jabotinsky was in London, trying to convince the

opponents of partition by means of rational and positive arguments (among which the difficulty of defending a Jewish state within the boundaries of the Partition Plan, and the intolerable population pressure within the area allocated to the Jewish state), publications along the entire spectrum of Revisionist opinion were talking in theo-political and emotional terms, portraying the advocates of partition in pejorative terms as a band of traitors, who had lost all spiritual and ideological bonds with the Zionist idea and with Zionist hopes and aspirations. Reading the countless exhortations against partition in Revisionist literature, one cannot help being impressed by the intensity of the belief in the territorial integrity of Eretz Israel in the consciousness and world-view of the Right. The fact that in Mapai, too, there were many who objected to the Partition Plan, did not prevent the Right from regarding Mapai and its leaders – whose leadership they claimed was usurped, and therefore illegal and immoral – as the instigators (together with Weizmann) of a treasonable conspiracy. Members of the workers' parties who did support the Partition Plan were portrayed as addicts to the socialist ideology, which had seeped like poison into their veins. Socialism's anti-national ideology – not to speak of its affiliated economic interests – had turned them into a herd of sheep, led by a well-oiled bureaucracy and a treasonable political leadership which had renounced the Jewish national vision and was now ready to surrender a large part of the historical homeland to Arab rule.

To this already established foundation of hostility and hatred, based on disparate reactions to historical events, opposing nationalist views, and conflicts about the evaluation of political opportunities, strategies and tactics, to mention only a few, several new layers were added during the 1940s. These conflicts lay in the political sphere. The IZL (preceded by Lehi) had come to the conclusion that the Jewish Agency and Mapai were following a defeatist policy. The fact that the *Haganah* – both its political arm and the underground defence organization – objected to the armed exploits of the two underground groups, and from November 1944 onwards undertook steps to try and eliminate the IZL, both by themselves and in cooperation with the Palestine Police and the British Secret Service (the so-called '[Open] Season'), resulted in their being labelled informers and traitors. The public condemnation of the IZL, and the attempts to boycott the organization and persecute, arrest and extradite its members and suspected sympathizers, created an undertow of resentment that was never forgotten or forgiven. In his notorious manifesto of February 1945, Menachem Begin denounced the *Haganah* as 'Cains' for persecuting and killing his brothers, accusing it of collaborating with the 'nazi-British' occupational regime in Eretz Israel. Here, too, the blame was not placed merely on the political leadership, but on the entire movement, including the rank and file which – according to Begin and his friends – displayed utter indifference to the Holocaust, and to the plight of the refugees and displaced persons in Europe, but who were ready to collaborate with the British 'Gestapo' in Eretz Israel. In his aggressive manifesto Begin repeated the well-worn characterization of the Zionist Left as a brutal and violent bolshevik movement, ready to resort to violence against fellow-Jews of divergent persuasions; a movement that refused to sacrifice its vested economic and political interests for the sake of the liberation of the Homeland; a movement ruled by a bureaucratic clique, which practised a rule of economic terror over its members; a movement which avowed Socialism, but used fascist and totalitarian methods; a movement, finally, which instead of by liberal and socialist thinkers, had been indoctrinated by Quisling, Laval, Degrelle and others of their ilk. Begin concluded this intemperate and rather pathetic manifesto, whose bitterness reflected the full intensity of his innermost emotions about the Left, by saying:

> Cain, remember! The Day of Judgement will come. The people will rise, their anger will pour forth, and for your crimes and betrayal, and for your machinations and treachery – in the name of the suffering nation, in the name of the enslaved homeland, in the name of the sacred victims, and in the name of our incarcerated brothers, in the name of their bereaved mothers and in the name of their abandoned children, in the name of our holy war and in the name of our blood that has been shed – we shall as yet repay you, Cain![8]

The decision by the workers' parties to accept, without serious internal opposition, the United Nations' Partition Plan of 29 November 1947 – including its implicit agreement to the division of Jerusalem – was considered the height of treason on the part of Mapai, under the leadership of David Ben-Gurion, and its partners.

Certificates, Transfer and Blood Libel

Our review of the basic causes of the negative attitude towards the

Zionist Labour movement and its goals would not be complete without a brief mention of the following events and phenomena:

1. Mapai and its socio-economic arm, the General Federation of Labour (*Histadrut*), were accused of abusing their monopoly of the labour market to prevent the employment of Revisionist workers. There is no doubt that the labour market was indeed controlled by a national network of *Histadrut*-run labour exchanges, which enabled it to exercise political and administrative control over this vital market, and in practice give preferential treatment to *Histadrut* members. Under the prevailing socio-economic conditions in Eretz Israel this meant that a person could be refused employment on political grounds, and such cases did indeed occur. It is not surprising therefore that the Labour movement was accused of using its monopoly position to deny Revisionist labourers the right to work, and in so doing virtually condemn them to starvation.

   The violent clashes on the labour front throughout the 1930s, and the organized as well as spontaneous coercion of Revisionist workers who refused to acknowledge the *Histadrut*'s control of the labour market, formed a constant and festering inducement to violence and hatred. Of course the two sides blamed each other for this violence, and the Revisionist camp portrayed the Labour movement as a bolshevik and totalitarian movement, that waved a 'red swastika' to protect its economic and political monopoly, while taking the bread out of the mouths of its political opponents. There were countless confrontations and clashes, all of which contributed to promoting a climate of unceasing political violence throughout the 1930s. There is insufficient space here to describe them in detail; the important thing to remember is that in a developing society which as yet lacked social services and a governmental social service system, the labour market was bound be a primary focus of social tensions.[9]

2. In the course of the 1920s Jewish immigration into Palestine turned into a party-political issue due to the mandatory government's immigration regulations. With the approval of the Zionist Executive, the mandatory authorities had fixed immigration quotas according to certain set criteria, that were partly determined by the political affiliation of the applicants. Immigrants belonging to the category of 'labourers' formed over half of the total number of newcomers during the 1930s, and they applied

for, and received, their immigration certificates through the so-called 'Palestine offices', a type of Zionist 'consulates' in a number of European cities. Consequently, the only possibility of immigration to Eretz Israel for the multitude of penniless immigrants – including the majority of the members of *Betar* – was the possession of one of these certificates. During the 1930s the demand for scarce certificates increased even further, and the allocation of certificates became an important source of political power, something of which all concerned in Zionism were only too well aware. To a large extent the affiliation of the newcomers became the key to the political composition of the Jewish population of Eretz Israel. The key according to which immigration certificates were allocated was the number of *hachsharah* (agricultural training courses) participants of the various movements abroad, subject to a computation by the Jewish Agency's Aliyah Department of the manpower required in the Palestinian labour market. Since the number of certificates was limited, and the distribution criteria were political, demand outstripped availability by a wide margin. In an effort to adjust itself to this situation, *Betar* created its own *hachsharah* organization. At the same time it utterly rejected the certificate policy, for two reasons of principle: firstly because it reflected a selective immigration policy, the result of collusion between Great Britain and the 'official' Zionist authorities, and secondly because it was in the view of *Betar* an expression of political and ideological prejudice, which favoured one particular group over another – Eastern European – group.[10]

It is not surprising that the Revisionists considered themselves seriously discriminated against, and regarded the existing immigration policy as a clear attempt to prevent their immigration to Eretz Israel.

Nor, for that matter, did Mapai spokesmen hide their desire to prevent Revisionist immigration, which was liable to change the demographic and political balance of power within the *yishuv*. Since Revisionist attempts to circumvent the certificate arrangements ended in failure, the pressures, bitterness and hostility – augmented by several tragic incidents – became the fundamental causes of the inhuman portrayal of Mapai as a party which for narrow party-political reasons was actually prepared to thwart the immigration of Jews to Eretz Israel.

3. The opposition of the Mapai-controlled Zionist Organization to the 'Evacuation Plan' of Polish Jewry which Jabotinsky had

formulated in 1933, was interpreted as yet another manifestation of the profoundly anti-Zionist attitude of Mapai. Mapai's opposition to the Evacuation Plan seemed a clear sign of its partisan and Palestine-centred attitude, and its refusal to acknowledge that Zionism was a movement intended to rescue Jewish lives; it was an opposition dictated by an elitist socialist ideology, which objected to the introduction of lower-class bourgeois elements into Eretz Israel that might interfere with their plan for the creation of a socialist society. From here it was only a small step to accusing Mapai of indifference and callousness towards the threat hanging over the heads of European Jewry and – eventually – of both direct and indirect responsibility for its fate during the Holocaust.[11]

4. Mapai's stand on the so-called 'Transfer', an arrangement for the transfer of German Jewish capital in the form of German export goods, which had been approved by the majority in the Zionist movement, was similarly regarded by the Revisionists as an act of high treason. In April 1933 Haim Arlosoroff, the chairman of the political department of the Jewish Agency, went to Nazi Germany to negotiate an agreement with Nazi authorities, and in June of that same year he was murdered on the Tel-Aviv seashore. During the intervening four months emotions ran wild. The Revisionists objected to the Transfer Agreement because it counteracted their plan for a world-wide Jewish boycott of German goods, which they believed would weaken the Nazi regime. A second reason for their opposition was their belief that the importation of goods and capital from Germany was basically intended to strengthen the *Histadrut* economy. The finer points of the issue need not concern us here, so that we shall not analyse the conflict in detail; it is sufficient to record that the Revisionists pointed at the transfer agreement as the ultimate proof of the despicable indifference of the Labour movement towards the distress of European Jewry. The bitter controversy, and the vituperative and demonological name-calling throughout the entire period were among the main factors contributing to the poisonous atmosphere and the deepening of the chasm between the two movements.[12]

5. The unsolved assassination of Dr. Haim Arlosoroff on 16 June 1933, resulting in accusations against a group of Revisionists and, by implication, the movement as a whole, was decried in Revisionist circles as 'blood libel'. The dramatic events around the trial and the acquittal of the accused (a verdict which Mapai

and its partners refused to accept as final), only added fuel to the already highly charged emotional and violent atmosphere. Mapai and its partners exploited the lingering suspicions as a lever for denouncing the Revisionists, to try to isolate and excommunicate them from *yishuv* society. The latter regarded this attempt as yet another demonstration of the 'bolshevik Stalinist' practices of the Labour movement, which in turn used the existing suspicion, and hostility to Revisionism to bolster the demoniacal image of a party that did not shy away from political terror to grasp the reins of government.[13]

These political dramas during the 1930s, which touched the most sensitive nerves in the Zionist body, were transformed into historical traumas which determined the relational patterns within the Zionist movement and the *yishuv* no less – and possibly even more – than theoretical interpretations and factual, ideological criticism.

The Fundamental Elements of the Negative Attitude of the Right towards the Left

The foundations of the critique of the ideology and methods of the Labour movement were, as mentioned before, laid in 1925, following which the selfsame arguments continued to be repeated in all subsequent arguments and controversies with the Labour movement about its institutions, its Zionist and settlement policy, as well as its national and social ideology. In the course of these controversies different – and often contradictory – arguments were raised, some far-fetched and marginal, some demagogic and intended merely to raise the hackles of the opponent, some dragged in merely for the sake of argument – as against others that were indeed rational and to the point.

The Revisionist leadership was fully aware of the special nature of the Zionist Jewish Labour movement: a synthesis of socialist ideology and internationalism with nationalism and constructivist Socialism. The criticism was therefore aimed at this synthesis, and focused on the various interpretations of this synthesis. Every single one of its elements was targeted for ideological or pragmatic criticism. It was said to have diverted the labour parties from the adoption of a simple, direct and consistent stance. By opting for 'having their cake and eating it', they had sacrificed 'their integrity and mental sanity'.[14] For Socialism was the antithesis of Zionism. Zionism functioned against a political and national perspective, whereas Socialism operated on an economic and class basis. Such opposites were impossible to reconcile, for no dialectics existed, either on the theoretical level, or in the realm of human history. Human history had to move along a simple, straight and one-dimensional track, rather than along a compound, problematic track. Any attempt to create a synthesis between the (Zionist) thesis and the (socialist) antithesis would necessarily result in a value system and behavioural patterns that were intrinsically dualistic, hypocritical and erratic; the result would be chaos.

Given this fundamental impossibility of a synthesis between Zionism and Socialism, it was only natural that it would give rise to hypocrisy; each and every one of its components contained an element of hypocrisy. One of the results of the synthesis of ideology and praxis was the constructivist Socialism of *Ahdut ha-Avodah*. What were the consequences of this constructivist Socialism? According to the Revisionist critics it had led to a loss of national élan and of political activism. Socialism had lost its creative drive and revolutionary perspective. When the socialist Zionists, under pressure of their objective circumstances, were forced to make the change to constructivist Socialism, they had needed capital to finance their initiatives. In Eretz Israel capital was created not by people's independent labour, but by importing it from abroad. The sources of capital were public funds, contributed by middle class Jews all over the world – the very bourgeoisie which the Jewish Socialists 'despised and did their best to help eliminate' in Eretz Israel. The workers' parties had established their collective agricultural society with the help of Jewish bourgeois money, while practising an anti-bourgeois ideology. This was moral duplicity, claimed the Revisionists. Worse than that, this bourgeois Jewish money was being used for strengthening political parties and the creation of a society which rejected large-scale immigration of middle-class refugees to Eretz Israel. Bourgeois money was used to create a socialist society which rejected the legitimate historical and Zionist right of middle-class Diaspora Jewry to emigrate to Eretz Israel. The synthetic ideology of socialist Zionism, wrote Uri Zvi Greenberg, is a 'pathetic' ideology, that is neither messianic, national nor sovereign. It is a 'huckstering' ideology which, while rattling collection boxes, has abdicated the national aspirations because of exilic flabbiness and love of comfort. Constructivism reflected a narrow perspective, subjection to economic and institutional interests, submission to the 'money lords' in the Zionist Organization and the Jewish Agency. From a national and political point of view it has turned the Labour movement into a 'petty bourgeoisie'.[15]

On the other hand, the Right claimed, Constructivism was unable to hide an ideology based on a class struggle and the nationalization of the means of production. Constructivism and the class struggle were two sides of the same coin, and they had the same purpose: to seize control of Jewish society in Eretz Israel and the Jewish people as a whole. According to the Right, the slogan 'From a class to a people', that Ben-Gurion had put forward in the early 1930s as the new ideology of the Labour movement,[16] merely meant that one class would dominate the nation through the ideology and praxis of the working class, subordinating the interests of the entire nation to these sectarian interests under the pretext of equality for all. Achimeir, so wrote Y.H. Yevin, regarded Marxism as 'a diabolic entity which, if it should succeed in controlling our lives, would wipe the image of God from the human face and drown it in the abyss of pollution.' 'In this respect,' Achimeir believed, 'there was no difference between Communism and Social-Democracy, or between Reformism and Bolshevism,'[17] and he was neither the only one, nor the most extreme holding this view.

The prevailing view among Revisionists, particularly during the 1930s, was a kind of demonology which equated Socialism with Communism, and socialist Zionism with both. Socialism, determined Achimeir in 1932, is one of the most negative occurrences in the whole wretched history of mankind ever since Tamerlane and Ghengis Khan. Even so his explanation of this socialist ideological hegemony of the *yishuv* was rather surprising and strange. The reason why Socialism was so firmly entrenched, he claimed, was the *absence* in Eretz Israel of a strong working class! For him Socialism was essentially the ideology of an aggressive and violent elitist political minority. This ideology had been internalized by the Jewish intelligentsia that had lost its geographical and cultural bearings which had been rooted in the Russian-Jewish civilization. In the transfer between two modes of life it was now passing through an identity crisis, apart from which these intellectuals anyway tended towards the kind of scholastic discussion of *yeshiva* students and autodidacts. Achimeir even maintained that 'the people of Israel, after giving birth to Christianity, had turned its back on it after first foisting it on the cruel Romans. Now history was repeating itself: the people of Israel had given birth to Socialism, and after using it to punish the cruel Russians, it was also turning its back on this deceitful doctrine.'[18] And so, 'the historic task of our movement is to reveal the incompatibility of Socialism – a typical intellectual, vacillating and [therefore] temporary movement – and the population at large and, in particular, the masses of working-class youth who are confidently looking forward to the national revolution.'[19] Socialist Zionism is a mental aberration, a pathological phenomenon, which deserves unrestrained hatred, he wrote.

In the demonology of the Right during the 1930s, Mapai was portrayed as a bolshevist-stalinist mob, which had even adopted marxist-internationalist symbols, such as the Red Flag and the Internationale, but which at the same time was prepared to kiss Hitler's boots, merely for the sake of money. In other words, it was a sick movement through and through, which out of sheer lack of principles had mortgaged the vital national interests to those of its own narrow partisan bureaucracy.

The most comprehensive critique of the synthesis, which influenced an entire generation of *Ha-Zohar* and *Betar* members, and which contributed materially to shaping their world-view, was formulated by Jabotinsky in his article 'Sha'atnez or the Glory of the Idea'.[20] [*Sha' atnez* is a ritually forbidden mixture of linen and wool.] In this article he repeated his firm conviction that there was nothing to distinguish between Communism and other socialist doctrines based on class principles.

> Socialism and Communism have their principal characteristics in common: the idea of social revolution has only one standard bearer, the working class, particularly the manual workers. The path to reform leads via the victory of this class and their domination of all other classes. The decisive step in this process of domination will be taken in the name of the 'Socialist Revolution' – in other words not by common consent, but by an act of violence. The only difference between Communism and Socialism is one of temperament – its intensity and its drive – but the aims remain the same.

Zionist Socialism, so claimed Jabotinsky, was Socialism which disguised its real intentions for tactical purposes. In its platforms the definition of its final aim was toned down, in order to receive financial assistance from 'bourgeois' national funds, and the political cooperation of the non-socialist parties. It also cooperated with the mandatory government in Palestine, which explained why it could not engage in political activism. According to Achimeir it was clear that the Palestine government used a policy of 'divide and rule' to control the *yishuv*. Since the workers' parties were minimalist in their attitude, they had been entrusted with the key for the allocation of immigration certificates, and this power was used against the Revisionists to restrict their immigration. The *yishuv* was ruled by an unholy triumvirate consisting of the Palestine government, the Jewish Agency and the *Histadrut*. In one of his more dramatic exhortations, Jabotinsky expressed himself in a similar vein:

> I [Jabotinsky], being of sound mind, do hereby declare and sign with my own hand, in the presence of witnesses: that the socialist parties, particularly those in Eretz Israel, are [not fighting the government, but that they are] subservient to the Palestine government and support it, and that the government would commit a tremendous folly if it persecuted or rejected its most loyal friends [i.e. Mapai and its allies].[21]

Again he railed at the duplicity of the workers' parties: superficially they were moderate and accommodating, because they operated in a non-sovereign society, in which they were unable to use the same revolutionary tactics as in a sovereign state. But inside their autonomous society they tried to eliminate another class – the middle class – and to take over the economy. Socialist Zionism tried to legitimize the attempt of a single party and a single class to dominate the Jewish society in Eretz Israel, and world Jewry in general; its aim was the domination of the salaried class. A victory of the labour parties (*Ahdut ha'Avodah*, or Mapai) would lead to a minority ruling the majority.

The agricultural collective settlements were portrayed as 'greenhouses', whose inhabitants lived at the expense of the general Jewish public, but at the same time were separated from it; who cared only for themselves and their own quality of life; and who were cut off from the principal issues of the Zionist revolution, assuming that they even worried about them. The *kibbutz* was like a monastery, an escapist institution which bred a 'degenerate' type of pioneer who cared only for his own salvation and that of his followers.

The ideology of the class struggle was intended to implement a classless society, something which might be suitable for the industrialized European nations, but not for the kind of settlement economy existing in Eretz Israel. The disastrous consequence of this ideology was that it prevented the establishment of a private . economy, and the immigration of an entrepreneurial middle class that could provide the needed momentum for the creation of a flourishing economy, which in turn would stimulate large-scale immigration. The shackling to Socialism meant enslavement to an alien ideology, and efforts to impose it upon the Palestinian and Jewish reality by artificial means.

Yet another aspect of the intrinsic contradiction of Zionist Socialism, according to the Revisionist interpretation, which revealed its duplicity and destructive inner conflict, was the unavoidable antithesis between internationalism and nationalism. Jabotinsky was of the opinion that the protestations by the labour parties – in particular *Ahdut ha-Avodah* (later Mapai) – of solidarity between Jewish and Arab workers in Eretz Israel, and their solidarity with the international working class, were patently dishonest. Fundamentally, he claimed, the proletariat could not possibly be internationalist; in fact, it was nationalist, and so were the workers' parties. The ideology and practice of 'Hebrew labour' and the 'Conquest of Labour' showed the very opposite of workers' solidarity, and if anything reflected a lack of solidarity and a clash of interests. The constant repetitions of the solidarity theme by the Labour movement were mere ritual restatements of an ideology that was detached from a reality which, as soon as it was put to the test, collided with the aims of Zionism. In effect this ritualization had created all kinds of rights and principles for the organized working class of Eretz Israel which contradicted its inner substance. This was yet another example of an unlawful mix of ideology and values, that produced the fickle and venal behaviour of the Labour movement, with as the only result alienation from the policies and aims of the Zionist movement. The labour parties were philistine parties, which looked after their own narrow interests only, while aspiring towards domination of the majority; they were immoral, violent, and totally lacking in ideological reliability and honesty.

Criticism of the Party System and the Histadrut[22]

The criticism of the structure and methods of the *Histadrut* centred on the assertion that *Ahdut ha-Avodah* (Mapai) had taken over what was supposed to be an apolitical trade union movement, turning it into a party-controlled organization and using it to increase the Labour movement's hold on the *Histadrut*, the *yishuv* and the Zionist Organization. To further this purpose an apparatus had been created of administrators and activists to run the party, and this bureaucracy exploited organized labour with the chief purpose of strengthening and enriching the party. The party was exploiting the *Histadrut* to achieve total ideological and economic control over organized labour. This process of politicization, as well as the political use of the *Histadrut*, had turned the Mapai–*Histadrut* complex into a powerful establishment with effective propaganda tools and the capacity to impose social and economic sanctions, which did not shy away from discriminating against, or even starving those who were not members. The election system and nomination procedures of the *Histadrut* were also rigged towards ensuring absolute control of the largest party, apart from which there existed an identity of interests between the *Histadrut* as an employer, and the *Histadrut* as a labour union entrusted with the protection of the workers' labour conditions. The political and class struggle of the *Histadrut* within the *yishuv* and the Zionist movement was aimed solely at the accumulation of material strength and at securing control of the labour market (through the labour exchanges) and the local economy.

The most outspoken manifestation of this point of view was Y.H. Yevin's *Jerusalem Waits* . . . .[23] According to this slanderous *roman à clef* even the *Histadrut* party bigwigs no longer believed in Zionism. They merely continued to wave the (ideological) Zionist banner to prevent them from losing their grip on the *yishuv*.

The socialist ideology, wrote Jabotinsky, arose to serve the proletariat of the industrialized countries of the Western world. During the present era – the 1930s – neither Western proletarian society, nor the *yishuv* were either hungry or poor. Organized labour had achieved social rights; it was neither starved, nor exploited by the well-to-do middle classes or the capitalist employers. 'The attraction is gone, the glorious era of the sacred Proletariat has come to an end,' wrote Jabotinsky in 1932 at the height of a heated debate on social issues. Organized labour had become an immensely powerful social class; it no longer struggled to improve its living conditions, but only to 'grasp power'. The only people worthy of the name proletarians were the lower middle classes, and they were self-employed and not unionized. They formed the masses of the poor: farmers, craftsmen, artisans, petty merchants, civil servants and clerks in private organizations. Manual labour was no longer physically exhausting; in the industrial era this kind of work was far less exhausting than that of farmers, merchants, clerks or intellectuals. The real proletariat was the lower middle class.

'What was the material position of the labourer?' he asked, and continued by answering his own question:

He works about half the number of hours of the farmer, or of a poor housewife, a mother of six small children. His labour unions own vast amounts of national capital, [as well as] banks, warehouses, hospitals, newspapers, libraries and clubhouses; his political influence outweighs that of anybody else; the statute books are full of labour laws protecting his rights; his wages allow him to live comfortably, and even save, and his banks have flourished and expanded on his savings; and if there should be a crisis, and the farmer and the merchant, or a young doctor or beginning lawyer should go hungry, and have nowhere to turn for assistance – then he, the salaried worker, will be supported out of public funds.[24]

According to Jabotinsky, the reality of the *Histadrut* society was living proof of this representation. A prosperous, powerful and bureaucratic *Histadrut* was threatening an impoverished and divided middle class, the mirror image of the Jewish lower middle classes of Eastern Europe, with pauperization and nationalization. The Zionist Organization had showered its bounties upon the *Histadrut*, enabling it to establish a burgeoning and affluent party-political apparatus, as well as palatial buildings, institutions, offices and countless branches, creating a sense of intoxication with their own power. The *Histadrut* was 'like a stalk planted in over-fertilized soil, and if we fail to subdue its outgrowths, its psychology will poison the entire Zionist enterprise, and once these people have come to power it will be impossible to breathe in Eretz Israel'.[25]

The above tirade was followed by a detailed description of the methods and tactics by means of which the *Histadrut* and Mapai tried to subjugate the entire Jewish society in Eretz Israel. The principal tactic, according to the Revisionist view, was the creation of an autonomous, centrally-controlled closed society, that would use its accumulated power to impose its will upon the various components of the surrounding society. To this end the *Histadrut* had created a tyrannical bureaucratic apparatus, and implemented its own cultural policies and an independent foreign policy.

Since the *Histadrut* was unable to take over the *yishuv*'s economy by coercive means (nationalization), and in view of the fact that the *yishuv* was an autonomous society – so the argument continued – it had developed a host of methods aimed at subjugating the rights of private capital owners in Eretz Israel. The economic aim of the *Histadrut* was to dispossess all private capital in the *yishuv*, to become its principal employer and the owner of nearly all assets.

The *Histadrut* itself was unable to impose restrictions upon the import of private capital, but it could try and prevent its transfer or, failing this, try and lay its hands on it after its arrival in Eretz Israel. This is why the *Histadrut* employed a two-pronged strategy: internally, segregation, and externally, expansion. From the moment the necessary apparatus had been created, and the necessary assets had been acquired, the immanent and natural urge to expand and dominate had to be given free rein. This was the 'natural philosophy' of organized wealth. The national capital, derived from public funds, was being turned into the 'private' capital of the *Histadrut*, since the major part of its contributions were transferred in the form of assistance and subsidies for its economic enterprises, and were invested in its organizations and institutions. The capital originated from public funds, but passed into the exclusive control of the *Histadrut*, which alone enjoyed the fruits. Private assets were expected to pass into the hands of the *Histadrut*; the opposite would be impossible. With the help of national capital resources the *Histadrut* would gradually succeed in appropriating the private sector of the economy and limit the economic freedom of the *yishuv*. This would be accomplished by a combination of compensation, exertion of financial pressure, and a monopoly of the labour market.

The *Histadrut* was maintained by 'other people's money', apart from which its economic enterprises were immune from strikes that could hamper their growth or stability. The *Histadrut* was both employer and trade union, it provided work to some and referred others; it was an autocratic and imperialist organization, a contractor who exploited the worker while fighting for his rights, who built one part of the economy while engaging in destructive competition with the rest. The *Histadrut* complex represented an autonomous, centralized society within the weak and unorganized Jewish Palestinian society, and consequently the main source of power within the *yishuv*. According to a calculation by Ben-Yerucham for the period 1932–1937, the *Histadrut* received by way of contributions, participations in commercial and industrial enterprises and profits an amount of Pal. Pounds 17,250,000 during this period alone.

Did the *Histadrut* society, which owed its creation to accumulation of power, indeed reflect the social ideals its builders had heralded and were still bragging about? The Revisionist answer to this question was a resounding 'No'. Did the *Histadrut* society indeed realize the Zionist ideals in an efficient and purposeful manner? The answer to this question was likewise negative.

Imperialism and autarky, the characteristics of the *Histadrut* society, were harmful phenomena, and there was a yawning gap between the pragmatic policies of the *Histadrut* and some of its activities, both internally and in the outside world.

Even the ideology of 'organized Hebrew labour' came under fierce attack. From a national rallying-cry, the ideology of organized Hebrew labour had turned into a party-political slogan, and the labour parties, particularly *Ahdut ha-Avodah,* i.e. Mapai, had to employ all kinds of tortuous dialectics to try and square their ideology with the internationalist ideology of the solidarity of the working classes. The outcome of these attempts at synthesis was the joint organization of the economy, with the aim of increasing the wages of Arab labourers, in order to prevent them from competing with their Jewish counterparts. But 'joint organization' ran counter to the Zionist objective, which was to provide employment for Jewish immigrants to Eretz Israel. There was an intrinsic contradiction between the struggle for the employment of Jewish labourers in the citrus groves, and attempts to impose the joint organization, and only during the riots of 1936 did the whole scheme come unstuck, when the Arab labourers abandoned their work places in the Jewish sector.

The Dialectic of Antagonism

There were those, of course, who regarded the above-described developments as superfluous and dangerous. The reader may remember that as early as 1927 some moderate Revisionists had warned against intensifying the struggle with Labour, as well as against the implied dualism of attempts to represent Revisionism as a movement that carried 'the eradication of Socialism from the Jewish community' in its banner. However, their efforts to deflect the course of events were in vain. Jabotinsky was at times forced to admit that an inbred hatred existed between the two camps, even though he was of the opinion that it was the other side which was to blame. In effect, several attempts were made to arrive at a compromise between the parties (such as the agreement between Ben-Gurion and Jabotinsky at the end of 1934, which was rejected by a *Histadrut* referendum in March 1935).[26] But these attempts usually came about under pressure of circumstances, and were mainly intended for external, tactical purposes. The continuing organization of the Zionist political culture into opposing Right and Left camps was never seriously contested.

The Right challenged the dominance of the Left, but to a much greater extent it was the Left which formed a continuous challenge to the Right, which was deeply disturbed and intensely frustrated by the fact that the Left succeeded in clinging to its political power, and continued to be identified with the realization of the Zionist effort and the building up of the National Home – and eventually – the rebirth of the State of Israel. As a consequence the entire Revisionist world became heavily dependent upon this confrontation and its outcome.

CHAPTER TWELVE

Revisionism and Fascism – Image and Interpretation

The Crystallization of the Fascist Image of Revisionism

The emergence of Revisionism as a political party, the fact that it presented itself as an alternative to the workers' parties, as well as its fierce criticism of their Zionist methods, their national views and their social and human character, within a short time resulted in its being equated with Fascism.[1] Almost from its inception Revisionism was portrayed as a nationalist movement which regarded the State and its coercive instruments as the supreme value. As a party, it was accused of wanting to destroy all that the organized working class had achieved. This negative interpretation failed to distinguish between programme, *Weltanschauung* and political behaviour, but apart from this it was simply unable to appreciate the singular character of the Zionist Right: Revisionism simply was fascist, inside and out.

In effect it was this very problem – the intense rivalry with, and deep-seated hostility to the workers' parties – which in essence produced the fascist image of Revisionism. Of the remaining elements of the above-mentioned interpretation, some were of a universalist nature and others specifically connected with Zionism or Eretz Israel. The fact that the launch of Revisionism during the middle of the 1920s coincided with the emergence of Fascism as a revolutionary and reactionary force in the international social and political arena, made this highly derogatory designation even more effective. The Left, which viewed itself as an *avant-garde*, as the representative of 'the People' and guardian of the higher national interest, could not afford to remain indifferent to this new and ambitious movement which, no less than itself, pretended to represent the overall national interest.

We shall introduce this chapter with a brief description of the evolution of the image of Revisionism as 'Zionist Fascism', resulting from a specific set of internal characteristics, combined with the generalized interpretation of outsiders.

The Image of Jabotinsky as a Political Demagogue

Even before the emergence of Revisionism as a movement, the leaders of the workers' parties portrayed Jabotinsky as a rather simple-minded nationalist leader whose mentality was worlds apart from their own spiritual climate: a cold personality, utterly lacking in human empathy and understanding of the mentality of the labour pioneers; a man attracted by the glitter and ostentation of external things, whose Zionism was devoid of inner content; a man who only knew the word 'demonstration', and whose idea of glory was confined to 'plumed helmets, riding boots and gold epaulettes'. Little by little this negative image of Jabotinsky took hold, until gradually only bad qualities were associated with his person. Jabotinsky's 'Russian period', that of the feuilletonist, journalist, translator, orator and propagandist, as well as the period during the Great War, when Jabotinsky founded the Jewish Brigade, were belittled and pushed into the background until they were mere nostalgic legends. The overriding image was that of Jabotinsky the charlatan, the demon, the demagogue and fascist . . . . 'Jabotinsky will never succeed in creating a movement; all he does is make waves and whip up froth. He doesn't have many followers, nor will he attract many. He acts like a knight in shining armour in search of past adventures in a new world.'[2] In 1931 the author Shlomo Zemach wrote a psychological analysis of the personality of Ze'ev Jabotinsky, in which he concluded that Jabotinsky lacked power of concentration, that he was unable to devote himself to a single cause, and that this explained his psychological tendency to scepticism, his demagogy, his belief in personal strength and his innate weakness of character – despite which, unfortunately, he happened to become an idol of many.[3] The attitude towards Jabotinsky within the Labour movement and 'liberal' Zionist circles had from the very beginning been ambivalent. He was faced with hostility from the side of *Ha-Po'el ha-Za'ir* and with a carefully reserved attitude on the part of the members of *Ahdut ha-Avodah*,[4] which after 1925 turned into general and unrestrained hostility. Until 1923 Jabotinsky had only been a public personality without a party; after 1925 he was the leader of a party which actually succeeded in attracting a mass following. The Jabotinsky who stood at the head of a competing political party was an enemy. Since the

Revisionist movement was identified with Jabotinsky, the party became the personification of the man: Revisionism had been created and moulded according to the image and the interpretations of the leader, and as such was nothing but his reflection – and conversely, the attributes of the leader corresponded with the collective characteristics of the public he led.

The Collective Image

The shift from a derogatory personal image to the negative fascist image of Revisionism as a whole, proceeded smoothly and virtually unimpeded.

The launch of Revisionism in 1925 had evoked a variety of reactions. At first interest was focused mainly on the group of activists around Jabotinsky and *Razsvet*, which functioned within the framework of the Zionist Organization. For a short while the movement in Eretz Israel was regarded as a centrist rather than a rightist party. The representatives of *Ha-Zohar* in the Elected Assembly of the *yishuv* voted with the *Ahdut Ha-Avodah* faction in several critical divisions (on a few occasions also against *Ha-Po'el ha-Za'ir*), but already in the Tel-Aviv municipal elections in December 1926 *Ha-Zohar* threw its support behind the liberal 'citizens' lists.

In any event, it was not *Ha-Zohar* in Palestine which aroused the concern of the workers' parties, but Revisionist activity within the Zionist Organization. Several elements of Revisionism caused considerable concern, among them the party's popular appeal and its potential flourishing as a movement capable of attracting the Jewish masses in Eastern Europe. It should be remembered that reactions to the appearance of the Revisionist movement cannot be divorced from the general – political and ideological – background. The 1920s were characterized by an intensifying struggle between the 'Right', the 'radical Right', Socialism and Communism for the 'European soul' and its political control. The rise of Nationalism in the newly-independent states that had been founded on the ruins of the Habsburg and czarist empires, the world-wide economic depression of 1929, the chronic crisis of the Weimar Republic, the fascist rise to power in Italy, Pilsudski's rise to power in Poland, Hitler's rise to power in Germany in 1933, the forcible suppression of the Austrian Social-Democrats by Dollfuss in 1934, as well as the Civil War in Spain – all these facts contributed to creating an all-pervading climate of overt and covert civil disobedience in Western society. The resulting sense of crisis provided a feeding ground for missionary ideologies competing with each other in the creation of a new world and a new society. In light of the above, events in Eretz Israel – despite the fact that the basic situation there was unique and very different from that of Europe – often seemed the mirror image of the struggle in the West. Earlier it was mentioned that party-political propaganda in Eretz Israel was rooted in this same consciousness, and in turn nourished by it. Against this background, and on the basis of a generalized historical and social interpretation of Revisionism, the labour parties described the Revisionists as 'fascists'. This interpretation, and the resulting fascist image, were due to a conjunction of the, in the view of the Left, two main characteristics of Revisionism, namely its conservative and reactionary nature and Jewish *petit bourgeois* membership, and the romantic nationalism and militarism of the party. Analysing the results of the 1925 elections for the Elected Assembly, the newspaper *Davar*, the official organ of the *Histadrut*, commented that Revisionism (i.e. *Ha-Zohar*) was a party feeding on the political dissatisfactions within the *yishuv* and the lack of stability of the middle-class parties. *Ha-Zohar* had no roots in this country, and its success could only be attributed to the fact that the members had 'a sturdy oak, Jabotinsky, to lean on'.[5]

Eliyahu Golomb, one of the spokesmen of the Labour movement, provided a simplistic explanation of the political and ideological stand of the *Ha-Zohar* leadership. Most of them, he wrote, were exiles from the Soviet Union, and therefore harboured a grudge against Socialism: '*Ha-Zohar* is the very flesh and blood of the bourgeois class, and its lack of regard for the Labour movement stems from the spiritual kinship of its creators with the bourgeoisie.' According to him the class-oriented social leanings of the leaders of *Ha-Zohar* were aimed at preserving the Jewish 'social pyramid', in an effort 'to maintain the Diaspora social structure of the Jewish nation.'[6] Even this 'bourgeois' definition was insufficient, inducing Golomb to add the supposition that Revisionism did not represent the 'successful bourgeoisie' – the capitalists and productive entrepreneurs – but the 'failures': reactionaries, *rentiers*, speculators, landlords who had seen their rental incomes decline during the depression, and so forth. According to him Revisionism represented the 'parasitic' elements in the Jewish Diaspora society. Another hostile analyst suggested that *Ha-Zohar*'s supporters

belonged to the misfits and the deprived elements among the

well-fed middle class, in particular the younger, idle and
marginal elements among the bourgeoisie who were trying to
find an outlet for their energy in pseudo-masculinity and
vainglorious heroic exploits. A generation of youths was growing up in Eretz Israel that lacked all substance and cultural and
social weight.[7]

It is this interpretation which became the prevailing view.

The socio-political analysis of Revisionism in Labour publications was in many ways informed by marxist methodology and the
marxist-socialist interpretation of European Fascism. According to
these, Revisionism was a party of lower-middle-class speculators,
rack-rent landlords and lower-middle-class youth 'living in a fantasy
world of militarism and organized sports'. Had not Jabotinsky
himself admitted, even in writing, that Revisionism was a movement which looked after the interests of the lower middle class,
which was a treacherous underworld, using catchphrases about
physical force and trigger-happy nationalism? *Ha-Zohar* supported
the Fourth Aliyah, which introduced a 'profusion of centrifugal
forces' into the country that progressively confused the national will
and turned Eretz Israel into 'a never-never land of would-be gold-
diggers'. Jabotinsky was 'like a knight in shining armour in search of
past adventures in a new world,' a man who thought he could
transplant the kind of national Romanticism found in historical
novels to a totally different reality from that which had produced the
European liberation movements. Yet another persiflage describes
one of the 'grandiose visions' of Jabotinsky's, by portraying him as
the leader of a band of screaming 'Jabotinsky Youth', striking
heroic poses reminiscent of the Latvian and Lithuanian student
organizations.[8]

The first serious and unbiased attempt at analysing the nature of
the Revisionist movement was an article in *Kuntres* in 1929, entitled
'On the Social Roots of Revisionism'.[9] According to its author the
ideology of bourgeois Zionism was characterized by two elements,
neither of which existed in Revisionism: (a) the insistence on being
the leading force in the establishment of a Jewish society, which
preserved Capitalism, while accommodating the demands of the
rising working class and its institutions – in other words, coexistence
between Capitalism and the rights of the working class; and
(b) acceptance of the idea of a minimum social level of existence,
and cooperation with the workers' parties, who constituted the
constructive element of the *yishuv*. For this reason the author

distinguished between the 'progressive bourgeoisie' and the 'reactionary bourgeoisie'. The progressive Zionist bourgeoisie did not regard the Labour movement as an enemy which had to be fought tooth and nail. As representatives of the Jewish capitalist industrialists in Eretz Israel, whose economic interests conflicted with those of the plantation owners, they too supported the principle of the nationalization of land resources. Capitalist industrialists in Eretz Israel had a stake in the commercial and industrial expansion of the domestic market, which meant that they were interested in Jewish labour, the demographic growth of the *yishuv* and the expansion of the collective settlements. It also meant that they respected the workers' pioneering efforts and could be trusted to act from Zionist considerations and take a realistic view of the special conditions prevailing in Eretz Israel – conditions which did not allow large-scale private initiative. The progressive bourgeoisie was therefore the ally of the working class, and had not the slightest desire to engage in social and political warfare against it.

According to this analysis, Revisionism in Eretz Israel was a political tool of the 'reactionary bourgeoisie' in its fight against the workers' parties. However, the author also distinguished between Revisionism and 'reactionary bourgeoisie', rather than lumping them together. It was a tool, but also an immanent socio-cultural development and phenomenon. According to him, Revisionism was a special kind of Jewish Palestinian Fascism, which developed as a result of the conditions in the country and its particular national environment. Fascist Revisionism was a mixture of syndicalism, early industrial capitalist notions, and ideas about 'absolute state control', combined with nationalist Romanticism, political dictatorship, hero worship and totalitarianism. Revisionism acknowledged the conflicting interests of the classes, but opposed class struggle and wanted to neutralize class dynamics by compulsory means. Despite the fact that Revisionism did not originate from the middle classes or represent its economic interests, it had adopted – just like Fascism – the social pathos of the bourgeoisie and accorded it moral legitimation. Hence its distinction between intellect and labour, and between physical and spiritual foundations; hence, also, its inclination to enforce social patterns by political means, through the instrument of fascist-style 'corporations', intended to reconcile the contradictions between capital and labour through a mechanism of compulsory arbitration that would deprive the worker of his legally guaranteed social protection. On these grounds the author concluded that Revisionism in effect conflicted with the interests of the Jewish middle class in Eretz Israel, as well as with middle-class Zionist ideology. Revisionism wanted to use the national funds as an instrument for expanding private ownership of both land and property, it glorified free enterprise, the acquisition of private wealth, settlement through war, and a no-holds-barred struggle with the Labour movement. Revisionism's fight against the American-Jewish plutocracy and its struggle for democratization of the Zionist Organization barely disguised its national Romanticism and the leadership *myth*. Revisionism, the writer of the article concluded his analysis, had its base in the 'murkiest elements' within the bourgeoisie – particularly bourgeois youth.

The qualification of Revisionism as European Fascism was hardly contested within the Labour movement. It was exploited for propaganda purposes in violently libellous documents, one of which, called 'The Labour Movement and Revisionism', was written by David Ben-Gurion on the eve of the elections to the Zionist Congress in 1933. This phenomenon was by no means uncommon, cropping up not only in published texts, but also in personal documents such as private letters. Ben-Gurion used this analogy not only to whip up fear of Jewish Fascism among certain circles of the Jewish public in Eastern Europe during the election period. In private letters written during critical moments of the struggle, he also compared Revisionism with Fascism and Nazism. Both the literature and propaganda materials of *Ha-Shomer ha-Za'ir* showed clear signs of being inspired by marxist interpretations and historiography, as can be seen from the bibliographies of books and articles written during this period. Ben-Gurion also defined Revisionism in marxist terms, using expressions such as 'the black, warlike wing of feudal Zionism'. Revisionism, all of whose distorted pathos derived only from class hatred and malice towards organized labour, had become the main support of those who were undermining Jewish labour in Eretz Israel. It organized gangs to break up strikes, and interfered with the activities of the labour organizations. By inciting the lowest class instincts of the employers, it created a class-oriented ideology which as good as justified the boycott of Jewish workers. As for the Revisionist leader, he even attempted to prove 'scientifically' that labour in general was by now of little value, and that its importance would continue to decrease with the advance of capitalist society.[10]

Here and there someone claimed that Revisionism was not a homogeneous body, and that actually only one specific segment of it (i.e. *Betar*) was fascist and militant. However, during the 1930s even this distinction disappeared in the welter of virulent debate. Alternatively, the Labour movement sometimes evoked Revisionism in order to stifle dissent, and more than once it was used as the bogeyman in internecine party struggles. At any rate, all the workers' parties, from *Ha-Shomer ha-Za'ir* to Mapai, evolved an anti-Revisionist demonology to keep the ranks united, but even then this 'fear' of Revisionism was not whipped up for purposes of political manipulation alone.

During the 1940s the IZL, and even more so Lehi, were portrayed as fascist organizations, and this not merely because of their links with the Revisionist mother-organization. The IZL was perceived as trying to obtain political clout by terrorizing the *yishuv*. The definition of the IZL as a fascist organization (a distinction which, incidentally, it shared in official British documents with the *Haganah*) was therefore not a result of its preparedness to use violence in the struggle against Britain, but to its refusal to submit to the authority of the political organs of the *yishuv*. Its perception as the secret military arm of Revisionism served only to reinforce this image. It is ironic that on more than one occasion the IZL portrayed Mapai as a fascist party, especially following the latter's attempts to eliminate the IZL by violent means during what is known in Israeli history as 'the Season', whereas Lehi made intensive efforts to escape the fascist stigma that was being attached to it.

Jabotinsky's Interpretation of Fascism

At this point it is worth noting that Jabotinsky's sociological interpretation of Fascism was similar to that of the Labour movement. Towards the end of his earlier-mentioned article 'Basta!' of 1925, Jabotinsky commented that without an equitable division of the national funds between the private and the *Histadrut* sector, it would be impossible to maintain the economic independence of the lower middle class in the *yishuv*. Without a stable organization of the economy the middle class would have no choice but to express its suffering and frustration through organized political militancy, 'like what they now call Fascism,' he added.[11]

Jabotinsky therefore considered Fascism a militant political manifestation of the plight of a middle class threatened with pauperization and proletarization, in this particular case − a reference to the Palestinian situation − by an organized working class that was wealthier and stronger than the independent middle class. Fascism was a middle-class movement whose members were merchants, lawyers, clerks, and so forth. In sociological terms Jabotinsky's description was a near perfect definition of the nature of his movement. A distinction should be made, however, in the social structure of Revisionism as a mass movement between the situation in Poland and the other Eastern European states, and that in Eretz Israel. Jabotinsky's contention that craftsmen and skilled labourers formed the mainstay of the radical Right was correct as regards various European societies, but did not apply to the situation in Eretz Israel. The Revisionists in Eretz Israel counted very few craftsmen among them, and neither could it be said that their economic status was declining; on the contrary, except for periodic depressions during the mandatory period affecting the *yishuv* as a whole, it improved steadily. Politically, Revisionism viewed the middle class in Eretz Israel with suspicion and contempt; in economic terms, however, Revisionism did not harbour syndicalist or pseudo-socialist ideas about an all-out struggle against monopolies and cartels, or capitalists in general. There simply were too few of them in the Palestine of those days.

Even assuming that Fascism did derive its social power from a declining middle class − on whose behalf it promised to fight the moneyed interests, but which ultimately was rewarded with Nationalism and anti-Semitism − Revisionism certainly did not suggest an economic struggle against Jewish capitalists and the employers in Eretz Israel. Its negative attitude towards the 'American-Jewish plutocracy', in other words well-to-do, non-Zionist American Jews who had joined the Jewish Agency Executive in 1929, was not prompted by socio-economic considerations, but by its views about the proper political structure of the Zionist Organization. Leading entrepreneurs such as Pinchas Rutenberg, who established the Palestine Electric Corporation, and Moshe Novomeysky, the founder of the Dead Sea phosphate works, were highly regarded as Zionist pioneers. Although the Revisionists lacked confidence in the political methods of the Palestinian factory owners, they were unstinting in their praise of the important, if not vital, contribution of private industry to the economy of Eretz Israel and the realization of the Zionist scheme. Revisionism was therefore not a protest against Jewish capitalism in the *yishuv*. On the contrary: we have seen that it enthusiastically supported the uses of capitalism, both in principle and in practice. It did not object to capitalism as a socio-economic order, to capitalism as employer and entrepreneur, or to capitalism as a social or cultural ethos. With the exception of Uri Zvi

Greenberg, whose writings during the 1920s were inspired by his expressionist contempt of bourgeois values, capitalism and private property, it enjoyed general approbation, and even admiration.

National Arbitration and the Corporatist Régime

The Revisionist model of a socio-economic class structure and its proposed national reconciliation mechanism for the solution of labour conflicts in the Palestinian economy probably formed the most tangible meeting points of fascist ideology and praxis, and the socio-political programme of Revisionism.

The idea of a corporative state as a solution to the crisis of the industrialized nations, and as a method of achieving industrial peace, spread during the 1920s and 1930s all over Europe in a variety of forms. In its most moderate version – such as, for instance, that proposed in Great Britain – there was no suggestion of abolishing the parliamentary party-political structure. But the proponents of the corporatist idea believed that the individual in an industrial society was both *homo politicus* and *homo economicus*, since most of his life was spent in economic activity. For this reason they wanted to organize the 'industrial man' in the economic field as well, as an extension of the anthropological concept of the *homo economicus* of classical Liberalism. Lytton Strachey, in his book *Revolution by Reason*, followed by Oswald Mosley – who at that time was merely one of the leaders of the British Labour party – developed the idea of state control of prices and wages. Against the background of the general strike of 1926 Italian Fascism seemed an efficient way of solving the crisis affecting the industrial societies, by rehabilitating their economies and fighting unemployment and inflation. The Macmillan–Boothby–Stanley group within the British Conservative party, in their essay 'Industry and State', formulated a plan for an 'Industrial General Staff' with compulsory authority over industry, based on the experience with centralized planning during the Great War. However, no changes were envisaged in the political structure. Mussolini himself formulated his corporative ideas only in 1932, by proposing a harmonious society in which all individual interests would be subordinated to the common cause, as determined by the state. His corporative model, tailored to the Italian situation, consisted of a comprehensive network of 24 corporations which together covered all branches of production, to be controlled by a National Corporative Council composed of representatives of the workers, the employers and the government, that would decide all issues concerning wages, prices, profits and labour conditions.[12] The principal problem was to strike a correct balance between the organizational autonomy of each of the corporations and the compulsory authority of the State. Who was to decide what constituted the 'good of the state'? That was the key question. The fascist answer was very simple: the fascist party, which controlled all aspects of life in the totalitarian-fascist state.

Both conservative and non-conservative commentators in Europe viewed the corporative system as *the* solution to critical problems such as labour–management relations, the distribution of income and the expansion of industrial output. They believed in the establishment of 'industrial peace' and social harmony through regulation and direction from above, i.e. by the state in its capacity of an 'objective' authority. The Labour movement, on the other hand, regarded the corporative régime as an instrument for the exploitation of the working man by the fascist party and the capitalist employers.

The corporative theory did not meet with a universally favourable response within the Revisionist party. Dr. Mordechai Avniel, a moderate Revisionist public figure, rightly concluded in 1939 that Corporatism was not going to bring prosperity to the salaried worker, whereas Jabotinsky, when broaching proposals for the most suitable social mechanism, usually – but not always – avoided referring to the Italian fascist régime, preferring to take his examples from Léon Blum's 'Popular Front' policy in France.[13] Replying to a letter from Shlomo Jacobi, demanding that Jabotinsky assume 'fascist control' over the party, Jabotinsky wrote on 4 October 1933 that Revisionism was not fascist, and that the only thing it had in common with Italian Fascism, apart from its rejection of the class struggle and the demand for compulsory arbitration of labour disputes, was the view that national interests transcended class interests. Revisionism, as opposed to Fascism, wrote Jabotinsky, believes in democracy, parliamentary government, freedom of speech and thought, and freedom of the press.[14] Even so, many Revisionists viewed Fascism as practised in Italy in a positive light, due to what they believed was the fascist desire to reconcile the social classes, and because of its social legislation, as a result of which intensive studies of the structure of the Italian corporative régime were undertaken.

Achimeir, for instance, regarded corporative government as an intrinsic part of the fascist economic régime, equating it with a nationalist and protectionist form of government. 'What is good for the middle classes, is good for the proletariat, and when the middle classes flourish, the proletariat will flourish as well,' he wrote. The middle classes and the workers have the same purpose: to capture and enlarge the market.[15] The Revisionist monthly *Betar* published translations of two Italian analytical essays of the corporative economic régime. Aldo Roki, the Italian minister of Justice, described Fascism as a way of transforming the liberal-democratic state into an authoritarian form of government representing the majority only, and invested with sole authority to govern in pursuit of what it considered the common good.[16] Professor Camillo Sorino, in his article 'Wages and Profits in a Corporative Administration' attempted to prove that Fascism did not contradict the classical laws of political economy, but represented a higher stage of development. Under a fascist régime, he wrote, it is the state which supervises the essentially opposing interests of capital and labour, thereby creating the right conditions for harmonic growth without interfering with the laws of political economy. The fascist economy differs from the liberal economy only in that it is protectionist, in other words aimed at promoting the national economy rather than international economic interests or free trade, and that it regards the public benefit as the determining factor rather than private gain or the economic market forces. The fascist economy applies a distinction between the way a company is managed, and its ownership and the way its profits are shared. Without profit there is no motivation to work; the overarching management of the economy by the state (or the party) does not mean a denial of the conflict between capital and labour. Fascism is Keynesian in its recognition of the fact that raising wages increases productivity and the standard of living, and therefore profitability. On the other hand, Fascism is very much aware of the considerable power which the labour unions have gained in the industrialized nations, as well as of the fact that industrial conflicts have caused a flight of entrepreneurial capital, thus resulting in a decline in profits and wages. For this reason Fascism considers it its task to put an end to labour conflicts and restore the equilibrium between the power of the labour unions and that of the producers. This will result in raising productivity and wages. The law of 3 April 1926 prohibited strikes as well as lockouts, and (in para.12) decreed a minimum wage; above this minimum, wages were to be determined by productivity, profits and the value of the productive output. This procedure would result in lower prices and higher wages, so that Fascism could indeed be regarded as a régime that was capable of regulating the laws of political economy.[17]

Zvi Kulitz, another Revisionist public figure and writer, considered the corporative régime the crowning glory of all that Mussolini and Fascism had wrought. Here was a régime which had realized the fundamental equality of all workers on the principle that labour was not a negotiable commodity, but a national duty. Such a principle did not acknowledge class differentials. The harmonic society would be based on a centralized régime and the intervention of the political apparatus in the economy – not for the benefit of one sector only, but in order to create an equilibrium and cooperation between capital and labour. The corporative state made itself responsible for the workers' welfare through the 'syndicates', the trade unions which formed a part of the corporations.[18]

The Revisionist proposals for compulsory arbitration and the establishment of a Supreme Economic Council, which represented major items in the Revisionist programme, were in essence inspired by the Italian fascist model. The difference, however, was that Revisionism wanted to implement this model, whose main strength lay in its enforced application, in an autonomous and voluntary society. Even more so, it considered applying it in a pre-industrial society which as yet lagged decades behind even a backward industrial country such as Italy – not to speak of industrialized societies such as Great Britain or Germany. The Revisionist theory of compulsory arbitration and a Supreme Economic Council was therefore a mere shadow of the Italian corporative model. *Ha-Zohar*'s platform simply contented itself with raising the idea, and only in Revisionist publications was the programme worked out in greater detail. The purpose of the idea, within the context of Eretz Israel, was mainly to weaken the power of the *Histadrut* and undermine its virtual monopoly of the domestic labour market. Revisionism differed from Italian Fascism in its assumption that it would be possible to achieve harmony between the various economic sectors without the use of compulsion, through a neutral, non-party constitutional authority. The idea behind it was not to create an egalitarian society, but to establish a balanced and peaceful relationship between the disparate components of the social system, in order to facilitate their smoother integration into the national political struggle – all this on the assumption that class distinctions were a natural and even positive phenomenon.

Fascism as a Model of a National Movement

Until 1933 the maximalist wing of Palestinian Revisionism evinced almost boundless admiration for the fascist ideology. This positive attitude was not necessarily due to a belief that Fascism had indeed brought political stability to Italy and prevented a communist takeover, which were the reasons for the approbation of Italian Fascism among various conservative and intellectual circles in Europe. The favourable attitude among maximalist circles within *Ha-Zohar* and *Betar* had a much deeper cause, being anchored in the fundamental historiosophic conception of the maximallsts. Abba Achimeir testified that his close friend Joseph Katznelson was among the first 'to welcome the Blackshirts in Italy'.[19] Achimeir himself in 1923 still showed an ambivalent attitude towards Fascism, comparing it to Russian Bolshevism, which he loathed. His conclusion, however, was that Italian Fascism was less dangerous than Russian communist Imperialism. It had induced a new spirit into Italian youth; it was a people's movement led by journalists, lawyers, party politicians, and so forth, whose strength lay in political demagogy. According to him, Fascism owed its success to the degeneration of Italian Liberalism into fascist Bonapartism; it was a movement of the urban, politically activist masses, functioning through mass-meetings and the mass-media. Fascism was a mass-oriented national liberation movement that aspired to restore the national historical past. As such it had much in common with Zionism, which itself was far removed from internationalist Communism, because the latter denied the past. The difference between Fascism and Bolshevism lay in their ideological content, rather than in the mentality or psycho-political attitudes of the two movements. Fascism was preferable from the ideological point of view, since it supported national rather than class egoism. For this reason Achimeir said that, if forced to decide between the two, he would choose Fascism. At the same time his article of the year 1923 was a mere theoretical and hypothetical exposition. Meanwhile the best alternative to Fascism, according to Achimeir, was the democratic republic, provided that it was fortunate enough to be guided by a popular Republican-Democratic mass movement.[20] If this failed, the only way to save European culture from Russian-Asiatic barbarism, and European society from anarchy, was Fascism.

In 1928, the year Achimeir began writing for *Doar ha-Yom* which at that time was still edited by Itamar Ben-Avi, his estimation of

Fascism as a preferable alternative to a threatening Bolshevism and a decadent Democracy was strengthened even further. Earlier it was mentioned how profoundly he was influenced by Oswald Spengler's monumental study of the decline of the West, but his Zionist orientation caused him to adapt its ultimate conclusions. His basic assumption was that Liberal bourgeois European culture was degenerate, deeply eroded from within by an excess of liberalism and individualism. Socialism and Communism – in contrast to Zionism – were portrayed as 'overcivilized' ideologies. Fascism, on the other hand – like Zionism – was a return to the roots of the national culture and the historical past. Apart from this, Italian Fascism was not anti-Semitic, whereas communist ideology and praxis were intrinsically anti-Semitic. Communism was anti-Zionist; Fascism was not.

However, there was more to Achimeir's approbation of Fascism than his comparison of Fascism and Zionism as two movements espousing national and intellectual Romanticism. He also developed a favourable attitude towards fascist praxis and its psycho-politics, such as the principle of the all-powerful leader, the use of propaganda to generate a spirit of heroism and duty to the homeland, and the cultivation of youthful vitality (as manifested in the fascist youth movements). When Achimeir wrote his series of articles under the title 'From the Notebook of a Fascist',[20] he was not trying to engage in journalistic provocation; he simply did not see anything wrong in calling himself a 'Fascist' – the opposite was the case! At the same time it should be remembered that at this particular moment Achimeir was not yet a member of the Revisionist movement, and that *Doar ha-Yom* represented the editorial views of Ben-Avi and his associates in *Benei-Benyamin*.

In the above-mentioned series of articles Achimeir portrayed Jabotinsky as a *'duce'*, the leader of a minority movement who was destined to rule Zionism through armed force as well as through the strength of his convictions. What Jabotinsky should do, he stated, was establish an elite 'national guard'; rather than put himself out trying to round up the 'herd', i.e. create a majority or a mass movement, he should invest all his efforts in organizing an elite revolutionary group in the style of the fascist 'Blackshirts'. His evaluation of 1928 depicts Fascism as a movement consisting of a tightly-organized minority, which is loyal and obedient to its leader, and which controls the people at large. It was in the same spirit that Achimeir welcomed Jabotinsky when the latter visited Eretz Israel in 1928, in the belief that Jabotinsky had decided to settle permanently in the country. 'I am not a Democrat, and it is my firm conviction that the only kind of government is an active minority ruling a passive majority.' Democracy was degenerate and corrupt. The government had to be given over to professional politicians, rather than remain in the hands of party hacks, even if they happened to have money and property. The Messiah will not come 'riding an ass, like a pauper; he will come driving a tank! He will not walk across a paper bridge, but across a bridge made of iron. The world is moving in the direction where the minority, or even a handful of people, will rule the majority by force of arms and through the power of their convictions.' For this reason Achimeir advised Jabotinsky not to waste his strength on the 'herd', but to concentrate on the establishment of a fanatical elite. 'When the city is under siege, and the nation is in the throes of liberation, there is no room for luxuries such as "Liberalism, human rights and Socialism." '

In light of the above, it is not surprising that the *Ha-Zohar* leadership accused Achimeir and his friends of infecting Revisionism with, of all things, the evil Leninist and communist revolutionary spirit! Both his Leninist association and his deliberate and overt identification with Fascism shocked and alarmed the *Ha-Zohar* leadership, first and foremost Jabotinsky himself. The reader will remember that in 1932 Achimeir participated in the Revisionist convention in Vienna with a platform that was outspokenly fascist in tenor and content. In an article entitled 'Zionist-Revisionist Trends', which appeared in August 1931, several months before the convention, in the Revisionist weekly *Ha-Am*, he wrote:

> Fascism has brought about a synthesis between Nationalism and class-consciousness; between the revolutionary national movement and the proletarian movement. It is a people's revolution against bourgeoisie and Capitalism. The keystones of Fascism are youth, authority, the leader, emotional and rational rapport between the leader and his movement, the impulse to revenge, and a totalitarian attitude which sacrifices private interests on the altar of the community.[21]

When Achimeir wrote an ideological manifesto for *Betar*, he again and again insisted that *Betar* organize itself as a zealot army, just like Cromwell's Puritans who rushed into battle armed with rifles and the Bible, or the conquering host of Mohammed, the prophet of Islam!

The earlier-mentioned book by Kulitz was unstinting in its praise of Italian Fascism also from an national point of view, making a distinction between Fascism and Nazism. Kulitz depicted Italian Fascism as the foremost phenomenon of the 20th century – a movement that had imbued a prostrate, oppressed and depressed nation with new national vigour and pride, and stimulated it to mighty deeds.

> This Italy can teach us something. In particular we, the Jews, who have never learned to raise our national philosophy to the level of a monolithic creed that is the sole criterion for every aspect of our existence, should study the miracles which the fascist movement has brought about, especially in the area of nationalism.[22]

Kulitz quoted extensively from Mussolini's speeches, adding laudatory comments about *Il Duce*'s personality, his international diplomatic acumen (for instance his intervention in 1934 to preserve Austria's territorial integrity), his national leadership, and the new régime which he headed. 'At this moment, during these very days, following numerous political and social experiments in all kinds of countries and by all kinds of leaders, we may confidently state: Democracy, which was created for the good of the people, runs counter to the psychology of the masses.' The masses need a charismatic leader with whom they can identify and whom they will obey, a leader whom they trust to lead them and the nation in a pleasant, paternalistic manner.

The periodical *Betar* describes Fascism as a national freedom movement that owed its emergence to the bankruptcy of Socialism. The movement, which had emerged in a rather empirical fashion, had been moulded into a 'magnificent vision'; into a people's movement that attempted to create a new kind of society, a new constitution and a new and harmonious socio-economic order which would rehabilitate Italy through grand enterprises and a cultural renaissance. The basis of Revisionist policy was 'the redemption of the country, and the redemption of the soil. Here too, prosperity will not result from welfare policies, but from industrialization, modernization and national arbitration'. In a similar vein yet another writer portrayed Fascism as 'the realization in our days of the true social synthesis' – a régime that did not allow class competition to detract from national unity; a system that lacked the exaggerated individualism of capitalist societies.[23] Following this, Kulitz defined the basic fascist philosophy as follows:

1. Fascism is a realistic ideology;
2. Fascism is an all-embracing frame of mind;
3. Fascism views life as a war in the positive sense of the word;
4. Fascism embodies the moral view that life is a serious and responsible struggle;
5. Fascism embodies a religious view of humankind;
6. Fascism strives towards the elevation of mankind;
7. Fascism is against individualism and totalitarianism, and for political freedom and freedom for the individual within the state;
8. Fascism is against Socialism and supports the corporative organization of the state;
9. Underlying Fascism is the idea of the unity of the nation;
10. The State is the creation of the nation, and it is to the State that the nation owes its united will and actual existence;
11. Nation and State are moral entities;
12. The authority of the State is unlimited, and internal discipline is essential;
13. The authority of Fascism is based on education and faith.

A far more reserved, and much more critical view on these features of Fascism was voiced by the earlier-mentioned Dr. Benyamin Avniel (who was a member of the *Ha-Zohar* Executive and a consultant on labour relations to the Palestine Manufacturers' Association). His book *Fascism*,[24] published in 1939 reflects the worsening attitude of Fascism towards the Jews following the signing of Italy's 'Pact of Steel' with Nazi Germany. In his view Fascism had brought Italy national unity and a feeling of national pride. Under its guidance a divided Italy had become an international power. Fascism had emerged at a time of crisis, like the dictatorship in historical Roman times. The positive side of Fascism was its desire to conciliate the classes, establish industrial peace and lead society in a harmonious manner. There was, however, a big gap between ideals and reality, for Fascism had not succeeded in bringing class harmony. Instead it had effectively neutralized the power of the working class to protest against the stranglehold of all-embracing state control. Theoretically Fascism had very useful aspects, depending upon the particular place and time, but its implementation had proved to be a failure. In practical terms Fascism represented suppression, tyranny, dictatorship and imperialism, as well as political and social injustice. Knowing that its social power rested in the masses, Fascism had launched large-scale public works projects in order to solve unemployment. But it had neglected to abolish the capitalist monopolies, and it had encouraged the armaments race for the benefit of the big industries and their capitalist owners. Socially the fascist régime was based on inequality. It had subjected the working class to all kinds of legal restrictions, but had failed to impose parallel duties upon management. Fascism sided with the strong – the rich employers – instead of implementing a balanced social policy, for this would have meant infringing the sacred rights of capitalists and property owners, and nationalist imperialism based upon rearmament which are 'the very soul of fascist theory'.

Avniel juxtaposed Fascism to liberal democracy, which he considered the most fitting alternative, expressing the hope that liberal democracy would succeed in renewing and rehabilitating itself. This would, however, be subject to the adoption of several of the solutions of the fascist régime.

> We should abolish all the frills of democracy, with its fragmentation and plethora of political parties, while preserving its spirit and soul: the people should have an opportunity to criticize the government at set times, but in the intervening period the government should be free to act and implement as it saw fit – as under a fascist régime.

What was needed, in other words, was a synthesis of the political freedom of liberal democracy and the absolute authority and compulsory powers of Fascism. A kind of nationalism that was not bellicose or aggressive, but positive, and without mystique; a social régime characterized by a balanced distribution of national wealth. Avniel warned that if Fascism emerged supreme, like in Italy, humanity would enter an era of darkness, oppression and world-wide war. Fascism would halt progress and thrust mankind back into the Middle Ages. Rather than realizing the rejuvenation of man's spirit, it would herald a period of barbarism and chaos.

Particularly critical was Jabotinsky, choosing his public appearances to criticize Achimeir's attitude to the Italian fascist régime and ideology. Jabotinsky did not believe that Fascism would be a lasting success, regarding it as national patriotism built entirely on the myth of the leader.[25] He pilloried the maximalist group within *Ha-Zohar* in Eretz Israel, whose publications employed fascist terminology. In 1933, in a letter to the editor of *Hazit ha-Am* he wrote that the paper's fascist orientation, quite apart from the completely mistaken understanding it showed of the essence of Fascism, was a knife in the back of the movement.

On 9 August 1932 Jabotinsky wrote to tell Abba Achimeir that his romantic ideas, like the zeal of his followers, were considered excessive. *Ha-Zohar*, he wrote, was a democratic political movement of a patrician, rather than populist or romantic kind. As a consequence the behaviour of Achimeir and his friends threatened his [Jabotinsky's] cherished movement, and if Achimeir's views were indeed similar to those which he expressed in his articles and letters, there was no room for the two of them in the same political camp. As may be expected, Achimeir reacted by claiming that hostile circles in *Ha-Zohar* had fed Jabotinsky false information, but the facts spoke for themselves. When Jabotinsky wrote to Jacobi, informing the latter of his formal decision to assume absolute control of the Revisionist movement, his sole intention was to extricate Revisionism out of the crisis in which it had sunk. The national views of Revisionism, he wrote in a tone of apology, did not originate from Fascism, but from nineteenth-century European nationalism. The problem was that the dividing line between national and nationalist policy, between power and violence, between national romanticism and Fascism, was a very thin one. Even if there existed a link with, and a positive evaluation of Fascism on the part of Revisionism in Eretz Israel, it was only a very small – though admittedly influential – group which expressed a sufficient degree of admiration for a fascist régime and Italian fascist ideology as to consider them fitting examples for the Zionist movement, and fitting models for the Zionist Organization and the socio-political régime of the *yishuv*.

The Italian Orientation

Jabotinsky, as well as – at a later date – Avraham Stern (both of whom had, although during different periods, studied in Italy), was hard put to separate his sympathy for the Italian people and culture, and his liking of its fascist régime. Like many other discerning persons inside and outside Italy, he found it difficult to understand the nature of Italian Fascism, although it did not enter his mind to regard it as an anti-Semitic or racist movement. Even during the 1930s he considered Italy a democratic country. His efforts to enter into a diplomatic dialogue with Italian Fascism (mainly as a means of exerting pressure on Great Britain) and the Revisionist activities in

Italy proper (in particular those concerning the Betar naval school in Civitavecchia near Rome) followed from a decision that it was impossible to disregard Italy's international status – in particular its aspirations in the Mediterranean basin – and that it was worthwhile to try and exploit these aspirations wherever possible for the benefit of Zionism. In the autumn of 1936 Jabotinsky believed Italy to be the strongest power in the Middle East, so that every effort had to be made to try and rally it behind the Zionist cause in Eretz Israel.[26] However this may be, Revisionist diplomatic activities in Italy, although assisting its opponents in tagging a fascist label on the movement, were not in any way connected with any real or presumed fascist characteristics of Revisionism as either a political or social movement.

Revisionism and Fascism: a Re-Evaluation

The rise of Fascism in Italy and Spain and its progression across European societies in general, projected a shadow across the Middle East, turning Fascism, however elusive as a phenomenon, and however difficult it was to characterize and describe in unequivocal terms, into a kind of *topos* and criterion for the characterization and evaluation of ideologies and social movements that arose during the two world wars, and even after World War II. In certain Middle Eastern countries Fascism even became a model for imitation. The polemical and research literature on the subject is of vast proportions, but it is not our purpose or intention to discuss here the sundry definitions of Fascism or suppositions about its origins and elements that have been suggested. There is no doubt that the fascist image of Revisionism to a very large extent resulted from the writings of a group of intellectuals and men of letters who viewed Italian Fascism as a positive national and political phenomenon and a model worth emulating, and in whose ideas can be discerned many parallels with what usually is considered as constituting Fascism. This group, even though consisting of only a small circle within the Revisionist movement, exercised considerable influence on the shaping of the ideology and *Weltanschauung* of the Zionist and Israeli Right. The official Revisionist party was a democratic political movement which neither in theory nor in practice contested the nature of the democratic parliamentary methods customary within Zionism or the *yishuv*. The opposite was the case, for most of its criticism was directed at what it considered the undemocratic political structure of Jewish society in Eretz Israel. In effect, the Revisionist social platform spoke of a separation of 'economics', 'politics' and 'party politics', and advocated social and political pluralism, rather than centralization and political control of the economy.

The marxist explanation of Fascism being the product of a crisis within the *petit bourgeoisie* which was fearful of proletarization, did not apply to the middle class in Eretz Israel; even less credible was the claim that Fascism resulted from a capitalist crisis, either in the Jewish societies in Eastern Europe, or in Eretz Israel. The movement's social and political militancy was directed against the labour parties – specifically, according to the prevailing Revisionist argument – due to the latter's political hegemony, their monopoly of the labour market and the vast material assets in the hands of the working class.

At the same time we should remember that the fascist image of Revisionism among at least part of the Zionist Left was due to the fact that the Revisionist *Weltanschauung* had turned the 'State' into both a national objective and a national value. These circles regarded the 'State' as fundamentally 'fascist' in nature, for which reason they preferred to talk in terms of a 'society' (*Gesellschaft*), whose world-view was based on the voluntary activities of the community (*Gemeinschaft*); the State, on the other hand, was essentially an instrument of compulsion. This view, which contradicted the Hegelian (as well as marxist) outlook which had been deeply rooted in Zionist thinking ever since the days of Herzl, resulted not merely from their moral opposition to the State concept, but from fear that the Jewish state might turn out to have bourgeois values, and their opposition to the possibility that a Jewish State would be forced to rule over non-Jewish citizens (in other words, Arabs). It is evident that attaching a fascist label to a political movement, only because it viewed the 'State' as a central objective and an essential instrument (or even a 'value' of profoundly historical importance) for the realization of the national goals, could only have come about within the context of the Zionist ideology between the two world wars. In a similar way the claims about the 'militant' and 'militaristic' Revisionist ideology were interpreted within the Left as proof of its nationalist and militarist values, even though for the majority of Revisionists (the exception being the radical stream) militarism merely meant serried ranks of soldiers and the attendant military pomp and circumstance, rather than a military ethos or value, let alone militarism as a character trait or 'national spirit'. During part of the mandatory period any talk about a British-style regular Jewish army was viewed by the Left as a sign of ideological and psychological deviation. Revisionism did indeed glorify nationalist catchwords such as 'State', 'Nation', 'Homeland' and 'the purity of the national culture'. As regards its view of the nation as an organism and the individual as one of its 'members', there indeed was more than a passing resemblance between integrative nationalism and Fascism.

'External' elements also contributed, possibly even more than the ideological aspects, to the shaping of the fascist image and interpretation of Revisionism, to wit the cult of the undisputed leader, the uniforms (brown shirts and leather bandoliers), the disciplinary hierarchical organization of *Betar*, the propaganda style and populist appeal, and the conviction among its opponents that Revisionism was ready – and willing – to achieve its objectives through organized violence and political terror.

As it happens, the Revisionists were in any case unable to put their 'fascist characteristics' to the test, either in Poland or in Eretz Israel. Their formula for 'national arbitration', for instance, was devoid of meaning in a voluntary society which lacked the political means for its enforcement. The violent attacks on the Zionist Left, which gave Revisionism its fascist image, were largely born out of a sense of frustration due to its fundamental weakness and its lack of practical political clout. The most frustrated element among Revisionism was in effect its cultural and political elite.

At any rate there is little use in asking ourselves whether specific characteristics of Revisionism reflected the influence of European Fascism, whether they must be seen as a reaction to the contemporary historical reality, or whether we are dealing here with national ideas anchored in a Jewish ideological and political tradition. The principal and decisive question is to what extent there existed a parallel between Revisionism as a phenomenon in its own right, and Fascism. Of particular importance from a historical perspective is the profound effect of this fascist image, and the intensive manner in which it was exploited in the ideological and political struggle inside the Zionist movement and the Jewish community in Eretz Israel. However, the proper period in which to examine the manner in which the Zionist Right transformed its ideological values into practical political behaviour, while attempting to change and shape the nature of the society and the government, is not the mandatory era, but the period following the establishment of the independent Jewish State in May 1948.

A Historical Perspective –
The Political Heritage and
Tradition of the Right

Types of Activities

Any summary of the history and vicissitudes of the Revisionist movement and its various – official and unofficial – offshoots during the period 1925–1948, as related in this book, is liable to be incomplete so long as we concentrate on ideology, political activities and the struggle of the underground movements. The involvement of the Right also left an imprint on other areas of Zionist history and on the evolution of the Jewish community in Eretz Israel. The fact that throughout this period the Right was in opposition, its virtual isolation from the sources of power in the *yishuv*, as well as its organizational and financial weakness in the Diaspora, seriously inhibited the freedom and scope of its development and initiative. The Revisionist ideology, which on grounds of principle objected to the interference of political parties in the economic and social life of the country, presented a further serious theoretical and practical obstacle to such an involvement. The Right proved unable to build up a centralized and multi-disciplinary social and political network, such as the Zionist Left had succeeded in creating for its activities in Eretz Israel. Even so, the need of the movement and its members to engage in practical activities impelled them to undertake a variety of initiatives, some of a pioneering nature. These were only possible due to the circumstance that the movement was not subject to the authority of the Zionist Organization or the institutions of the *yishuv*, as well as to the fact that various groups within the movement wanted to direct their activity into new and hitherto unexplored channels outside the existing political and ideological-educational frameworks, which in many cases were considered sterile.

A comprehensive historical review of the Zionist Right should therefore look beyond the personality of Ze'ev Jabotinsky or the IZL and Lehi's armed struggle against the British Mandate.

Little attention has been devoted in the previous chapters to a description of the involvement of Revisionism in various other Zionist spheres of activity, either in Eretz Israel or the Diaspora. Neither do I intend to elaborate here, except to review briefly these areas to provide the reader with a more correct and balanced perspective.

Educational Activities

Revisionism was an educational movement. Tens of thousands of Jewish youngsters owed their consciousness of and involvement in Zionist affairs to the personality of Jabotinsky and the ideas of Revisionism and *Betar*. Jabotinsky's Revisionism educated towards an active national Jewish sense of identity, and as such helped to mould the awareness and character of the generation that grew up between the two world wars. This educational activity, both oral and in writing, was carried out within the framework of *Betar*, through 'pioneer training' (conducted in special training facilities in the Diaspora, where Jewish youth prepared themselves for immigration to Eretz Israel and employment in much-needed – particularly agricultural – occupations) and by various other means. As such it contributed materially to turning Zionism into a national mass-movement among the Jewish public as a whole. Even though Revisionism did not attach any particular moral or ideological value to pioneer training (the reader will remember that all immigrants, regardless of their occupation or profession, were considered equally worthy of encouragement and assistance), several Revisionist *hachsharah* centres in Poland prepared thousands of Eastern European Jewish youngsters for their immigration to Eretz Israel, which was the more important because this basic training was a prerequisite for the receipt of an immigration certificate. However, para-military training, consisting more of a glorification of martial values than actual military practice, played a far more important role in the estimation of *Betar*. The various Revisionist journals and training manuals, and the ideological and fictional literature used by the movement, or produced within the ranks, also contributed to creating a profound ideological and cultural infrastructure for Revisionism.

Social Organizations and Activities

The Revisionists in Eretz Israel became embroiled in a number of political and social conflicts, some of which have been described in the course of the previous discussion. A separate activity which deserves special mention were the so-called 'Work Brigades' (subsequently called 'Mobilized Groups'). These brigades were established by *Betar* for the purpose of absorbing young immigrants by providing them with employment within a collective framework. Each brigade consisted of several dozen youngsters, who lived together for relatively short periods in a communal life-style. Most of them were employed as agricultural labourers in the veteran farming settlements, particularly in Upper Galilee and in the coastal plain, usually under conditions of considerable hardship which no unionized labourer would have accepted. In the course of the 1930s several hundreds of *Betar* members, both new immigrants and Palestine-born youths, passed through these mobilized brigades. Although the brigade members occupied themselves with discussions about their place within *Betar*, and the most desirable pattern of communal existence, the underlying reason for the establishment and maintenance of the brigades was neither social nor ideological, but purely an effort to find the most efficient way of guiding certain kinds of young immigrant who lacked either a family or material possessions during the initial phases of their life in Eretz Israel. A second purpose was to try and cast *Betar* members into a more or less uniform mould, to try and prevent – even temporarily – their return to the anonymity of private life with an only partial commitment to the movement. Participation in a brigade contributed to a more complete integration into *Betar*, and the mobilization of the individual members to a life of service to the movement.

To a certain extent the brigades played a role in the development of the cooperative villages, apart from which they served as training grounds for new *Betar* members in Eretz Israel, and as a convenient basis for the expansion of the IZL outside the cities. However, all attempts to compel immigrant members of the *Betar* movement to join the brigades, or to continue their involvement for a set period of time were in vain. In contrast to the Labour movement's *hachsharah* activities, the 'pioneer training' of *Betar* did not result in the establishment of cooperative settlements, but served merely as a half-way house to their absorption in civilian life.

The founding in 1934–35 of the National Labour Federation committed Revisionism to the establishment of a socio-economic sub-system, in order to provide the members with various social and welfare services, in particular medical care. To this end it established the Nationalist Workers' Sick Fund and various other social services parallel to the facilities provided by the *Histadrut* (including a housing company) – all of these however on a far more modest scale than those provided by the Histadrut.[1]

Illegal Immigration and Military Activities

The Revisionist movement and its affiliates were actively involved in the organization of illegal immigration.[2] In fact, organized illegal immigration into Palestine may be said to have begun at the initiative, and with the support of the Revisionists. During the second half of the 1930s, specifically during the years 1939–40, the Revisionists and affiliated elements brought in some 15,000 immigrants in 25 ships, a number accounting for some 40 per cent of the total number of illegal immigrants arriving by sea during this period. In this connection it is worth mentioning various Revisionist-initiated activities in the naval sphere. Thanks to the initiative of Yermiyahu Halperin, one of the more colourful personalities within the movement, a naval school was established in Civitavecchia near Rome, from which three classes of Jewish naval officers graduated.

There were a number of other Revisionist activities in similar fields.[3] From the end of 1936 hundreds of Revisionists served in the Jewish Settlement Police, and during World War II approximately 3,500 members (among whom a number of activists of the IZL) enlisted in the British Army, fighting in various British units in the Western desert and in Europe. During the war an IZL delegation founded the Hebrew Committee for Jewish Liberation in the United States which, together with several affiliated front organizations, undertook intensive and dramatic attempts to mobilize American public opinion for the rescue of European Jewry and, following the war, the establishment of a Jewish state in Eretz Israel. In 1948 the IZL provided some 5,000 soldiers for the Israel Defence Forces, which – together with 500 Lehi recruits – amounted to some 10 per cent of the trained manpower of the newly-established Israeli army.

Revisionism – a Historical Appraisal

The above organized involvements and activities, together with a number of initiatives by individual members outside the official party framework, show that Revisionism was an integral part of the Zionist revolution and its realization. At the same time the nature of these involvements demonstrates the limitations of Revisionism as a social and political force in Zionism under the prevailing historical circumstances.

As a political movement Revisionism failed to achieve most of its objectives. Every political movement aspires towards taking over the reins of government and achieving hegemony, or at least reaching a position which enables it to exercise a measure of direct influence on the political, social and economic environment in which it operates. Revisionism succeeded neither in taking over the government, nor in achieving hegemony, whereas its influence on Zionist policy making was negligible. For all its posturing and attempts Revisionism failed to become a leading force within the Zionist movement, in the same way as it failed to influence British policies towards Zionism and the Jewish community in Eretz Israel. From the moment of its foundation in 1925 the Revisionist movement was in opposition to the ruling coalition within Zionism and the *yishuv*. When it despaired of its fruitless struggle within the existing system, it seceded and established its own independent framework, which existed for eleven years (from 1935 till 1946). Even this new framework, the 'New Zionist Organization', failed however to make any significant political gains. Political Revisionism, operating outside the scope of the Zionist Organization, proved unable to influence or change either Zionist or British policies. This explains why Revisionist schemes were never put to any practical test, let alone succeeded in achieving political or diplomatic implementation, and thus remained within the realm of mere ideas, proposals and – of course – criticism. Such, typically, is the fate of an opposition movement, and as such an essential feature of the vicious circle within which it finds itself forced to act.

At the same time, in those cases where Revisionism attempted to implement its methods, it failed. Here we should allow for the fact that, as an opposition movement, the Revisionists intrinsically were in a weaker position. Yet it would seem as if the Revisionist political outlook was anchored in an optimistic world-view that was notably detached from everyday political reality and the forces acting upon it. The Revisionists believed that the sheer moral and political strength of Zionism was capable of overcoming all obstacles, but their assumption that it would be possible to prevail on Great Britain to conduct an active and wide-ranging pro-Zionist policy was utterly devoid of realism. The expectation that Britain would transfer to the Zionist movement the necessary constitutional instruments for the implementation of a large-scale, modern Jewish colonization policy was similarly based on false hopes.

Revisionism offered Zionism a way it could not possibly follow. It suggested that Zionism concentrate on conducting a political struggle and on creating a political framework and political instruments, while at the same time neglecting to strengthen the already existing foundations of the National Home. It went against the Revisionist grain to agree to the realization of Zionism by slow, evolutionary means, or as a process with a constructivist or positivist imprint – in other words to build a society as a national organism by relying on the internal strength (in terms of economic resources) of Zionism and the – in spite of everything – considerable scope granted by the British Mandate. The failure of Revisionism during this period represented the resounding failure of an in itself distinctive nationalist and populist rightist party that proved unable and unwilling to adapt itself to the prevailing circumstances and the patterns of conduct of a voluntary society under a mandatory administration. Its political approach and national romanticism were able to sustain ideas and sentiments, but they were incapable of making a significant contribution to the creation of society as such.

The tensions between expectations, intentions and leadership aspirations, on the one hand, and the power and means to implement them, on the other, caused a profound ferment within Revisionism, that manifested itself both on the ideological level and in the earlier-mentioned schisms and organizational initiatives. Ideas which germinated and flourished within Revisionism during the period under discussion fertilized and nurtured Zionist (and non-Zionist) currents along virtually the entire Zionist ideological spectrum. Apart from this, the feelings of bitterness and frustration which were aroused at this time were intensified by a series of dismal and dramatic conflicts that became part and parcel of the world-view of the Israeli Right, thus helping to shape its attitudes with regard to future developments.

The Function of the Mandatory Past in the Israeli Present

Any evaluation of the historical role of Revisionism during the mandatory period should therefore take into consideration the sum total of all its activities – both successes and failures. Revisionism constitutes one of the central aspects of the – at times unrealistic – quest of Zionism for ways and means of realizing its goals. The history of Revisionism is to a large extent a variation on a central Zionist theme, namely the tension between redemptionist expectations and their fulfilment, and the practical limitations and historical forces which it was unable to control. From a Zionist political point of view, however, Revisionism nevertheless produced – the changes and reversals to which it and Jewish society in general were exposed notwithstanding – a deep-rooted and organic political tradition based on an awareness of solidarity and a stable set of beliefs and values. During the early years of the State (1948–1967) this value system was forced to lead a more or less marginal existence within Israeli society, which does not mean that it eroded or was doomed to gradual extinction; on the contrary, it continued to exist, gradually gathering strength within the evolving Israeli society, to emerge with renewed force following the Six-Day War in June 1967. During its years in opposition the Right preserved its political tradition, while gradually gathering strength. After 1967 this political tradition adjusted itself to the *Weltanschauung* of the general Israeli public, paradoxically finding itself more moderate and 'pragmatic' than the radical nationalist sectors among this public. As such this political tradition became a part of the mainstream of the prevailing Israeli political and ideological reality.

The way in which the Right adjusted to sovereign statehood and strengthened its hold on Israeli society, its method of operation and its choice of partners, while – surprisingly enough – preserving internal stability and continuity – as well as the way in which it contributed to shaping Israeli society and the history of Israel in the Middle East, will form the subject of the next volume.

Supplementary Remarks

Since this book was written, the debate on the nature and character of 'Revisionism' and on Jabotinsky's world-view and political thinking has continued unabated. It has been carried on in the press as well as in scholarly studies. This debate has concentrated on two main subjects:

A. What was the 'true' and 'real' nature of 'Revisionism', and what were the 'true' ideas of Jabotinsky himself?

B. To what extent were the *Herut* movement − and later the *Likud* governments − genuine followers of 'Revisionist ideology' and of Jabotinsky's principles, or to what extent, on the contrary, did they deviate from it?

Veteran Revisionists as well as newcomers, supporters as well as opponents, are drawing on his writings to justify their positions and invoking his name in order to silence critics. His disciples swear their loyalty to him as mentor and guide more than 45 years after his death. As a result, the Revisionist ideological tradition has become a subject of internal debate. Different, even contradictory interpretations, have been given to his utterances in order to support ideological interests, new thinking and trends. One of the ironies in the course of this debate in recent years, is the fact that opponents are now emphasising Jabotinsky's liberalism and rationalism and even his 'moderate' political stands, instead of the more traditional view of him as a 'pure nationalist', and even a quasi-fascist! Thus, one can find in recent years both followers and opponents borrowing from Jabotinsky's writings quotations that will support their own political views or political criticism.

The *Herut* movement was − and still is − committed to its historical heritage; even so it has undergone basic changes in its social structure and political status. However, very often it seems as if its history is reduced to the biography of one man, and that the main − if not the only − question at stake is: to what extent was the movement able to apply this man's thinking in the realm of reality? In this volume I have attempted to interrelate the history and the profile of the movement and of the man, and claim that already in his lifetime Jabotinsky was not the single undisputed leader and thinker who created and shaped the 'nature' of the Zionist 'Right'. Furthermore, his personal ideological and political development passed through different phases. Therefore it is not always easy to determine what were the fundamental cornerstones in his political thinking, and which of his ideas and arguments were mainly the 'fruit of the time'. It is even harder to predict how he would have reacted and behaved in different historical circumstances.

It is important to note here that while the present book is dedicated to the Revisionists' political and ideological world during the pre-state period, and therefore Jabotinsky's role in it is pivotal, and his presence dominates a large part of its chapters, its sequel will not follow the conventional interpretation and evaluation, i.e. that *Herut* ideology and policy must be understood as a mere mirror − a negative or positive mirror − of Jabotinsky's thinking. The history of the descendants and heirs of Revisionism should not be misjudged or reduced to the question whether his disciples followed his line or deviated from it. The *Herut* movement from 1948 onward has its own history. It is a history deep-rooted in its own past and tradition, but it is not a mere continuation, reflection or realization of it.

NOTES

N.B. The names of all non-English books and articles have been translated into English. Many of Jabotinsky's articles appeared in several languages at one and the same time in the various publications of the movement.

INTRODUCTION

1. Ernest Nolte even considers anti-Marxism, i.e. the negativist aspect of Fascism, as its outstanding characteristic: E. Nolte, *Three Faces of Fascism*, pp.16–21. As regards the characterization of 'Left' and 'Right' in Central and Eastern Europe, it should be taken into account that (at least prior to 1945) certain criteria and elements, for instance their relationship to national minorities, or their attitudes to territorial questions, were not relevant to Western countries. See also B. Vago, 'The Attitude towards the Jews as a Criterion of the Left–Right Concept', in B. Vago & G.L. Mosse (eds.), *Jews and Non-Jews in Eastern Europe 1918–1945*, pp.21–56.

   A contemporary testimony about the relationship of the Polish Right and Left versus the Jews states that '. . . if the Right is intolerant to the Jews, the Left treats them with coolness and indifference' (W.K. Korostowetz, *The Rebirth of Poland*, London, 1928, p.97). (See * on p.407 for addition to Note 1.)
2. H. Seton-Watson, 'Fascism, Right and Left', in W. Laqueur & G.L. Mosse (eds.), *International Fascism 1920–1945*, pp.183–187.
3. 'When speaking about the good of the people, everyone had his own good in mind' – Sallust, *Catiline's War*.
4. See Chapter 5.
5. On this concept see, A. Walicki, *The Slavophile Controversy*, pp.1–15; see also, Karl Mannheim, *Essay on the Sociology of Knowledge*, New York, 1952, pp.33–8.

CHAPTER 1

1. Z. Jabotinsky, *The Story of my Life*, p.84–85. Jabotinsky's articles about contemporary Poland were published in *Razsvet* (in Russian) in April 1905, March 1911, and later. All of them reveal a lack of enthusiasm about the prospect of Poland becoming independent.

   Interesting is a report dated 7 October, 1927 from the German Embassy in Warsaw to Berlin, according to which Pilsudski did indeed fight anti-semitism, but without much success. 'Even so', the report states, 'the Jews have every reason to be grateful to his Government'. (*Politisches Archiv, Auswärtiges Amt: Juden in Poland*, Bd. 2, L360763.) A report dated November 1931 states that the hatred of the Jews in Poland is an inseparable part of the Polish National-Democratic ideology, ibid. L360836.
2. Z. Jabotinsky, 'The Evacuation Plan', in *Unser Welt*, no. 3 (63), October 1933; see also *Speeches*, pp.212–217.
3. About the election struggles in Poland, see my article 'Eretz Israel and Poland as a Political Poly-System', in *State, Government and International Relations* (Heb.) Jerusalem, Spring 1986, pp.148–160.

4. The best analysis of the political system of the *yishuv* is that by D. Horovitz and M. Lissak, *The Origins of the Israeli Polity*.
5. See N. Gross, 'The Economic Policy of the Mandate Government', in Y. Porat and Y. Shavit (eds.), *The History of Eretz Israel*, Vol. IX , pp.106–137.
6. *Masuot*, Issues 8–9, 1929, contain a letter by Jabotinsky addressed to the members of *Betar*, in which he describes the movement as follows: 'Not a new political party, and not a new framework, but a new world, and a new spiritual race.' See also his article 'Das Farben Lied', *Razsvet*, 17.4.1927. See also Chapter 2.
7. Jabotinsky devoted several articles to sketching a profile of Herzl, in which he attempted to understand Herzl as a 'leader', and an archetypical example of the 'new Jew'.
8. Schechtman, in an article called 'The Political Contents of Revisionism' (*Razsvet*, 27.12.1925), wrote: 'Ideologically it suits any social or religious point of view, and is acceptable to any Zionist group.'
9. On the two utopias in the Russian way of thinking during the 19th century, see A Walicki, *The Slavophile Controversy*, pp.445–455. An utopia tries to describe the personality of a society and of a human existence that is as yet not realized, but whose desired image exists in theory.
10. N. Davies, *God's Playground*, Vol. II, p.8. A. Walicki, in *Philosophy and Romantic Nationalism: the Case of Poland*, p.3, writes: 'It seems justified to treat the Poland of this time as a classic country of romantic nationalism.' See also my article 'Politics and Messianism: the Zionist Revisionist Movement and Polish Political Culture', in *Studies in Zionism*, Vol. 6, no.2, Tel-Aviv, Autumn 1985, pp.229–246 (Engl.), and an expanded version in my book *The Mythologies of the Zionist Right Wing*. The correspondence between the national aspirations of Poland and those of Zionism is well summarized in the lines of the poet Uri Zvi Greenberg written during 1933–34: 'Poland has been revived and her white eagle is screaming from the shores of the Baltic to the Black Sea' (from: *The Time Will Come*).

CHAPTER 2

Chapter 2A

1. 'Constructivism' refers to the dominant socialist ideology of the Labour movement in Eretz Israel, which from the period of the Second Aliyah onwards decreed that the socialist society in the country would be built from scratch by the organized working class, rather than first being built by the bourgeoisie, and only then transformed into a socialist society.
2. Y. Drori, 'General Zionism in Palestine during the 1920s', *Zionism* (Heb.), Vol. X, 1985, pp.88–138.
3. Not to be confused, of course, with the revisionist school in Marxism (of Eduard Bernstein and others); another common name was 'State Zionism'.
4. *Berit Trumpeldor* wrote the name of its hero with the Hebrew letter *Taf*, rather than with a *Tet*, as is customary in other circles, in order to make the abbreviation of the organization bearing his name identical with the word *Betar*, the last stronghold of Bar-Kochba.
5. Jabotinsky's Movement, the Union of Zionist Revisionists (*Berit Ha-Zohar*) received 2,812 votes during the elections (9.7%), whereas the *Herut Movement* established by the *IZL* received 49,782 votes (11.5%) and 14 mandates (out of 120 mandates). *Lehi*'s 'Fighters' List' received 5,363 votes (1.2%) and one representative in the First Knesset.
6. On the early days of *Ha-Zohar*, in addition to Schechtman's biography, and the book by Schechtman and Benari, see also M. Grossman, 'The Beginnings of the Activist Movement', *Ha-Ummah*, June 1964, pp.25–38, and J. Nedava, 'The

Background to the Growth of the Revisionist School', in J. Nedava (ed.), *Issues in Zionism 1918–1948*, Haifa, 1979, pp.23–43. See also J. Nedava, 'The Relations between Weizmann and Jabotinsky', *Ha-Ummah*, no. 53, December 1977, pp.114–125. The review in this chapter is based upon existing literature and the copious archival material.

The majority of the founders of the party were mainly the members of the activist faction during the 8th Assembly of the Russian Zionists in May 1917, who emigrated from Russia before the Revolution and established the Federation of Russian and Ukrainian Zionists. It is among them that Jabotinsky found his first followers, and they formed the initial leadership elite of the movement.

7. The letter of resignation, dated 18.1.1923, appeared in *Razsvet* on 28.1.1923. See also Jabotinsky's explanation of his resignation in *Razsvet* on 4. 2.1923. A discussion about the reasons for his resignation, namely his opposition to the White Paper, the criticism of his discussions with the representatives of the Ukrainian leader Petlyura, etc., fall outside the scope of this study. See his article about the question of Petlyura in *Razsvet*, 8.3.1925. On the general background of Zionist political activity during this period, and Jabotinsky's contribution, see A. Priesel, *Zionist Policy after the Balfour Declaration, 1917–1922.*

8. Letter to E. Ben-Horin, dated 4.8.1925, JI 15/2/1 A. See also the letter to A. Weinshal, dated 13.10.1925, JI 14/2/1 A.

9. During the 14th Zionist Congress in 1925 the Revisionists were represented by 5 delegates, at the 15th Congress in 1927 by 10 delegates, and at the 16th Congress in 1929 by 21 delegates. At the 17th Congress in 1931 they had 52 delegates (21%), and at the 18th Congress in 1933, 45 delegates (14%). The separatist Jewish State Party received 2 delegates (2%). In 1933 the Labour faction was represented by 138 delegates (44%).

10. E. Mendelson, 'The Dilemma of Jewish Politics in Poland: Four Responses', in B. Vago and G. Mosse (eds.), *Jews and Non-Jews in Eastern Europe 1918–1945*, pp.203–220.

11. A. Achimeir, *The Death of Joseph Katznelson*, p.91. Nalevki was one of the poorer quarters of Warsaw. In November 1935 Jabotinsky wrote to Achimeir: 'Only in Poland do we have in the Jewish streets a force with which no other party could compete. Only if we are able to add to this a world organization with all its prestige, will we be able to make up for our weakness in Jerusalem and in London', *Letters*, p.25.

12. For a balanced picture of the formal growth of the Zionist movement, see my article, 'Eretz Israel and Poland as a Political Poly-System', pp.148–160. Suffice here to mention that in 1933 the number of *shekels* purchased amounted to 694,393 (about a quarter million of which in Poland). It is also important to remember that the Zionist *shekel* purchased in Eretz Israel was worth twice the *shekel* purchased abroad.

There are no researches available on the Revisionist movements in the various countries, and on the nature of their local leaderships. On Revisionism in Germany, see the first chapter (out of two) in F. R. Nicosia, 'Revisionist Zionism in Germany: Richard Lichtheim and the Landesverband der Zionisten-Revisionisten in Deutschland, 1920–1933', *LBI Ybk*, Vol. XXXI, London 1986, pp.209–240.

13. N. Sokolow, 'Journey through Poland in 1934', in *Watchman unto the House of Israel*, Jerusalem, 1961, p.256.

14. See the discussions of the Cracow Assembly in January 1935, JI 6/3/2. Uri Zvi Greenberg expressed confidence in 'common sense' and in the 'simple Jew' by saying that 'the man in the street' was to be preferred over ideologically motivated pioneers, since he at least had a pure faith, untainted by 'formulas and dialectics'.

15. See the article by E. Rubinstein, 'From Community to State: Institutions and Parties', in B. Eliav (ed.), *The Yishuv during the Period of the National Home*, Jerusalem, 1976, pp.170–184.

16. A. Achimeir, *The Trial*, pp.8–13. In Revisionist terminology the ideology of the

avant-garde was called 'the Doctrine of the Few', the 'few' being the ones who strode ahead of the masses, thus providing the driving force which steered the heavy and cumbersome vessel on its desired course.

17. A. Achimeir, 'Letter to the Betar Youth', *Revolutionary Zionism*, p.59.

18. Betar succeeded in something that has so far eluded *Ha-Zohar*, namely a comprehensive historical documentation, written by Ch. Ben-Yerucham, of which so far three volumes have appeared. For other sources, see the *Rules of Betar* from the year 1931; Z. Jabotinsky, *The Teachings of Betar* (an anthology), Tel-Aviv, 1943; *Berit Trumpeldor, its Present Development and Status, Report on the Betar World Conference in Danzig 1931*, Vienna, April 1931; Betar 1924–1934 (on the occasion of the 10-Year anniversary of *Betar*), Riga, 1934. See also A. Z. Propes, 'Between Ha-Zohar and an Educational Youth Movement', *Ha-Ummah*, no. 1, May 1981, p.63; E. Ashkenazi-Stein, 'Jabotinsky and Betar during the Formative Years of the Movement', *Kivunim*, no. 15, Jerusalem, May 1982, pp.117–134; and Y. Oppenheim, 'The Pioneering Training of Betar', *Proceedings of the 6th World Congress on Jewish Studies*, Jerusalem, 1975, pp.295–305.

Uri Zvi Greenberg viewed *Betar* as a 'messianic army' (even if after a while he transferred his affections from *Betar* to the *IZL*) when he wrote: 'We already have in the Zionist Revisionist movement, and in *Betar*, that same Trumpeldorian foundation that our messianic movement is in need of – an element such as this can be presented before an empire that might want us as a partner . . .!' (*Ha-Yarden* on 5.11.1938).

19. See note 54.

20. According to this agreement, which preceded the Calais Compromise, Jabotinsky, in his position of Head of *Betar* and President of *Ha-Zohar*, was the authoritative and unifying personality of the two movements. Jabotinsky protected the right of adult *Betar* members to be involved in political questions, but not the right of *Betar* as such. See his letter to the Executive of *Ha-Zohar* dated 15.8.1931, JI 2/21/2/1 A. This attitude changed as a result of the events at the Zionist Congress.

Chapter 2B

21. Letter to S. Gafstein, dated 5.5.1929, JI 30/10 C.

22. To M. Grossman, 7.12.1932, JI 2/20/2/1/ A and 2/21/2/1 A.

23. To E. Ben-Horin, 14.10.1931, JI 2/21/21/2 A.

24. There is no doubt that Jabotinsky feared the radical-revolutionary ideology of Achimeir and his group, and the possibility that his radicalism would scare away large numbers of moderate and liberal *Ha-Zohar* voters. The slogans about a movement for national liberation failed to appeal to him.

25. To M. Schwartzman, 8.10. 1933, JI 2/23/2/1 A. On the stormy meetings in Vienna, see *The Book of Betar*, Vol. I, pp.345–354, as well as the reports in *Ha-Aretz*, 31.8.1932, and in *Hazit Ha-Am*, 7.10. 1932.

26. Jabotinsky hesitated to take a stand against the radical faction in the movement; on the one hand he regarded the performance of the 'Radicals' in Vienna as an 'exotic show', but on the other hand he found it impossible not to appreciate their contribution to the spirit of the movement; see *Ha-Aretz*, 15.9.1932. It is impossible to know how things would have developed, but for the storm around the Arlosoroff murder after June 1933.

27. *Contemporary Recollections*, p.216; 'A Leader', *Der Moment*, 13.7.1934.

28. Letter to A. Dissentchik, JI 2/21/2 A; see also Dissentchik's memoirs in *Ma'ariv*, 15.7.1977. Some are of the opinion that Jabotinsky soon regretted the loss of his old friends, to whom he felt a cultural affinity, and that he looked for ways to bring them back into the movement. This may have been his private feeling, or perhaps this is what the Revisionist oldtimers believed, who found themselves outside the Revisionist party as members of a related, but rival movement.

29. JI 2/21/2/1.
30. Notwithstanding the fact that the *Ha-Zohar* central leadership in Eretz Israel was not over enthusiastic about Achimeir and his friends, they were forced to rally behind them. As a result, Jabotinsky's and his movement's support of the accused in the Arlosoroff murder, and the subsequent campaign to clear their name, became a foremost unifying element.
31. See Chapter 11, and Jabotinsky's articles on the 'Transfer': 'The Transfer Agreement', *Ha-Yarden*, 4.12.1934; 'The Boycott', *Hazit Ha-Am*, 15.1.1934; and 'Germany after the Slaughter', *Haynt*, 15.1.1934, etc. See note 27, Chapter 7.
32. Letter to S. Jacobi, in J. Schechtman, *The Vladimir Jabotinsky Story*, Vol. II, p.235, as well as the letter to Schwartzman, dated 8.10.1933, JI A1/2/23/2. Pilsudski was the only one among the European statesmen during the interwar period to be warmly praised by Jabotinsky, due to the fact that, according to Jabotinsky, he 'had turned Poland into a national state with a Western character'.
33. 'Wanted: a Plan', *Ha-Mashkif*, 3.4.1939.
34. Not only the moderate camp believed that it was possible to maintain the movement without Jabotinsky, and practical steps and propaganda preparations for such an eventuality were in fact taken. The Radicals also wrote publicly that the activist public in the movement stood behind them, and that, if they should fail to release Jabotinsky from 'imprisonment' by the Moderates, it would be possible to run the movement without him. One of the heads of the 'Moderates' believed that the party was being propelled by false pathos, since all factions were invoking Jabotinsky's name, even in matters where their own views totally disagreed with his own. As a result they were transforming him into a kind of Lenin, who against his will was expected to head a violent revolution; see *Die Welt*, 24.2.1931. At this stage Jabotinsky still tried to protect his moderate colleagues in Eretz Israel against attempts by the more extreme members to oust them.
35. See my article,' "Fire and Water", Zeev Jabotinsky and the Revisionist Movement', in *Studies in Zionism*, no. 4 (Engl.), October 1981, pp.215–236.
36. 'Fascist Zionism', *Razsvet*, 20.11.1925.
37. On Jabotinsky's letter to Mrs. Miriam Lang, see my article in ibid. p.224. This letter, in which he among other things attacked the leadership cult within the movement, includes the following poignant comment: 'The present composition of the movement is far from elitist: perhaps even the contrary is true. This is nothing new. Movements of the kind which sanctify moral purity within their ranks, usually contain impure elements.' Jabotinsky's status within the party is reminiscent of what was written about Herzl and his kind: '[They] possessed the peculiar gift of answering the social and spiritual needs of their followers by composing ideological collages made of fragments of modernity, glimpses of futurism and resurrected remnants of a half forgotten past'; see C.E. Schorske, 'Politics in a New Key: an Austrian Trio', in *Fin-de-Siècle Vienna: Politics and Culture*, pp.116–180.
38. Letter to D. Ben-Gurion, dated 30.3.1935, *Letters*, pp.42–45.
39. Uri Zvi Greenberg, 'When There is No Way-Out', *Kuntres*, no. 234, Volume 12, 1925. His example was the Soviet Union, which had 'a regime dominated by a single idea, that does not allow deviations or dissonances.'
40. See also Chapter 12.
41. Such was the nature of the editorials in the paper, that Jabotinsky authorized A. Weinshal to put the editorial affairs of the paper in order (JI A1/2/24/1). On 17.5.1933 he wrote to the editor of *Hazit Ha-Am* that the nasty articles appearing in the paper were a stab in the back of the movement. 'If these foul stories do not disappear from the columns of the paper,' he wrote, 'and if it continues to publish things which seem to approve of Nazism, I will demand the dismissal of the editorial staff from the movement, and break off all personal relations with the people who obstruct me with their cheap and opinionated behaviour' (JI A1/2/23/1). See also his article, 'Admirable Haste', *Hazit Ha-Am*, 14.7.1933.
42. Basically the Labour faction and its supporters invoked the disciplinary clause of

the constitution of the Zionist Organization, which forbade independent political activities by the political parties. The implementation of the disciplinary clause meant a total ban on any political and diplomatic activity of Revisionism, which *Ha-Zohar* would not have accepted in any case. See the detailed description in Y. Goldstein, *The road to Hegemony*. The issue of the legitimization of independent Revisionist political activity, and the resulting secession of the party from the Zionist Organization, occupied Jabotinsky intensely. See 'About Unity', *Ha-Yarden*, 19.5.1935; 'The Ethics of Independence', *Ha-Yarden*, 24.5.1935, and so forth. At the same time *Ha-Zohar* resisted any independent activities inside the movement (for example by the *IZL!*).

43. On *Ha-Zach*, see among others, *Kongresszeitung der neuen zionistischen Organisation*, Vienna, 1935, and *Political Zionism: the Programme*, Warsaw, 1935. On the election system of *Ha-Zach*, see *Voting Rights for All*, Tel-Aviv, 1935. Jabotinsky defined his new-style Zionism not as 'Revolutionary Zionism', but as 'Lofty Zionism' (*'Hochzionismus'*).

44. D. Sha'ari, 'Unity and Division in the General Zionist Camp', *Studies in Zionism*, Vol. X, pp.151–198.

45. On the attitude of the organized bourgeoisie within the General Zionists, see J. Sapir, 'How the Leftists Dominate our entire Lives', *Bustena'i*, organ of the Farmers' Union, July 1933. See also 'The Workers', *Razsvet*, 17.3.1929.

46. See, for instance, his article, 'The Industry in Eretz Israel', *Haynt*, 4.12.1928. See also J. Brutzkus, 'The Class Struggle in Eretz Israel', *Razsvet*, 30.4.1934.

47. Letter to J. Schechtman, JI A1/19/2.

48. To A. Achimeir, *Letters*, p.29.

49. 'The General Zionists "B" ' in Eretz Israel represented the economic circles who fought the *Histadrut*; generally they were regarded as having a conservative socio-economic outlook.

50. I. Remba, 'Ha-Zohar and the Zionist Parties (the General Zionists "B")', *Ha-Yarden*, 15.5.1935.

51. E. Shostak, 'On the 13th Anniversary of Betar', *Ha-Yarden*, 11.2.1937.

52. See Chapter 11.

53. Z. Jabotinsky, 'Our Propaganda Problems', *Ha-Yarden*, 10.8.1934. To his friends he wrote that, given the nature of their rivals in Eretz Israel, he understood the character of the propaganda of the Popular Front. See also his article, 'Following Moscow's Example', *Hazit Ha-Am*, 11.8.1933.

54. A census undertaken in 1939 among 194 groups comprising a total of 16,000 members (of whom 60% were boys), showed that 37.5% were school pupils and 2% students (*The Book of Betar*, p.183).

55. Jabotinsky hesitated to state unequivocally that the intelligentsia indeed formed a part of the bourgeoisie (to S. Jacobi, 28.8.1928, JI A1/2/18/2). See also *Weizmann Letters*, Vol. 4, Jerusalem, 1973, p.231 (Hebr. ed.). Although, on the one hand, the Jewish intelligentsia was believed to be detached from its own milieu, it was also regarded as lacking its limitations, and therefore suited to unbiased and dis-interested political activity. This explains the central role of lawyers, journalists and similar professionals in the national movement. See A. Achimeir, *The Death of Josef Katznelson*, p.151.

Chapter 2C

56. Z. Jabotinsky, 'Middle Class Youth', ibid. See also Y. Halperin, 'Berit Ha-Hayil and the Jewish State', *Ha-Yarden*, 8.6.1934.

57. Except for most of the letters by A. Achimeir, and the collection by Y. Achimeir and S. Shatzky, *Berit ha-Biryonim: the First Anti-British Organization. Documents and Evidence*. The other sources are a (stenciled) newssheet, entitled *Ha-Biryon* ('The Brigand'), the organ of the group, and the newspaper *Hazit Ha-Am*.

58. The *Sicarii* were the extremists among the *Kannaim* ('Zealots'), called after the *sica*, the dagger they carried hidden under their garments as a terror weapon.
59. A. Achimeir, 'The Scroll of the Sicarii', in *Berit Ha-Biryonim*, pp.217–223.
60. JI C.10/69.
61. To Y.H. Yevin, 9.8.1932, JI A1/2/22/2.
62. The epithet used by Jabotinsky to describe activities of this kind was 'impressionism', as opposed to 'adventurism', which included activities forming part of a broader framework, which served as a lever for exercising pressure.
63. The hanging of Ben-Yosef in Acco jail, despite intensive efforts to obtain a pardon, turned him into a victim for the cause, the first martyr of the movement. Jabotinsky did not regard him as a pioneer of the armed struggle, but as a symbol of exemplary behaviour in the face of death.
64. See his article 'Adventurism', *Haynt*, 26.2.1932. (He used the Italian word 'Avventurismo.')
65. The principal source, besides the available archival material, is Y. Ophir, *The History of the National Labourer*; see also Y. Shavit (ed.), *A Collection of Sources on the History of the National Labour Federation.*
66. JI A1/2/19/1.
67. See in particular the six volumes of D. Niv, *The Battle for Freedom: the IZL.* The various biographies of Begin deal virtually exclusively with this chapter in his life.
68. The debate on this question in the Zionist Executive in 1921 was one of the most basic discussions, which revealed the fundamental differences of opinion about principle and tactics relating to the use of force in the realization of Zionism.
69. Z. Jabotinsky, *The Question of the Defence of Eretz Israel*, 1929. See also the many articles he wrote on the re-establishment of the Legion: 'The Legion', *Razsvet*, 10.5.1925; 'The Legion', *Der Morgen Journal*, 21.8.1932; and 'About Militarism', *Haynt*, 25.1.1939; and others.
70. See Y. Shavit, *Self-Restraint or Reaction.*
71. The C.I.D. closely followed the Paris talks; see its report in J. Achimeir, (ed.), *The Black Prince*, pp.22–28.
72. There exist a number of writings on the history of *Lehi*, but so far no comprehensive study, although one, written by J. Heller, will be published in the foreseeable future.
73. On 9 September 1938, *Jeruzolima Wyzowolna* ('Liberated Jerusalem'), the *IZL*'s Polish-language organ, printed a collection of Pilsudski's sayings entitled, 'The Politics of the Practical War' (*Polityka Walki Czynnej*), which included a passage entitled 'How to Educate for a National War of Liberation':

> The blood that is spilled today, the life that is extinguished today, will yield its blessings in the future . . . . Meanwhile we should take into account that at no time in world history there was a political ideal, or a slogan, that was not at first greeted with derision. We always see that the same approaches that at first are extremely unpopular, are the ones to emerge victorious . . . . This will also happen with the slogan of the armed uprising. Today it seems like an Utopia, but when the war comes, and once it has passed, it will be remembered as a reality by those same people who reject the slogan today. No sane public will suffer the rule of thieves supported by a government, or of a government supported by thieves, without preparing for armed resistance . . . . The quicker we conclude that the only escape from the present situation is armed warfare, the better it will be for us . . . . Nearly every popular rebellion movement has been preceded by a lengthy period marked by all kinds of manifestations, demonstrations, skirmishes and other conflicts, which were not only caused by, but also helped to prepare the special mood and atmosphere which readies an ever larger group of people for war.
>
> (Hebrew translation in *Omer La-Am* (a one-time publication), 29.7.1939)

74. A letter by D. Raziel, dated 7.5.1939, part of the *IZL* archives that were buried in a

jar during the 1940s, and are in the possession of the Stern family.
75. A letter by D. Raziel, dated 28.3.1939. On this relationship, and the episode involved, see my article, 'Father of the Revolt', in *The Mythologies of the Right Wing*, pp.103–110, and in particular Note 20, ibid, pp.116–117.
76. See the letter dated 5.7.1940, which the Stern group wrote to Jabotinsky before the latter's death, JI K 4/1/10.

CHAPTER 3

1. It is clear that from this point of view all three belong to a larger and more varied group of thinkers, whose transition from a theocentric to an ethnocentric ('natural') world-view obliged them to provide new answers to such questions as the sources and contents of the 'Jewish spirit', the 'singularity of Jewish history', the 'Jewish identity', etc.
2. There exist a large number of essays on the national outlook of Jabotinsky, only some of which are listed in the bibliography of I. Yavarovitch, *The Writings on Ze'ev Jabotinsky*, 1980. Partly they are scholarly essays, but most of them are political essays of various kinds. See, for instance, the chapter 'Integralist Nationalism and the Illusion of Power' in S. Avineri's book, *Varieties of Zionist Thought*, pp.182–215. See also my article 'Ze'ev Jabotinsky's National Theory and his Mutual Relationship with his Movement', in my book *The Mythologies of the Zionist Right Wing*, pp.207–228.
3. In Z. Jabotinsky, *Nation and Society*, pp.15–71.
4. Ibid. pp.193–222. The original Hebrew version is preserved in the Jabotinsky institute; the second version was first serialized in *Ha-Mezuda* in January and March 1938. Jabotinsky apparently intended to complete the writing of this theoretical essay, but he failed to do so. Both versions are included in the volume *Nation and Society*. This volume, and his volume *Early Zionist Writings*, contain mainly articles on the subject of the historical and national outlook, and as such do not comprise a complete or comprehensive selection.
5. About Labriola, see G.D.H. Cole, *The History of Socialist Thought*, Vol. III, part II, pp.731–748. Since this chapter is not intended as an intellectual biography of Jabotinsky, this is not the place to enter into details on the various influences to which Jabotinsky was exposed from his Russian period onwards; see also the discussion in Chapter 9.
6. J. Nedava, 'Jabotinsky in Vienna', *Gesher*, no. 1/110, Spring 1984, pp.56–67.
7. See my article, 'The Works of H.T. Buckle and their Application by the Maskilim of Eastern Europe', *Zion*, Vol. XLIX, 1984, pp.401–412.
8. Z. Jabotinsky, *Race*, first published in 1922 in Russian, and subsequently in *Early Zionist Writings*, pp.123–136.
9. S. Avineri perceives in these articles by Jabotinsky a racist outlook, but similar expressions were used by many other Jewish writers during this period, such as Chaim Jetlovski, one of the founders of Jewish National Socialism, in his Russian essay 'Thoughts on the Historical Fate of Judaism', Moscow, 1887. The concepts 'race', 'nation' (*folk; narod*) were used variously in the new ethnocentric view, but they did not refer to deterministic, biological 'racism', and obviously bore no relationship whatsoever with the conclusions that were eventually drawn from them.
10. Z. Jabotinsky, *Race*. Subsequently he reiterated these words in his book, *A Jewish State: a Solution to the Jewish Problem*, pp.23–27, where he writes that the psyche shapes the objective environment, rather than the reverse.
11. Z. Jabotinsky, 'Letter on Autonomism', was first published in 1904, in Russian. From this it follows that Zionism is first and foremost a renaissance of the national psyche which tries to return to its 'natural place'.
12. *The Idea of Betar*, 1934.

13. 'The Language of Education' initially was a lecture Jabotinsky gave at the congress of the Russian Zionists in Vienna in 1913. It was published in *Ha-Sheloach*, Odessa, Vol. 30, no. 5, May 1914 and no.6, June 1914. This view of Jabotinsky was severely criticized in writing by no less than Joseph Klausner.
14. The story *The Little Master* was originally written in Russian, and reprinted in *Razsvet* in 1911.
15. See, for instance, 'I. Remba, 'Religion and Tradition in his Life and Teaching', *Ha-Ummah*, Vol. 3, no. 9, June 1964, pp.146–166; Avraham Heller, 'The relationship of Jabotinsky to Religion and his Letter to Eri', *Ha-Ummah*, no. 58, September 1979, pp.356–361. See also my article 'Zeev Jabotinsky's National Theory', in *The Mythologies of the Right*, pp.216–220.
16. 'Out of Bounds', *Hadashot ha-Aretz*, 22.10.1919.
17. Letter from Jabotinsky to J. Schechtman, dated 18.6.1925, JI A1/2/15/1.
18. E. Jabotinsky, *My Father, Ze'ev Jabotinsky*, p.101. Eri, his son, was a convinced atheist. The principal articles by Jabotinsky on this subject are: 'A Matter of Tradition', *Der Moment*, 5.8.1934; 'Religion', *Der Moment*, 19.7.1935 (and also in *Ha-Yarden*, 2.8.1935); 'Reflections on Religion', *Der Moment*, 10.6.1936; 'A Letter', *Unser Welt*, 21.5.1937; etc.
19. Z. Jabotinsky, 'Building', in *Hadashot ha-Aretz*, 27.10.1919. By contrast, see his new attitude as expressed in his article 'Those who Saved', *Der Moment*, 27.7.1934 (about those who intervened on behalf of the accused in the Arlosoroff murder trial).
20. 'The Great Albania', in Z. Jabotinsky, *Nation and Society*, pp.113–122.
21. 'Syria and the Arab Crisis', *Ha-Aretz*, 9.8.1920. See also Chapter 9.
22. On his articles from this period, see Y. Shavit, 'The Articles of Z. Jabotinsky 1919–1920: Zeev Jabotinsky on the Status of the Jewish Community and on the Crystallization of the National Society in Palestine', *Zionism*, Vol. VI, Tel-Aviv, 1981, pp.323–358.
23. Z. Jabotinsky, 'The Hashmonean from Riga', *Razsvet*, 28.2.1926, and in the volume *Notes* of Jabotinsky's writings, pp.189–198.
24. On Jabotinsky's attitude towards the role of translating from a foreign-language into a 'national literature', see Zohar and Yaacov Shavit, 'Translations versus Original in the Process of Establishing the Hebrew Literary Center in Eretz Israel', *Ha-Sifrut*, no. 25, October 1977, pp.45–68. Jabotinsky was among those who encouraged the translation of crime stories, and in particular detective stories, into Hebrew.
25. This outlook is evident in all his articles about the nature and quality of the East; see Chapter 8.
26. For more details, see the discussion in Chapter 6.
27. Idem.
28. The relevant writings of Klausner comprise numerous books and countless treatises and articles. It is surprising that no biographies or monographs have been written about Klausner, the man, his works and his thoughts. A bibliography of writings and articles about him is included in the *Klausner Jubilee Book*, published in his honour in 1937. Supplementary bibliographical material has been published in *Zionism*, Vol.XI, 1986, pp.413–430. See also the only existing monograph about Klausner by Y. Beker and H. Toren, *Joseph Klausner, the Man and his Work*, Tel-Aviv, 1947. The following summary is based on a considerable part of his writings, in particular *Flames and Humanity*, 2 vols., 1955 (4th revised and expanded edition of everything written since the beginning of the century).

> *Jewish History*, Odessa, 1909.
> *The History of the Second Temple*, 1924–1925. A five-volume study by the same name was published in 1949.
> *The Messianic Idea in Israel from its Inception till the Present Day*, 1927.
> *The Prophets, Essays on the Morality of the Prophets and the World-View of the Prophets of Israel*, 1951.

When a Nation Fights for its Freedom: Historical Essays, 1939.
New Researches and Ancient Sources, 1952; etc.
Here I have presented only the essentials of his outlook, without discussing his intellectual and scientific development, his various formative influences, or his research work and public activities.

29. Neither do we have a monography about Achimeir. My summary is based on his writings (see Bibliography). Not all his articles are included in his collected writings. See also J. Nedava's introduction to the volume of collected articles *Berit ha-Biryonim*, but in general the discussion about Achimeir concentrates on his political views rather than on his historiosophical outlook; there are also differences of opinion about the extent of his influence on *Betar*, the *IZL*, and *Lehi*. It is my view that this influence was marked and important, even though, for a variety of reasons, efforts have been made to degrade it.

30. About Joseph Katznelson, see J. Achimeir (ed.), *The Black Prince: Joseph Katznelson and the National Movement in the 1930s*, Tel-Aviv, 1983. He was born in Bobroisk (White Russia, the birthplace of Berl Katznelson), he studied law at Kiev University, philosophy and history at Vienna University. He immigrated to Eretz Israel in 1927 and worked as a clerk. In 1938 he was elected to the World Leadership of *Betar* and was placed in charge of the illegal Revisionist immigration centre in Poland. He died of an illness in Nazi-occupied Warsaw. Achimeir's narrative about him in *The Black Prince* is a moving document.

31. He served as an army doctor in the Russian army, and emigrated to Palestine in 1924. Editor of *Hazit ha-Am*. He also wrote historical novels.

CHAPTER 4

1. See the article by M. D. Herr, 'Between Realistic Political Messianism and Eschatological Cosmic Messianism in the Writings of the Jewish Sages', in *Tarbiz*, Year 54, no. 3, April/May 1985, pp.331–346. The article includes an extensive bibliography on the subject. See also the article by B. Oppenheimer, 'From Prophetic Eschatology to the Apocalypse', in Zvi Baras (ed.), *Messianism and Eschatology*, Jerusalem, 1984, pp.27–72. On Millenniarism, see the collection of articles by Sylvia L. Thrupp (ed.), *Millennial Dreams in Action: Essays in Comparative Study*, The Hague, 1962.

2. See Klausner's views, as expressed in his book *The Messianic Idea in Israel*, as well as the voluminous essay by G. Sholem, *The Messianic Idea in Judaism, and other Essays on Jewish Spirituality*, New York, 1971, pp.1–36. See also A.H. Silver, *A History of Messianic Speculation in Israel*, Gloucester, Mass., 1978 ed.

3. In his article 'About the Messianic Idea and Jewish Independence' from 1842.

4. The question of the messianic source of Zionism, on the one hand, and the messianic contents of Zionism, on the other, continues to form the subject of vigorous polemics and research. However, if we were to categorize every expectation of 'national redemption' or any action directed at national redemption as Messianism, we would be faced with such a broad definition that it would lose its meaning. The essence of the messianic idea is fraught with questions about the sources and bearers of redemption, not to speak of its spiritual contents. The national-territorial and political visions of Uri Zvi Greenberg have been defined here as historical-realistic eschatology, not because of their visionary realism, but because they called for action on the part of human beings in order to change the course of history – in other words for immediate historical activism for the sake of implementing concrete political programmes. He and his followers, as well as other currents in Zionism, rejected any comparisons between Zionism as a national movement and European national movements. See the same idea in Martin Buber, *Between a Nation and its Land*, 1939 (2nd. ed., 1984). This is a fundamental outlook in Judaism, which within the Right received rhetorical and political, as well as

concrete and topical expression. See also H. Fisch, *The Zionist Revolution: a New Perspective*, London, 1978.

5. For a brilliant intellectual analysis of *Gush Emunim*, see Uriel Tal, 'Totalitarian Democratic Hermeneutics and Policies in Modern Jewish Religious Nationalism', in *Totalitarian Democracy and After: International Colloquium in Memory of Jacob L. Talmon, 1982*, Jerusalem, 1984, pp.137–152.

6. On the difficulty of distinguishing between Western elements and original Russian elements, see Michael Confino, *Russian and Western European Roots of Soviet Totalitarianism*, ibid., pp.104–117. The interconnection between non-religious eschatology as current within the Right, and religious eschatology, was provided by several organizations on the periphery of Revisionism, such as the *Berit ha-Kana'im* and the *Berit ha-Hashmona'im*, whose members included observant religious individuals who foresaw national redemption and an Israeli kingdom according to the laws of the Torah.

7. The essays on Uri Zvi Greenberg, his poetry and world-view are multifarious. See the bibliography by J. Arnon. Not all his writings have been included in his collected works; this applies in particular to his journalistic articles. Neither do they contain a comprehensive biography and monograph of this singular personality, who was both revered and hated, and who became a legend and myth in his lifetime. See my discussion about his prophetic status, in 'Uri Zvi Greenberg's Status as an Eschatological Poet', in *The Mythologies of the Right Wing*, pp.181–206. On the Polish model of the prophetic poet, see the article 'Between Pilsudski and Mickiewicz', ibid., pp.23–25, and on Mickiewicz's development as a prophetic poet similar to Greenberg, see V. Weintraub, *Literature as Prophecy; Scholarship and Martinist Poetics in Mickiewicz's Parisian Lectures*, The Hague, 1959. See also V. Ehrlich, *The Double Images: Concepts of the Poet in Slavic Literature*, Baltimore, 1964.

8. Clearly we should draw a distinction between the prophecies of the Last Days, concerning the end of the world and its civilization and culture, and other messianic prophecies with a defined national or religious background.

9. See S. Lindenbaum's study of the early Greenberg, *The Poetry of Uri Zvi Greenberg (Hebrew and Yiddish): an Outline*.

10. 'The Naked Truth', in *Doar ha-Yom*, 20.5.1930, and in *Hazit ha-Am*, 26.5.1933. The irony is that after 1945 the 'Faustian myth' was regarded as an expression of the 'German spirit', which ultimately led to Nazism!

11. As mentioned, a similar mytho-geographic idea is found in the writings of Buber and others, and its roots lead back to *Ha-Kuzari* by Rabbi Yehudah Halevi.

12. See the series of articles 'The Tortuous Road to Redemption in the World', published in *Ha-Mezuda* (the IZL organ in Jerusalem) in 1929, and subsequently in *Lehi Writings*, Volume I, pp.341–350.

13. So far no monography has been written about Scheib, who following the establishment of the State became the foremost intellectual of the Right. From the 1960s onwards he was more and more rescued out of his public isolation. The *Sulam* group and its influence will be discussed in detail in the second part of this study.

14. In this series, which was published in *Ha-Hazit* at the end of 1943, Eldad in effect collected the various dispersed ideas of Greenberg, in order to formulate an initial platform of the national Eschatology against his own intellectual background. An earlier formulation, which Eldad apparently acknowledged only later, was contained in a book by P. Heller, *National-Revolutionär Zionismus: Untersuchung und Proklamation*, Vienna, 1938. Heller, who was born in Nuremberg and grew up in Vienna, at first belonged to the group of Buber in *Der Jude*, before joining radical Revisionism.

15. Thus Scheib attempted to unite the theocentric and ethnocentric view into a single 'organic' outlook.

16. See note 13.

17. In this historical division the Middle Ages and the Pale of Settlement were transformed into an era in modern Jewish history characterized by idyllic and

harmonious relations between religion and nationalism.

18. This, too, reflects the development and actualization of an idea which already existed during the 19th century among nationalist Jewish intellectuals who were disillusioned with 'European' progress, and therefore created a distinction between culture (in the sense of morality) and 'material culture'.

CHAPTER 5

1. About Shevchenko, see C.A. Manning (translation and introduction), *T. Shevchenko, Selected Poems*, New York, 1945. It is interesting to note that Shevchenko's status as a 'national poet' of the Ukrainian people to a certain extent influenced Jewish national attitudes towards the status and role of the poet in a national revival movement.
2. 'Lessons from Shevchenko's Jubilee', an article published in 1911 in *On Literature and Art*, pp.133–141.
3. On this, see, for example, R. Kirk, *The Conservative Mind*, Chicago, 1953, and also Y. Harkabi, *Fateful Decisions*, pp.89–109. Harkabi's description and categorizations seem to me too schematic; neither does he credit the fact that the same basic attitudes exist among many individuals within the Labour movement. He even believes in the existence of an unequivocal deterministic link between a system of beliefs and the actual political behaviour of a group in a 'closed system'. I refer to the efforts by various ideological systems to provide answers to the most common questions about human life and behaviour.

   I have not concerned myself here with the history of 'mentality' in the broad sense of the word. It would be interesting to examine whether the Right exhibits a similar special affinity to broader human concepts such as love, birth, death, and so forth, or whether its singular mentality remains confined to the area of nation and society.
4. See A. Arian, *The Choosing People*. No field researches from the mandatory period are available. We should, however, remember that the questions that are asked in this kind of interview often are of a very general character. If someone is asked whether he is a 'Socialist', he will be hard put to give a correct definition of this concept.
5. The Rightist individual is not so much a traditional individual as a 'traditionalist', in the sense that he tends to rely on tradition as a response to modernism, and therefore clings to traditional values in a modern, post-revolutionary way.
6. The Rightist individual will use the term 'revolution' to refer to the revolutionary changes in the status of the Jewish people that have been achieved by the Zionist movement. At the same time 'revolution' also has negative connotations as a dangerous attempt to rupture the continuity of Jewish history. In this respect the Rightist individual represents a predominant tendency in the contemporary Jewish world-view, which emphasizes the organic quality, and the importance of historical continuity in Jewish history.

CHAPTER 6

1. See his article, 'Return to the Charter', *Die Tribune*, Copenhagen (Yiddish), 15.11.1925 and 'Activism', ibid., 10.10.1915. The origins and contents of the 'Colonization Regime' are discussed in detail in my book *Revisionism in Zionism*, pp.137–151.
2. For the contemporary criticism of the plan, see M. Medzini, *The Teachings of Zeev Jabotinsky: a Criticism on the Revisionist Programme*, Tel-Aviv, 1927. See also Z. Jabotinsky, 'The Secondary Functions of the Founding Meeting of the Revisionist Party', *Razsvet*, 19.4.1925, and his article 'The Duty to Pressure', *Ha-Aretz*, 21.6.1925; see also J. Shechtman, *The Vladimir Jabotinsky Story: Rebel and Statesman*, Vol. II.

3. *Grundsätze der Revisionismus* [Basic Principles of Revisionism], Paris, 1929; see also J. Schechtman, *The Vladimir Jabotinsky Story: Rebel and Statesman*, Vol. II, p.36.
4. See the description of the debate, which also was a turning point in the ascendancy of Mapai and its hegemony in the Zionist movement, in D. Ben-Gurion, *Memoirs*, Vol. I, 1971, pp.483–484. The issue is extensively dealt with in Y. Goldstein's study, *The Road to Hegemony: Mapai, the Crystallization of its Policy 1930–1936*.
5. For a discussion, in a different context of the Revisionist opposition to Partition, and its demand for the immediate establishment of a State in the year 1937, see Chapter 7. There is a wealth of material on this subject available: see *Board of Governors of Ha-Zach*, 27.6.1937, JI10/C; B. Lubotzky, 'The Abortive Scheme', *Ha-Yarden*, 9.7.1937; as well as Y. Avraham, 'The Revisionist Opposition to the Partition Plan', *Ha-Ummah*, no. 53, December 1977, pp. 126–132. The author of the latter article suggested the totally unpractical idea that it would be possible to pressure Great Britain into establishing a Jewish State in the whole of Western Eretz Israel in 1937. However, Benyamin Akzin testified that Jabotinsky believed that it would be possible to agree upon a plan, provided only that one could put faith in the seriousness of Great Britain's intentions; after all, Italy, too, had evolved out of the small state of Piedmont. See also 'The Attitude of Ha-Zohar to the Partition Plan', in *Studies on the Partition Plan 1937–1947*, Ben-Gurion Univ. of the Negev, 1984, pp.160–165.
6. See Jabotinsky's testimony to the Peel Commission, Z. Jabotinsky, *Evidence Submitted to the Palestine Royal Commission*, London, 1937.
7. Z. Jabotinsky, *The Jewish War Front*, pp.204–214.
8. See my book *The New Hebrew Nation: a Study in Israeli Heresy and Fantasy*, pp.33–36. See also my book *Revisionism in Zionism*, pp.43–45.
9. This is the red thread running through all of Ben-Gurion's critical articles during this period. See D. Ben-Gurion, *From a Class to a Nation*, 1933, pp.219–245.
10. In August 1913 Weizmann wrote to L. Greenberg: 'Differences in method matter very considerably when the *Endziel* ('final goal') is so remote . . .' With this he referred to the fact that tactical actions would be turned into facts. *Weizmann Letters, 1913–1914*, Series A, Vol. 6, p.126.
11. *Die Tribune*, ibid.
12. J. B. Schechtman, *The Vladimir Jabotinsky Story*, Vol. II, pp.36–37.
13. The discussion about the 'enlargement' of the Jewish Agency, a subject which falls outside the scope of this study, touched upon some of the essential aspects of the structure of the Zionist movement and its relations with the Jewish world. See also Jabotinsky's article, 'The Prospect of Government by the Plutocracy', *Razsvet*, 1.7.1923, soon to be published by the Jewish Agency.
14. Z. Jabotinsky, 'Majority', *Razsvet*; see also my book *Revisionism in Zionism*, pp.138–147, where I have related all the claims and complaints against the mandatory government.
15. See his principal speeches on this subject, 'A Useful Storm', *Ha-Yarden*, 30.10.1936; 'Transjordan and the Ten-Year Plan', *Unser Welt*, April 1938; 'About the Evacuaion Plan', *Unser Welt*, 30.9.1936; 'Poland will Assist and Gain from the Evacuation Plan', ibid., 1936; as well as his book, *A Jewish State*, 1937. In the course of 1936, apart from publishing a number of articles on this subject, he addressed public meetings and even broadcast about the Plan on various Polish radio stations. See also my article, 'The Polish Ghetto and the Holocaust Prophecy: between Catastrophe Rhetorics and a Rescue Policy', in *The Mythologies of the Right Wing*, pp.63–84. See further the discussion in the next chapter.
16. See the next chapter.
17. The basic claim against *Mapai* was that it preferred a 'selective' and 'pampered' form of Zionism destined for an existing elite, at the expense of the Jewish people as a whole. See, for example, his article 'Comments', in which he railed against the 'Transfer' arrangement with Nazi Germany (*Ha-Yarden*, 31.1.1936), and which

was published in Yiddish and German under the title: 'Alles für Reiche – nichts für die Armen' (*Medinah Ivrit*, 7.2.1936).

CHAPTER 7

1. Even though, as already mentioned, the Right claimed that the fundamental preference of the Left for building an exemplary society caused it to be satisfied with autonomy and prevented it from pursuing Zionism as a revolutionary national liberation movement.
2. The personality of 'Xerxes' as a Messiah derives from the prophecies of the second Isaiah. His example came to be used as a symbol of other world leaders who showed a preparedness to act on behalf of the Jews, including Napoleon, Czar Alexander II and Lord Balfour.
3. In the well-known lines of the poem 'Judea Today, Judea Tomorrow' (*Ha-Yarden*, 30.7.1938), Greenberg writes among other things:

   I can see the eagles of Amalek* streaking down from the Rhine,
   soaring above the high roofs of Westminster . . .
   I see the whole of India pulling up your anchors . . .

   * i.e. Germany

4. See his articles 'The Englishmen', *Der Morgen Journal* (Yiddish), New York, 6.8 and 13.8.1926, and reprinted in three instalments in *Razsvet* on 1.12, 8.12 and 15.12. 1929. The principles of the 'Pressure Theory' were formulated in the articles 'The Duty to Pressure' in *Ha-Aretz*, 21.6.1925, and 'Pressure' – three articles in *Razsvet*, published on 5.8.1923, 13.8.1923 and 19.8.1923.
5. The letter was buried with the secret *IZL* archive; see Chapter 2, Note 74.
6. The proclamations and articles in the *IZL* organ *Ba-Machteret*, as well as other publications since 1944, abounded in comparisons of the British with the Nazis, as well as claims that Great Britain and Nazi Germany were jointly responsible for the Holocaust.
7. Letter dated 28.12.1929, JI A1/2/29/2. This British orientation is described in my article, 'Father of the Revolt: an Examination of the Title, its History, and its Function in the Historical Tradition of Revisionism, the Irgun and the Herut Movement', in *The Mythologies of the Zionist Right Wing*, pp.85–124.
8. In J. Achimeir (ed.), *The Black Prince*, p.262. He addressed the Congress on 30.8.1932.
9. Z. Jabotinsky, 'At the Fireside' (*The New Alef-Beth*) *Zammelbuch für betarischen Jugend*, Warsaw, 1933. In 1927 he wrote that the purpose of Zionism was to *convince* Great Britain to remain in the East.
10. See the article 'Political Orientation and Lowdown Libellous Charges', *Ha-Yarden*, 14.10.1935.
11. See his articles 'England or . . .?', *Razsvet*, 13.10.1928, and 'England and Us', ibid., 25.3.1928.
12. Z. Jabotinsky, 'Did we Lose?', *Ha-Yarden*, 24.7.1936. He was convinced that Zionism would only stand to gain from the revolt!
13. These reactions are recalled in my book, *Self Restraint or Reaction*.
14. On this subject, see F. Martin, 'The Evolution of a Myth – the Easter Rising', Dublin, 1916, in E. Kamenka (ed.), *Nationalism, the Nature and Evolution of an Idea*, London, 1976, pp.57–80.
15. In any case, pride of place in this framework of analogies was reserved for the Jewish revolt against the Romans.
16. All these arguments about to Western Eretz Israel appeared were shared by other opponents of Partition; see S. Dothan, *The Partition of Eretz Israel in the Mandatory Period: the Jewish Controversy*.
17. Jabotinsky wrote about this to Winston Churchill on 16.7.1937. The letter was

reproduced in *Ha-Ummah*, 74/75, Spring 1984, pp.122–125.

18. Z. Jabotinsky, 'Precondition to the Ten-Year Plan', *Unser Welt*, April 1938. On the Rumanian and Polish opposition to the Partition Plan, see F. Nicosia, *The Third Reich and the Palestinian Question*, London, 1985, pp.125–126.

19. Z. Jabotinsky, ibid.

20. On the discussions in July 1938 and July 1939, see JI 2/19–43.

21. For a description of this activity, see Ch. Lazar-Litai, *The Book of the Illegal Immigration*, Tel-Aviv, 1957. The proclamation on the Paris Conference of 12.1.1940 is in JI K4/1/12.

22. Ben-Gurion wrote: 'Do you really think that Malcolm [Macdonald] or Neville [Chamberlain] have read the article in *Haynt*, or that they have heard about the protests in Pinsk?', in D. Ben-Gurion, *Memoirs*, Vol. III, 1974, p.105. Jabotinsky was convinced that Great Britain would not implement the policy of the White Paper, as he wrote in an article called, 'To Implement the Oath', in *Unser Welt*, June 1938, as well as in several private letters written during May–July 1939. As a result, the publication of the White Paper came to him as a bitter blow and a stunning disappointment! Among Jabotinsky's numerous articles on the Petition Plan, see 'Our Brothers', *Hazit Ha-Am*, 29.5.1934. Although the party placed much weight on the Petition Campaign, the 'radicals' treated it with contempt and scorn. See also 'The Petition: a National Protest', 11.1.1934, ibid.

23. Z. Jabotinsky, 'The Evacuation Plan' (Yiddish), *Unser Welt*, October 1933.

24. On this, see my article, 'Between Pilsudski and Mickiewicz', in *The Mythologies of the Right Wing*, pp.39–41. The letter to Schechtman in JI 1/29/2/1A, and an additional letter dated 22.12.1938, are in JI 2/18/2/1A. On this subject, see the discussion by D. Engel, 'The Failed Alliance: the Revisionist Movement and the Polish Government in Exile, 1939–1945', in *Zionism*, XI, 1986, pp.333–360, and in particular the discussion on pp.335–338.

In the course of the 1930s the idea took hold that Poland was a Great Power. Robert Machary wrote in 1936 that 'In 1934–1935 it was obvious that Poland had become a Great State, to be reckoned with accordingly'; *The Poland of Pilsudski*, London, 1936, p.13. On the general background, see E. Melzer, *Political Struggle in a Trap; the Jews of Poland 1935–1939*.

25. This issue is naturally a subject of historical controversy. Poland could have assisted the illegal immigration with arms and so forth, but there is serious doubt as to whether she could have influenced Great Britain to change her policies in Eretz Israel.

26. Nahum Sokolow, 'Journey through Poland in 1934', in *Watchman unto the House of Israel*, p.261.

27. Z. Jabotinsky, 'Zion Sejm', in *Der Moment*, 16–17.5.1939. Earlier, in an article entitled 'The Coming War' (*Ha-Mashkif*, 14.4.1939) he had stated that the danger of a war had receded thanks to the aggressive stance of Poland.

The various nazi authorities kept a close watch on Revisionist activities, in particular because of the central role the Revisionists played in organizing an anti-German boycott. In various German reports Jabotinsky is accused of being full of a *Hetze* against Germany (*Politisches Archiv, Auswärtiges Amt: Inland*, IIA/B, Bd.; see also the report on the Founding Meeting of *Ha-Zach* in Vienna, ibid, Bd. 3, 19.9.1935). The analysis by Jabotinsky and other Revisionists of the nature of Nazism and German policies between 1933 and 1939, as well as the debate about the boycott movement, have been the subject of several studies, although the last word on these subjects has not yet been spoken. Such a discussion within the framework of Zionist and Jewish historical polemics usually revolves around questions such as: 'Who foresaw more clearly the danger of Nazism?'; 'Would it have been at all possible to fight Nazism during the 1930s, and by which means?'; and 'Could more Jews have been saved from the Holocaust?' This is a very wide-ranging subject that falls outside the scope of this study and, in my opinion, should be dealt with in a different context. For this reason I intend to discuss it in a separate essay.

28. JI A1/2/29/2.
29. This subject is described in detail in my article 'Father of the Revolt', ibid., pp.96–102.
30. In a special issue of *For the Fatherland*, Tel-Aviv, March 1938. The entire group, except Menachem Begin, joined the *IZL* in Poland.
31. Y. Eldad (Scheib), *The First Tithe: a Book of Memoirs and Moralities*, pp.21–25.
32. J. B. Schechtman, *The Vladimir Jabotinsky Story*, Vol. III (Hebrew), 1959, pp.236–237.
33. Letter dated 7.8.1939, JI, A1/2/29/2.
34. *Report on the Third World Assembly of Betar, Warsaw, 1938*, Bucharest, 1940, pp.31–63. See also *Ha-Yarden*, 7.10.1938. Begin's speech was published in *Unser Welt* of 23.9.1938, but Jabotinsky's reaction was not published there. Several personalities insist on interpreting Begin's speech as an open call to revolt, and tried to mitigate and dilute Jabotinsky's fierce criticism of Begin.
35. Exchange of letters in the Yunitschman file (File Q106) in the Jabotinsky Institute.
36. JI A1/2/29/2.
37. JI A1/21/29/2.
38. See his optimistic perspective of Zionism after the war's end in his last book, *The Jewish War Front*, 1940.
39. For a detailed description of this programme, see my article 'The Father of the Revolt', pp.102–110, in which I analyse the various testimonies on the subject.
40. This document was published several times after it was first revealed in D. Yisraeli, *The Palestine Problem in German Politics*, pp.227–228. See also my discussion on the nature of *Lehi*'s proposal in my article, 'Between Idealism and Opportunism: an Attempt to Portray *Lehi* as an Underground Organization and an Ideological Group', in *The Mythologies of the Right Wing*, pp.161–163. See also the apologetic and unconvincing explanation in the new biography of A. Stern by Ada Amichal-Yevin, *In Purple*, p.223.
41. B. Wasserstein, 'New Light on the Moyne Murder', in *Midstream*, March 1980, pp.30–38; and M.J. Cohen, 'New Light on the Moyne Murder', in *Middle Eastern Studies*, October 1979, pp.370–371. These are only two of the articles that have been published during the last years; see also my article in 'Between Idealism and Opportunism', ibid., pp.165–170.
42. This dark and problematic episode in the history of the *yishuv* is described in my book *The 'Open Season': the Confrontation between the 'Organized Yishuv' and the Underground Organizations 1937–1945*.
43. The history of the IZL is detailed in Vol. VI of D. Niv, *The Battle for Freedom: the IZL*. J. Bell's *Terror out of Zion: IZL, Lehi and the Palestinian Underground, 1929–1949*, presents a dramatic running account, based mainly on interviews.
44. Press conference in Cracow, 12.1.1935. In *Ha-Yarden* of 4.1.1934 Jabotinsky wrote that 'we cannot exploit a war by raising arms against England, and neither would all of us favour this (I, for one, would not want it, even if we had all the guns [in the world]) . . .'.
45. The exchange of letters during January/February 1940 between Vilna and Tel-Aviv in JI, File P106 offers an interesting insight into the biography of Begin concerning the same period. See also my article 'Begin's Course to Revolt', in *The Mythologies of the Right Wing*, pp.137–140.
46. During the same period, Begin published his articles in the legal *Betar* newspaper *Ha-Madrich* under the pseudonym M. Ben-Zeev (after his father Zeev Begin).
47. Y. Shavit, ibid., p.144. There is no doubt that the reports on the Warsaw ghetto uprising in the summer of 1943 were a turning point which brought Begin to the conclusion that the battle against the White Paper (but not against Great Britain) had to be renewed soon, in particular in view of the danger that Britain would attempt to apply the paragraph about the establishment of an Arab state in Eretz Israel.
48. For the plan of the revolt, see JI, K/4/1/13.

49. For a description of the organization of the *IZL* in Europe, see E.J. Tavin, *The Second Front: the IZL in Europe 1946–1948*. The direct consequence of these efforts was the despatch of the arms ship *Altalena* from Marseilles to Tel-Aviv, and the resulting bitter confrontations in June 1948. This tragic episode has been described in numerous publications, and more recently in two studies, each reflecting a different point of view, viz.: S. Nakdimon, *Altalena*, Tel-Aviv, 1978, and U. Brenner, *Altalena: a Political and Military Study*, Tel-Aviv, 1978.

CHAPTER 8

1. The principal studies on this subject are:
   a. Y. Gorny, *The Arab Question and the Jewish Problem*. (An English edition will be published by Oxford University Press.)
   b. Several chapters in S. Almog (ed.), *Zionism and the Arabs*, Jerusalem, 1973, pp.73–94; for a discussion about the Revisionist view, see in particular Y. Shavit, 'Revisionism's View of the Arab National Movement'.
   c. J. Heller, 'Weizmann, Jabotinsky and the Arab Question – the Peel Committee Affair', in S. Ettinger (ed.), *Nation and History, Studies on the History of the Jewish People*, Vol. II, 1984, pp.285–306.
   d. Idem, 'Between Messianism and Political Realism – Lehi and the Arab Question 1940–1947', in *Contemporary Judaism, Yearbook for Study and Research*, Vol. I, Jerusalem, 1984, pp.223–247.
   e. Idem, 'Lehi and the Arab Question 1947–1948', ibid, Vol. II, 1985, pp.337–374.
   f. Among the relevant writings which express the rightist point of view, see S. Katz, *Battleground: Facts and Fantasy in Palestine*, Tel-Aviv, 1972.
2. Z. Jabotinsky, *The Story of my Life*, p.115. On his scepticism with regard to the 'magic of the East', see the story 'Ednée', 1912, in *Stories*, pp.99–107, as well as his articles 'The East', *Razsvet*, 16.9.1926, and 'The Pictorial East', ibid., 7.2.1932.
3. Letter to Oscar Rozenberg, dated November 1925, in *Letters*, 1959, pp.72–74.
4. See also A. Achimeir's article, 'Fiddlesticks' in *Ha-Yarden*, 12.2.1938.
5. On Orientalism and the traditional Western approach to and image of the Muslim world, see Edward Said, *Orientalism*, New York, 1978. In this work, which created a great deal of heated controversy, Said analyses only one aspect, although a central one, of the attitude of the West towards the Levant.
6. This outlook is summarized in an article by M. Nissan, 'The Face of the Political Culture of the Muslim Arabs', in *Ha-Ummah*, 78/79, Spring/Summer 1985, pp.19–27. Similar opinions are expressed in a list of essays and articles too long to be mentioned here.
7. See Jabotinsky's introduction to his booklet, *The Hebrew Accent*, 1930. In it, he creates both an ethnic and a linguistic link between the Hebrew people and the 'Arab Semitic nations'.
8. These literary reportages were first published in the year 1946. The irony is that they employ the same characteristic categories as are used in anti-Jewish literature, even though the arguments are different.
9. M. Avniel, *The Problem of the Arabs in Eretz Israel*, Tel-Aviv, June 1936, JI 151. The description of the Arabs as congenital traitors is a recurrent motif in this kind of literature. Time and again the Arabs are portrayed as capricious and immoral, and as people who are inconstant, whose word cannot be trusted and who are always ready to betray.
10. 'Principles and Conclusions', in *Omer la-Am*, special edition of the IZL (the future *Lehi* group), 29.7.1939. The article repeats the same arguments that had been presented throughout the years, but in much more outspoken language. See the article by Prof. Joseph Klausner, 'Arab Nationalism and Culture' in *Die Velt*, 28.5.1936. The Arabs, wrote Klausner, did not establish a culture in Eretz Israel, and for this reason they do not possess an inherent Arab nationalist consciousness,

which is the foundation of all culture. Already at the beginning of the century Klausner had written in *Ha-Shiloach* no. 17, 1907/1908, that the Jews lacked affinity with the East, and that Judaism had to be cleansed of every shred of Orientalism.

11. Y. Scheib, 'A Frank Look at Reality (about the Question of our Relations with the Arabs)', *Metzuda*, no. 18, January 1938.

12. See Jabotinsky's articles on this subject, 'The Terrible Islam', in *Der Morgen Journal*, New York, 22.6.1927, and 'Islam', *Razsvet*, 19.4.1924 and 15.5.1924. About the weakness of Islam as a political power, Jabotinsky had earlier written in his brochure *Turkey and the War*, predicting that Islamic unity would be a thing of the far distant future – if it ever would come to pass.

13. Achimeir rejected the attitude of the mandatory government towards the *yishuv*, among other things because he felt slighted by Great Britain's treatment of the Jews as 'natives', rather than kindred representatives of Western culture. In his article 'Egypt', published in *Hadashot ha-Aretz* of 23.11.1919, Jabotinsky wrote that in the long term Egypt was not a stronghold capable of ensuring British domination of either the Mediterranean, or the passage to India, and that for this reason there would come a day that the British people would 'inscribe the Balfour Declaration in golden letters in the annals of Britannia that ruled the waves', for the simple reason that only the Jews would prove to be secure and eternal allies . . . . (This prediction of the instability of Egypt had been made by British Imperialists as early as the 1880s.)

14. The Revisionist press often referred to the Biblical verse, 'Look now, you are depending on Egypt, that splintered reed of a staff . . .' [Isaiah, 36: 6], to describe the Arabs as fundamentally untrustworthy allies.

15. See my book, *The New Hebrew Nation*.

16. Z. Jabotinsky, *Turkey and the War*. However, before World War I, Jabotinsky preferred the continued existence of a united Turkish empire over its division, something which would result in the establishment of national Arab states; see his article 'The New Situation in Turkey' in *Die Velt*, no. 3, February 1909. At that time Jabotinsky hoped for understanding on the part of the Young Turks that Zionism would be able to assist them against Arab nationalism, which could cause the disintegration of the Ottoman Empire from within. Only after the war had broken out did he come to the conclusion that the fate of the Ottoman Empire had been sealed, and that its place would be taken by the European powers.

17. Z. Jabotinsky, 'Syria and the Arab Crisis', *Ha-Aretz*, 9.8.1920. In this article he writes that 'a national movement which denies the right of another nation, is not a national movement in the proper sense of the word'.

18. See J. Heller, 'Lehi and the Arab Question 1940–1947', pp.240–247, and pp.337–339. The memorandum was written by Nathan Yellin-Mor.

19. On this subject, see the memorandum by Yonathan Ratosh of 1938, JI: B/2/1/3. There is no doubt that memories of the Minority pact were, among other things, behind the Likud government's policy *vis à vis* Maronite aspirations in Lebanon during the 1980s, even though this view was not restricted to the Right only.

20. Proceedings of the Zionist General Council 1919–1921, Vol. II. In the sessions in July 1921 Jabotinsky for the first time used the expression 'Iron Wall', when he said that Zionism could not afford to give anything to the Arabs: today the Jews constituted a minority, but in another twenty years they would be the majority, 'and if we were Arabs, we would not accept this either. The Arabs are as good Zionists as we are, and the country is full of Arab memories'. Since there was no hope of a compromise, it was necessary to erect an 'iron wall' between the Zionist aspirations and the conflicting Arab aspirations, ibid., pp.280–289.

21. These two articles were reprinted a number of times. They were first published in *Razsvet* on 11.11. 1923 and 4.11.1924.

22. See the chapter, 'The Arab Problem – Without Dramatics', in the book *The War and the Jews*, pp.211–222. See also the introduction to S. Klinger's brochure, *The Ten-Year Plan for Palestine* (Engl.), London, 1938.

23. *Mivrak*, 13.6.1948.
24. The influence of these theoreticians of the national question on Jabotinsky is clearly visible in his dissertation, *Self-Rule of the National Minority* of the year 1912, originally written in Russian; see *Nation and Society*, 1950, pp.13–72. On this issue, see also the discussion in chapter 3.
25. In his article 'About a Bi-national Eretz Israel' in *Razsvet*, 3.1.1926. See also his articles, 'Majority', ibid., 21.10.1923; 'Useless Talk', *Haynt*, 12.9.1930; and 'Again about Bi-National Eretz Israel', in *Razsvet*, 16.10.1927.
26. See Z. Jabotinsky, *Self-Rule of the National Minority*.
27. 'The Arab Crisis', ibid.
28. For details of the programme, see his book, *The Jewish State*, pp.182–188.
29. 'Discussions with Zangwill', *Der Moment*, 27.7. 1939.
30. Here it should be noted that this referred not to the Arabs as a 'national minority', who had a right to autonomy, but to Arab citizens of a Jewish state, enjoying equal civic rights and the right to live their own cultural and religious existence. They would not, however, have the right of national self-expression, for this would be tantamount to granting them political rights.
31. Programme of the 'Israel Freedom Fighters' (*Lehi*), July/August 1948. See J. Heller, *Lehi and the Arab Question, 1947–1948*, p.367.
32. See my book *The New Hebrew Nation*, p.126.
33. *Sulam*, in numerous articles, quoted Biblical sources for its conclusion that the Jews should follow in the footsteps of Joshua or King David, and extradite any non-Jewish residents who refused to accept Jewish authority. (The forced conversion practised by several of the Hasmonean kings was not mentioned!)

CHAPTER 9

1. See J. Schechtman's article in *Ha-Zafon*, 12.6.1927. Schechtman wrote that the workers did not persecute the bourgeois, but that the opposite was the case. See also B. Lubotzky, 'Ha-Zohar and the Social Question', in *Ha-Yarden*, 28.10. 1935, and B. Avniel's article, 'We Won't Obey and we Won't Listen', in *Ha-Yarden*, 28.10.1935, which protest the claim that it was the declared purpose of *Ha-Zohar* 'to eradicate Socialism within the Jewish community'. Against this, see the reaction in *Ha-Yarden*, 4.11.1935, according to which it was indeed the duty of *Ha-Zohar* to put an end to the treacherous feelings of superiority of *Mapai*.
2. Z. Jabotinsky, 'Immigration', *Hadashot ha-Aretz*, 14.11.1919. A pronounced evolutionary view on the development of the *yishuv* was expressed as early as 1905 in the brochure, *What are we to do?*, in which he advocated 'grey work, without fireworks'; see also his article 'The Amount of Immigration', *Ha-Aretz*, 18.12.1919.
3. 'From the Side', *Hadashot ha-Aretz*, 17.9.1919. In this article he wrote that the composition of the Jewish population of Eretz Israel was as yet unbalanced, because the middle class was weak and the political party which represented it rather reactionary. At the same time there was not yet room for a middle class – as opposed to 'capitalists' – in Eretz Israel, for only after an intermediary period of growth and stability could the door for the immigration of the middle classes be opened.
4. On Grabski as a 'financial dictator', see R. Machary, *The Poland of Pilsudski*, pp.178–183. On the Fourth Aliyah, see D. Giladi, *Jewish Palestine during the Fourth Aliya Period (1924–1929)*. On the formation of immigration policy during this period, see M. Mossek, *Palestine Immigration Policy under Sir Herbert Samuel*.
5. December 1926, *Speeches*, Vol. I, p.315. See Jabotinsky's lecture, 'The Roots of the Crisis', at the World Assembly of *Ha-Zohar* in December 1926, in *Speeches*, I, p.315. Jabotinsky devoted numerous articles to the crisis of 1921–1923, followed by the crisis years 1922–1925; see, for instance, 'National Settlement and Private Initiative', *Ha-Aretz*, 16.5.1922. In effect, every economic crisis was explained as a

result of the misguided British policy, whereas any sign of prosperity was called merely illusory.

6. The profound crisis created among Polish Zionists by the Fourth Aliyah is surveyed in the study by E. Mendelson, *Zionism in Poland: the Formative Years 1915–1926*.

7. The 'New Economic Policy' (N.E.P.) was declared by Lenin at the 10th Communist Party Congress in March 1921. Its purpose was to stimulate private production; see E.H. Carr, *The Russian Revolution from Lenin to Stalin 1917–1929*, London, 1979. See also note 13.

8. Letter to Oscar Gruzenberg, dated 12.11. 1925, in *Letters*, pp.72–74.

9. Thus he wrote to M. Grossman that *Ha-Zohar* as a party represented the position of a liberal, national bourgeois centre (22.10.1928 and 4.10.1933, JI A1/2/18/2 and A1/18/12/23). See J. Schechtman, *The Vladimir Jabotinsky Story: Rebel and Statesman*, Vol. II, pp.309–312.

10. On Jewish craftsmen and artisans in Poland, see R. Mahler, *Polish Jewry between the two World Wars*, pp.43–48. The decline of the craftsmen and artisans, and their fear of proletarization and impoverishment are generally believed to have been responsible for the rise of Anti-Modernism and Fascism. See S. Volkov, *The Rise of Popular Anti-Modernism in Germany: the Urban Master Artisans*, New Jersey, 1972. See also Z. Jabotinsky, 'Things which have been Forgotten', *Razsvet*, 9.4.1925. Even so Jabotinsky was aware of the fundamental differences between the situations of Jews and non-Jews, as well as the differences between Eretz Israel and Poland. Jewish craftsmen in Poland wanted to emigrate in order to be able to pursue their professions, but as regards *aliyah* their fate was sealed in 1921. Meanwhile another 10,000 artisans who were already in Eretz Israel failed to qualify for assistance on the part of the Zionist institutions.

11. This brochure was first published in Odessa in 1905; see *Early Zionist Writings 1903–1906*, 1949, pp.75–106.

12. See his speech at the 12th Zionist Congress in Carlsbad, *Speeches*, Vol. I, pp.211–229, as well as his articles 'A Zionist N.E.P.', *Razsvet*, 29.7.1923; *Haynt*, 16.12.1927, and 'On the Zionist N.E.P. (a Second Time)', ibid., 29.3. 1928.

13. See note 9. It is interesting that Joseph Katznelson saw the N.E.P. as a sad testimony to the revolutionary spirit of Russian Communism (A. Achimeir, *The Death of Joseph Katznelson*, p.7). A policy similar to the N.E.P. was supposed to be in practice independent of British policy, whereas a colonization regime was by its very nature dependent upon it.

14. 'Funds for Eretz Israel', *Ha-Yarden*, 9.9.1934.

15. See Jabotinsky's greetings to the founding meeting of the National Labour Federation, *Hazit ha-Am*, 15.5.1934, and E. Shostak (ed.), *The National Labour Federation – the Tenth Anniversary of the Federation*, 1944, pp.3–7.

16. Uri Zvi Greenberg, *Sadan/ Manifest le-bitui*, Vols. I–II, Jerusalem, 1925. Greenberg regarded the Fourth Aliyah as something that had brought the Diaspora to Eretz Israel, including its negative human elements and all its other curses.

17. See 'The Revolt of the Aged' (originally in Russian), Paris, 1937, *Nation and Society*, pp.223–236. Elsewhere he called the 19th century 'the century of dishonour', because it was characterized by capitalist exploitation.

18. Z. Jabotinsky, 'The Young Middle Class', *Hazit ha-Am*, 13.4.1934, and 'The Middle-Class Youth', *Ha-Yarden*, 24.5.1934.

   The Zionist political dictionary was influenced by the German language, as a result of which the word *bourgeoisie* – in the sense of 'middle class' – is equivalent to the German word *bürgerlich*. Jabotinsky did not talk about a bourgeoisie in the sense of a uniform demographic class, but rather as a specific group, united by shared economic, cultural and political attitudes, even though the individual members might have quite different life-styles. See also P. H. Reill, *The German Enlightenment and the Rise of Historicism*, Los Angeles, 1975, pp.4–5.

19. Z. Jabotinsky, ibid.

20. On merchants as 'creators of our world', see Z. Jabotinsky, *Contemporary*

Recollections, p.41, and 'The Retailer', *Haynt*, 5.6.1927. See also, 'Lecture on the History of Israel', *Nation and Society*, p.164, and 'We are the Bourgeoisie', *Ha-Zafon* 8.5.1927.

21. See A. Achimeir, 'The Spirit of Tu-Bish'vat', in *Revolutionary Zionism*, pp.150–154. According to Jabotinsky, trading was one of the historical expressions of the adventurous spirit. See his articles in *Haynt*, 29.7.1937 and 31.7.1937.
22. For details of the programme, see my book *Revisionism in Zionism: the Revisionist Movement – the Plan for a Colonization Regime and Social Ideas 1925–1935*, pp.182–191. On Soskin's agricultural programme, see Z. Soskin, *Das Kolonisationsproblem*, Paris, 1929, and *Revision der zionistischen Politik*, Berlin, 1930. The paradox is that from 1937 onwards it became possible to implement Soskin's theories about intensive agriculture and hydroponics as a means of supporting the Partition Plan!

    On Revisionism and Hebrew labour, see the resolutions of the Fourth Assembly of *Ha-Zohar* in April 1928, JI 57/10 C, etc.
23. This issue was the subject of considerable polemics. See the discussion in my book *Revisionism in Zionism*, pp.202–235, as well as 'What do the Zionist Revisionists Want', in *Razsvet* 13.6.1926; B. Avniel, *Labour Problems in Eretz Israel*, 1941; and Z. Jabotinsky, 'Yes, Break It!', *Haynt* 4.10.1932, etc.
24. Only after World War II was social legislation in mandatory Palestine expanded.
25. See Chapter 12. As mentioned, Jabotinsky preferred to point at the government of Leon Blum as a forerunner in the field of organized labour relations. See S. B. Clough, T.M. Moodie, and C. Moodie (eds.), *Economic History of Europe: Twentieth Century*, New York, 1968, pp.259–260.
26. By 'utopia' I refer, as mentioned earlier, primarily to the description of an ideal social order.
27. During this period Jabotinsky keenly felt the absence of a theory as a basis for an ideology and a programme; see also the two versions of Economic Theory of 1938, and see his article, 'The Ideological Question' in *Ha-Madrich*, the organ of *Betar* in Eretz Israel, 1942 (apparently written in 1934).
28. As already mentioned, Jabotinsky was influenced by Antonio Labriola, but – according to his own testimony – no less by the Italian socialist and criminological theoretician Enrico Ferri, who in 1894 tried to formulate a synthesis between Darwinism and Marxism, which met with a lukewarm reception by contemporary marxist groups.
29. It is not clear whether Jabotinsky ever read *Das Kapital*, or whether his knowledge of Marxism was derived from other sources. In effect, all he wanted to say was that intellect is also a 'productive factor', and – most important of all – that creative intellect is not even class dependent.
30. Buckle believed that cultural progress is the outcome of the liberation of human society from the dominating influence of restricting 'external forces', and that as such it is mainly the product of 'free internal forces'.
31. As against this, he stressed the centrality of economic factors in the revival of Zionism among Polish Jewry!
32. See his article 'Social Redemption', in *Notes*, pp.293–314; 'The Crisis of the Proletariat' (originally in Russian), 19.4.1932, as well as in *Notes*, pp. 314–315.
33. See also Chapter 3. The summary is derived from his articles 'The Mission of Israel'; 'Our Spiritual Values'; and 'Prophetic Socialism', which were published in J. Klausner, *Judaism and Humanity*, Jerusalem, 1955.
34. As a result he considered Jewish morality superior, and thus preferable to Greek ethics.
35. See the chapter on 'State Capitalism' in M. Harrington, *Socialism* (according to the Hebrew translation of 1973).
36. Z. Jabotinsky, 'The Idea of the Jubilee Year', in *Nation and Society*, pp. 171–180.
37. 'Social Redemption', ibid.
38. *Social Insurance and Allied Services: Beveridge Report*, 1942. See also, J.R. Hay,

The Origins of the Liberal Reform 1906–1914, London, 1975, and A.J.M. Milne, *The Social Philosophy of English Idealism*, London, 1962.

39. See his earlier-mentioned articles 'The Middle-Class Youth' and 'The Revolt of the Aged'.
40. First published in *Zammelbuch far betarischen Jugend*.
41. A collection of his novellas, *Fantasies of a Realist*, was published in Vienna in 1894. Joseph Popper (1838–1921) was a writer, inventor and utopian, and one of the most interesting and talked-about personalities in Vienna during the closing days of the Empire. See the monograph by Y. Dorion, *An End to the Struggle for Survival*.
42. Z. Jabotinsky, 'A Working People', *Doar ha-Yom*, 5.12.1932, and 'The Right of the Individual', *Razsvet*, 25.12.1932.

CHAPTER 10

1. On this subject, see my article, 'Father of the Revolt', in *The Mythologies of the Right Wing*, pp.85–124. Some of the developments in the *IZL* between 1942 and 1948 are described at length in D. Niv, *The Battle for Freedom: the IZL*, Vol. VI.
2. This subject is discussed in my article, 'Between Idealism and Opportunism' in, *The Mythologies of the Right Wing*, pp.153–179. See J. Heller's two articles, 'Lehi and the Arab Problem', in the notes to Chapter 8. See also Y. S. Brenner, 'The Stern Gang 1940–1948', in *Middle Eastern Studies*, 2:1, October 1965, pp.2–30.
3. See P. Genosar, *Lehi Revealed: Proceedings of the Conference of the Israel Freedom Fighters (Lehi), March 1949*, p.102. In my view, however, the so-called 'Soviet orientation' of Yitzhak Shamir was not based on authentic socialist ideology or admiration of the Soviet Union as a socialist state, but on his respect for the Soviet Union as an emerging world power. Shamir is a prime example of a pragmatic doctrinaire! If the communist world power was prepared to assist the Jews in achieving their great national goal, then it was a welcome ally.
4. This description and interpretation is based on the many articles on the subject published in *Lehi* publications during the years 1947–1948 (collected mainly in *Lehi Collected Works*). The reasons for the leftist tendency in *Lehi* during this period are a matter of intensive dispute between former *Lehi* members; see also my article 'Between Idealism and Opportunism' in *The Mythologies of the Right Wing*.
5. See the programme of the 'Israel Freedom Fighters' (*Lehi*) in P. Ginosar, ibid. pp.133–135. See also my discussion in, *The New Hebrew Nation*, p.146–148. The most interesting developments within *Lehi* will be described in the second part of the study.

CHAPTER 11

1. 'Basta' [Ital.: 'Enough!'], *Razsvet*, 28.7. 1925. See also his articles, 'Revisionism and the Labour Movement', 2.3.1930; 'The Enemy of the Workers', 2.8.1925; 'The Left', 21.1.1925; and 'The Left', 12.7.1925, ibid. These are only four among his numerous articles on the subject. In an interesting interview he gave on 6.7.1928 to the Warsaw Jewish newspaper *Ha-Zefirah*, he protected the workers' settlement effort from its detractors in Poland by stating that Zionism was bound by ties of love to any groups which embraced the Zionist idea. He explains his own criticism as being directed against the agreement of the Labour parties to the plan for the enlargement of the Jewish Agency.
2. See S. Schwartz, *Jabotinsky, a Fighter for his Nation*, Jerusalem, 1943, pp.137–138. The author was of the opinion that the chasm between Jabotinsky and the Labour movement had already been created at the 12th Congress in 1924. For a detailed description of the conflict during the years 1925–1928, see Y. Goren, *The Decisive Conflict*. This research regards the year 1928 as the turning point in the relations between the Labour movement and the Revisionists, signifying the final parting of

the ways.
3. See the impact of the new party on the Labour movement in Y. Goldstein, *The Road to Hegemony*, and in J. Gorny, *Partnership and Conflict: Chaim Weizmann and the Jewish Labour Movement in Palestine*. There is no doubt that the emergence of Revisionism as a new right-wing force played a major role in the creation of *Mapai* out of *Ahdut ha-Avodah* and *Ha-Poel ha-Za'ir* in 1930.
4. Letter dated July 1925, in JI A1/1/2/15. The letter was a response to Schechtman's article 'A Second Basta', published in *Ha-Zafon* of 17.6.1927, in which Schechtman had tried to mitigate some of his sharp criticism of the Labour movement. See also Jabotinsky's letter dated 19.8.1929 to I. Klinov on the same subject. It did not take long for Jabotinsky to change his explanation that *Mapai*'s economic interests caused its hostility towards Revisionsm, to the more fundamental charge that it was a matter of intrinsic hatred.
5. I. Trivus, 'We and They', *Razsvet*, 21.5.1925.
6. For a detailed description of this bitter controversy, replete with mutual recriminations, see my study, *Self-Restraint or Reaction*.
7. Y.H. Yevin,*The Criminal Culpability of the Jewish Agency and the Abandonment of the Yishuv*, Jerusalem, April 1937. See also Yevin's novel *Jerusalem is Waiting . . . .*
8. M. Begin, 'We Shall Pay You Back, Cain!', February 1945. See Begin's book, *In the Underground*, 1959 (2 vols.), pp.221–223. The Cain referred to here is of course the Biblical murderer of his brother Abel. On the historical background of this pamphlet, see my book *The 'Open Season'*.
9. The social tension is described in detail in my book, *Revisionism in Zionism*, p.243–255, and in Y. Ophir, *The History of the National Labourer*. The subject also occupies a considerable part of A. Shapira's study, *Futile Struggle: the Jewish Labour Controversy 1929–1939*.
10. On this, see Y. Goldstein and Y. Shavit, *The Agreement between David Ben-Gurion and Zeev Jabotinsky and its Failure (1934–1935)*, pp.13–130. The situation is described in a letter to Ben-Gurion, dated 8.5.1936 (JI 10/74), written by Dr. Vernes Sentor, the head of the Immigration Department of the Jewish Agency. The episode forms a recurrent theme throughout the three volumes of Ch. Ben-Yerucham, *The Book of Betar, History and Sources*, (1969–1985) and other Revisionist sources. It should be noted that the struggle revolved entirely around immigrants who required so-called 'C-certificates', the allocation of which was determined by the British views on supply and demand in the labour market. It did not, therefore, concern certificates for people with independent means (the recipients of 'A-certificates').
11. See my article, 'The Polish Ghetto and Holocaust Prophecy', in *The Mythology of the Right Wing*, pp.63–84. The accusation was that *Mapai* and the Jewish Agency objected to the 'Evacuation Plan' and mass immigration into Eretz Israel. This evolved into a charge of cooperation with the Nazis, and even that they rejoiced at the misfortune of the Jews who had been left behind in Nazi-occupied Europe!
12. See Y. Gelber, 'Zionist Policy and the Ha'avara Agreement', in *Yalkut Moreshet*, no. 17, February 1974, pp.97–152, and no. 18, November 1974, pp. 106–113.
13. The Arlosoroff Affair and the public storm it aroused are described from two different points of view in, Ch. Ben-Yerucham, *The Great Libel: the Arlosoroff Case*, Tel-Aviv, 1982, and S. Tevet, *The Arlosoroff Murder*, Jerusalem/Tel-Aviv, 1982. Tevet's book was the immediate cause of Menachem Begin's controversial decision to establish a State Commission of Inquiry to re-investigate the case.

   In its report, which was submitted in June 1985, the Commission absolved the suspects, but was unable to determine who the real murderers had been. The Committee also rejected the traditional Revisionist claim that the entire case had from the outset been a libel organized by members of *Mapai*, and that those concerned had submitted perjured evidence during the trial.
14. Z. Jabotinsky, 'The Left', *Razsvet*, 12.7.1925. Ch. Ben-Yerucham summarizes the

various claims in his book, *Nation and Class*, 1942.
15. U.Z. Greenberg, *Watchdog*, 1929. See also Jabotinsky's article, 'Social Profile', in *Doar ha-Yom*, 28.1.1929, in which the negative image and interpretation of the 'bourgeoisie' prevails.
16. D. Ben-Gurion, *From a Class to a Nation*. This slogan referred to Ben-Gurion's view that the Labour movement should see itself not only as a vanguard, but as *the* representative of Zionism as a whole. The tactical and ideological implications of this slogan aroused a vigorous debate within the Labour movement. The 'Radicals' regarded it as a call for the transformation of *Mapai* into a 'reformist' social-democratic party.
17. A. Achimeir, *The Death of Joseph Katznelson*, p.54.
18. Y. H. Yevin, 'Achimeir', *Herut*, 15.7.1960.
19. Z. Jabotinsky, 'The Ideological Fifty-Fifty', *Hazit ha-Am*, 16.12.1932.
20. Z. Jabotinsky, 'Sha'atnez on the Glory of the Idea', *Haynt*, 18.1.1929.
21. Z. Jabotinsky, 'The Rule of the Fist', *Hazit ha-Am*, 11.11.1932.
22. See Ch. Ben-Yerucham's description in, *Nation and Class*, and Y. Avishai's [pseudonym] sarcastic response to Ben-Gurion's slogan: 'and Marxism – the Salvation of the People?'.
23. The novel was translated into Yiddish and was published in Poland. In Eretz Israel the Labour party tried to boycott it, as a result of which it was almost impossible to obtain. This added even more fuel to the fire, reinforcing the self-image of the Revisionists as a persecuted minority.
24. 'The Rule of the Fist', ibid. See also his article, 'A Warning', in *Doar ha-Yom*, 28.1.1928.
25. Ibid; see also his other articles, describing the dictatorship and terror of the *Histadrut*: 'Following the Example of Moscow', *Der Moment*, June 1933; 'Yes, Break It!', *Haynt*, 4.10.1932; 'The Danger of the Flood', *Der Moment*, 6.12.1933; etc.
26. This agreement, and the referendum, are described in Y. Goldstein and Y. Shavit, *The Agreement between Ben-Gurion and Zeev Jabotinsky*. It should be noted here that it was the first – and the last – time that the leadership of *Mapai* had recourse to a referendum among the members in order to determine its policy. The internal struggle between the proponents and opponents of an agreement with the Revisionists revealed the deep-seated differences of opinion about the interests of the Left and the *Histadrut*. In this respect the conflict proved more important for the evolution of the Left than for the history of Revisionism. There, too, there were opponents, but Jabotinsky's status within the movement, the failure to organize an independent Revisionist legal immigration effort, and various other Revisionist problems, combined to secure a majority for Jabotinsky's opinion.

CHAPTER 12

1. This, of course, was a direct result of the fact that anti-Socialism and anti-Communism were central features of the fascist ideology, and thus the Left automatically regarded any criticism of Socialism as fascist. For a good descriptive analysis of the 'positive' and 'negative' aspects of fascist ideology, see Z. Sternhell, 'Fascist Ideology', in W. Laqueur (ed.), *Fascism: a Readers' Guide*, pp.315–376.
2. Y. Yaziv, 'Jabotinsky (a Character Sketch)', *Kuntres* (official organ of *Ahdut ha-Avodah*), 26.10.1926.
3. S. Zemach, 'A Profile of Jabotinsky', *Ahdut ha-Avodah* (*Mapai* quarterly), Vol. I/II, July/August 1931, pp.41–46.
4. For a more detailed description of this attitude, and of the many articles during the early years of Revisionism devoted to portraying Jabotinsky as a personality and a leader, see my book *Revisionism in Zionism*, pp.27–35 and 57–63.
5. *Davar* (daily newspaper of the *Histadrut*), 14.12.1925. When Eliyahu Golomb met

Jabotinsky in London in October 1923, he tried to convince him to support *Ahdut ha-Avodah*, to prevent himself from falling between two stools. According to Golomb, Jabotinsky had a 'great mind', but was incapable of achieving practical results.

6. E. Golomb, *Kuntres*, 3.7.1925.

7. Ibid.; the same view was expressed in other articles, including one in *Kuntres* on 5.4.1927.

8. M. Beilinson, 'The New World of Mister Jabotinsky', *Davar*, 2.9.1925. See also his article, 'The Revisionist Conference in Paris', *Kuntres*, 12.6.1925.

9. E. Tabori, 'About the Social Roots of Revisionism', *Kuntres*, March/April 1929, pp.12–22. A similar analysis is presented in the article by M. Nemirovsky in *The Young Worker*, 28.4.1933, and in D. Ben-Gurion, *The Labour Movement and Revisionism*, 1933, as well as in numerous other articles.

10. For an example of a good bibliography about Fascism, listing some 60 titles, see M. Garson, *Fascism*, 1939, pp.198–200. See also H. Ben-Meir, *Revisionism – a Danger to the Nation*, 1938, and D. Ben-Gurion, *The Labour Movement and Revisionism*, 1933. Ben-Gurion distinguished between Revisionism in Poland and that in Eretz Israel, regarding them as two distinct social phenomena. In a private letter from January 1933, Ben-Gurion compared the nazi victory in Germany with a Revisionist victory in Palestine (*The Letters of D. Ben-Gurion*, Vol. III, 1974, pp.145). The majority within the Labour movement was of the opinion that Revisionism, both in Eretz Israel and in Poland, was tantamount to Jewish Zionist Fascism.

11. Z. Jabotinsky, 'Basta', *Razsvet*, 28.7.1925. See also his definition of a fascist party in his article 'Fascist Zionism', *Razsvet*, 20.12.1925, and his interpretation of national Fascism in Eastern Europe as a middle-class response, in 'Lessons from Shevchenko's Jubilee', *On Literature and Art*, pp.133–141. See also his article 'Jews and Fascism: Some remarks and a Warning', *Jewish Daily Bulletin*, 11.4. 1935.

12. P. Einzig, *The Economic Foundation of Fascism*; see, in particular, the fascist *Carta del Lavoro* ('Labour Charter'), pp.125–156.

13. Z. Jabotinsky, 'A Precondition to the Ten-Year Plan', *Unser Welt*, April 1938. See also his article 'Class Problems', in *Zammelbuch far betarischen Jugend*.

14. Letter dated 4.10.1933, JI A1/12/23/2.

15. A. Achimeir, 'The International Economic Crisis and its Origins', *Betar*, Vol.I, Jan./June 1933, pp.51–57.

16. A. Roki, 'The Changing Face of the State', ibid., pp.439–455.

17. C. Sorino, 'Wages and Profits in a Corporative Economy', ibid., pp.263–372.

18. See Z. Kolitz, *Mussolini, his Personality, his Teaching*, Tel-Aviv,1936, pp. 114–119. The book includes extensive quotations from Mussolini's speeches about the corporative state.

19. A. Achimeir, *The Death of Joseph Katznelson*, p.8. See Achimeir's initial reaction to Fascism in his article, 'Some Ideas about Fascism', *Ha-Toren*, Vienna, Vols. 4/5, July/August 1923, pp.150–155. It is clear that Achimeir's reaction was mainly influenced by his attitude towards Russian communist 'barbarism', and that he viewed Fascism as a countervailing force that might be able to save Western civilization from decadence and communist dictatorship.

20. This series of articles was published during October 1928 in *Doar ha-Yom*, which was at that time edited by Itamar Ben-Avi. These articles were not included in any collection of Achimeir* articles, published either during his lifetime or after his death.

21. 'The Aim of the Zionist-Revisionists', *Ha-Am*, 5.8.1931.

22. This was written by the publisher as an introduction to Kolitz's book.

23. See M. Karmon, 'Fascism – Ten Years in Power', *Betar*, January 1933, pp. 34–36. See also J. Or, 'The Real Synthesis', *Ha-Yarden*, 10.8.1934, and Kolitz, ibid., pp.188–191. Achimeir distinguished between Nazism, which he regarded as an ideology based on a fictitious, mythical past, and Fascism, which in his view was

rooted in a real historical past; see his article, 'On the Origins of Hitlerism', *Betar*, pp.188–191.
24. A. Avniel, 'Fascism', in *Contemporary Problems*, pp.184–189.
25. Z. Jabotinsky, 'Fascist Zionism', *Razsvet*, 20.12.1925.
26. Z. Jabotinsky, 'Italy in the Mediterranean', *Ha-Yarden*, 21.8.1936.

CONCLUSION

1. On the activities of the Revisionist labour movement and its independent trade union movement, see Y. Ophir, *The History of the National Labourer*; see also Y. Shavit (ed. and introd.), *Documents of the First Two Covenants of the National Labour Federation*. During this entire period the membership of the Labour Squads amounted to some 800.
2. On the Revisionist initiatives during this period towards illegal immigration, see A.L. Avneri, *From 'Velos' to 'Taurus': the First Decade of Jewish 'Illegal' Immigration to Mandatory Palestine, 1934–1944*, pp.193–260. For a detailed description, see Ch. Lazar-Litai, *The Book of the Illegal Immigration*. The question of who was the first to propose and organize illegal immigration into Eretz Israel is still being disputed. There is no doubt, however, that the first initiatives were taken by persons connected with the Revisionist movement, in particular Moshe Kriboshin (Galili), and that only later it became an organized initiative of the Revisionists and – eventually – (but on a far larger scale) of the Labour movement and its agencies.
3. On the *IZL* in Europe and in the United States, see A. J. Tavin, *The Second Front, the IZL in Europe 1946–1948*, and the study by J. Kaplan, 'The Rescue Activities of the IZL Delegation in the United States during the Holocaust', *Yalkut Moreshet*, no. 30, November 1980, pp.133–155, and no. 31, April 1981, pp.75–96. Other initiatives, for instance in the field of aviation, were undertaken by different Revisionist individuals and groups. All these initiatives formed a part of the Revisionist desire to extend their efforts beyond mere political activity into 'constructive' areas which they believed the Labour movement had neglected. About the maritime activities, see Y. Weinshal, *Irma*, 1968, the biography of Irma Halpern, the ideologue and moving force behind the naval activity of *Betar*.

*Karl Dietrich Bracher, in his *The Age of Ideologies: A History of Political Thought in the Twentieth Century* (Engl. Transl. Ewald Osers, London, 1984, p.86, note 1) correctly comments on Nolte's one-sided interpretation that: 'the prominent definition of Fascism *tout court* as anti-Communism or anti-Marxism emphasized also by Nolte, runs a double risk: firstly, of underestimating both the anti-Liberal and the "positive" elements of the right-wing ideologies, and secondly of misunderstanding the profound justification of bourgeois-liberal anti-Communism, and, at the same time overlooking the numerous affinities and convergences of right-wing radicalism.'

Bibliography

INTRODUCTION

The bibliography consists of two parts. The first part is a bibliographical survey of primary sources about the history of Revisionism, and the various publications and essays written by either Revisionists or former Revisionists, as well as contemporaries.

The second part contains a list of literature dealing with the history of the Zionist Right, and a selection of general literature about the European Right in general, the history of Zionism, the history of Palestine (*Eretz Israel*) during the Mandate, British policy, the Palestinian problem, and so forth.

The majority – if not all – publications and essays written by Revisionists or members of the underground organizations, or those who at one time belonged to the Revisionist movement, fall in the category of 'auto-history'; in other words they express partisan historical viewpoints, and their principal value lies in the fact that they contain a wealth of documentary material and evidence, despite the fact that, in the main, they are too expansive, as well as selective and subjective. The plethora of sources of this kind enable the researcher to compare testimonies and to examine witness reports and other sources of information from various points of view.

In the second part only a limited selection of general literature has been included, since detailed bibliographical lists of scholarly studies relating to the various subjects are readily available to the interested reader both in Hebrew and in English.

The sheer quantity of available primary sources, due to the intensity and profusion of the contemporary and subsequent polemics, made it impossible to present an exhaustive list of all the journalistic and scholarly articles that were consulted. The reader will find a detailed list in several of the bibliographies included in the list, as well as, of course, in many of the books included there. Only a small selection of the even more extensive available corpus of articles is listed in the footnotes, the majority of which refer to articles that are either quoted in the text, or constitute the primary source for the standpoint, idea or attitude under discussion, or on which I relied during my research for sources of information. The interested reader will therefore find supplementary bibliographical material in the footnotes.

All reference material printed in Israel was originally published in Hebrew, unless indicated otherwise. All literature published outside

Israel was published in English, unless indicated otherwise. Only the literature listed in the primary sources contains a transliteration of the original Hebrew title. English titles of Hebrew books represent either the title mentioned in the original publication, or its literal English translation; only in cases where no English title was available have I myself translated the title.

I. GUIDE TO PRIMARY SOURCES

1. ARCHIVES

The Jabotinsky Institute (*Machon Jabotinsky*: JI;   ) in Tel-Aviv possesses a wealth of material for researchers. The archives, which are as yet only partly organized, contain files of letters, minutes of meetings – both printed and hand-written – photocopies of documents from other archives, and so forth (in addition to collections of newspapers, brochures, pamphlets and books on our subject). An important part of the material was destroyed during World War II in the course of a German air raid on London, during which the headquarters of *Ha-Zohar* in Finchley Road was hit. Other material (particularly the IZL archives, which were secreted in an underground hiding place in Warsaw) was lost. Even so sufficient material is left to enable us to reconstruct the history of the Revisionist movement and its various subsidiary organizations.

The archival material is subdivided by subject, as follows:

a. *Berit Ha-Zohar*: the Union of Revisionist Zionists/the Head Office in Paris during the years 1924–1929 – marked 1   (C1); the Union of Zionist Revisionists/the Executive in London during the years 1929–1933 – marked 2   (C2); the Information Office of the Executive of the World Union of Zionist Revisionists in Tel-Aviv, 1933 – marked   2 (C2A); the World Union of Zionist Revisionists/the Executive in Paris/London 1933–1946 – marked 3   (C3); the Presidium of the New Zionist Organization, London, 1935–1946 – marked 4   (C4); the Head Office of *Ha-Zohar* in Eretz Israel, 1926–1946 – marked 10   (C10); the Head Office of *Ha-Zach* in Eretz Israel, 1935–1946 – marked   10 (C10 A). The above material encompasses some 660 files.

b. *Irgun Ovedei Ha-Zohar ve-Betar* ('Organisation of Ha-Zohar and Betar Workers'), 1930–1934 – marked 1   (D1); *Histadrut ha-Ovedim ha-Leumit* ('National Union of Workers')/the Executive in Tel-Aviv, 1934–1967 – marked 2   (D2); *Kupat Holim le-Ovedim Le'umiim/* Head Office in Tel-Aviv, 1933–1956 – marked 3   (D3). This material encompasses some 100 files.

c. *Keren Tel-Hai* ('Tel-Hai Foundation')/the Board of Management in London, 1929–1940 – marked 1   (G1). This material encompasses some 160 files.

d. *Berit Trumpeldor* (*Betar*)/the Headquarters in Riga/Vilna – marked
    1   (B1); the *Betar* Executive (*Shilton*), Paris/London, 1931–1940 –
    marked 2   (B2); the Directorate of the *Pelugot ha-Avoda le-Betar
    Eretz Israel* ('Betar Work Brigades in Eretz Israel') 1929–1934 –
    marked 5   (B5); *Nezivut Betar be-Eretz Israel* ('Betar Commission in
    Eretz Israel')/the National Leadership, 1927–1966 – marked 9   (B9);
    Ken Betar Tel-Aviv ('Betar Pack Tel-Aviv'), 1928–1948 – marked 10
    (B10). This material encompasses some 200 files.
e. *Berit ha-Biryonim* ('Brigands' League') – marked 14   (K14). This
    material encompasses 8 files.
f. *Berit ha-Hayal* ('Veteran's Union') marked 1   (L1).
g. *Mifleget ha-Medinah ha-Ivrit* ('Jewish State Party') – marked 6   (L6).
h. Revisionist party newspapers published in Eretz Israel – marked 7
    (L7).
i. Archives of the *Irgun Zeva'i Le'umi* ('National Military Organization'
    – IZL) – marked 4   (K4), containing some 400 files.
j. Archives of the *Lohamei Herut Israel* ('Israel Freedom Fighters' –
    Lehi) – marked 5   (K5), containing some 70 files.
k. *Mate IZL la-Golah* ('IZL Diaspora headquarters')/Paris – marked
    18   (K18).
l. The private archives and collections of Ze'ev Jabotinsky – marked 1
    (A1). This material comprises 560 files, including some 6,000 – mainly
    hand-written – letters. A key to the letters written between the years
    1901 and 1924 was published in 1972. The remaining keys, and
    summaries of the letters written from 1924–1940 in various languages
    (principally Russian, English and Hebrew), both typewritten and in
    handwriting, are to be found in the Jabotinsky Institute.
m. Numerous private archives belonging to personalities who worked in
    various capacities for the Revisionist movement. The material is
    contained in several hundreds of files, marked   (Q1).

For a review of the archive materials, see Pesah Gani, 'Archives and
Documentary Materials Stored in the Jabotinsky Institute', 2nd printing,
1979.

2. DAILY NEWSPAPERS AND PERIODICALS (SELECTION)

Doar ha-Yom ('Daily Mail')	Founded by Itamar Ben-Avi in 1919; became a Revisionist organ between 1928–1931.
Ha-Am ('The People')	National newspaper edited by Dr. W. von Weisl, which appeared in 1931 following the closure of *Doar ha-Yom*.
Ha-Mashkif ('The Observer')	Organ of *Ha-Zohar*, 1939–1949.
Ha-Yarden ('The Jordan')	Official newspaper of *Ha-Zohar* in Eretz Israel; as from 1934 published

	as a daily newspaper, and as a weekly from 1934–1936.
Ha-Zafon ('The North')	Newspaper on 'political, economic and literary affairs', edited by A. Weinshal, 1926–1927.
Herut ('Freedom')	Official daily newspaper of the *Herut* Party, first published in 1948.
Mivrak ('The Telegram')	Lehi daily newspaper, 1948.

Special Publications and Supplements

Ha-Biryon ('The Brigand')	Stencilled brochures (5 issues) of the *Berit ha-Biryonim*, first published in 1932.
Herut ha-Moledet ('Freedom of the Fatherland')	23.12.1937.
Le-Ma'an ha-Moledet ('For the Fatherland')	14.1.1938.
Mishmar ha-Yarden ('Watch on the Jordan')	Youth supplement to *Ha-Yarden*, 1934–1935 (12 issues).
Yediot Ha-Zohar ('Ha-Zohar News')	Bulletin dated 1.4.1935.

Newspapers published in Poland (in Yiddish)

Haynt	1926–1932
Der Moment	1937–1939
Die Velt	Weekly, 1933–1934

Various Periodicals

Iggeret ('Newsletter')	Bulletin of the World Directorate of *Betar*, Riga, 1928–1937.
Betar	Literary political monthly edited by Prof. Joseph Klausner, 1933–1934.
Eretz Israel	Monthly of the *Herut* movement, from 1971.
Ha-Hevrah ('The Society')	Organ of the *Benei-Horin* movement, 1940–1946.
Ha-Medinah ('The State')	Youth organ of *Betar*, Warsaw, Riga, and Kovno, 1933–1940.
Ha-Mezudah ('The Fortress')	Central forum of World *Betar*, 1932–1933
Ha-Ummah ('The Nation')	Quarterly, first published in 1962
Ha-Yishuv ('The Community')	Literary political weekly, 1924–1927.
Hazit ha-Am ('Popular Front')	Weekly, edited by the maximalist

	group in *Ha-Zohar*, and organ of the 'Organization of Ha-Zohar and Betar Workers', 1932–1935.
Sifriat ha-Pelugot ('Library of the Brigades')	1933
Razsvet ('The Dawn')	Published from 1924 till 1934 in Paris as a weekly and bi-weekly newspaper; the principal organ of *Ha-Zohar*. Numerous articles from *Razsvet* and other foreign-language party publications were translated and published in the Hebrew journals of *Ha-Zohar* in Eretz Israel.

Periodicals of the IZL and Lehi (Selection)

Ha-Mezudah ('The Fortress')	1932–1933
Ba-Herev ('By the Sword')	1939–1944
Jeruzolima Wyzowolna ('Jerusalem Liberated')	Published in Warsaw, in Polish, 1938–1939.
Die Tat ('The Deed')	Published in Warsaw, in Yiddish
Herut ('Freedom')	1942–1948
Ba-Mahteret ('In the Underground')	1940–1941
Ha-Hazit ('The Front')	1943–1944
Ha-Ma'aseh ('The Deed')	1946–1949

Lehi underground newspapers are collected in *Lehi Collected Works,* Vols. I–II, Tel-Aviv, 1959–1960.

A considerable part of the IZL publications are listed in Menachem Begin's book *Ba-machteret* ('In the Underground'), first published in 1959 in 2 volumes.

Most of the contemporary newspapers and periodicals, particularly those of the rival movements to Revisionism, also constitute an important source of information.

3. BIBLIOGRAPHIES

Yavarovitch, Israel, *The Writings on Ze'ev Jabotinsky, 1897–1940: a Bibliography*, Tel-Aviv, 1980.
— *Essays on Ze'ev Jabotinsky; a Bibliography*, Tel-Aviv, 1980.
Amrami, Yaacov, *Practical Bibliography*, Tel-Aviv, 1975. Contains a list of publications by the underground organizations, as well as testimonies, books and articles on the undergrounds. Also contains a detailed list of newspapers and periodicals (pp.233–238).
Arnon, Johann, *Uri Zvi Greenberg, a Bibliography*, Tel-Aviv, 1980. A voluminous bibliography of Greenberg's writings, articles and poetry.

The following two guides, published in 1982 by the Institute for the Research of the Undergrounds, Bar-Ilan University, Ramat-Gan, contain valuable bibliographical material:

> *Guide to the Private Archives of Abba Achimeir*
> *Guide to the Private Archives of Avraham Stern*

4. THE WRITINGS OF Z. JABOTINSKY

The multifarious literary output of Ze'ev Jabotinsky comprises approximately 2,200 items (not including his correspondence). For a list of Jabotinsky's articles from the year 1897 onwards, see the bibliography by Yisrael Yavarowitch (pp.420–424), which also contains a partial list of Jabotinsky's books and brochures.

Various collections of Jabotinsky's articles (translated by different translators) were published in the course of the years, some of which contain the same articles. Numerous other articles were not included in these collections, and still others have never been translated into Hebrew (in particular his articles in the Russian language that were published in Russia). Three volumes of Jabotinsky's collected works were published between 1936 and 1945, namely: *Golah ve-hitbolelut* ('Diaspora and Assimilation'), 1936; *Be-sha'ah harat olam* ('Historical Hours'), 1943; and *Ha-medini'ut ha'zionit* ('The Zionist Policy'). Following Jabotinsky's death, 18 volumes of his writings were published between 1947 and 1959:

a. *Megillat ha-gedud* ('The Story of the Jewish Legion'), New York, 1941 (Hebrew, 1957).
a1. *Sippur Yamai* ('The Story of my Life'), an unfinished autobiography, covering the years 1926–1936, 1957.
b. *Poems* (Poetry and translations), 1957.
c. *Pyatero*, a novel, written in Russian, 1936; (Hebrew: *Hamishtam*, 1957; Engl. transl.: 'The Five', 1957).
d. *Ne'umim 1905–1925* ('Speeches 1905–1925'), Vol. 1, 1957.
e. *Ne'umim 1927–1940* ('Speeches 1927–1940'), Vol. 2, 1958.
f. *Al sifrut ve-omanut*, 1904–1936 ('On Literature and Art, 1904–1936'), 1948.
g. *Sipurim* ('Stories'), originally written in Russian, 1949.
h. *Ketavim zioni'im rishonim 1903–1906* ('Early Zionist Writings 1903–1906'), 1949.
i. *Umah ve-hevrah* ('Nation and Society'), 1950.
j. *Samson the Nazarite* [1930; also published as *Prelude to Delilah* (1935)], a biblical novel, originally written in Russian (1926), and twice translated into Hebrew.
k. *Ba-derech la-medinah* ('On the Way to a State'), 1950.
l. *Ba-sa'ar* ('In the Storm'), 1953.
m. *Filitonim* ('Feuilleton', 1902–1932), 1954.
n. *Nechar* ('Foreign Land'), a play, written in Russian (Hebr. 1958).

o. *Spartacus* (and other stories), stories by Raphael Giovanioli, a translation from the Italian, no date.
p. *Reshimot* ('Notes'), no date.
q. *Zichronot ben-dori* ('Contemporary Recollections'), no date. Auto-
  biographical and biographical notes. The chapter on 'Turkey and the
  War' was written separately (in English) in London in 1917.
r. *Michtavim* ('Letters'), a selection of Jabotinsky's letters, 1959.

Two pivotal books written by Jabotinsky during the 1930s are:

> *Medinah ivrit: pitaron she'elat ha-yehudim* ('A Jewish State: a Solution
> to the Jewish Problem'), was published in 1937, in Hebrew, Yiddish
> and Polish.
> *The Jewish War Front.* This was Jabotinsky's last book. It was written in
> London in 1939, and published in the United States in 1940 under the
> title *The War and the Jews.* A Hebrew edition appeared in 1941 after
> the author's death.

Jabotinsky published a number of collections of his articles in Yiddish and
other languages, the principal ones being:

> *Zammelbuch für betarischen Jugend* (Yiddish), Warsaw, 1933.
> *Aktuelle Artikelen 1935–1936* (Yiddish), Riga, 1936.

The following is a selection from the numerous collections of Jabotinsky's
articles on a variety of subjects by various editors:

Bella, Moshe (ed.), *The World of Jabotinsky: a Selection of his Works
  and Essentials of his Teaching*, Tel-Aviv, 1972. An 'encyclopaedic'
  selection of Jabotinsky's statements and comments on various
  subjects.
Jabotinsky, Z., *Labour Problems (1925–1932)*, Jerusalem, 1933.
Nedava, Joseph (ed.) *Zeev Jabotinsky: the Man and his Teaching*, Tel-
  Aviv, 1980. A selection of articles, plus a wide-ranging biographical
  introduction.
— (ed.) *Guiding Principles for Contemporary Problems*, Tel-Aviv, 1981.
— (ed.) *The Road to Zionist Revisionism, 1923–1925*, Tel-Aviv, 1984.
— (ed.), *Zionist Revisionism: the Years of Consolidation, 1925–1929*, Tel-
  Aviv, 1985 – and two further collections in 1987.
Shavit, Yaacov, 'The Articles of Z. Jabotinsky, 1919–1920'. An introduction, followed by a selection of Jabotinsky's articles published in
  the Palestinian Jewish press during these two years. Zionism, Vol.VI,
  Tel-Aviv, 1981, pp.323–358.

5. REVISIONIST CONTEMPORARY LITERATURE AND DOCUMENTS

Al hurban shelishi ('Beware of a Third Destruction'), a brochure against
  the Partition Plan, Tel-Aviv, 1937.
Avishai, Y., *Ve-ha-marxism – yeshu'at ha-am* ('And Marxism – the
  People's Salvation?'), Tel-Aviv, 1938.

Avniel, Benyamin, *Ba'ayot be-yameinu* ('Contemporary Problems'), Jerusalem, 1939.

—— *Ba'ayot ba-avodah be-eretz israel* ('Labour Problems in Eretz Israel'), Jerusalem, 1941.

Basic principles of Revisionism, London, 1929.

Begin, Menachem, *Hashkafut ha'im ve-haskafah le'umit — kavei yesod* ('Outlook on Life and National Outlook — A Basic Outline'), 1952.

Ben-Yerucham, Ch., *Ha-am ve-ha-ma'amad* ('Nation and Class'), 1942.

Din ve-heshbon, Ha-ve'idah ha-sheniah shel ha-histadrut ha-ovedim ha-le'umit ('Report on the Second Assembly of the National Labour Federation'), 1935.

Din ve-heshbon shenati 1940–1941, Histadrut ha-ovedim ha-le'umit ('Annual Report 1940–1941 of the National Labour Federation'), 1941.

Grossman, Meir, *Das revisionistische Aufbauprogramm*, Paris, 1929.

Grundsätze des Revisionismus aus den Resolutionen der 1, 2, und 3 Weltkonferenzen der Revisionistischen Union, Paris, 1929 (in English: 'Basic principles of Revisionism', London, 1929).

Histadrut ha-ovedim ha-le'umi'im — mah he? ('What is the National Labour Federation?'), 1935.

Ha-kinus ha-olami ha-rishon shel berit trumpeldor ('The First World Assembly of Berit Trumpeldor'), Paris, 1931.

Ha-kinus ha-olami ha-slishi shel berit trumpeldor ('The Third World Assembly of Berit Trumpeldor'), Cracow, 1935.

Ha-Zionut ha-medinit/yesodot ha-revisionism ('Political Zionism/The Foundations of Revisionism'), Tel-Aviv, 1939.

Jabotinsky, Zeev, *Evidence Submitted to the Palestine Royal Commission*, London, 1937.

——, *The Threatened Partition of Palestine*, Address to Members of Parliament in July 1937, London 1937.

——, *Ha-Zach: ha-histadrut ha-zionit ha-hadashah* ('Ha-Zach: the New Zionist Organization'), Tel-Aviv, 1937.

Klinger, S., *The Ten-Year Plan for Palestine*, 1938 (Engl.).

Lichtheim, Richard, *Revision der Zionistischen Politick*, Berlin, 1930.

Lubotzky, Benyamin, *Betar 1924–1934*. Special Issue on the Ten-Year Anniversary of Betar, Riga, 1934.

Petition Submitted to the Mandates Commission of the League of Nations by the Central Committee of the Union of Zionist Revisionists in Eretz Israel 1934.

Programme of Action for the 22nd Congress, London, 1946.

Ratosh, Yonathan, *Eineinu nesuot el ha-shilton/hazit ha-mahar shel tenuat ha-shichrur* ('Aiming for the Government: the Future Front of the Liberation Movement'), Tel-Aviv, 1938.

Review of the Revisionist Programme, London, 1935.

Schechtman, Joseph B., *Judenstaats Zionismus, Grundsätze des Revisionismus*, Prague, 1933.

Shneiderman (Shenari), Arieh, *Anu ma'ashimim; ha-yeridah ve-harikavon be-histadrut ha-ovedim ba-eretz israel* ('We Accuse;

Emigration and the Corruption in the General Federation of Labour in Eretz Israel'), 1933.

Shostak, Elizier (ed.), *Pa'amei be-reshit – yovel ha-asor le-kupat holim le'umit be-eretz israel, 1933–1944* ('Birth Pangs: on the Tenth Anniversary of the National Health Fund in Eretz Israel, 1933–1943') Tel-Aviv, 1944.

— (ed), *Histadrut ha-ovedim ha-le'umit be-eretz israel – eser sh'not ha-histadrut* ('The National Labour Federation – the Tenth Anniversary of the Federation'), Vol. 1, 1944.

Soskin, Selig, *Das Kolonisationsproblem*, Paris, 1929.

Stricker, Robert, *Was ist Zionismus-Revisionismus*, Vienna, 1933.

The Hebrew War of Independence, a summary of the ideology and political thinking of the IZL, Tel-Aviv, no date.

Yalkut berit ha-biryonim – leket me- ha-itonut 1931–1932 ('Anthology of the Berit ha-Biryonim – A Summary of Press Reports 1931–1932'), Tel-Aviv, 1949.

Yevin, Y.H., *Pesha ha-damim shel ha-sochnut ve-hafkarat he-yishuv* ('The Criminal Culpability of the Jewish Agency and the Abandonment of the Yishuv'), Jerusalem, 1937.

Yizraeli, M. (ed.), *Hadar* ('Glory'), Tel-Aviv, 1951.

Was wollen die Zionisten-Revisionisten?, Paris, 1926.

6. SELECTED DOCUMENTS

Genosar, Pinchas (ed.), *Lehi Revealed: Proceedings of the conference of the Israel freedom Fighters (Lehi), March 1949*, Ramat-Gan, 1985.

Shavit, Yaacov (ed.), 'A Collection of Sources on the History of the National Labour Federation', Tel-Aviv, 1978 [with preface: The Constituent and Second Convention of the National Labour Federation].

— (ed.), *Self-Restraint or Reaction*, Ramat-Gan, 1983. A collection of source materials, with a lengthy introduction on the conflicts within the *Yishuv* about its reaction to the Arab revolt.

7. REVISIONIST WRITINGS: COLLECTIONS OF ARTICLES, ESSAYS, LITERATURE, ETC.

A large part of the writings of Abba Achimeir is contained in the following:

> *When the Cock Crows*, 1958.
> *Judaica*, 1961.
> *Revolutionary Zionism*, 1966.
> *The Trial*, 1968.
> *Berit ha-Biryonim*, 1972.
> *The Death of Joseph Katznelson*, 1974.

Kister, Joseph (ed.), *Achimeir and Betar*, Tel-Aviv, 1982.

Nedava, J. (ed.) *Abba Achimeir: the man who diverted the stream*, Tel-Aviv, 1987.

Achimeir's reminiscences about his imprisonment are collected in his book

Reporta'ge shel bahur yeshivah, 1933–1935 ('Notes from Prison'), Tel-Aviv, new edition, 1984.

A 3-volume edition of selected articles by Yisrael Eldad (Scheib) was published in 1980:

> *Hegyonot Yisrael* ('Reflections on Israel');
> *Hegyonot Yehudah* ('Reflections on Yehudah');
> *Hegyonot Chag* ('Reflections on Festivals');

A collection of articles by Menachem Begin in the underground press was published in *Ba-machteret* ('In the Underground'), 4 volumes, 1959 (2nd ed. in 2 vols., 1978).

Collections of poetry by Uri Zvi Greenberg published during the period under discussion are:

> *Kelev bayit* ('Watchdog'), 1929.
> *Hazon ahad ha-ligyonot* ('Vision of one of the legionnaires'), 1928.
> *Ezor magen u-ne'um ben ha-dam* ('The Speech of the Son of Blood'), 1930.
> *Sefer ha-kitrug ve-ha-emunah* ('The Book of Indictment and Belief'), 1937.

Among the books of Yehoshua H. Yevin are:

> *Jerusalem is Waiting . . .*, Tel-Aviv, 1934.
> *Ketavim* ('Writings'), Tel-Aviv, 1969.

The most important writings of Joseph Klausner within the context of this study are:

> *Ke-she umah nilhemet al herutah: masot historiot* ('When a Nation Fights for its Freedom: Historical Essays'), Tel-Aviv, 1939.
> *Yehudat ve-enoshut,* ('Judaism and Humanity'), 2 vols., Jerusalem, 4th ed., 1955.

The writings of Joseph Katznelson were collected in Hebrew by Achimeir, Joseph (ed.), *The Black Prince: Joseph Katznelson and the National Movement in the 1930s,* Tel-Aviv, 1983.

The poetry and notes of Avraham Stern (Ya'ir) appeared in Avraham Stern, *You Live Forever in Your Blood – Poetry,* Tel-Aviv, 3rd ed., 1976.

8. MEMOIRS

The most important among the numerous books of memoirs are:

Begin, Menachem, *The Revolt,* Tel Aviv, 1949 (since then a number of reprints have appeared).

Eldad (Scheib), Yisrael, *The First Tithe: a Book of Memoirs and Moralities,* Tel Aviv, 1950.

Eliav, Yaacov, *Wanted,* Jerusalem, 1983.

Katz, Samuel, *The Day of Fire,* Tel-Aviv, 1966.

Lankin, Eliyahu, *The Story of the Altalena*, Tel-Aviv, 1950.
Livni, Eitan, *IZL – Operation and Underground*, Tel-Aviv, 1987.
Yellin-Mor, Nathan, *Lehi: People, Ideas and Deeds*, Jerusalem, 1974.

9. CONTEMPORARY ANTI-REVISIONIST POLEMICS

Ben-Zakkai, Y., *Neged kevutzot ha-terror, ha-etzel ve-ha-lehi ve-hashkafat olamam* ('Against the Terror Groups, the IZL, Lehi and their World-View'), 1946.
Ben-Meir, H., *Ha'Revisionism – sakanah la-am* ('Revisionism – a Danger to the Nation'), 1938.
Ben-Gurion, David, *Tenuat ha-poalim ve-ha-revisionism* ('The Labour Movement and Revisionism'), 1933.
Bo'u heshbon, eser she-elot le-miflagah ha-revisionistit ('Tell us Frankly: Ten Questions to the Revisionist Party'), 1935. A polemic against Revisionism by an anonymous former party member.
Libestein, E., *Wo steht der Revisionismus?*, Berlin, 1943.
Medzini, M., *Torato shel Ze'ev Jabotinsky / Bikoret shel ha-tochnit ha revisionistit* ('The Teachings of Zeev Jabotinsky / a Criticism of the Revisionist Programme'),Tel-Aviv, 1927.
Shuchman, Y., *Mah garam le-shvitat Frumin?* ('What caused the strike at Frumin?'), 1932.
Schwadron, Avraham, *ha-nihyeh shutfei shutfav shel amalek; be-inyan shel ha-reviziah shel ha-revizionism* ('Should we be the Accomplices of the Henchmen of Amalek; about the Revision of Revisionism'), Jerusalem, 1935.

10. OTHER GENERAL SOURCES

Protokoll der Verhandlungen des XIV Zionistenkongresses: Vom 18. bis 31. August 1925 in Wien, London, 1926.
Protokoll der Verhandlungen des XV Zionistenkongresses, Basel, 30 August bis 11 September 1927, London, 1927.
Protokoll der Verhandlungen des XVI Zionistenkongresses und der Konstitutionenden Tagung des Council der Jewish Agency für Palästina, Zürich, 28 bis 14 August 1929, London, 1929.
Stenographisches Protokoll der Verhandlungen des XVII Zionistenkongresses und der zweiten Tagung des Council der Jewish Agency für Palästina, Basel, 30 Juni bis 17 Juli 1931, London, 1931.
Stenographisches Protokoll der Verhandlungen des XVIII Zionistenkongresses und der dritten Tagung des Council der Jewish Agency für Palästina, Prag, 21 August bis 4 September 1933, London/Vienna.
Yogev, Gedalya and Freundlich, Yehoshua (eds.), *The Minutes of the Zionist General Council 1919–1921*, Vol. II (Feb. 1920–Aug. 1921), Jerusalem, 1985.

I. SELECTED GENERAL LITERATURE

1. REVISIONIST SELF-WRITTEN HISTORY

Achimeir, J. and Shatzky, S., *Berit ha-Biryonim: the First Anti-British Organization. Documents and Evidence* (2nd ed.), Tel-Aviv, 1978.

Axelrod, Avraham, *The Social Doctrine of Ze'ev Jabotinsky*, Tel-Aviv, 1965.

Ben-Yerucham, Chaim, *The Book of Betar. History and Sources*, 3 vols., 1969–1985. A comprehensive and wide-ranging portrayal of the history of *Betar* against the general background of Revisionist and Zionist history.

Katznelson, Kalman, *The Decline of Jabotinsky's Movement*, Tel-Aviv, 1952.

—, *Conquerors in Distress*, Ramat-Gan, 1980.

Lev-Ami, Schlomo, *Through Struggle and through Revolt*, Tel-Aviv, 1972.

Lazar-Litai, Chaim, *The Book of the Illegal Immigration*, Tel-Aviv, 1957.

Lubotsky, Benyamin, *Ha-Zohar and Betar*, Jerusalem, 1946.

Niv, David, *The Battle for Freedom: the IZL*, 6 vols., Tel-Aviv, 1965–1980. The comprehensive history of the IZL.

Nedava, J. (ed.), *Sixty Years of Ha-Zohar*, Tel-Aviv, 1985. A collection of articles and testimonies from various periods.

Ophir, Yehoshua, *The History of the National Labourer*, Tel-Aviv, 1959.

Schechtman, J.B. and Benari, Y., *History of the Revisionist Movement*, Vol. I, Tel-Aviv, 1970. The first volume covers Revisionist history until the 1930s; the second volume was never published.

Sokolsky, S., *The Educational Doctrine of Betar*, Tel-Aviv, 1947.

Stein, Moshe, *Days of Service*, 1986. The history of the 'mobilized Brigades' of *Betar* and the reminiscences of one of its members.

Tavin, Eli J., *The Second Front: the IZL in Europe 1946–1948*, Tel-Aviv, 1973.

Yishai, David, *Between Blue-White and Red: about the History of the Non-Socialist Labour Movement*, Tel-Aviv, 1980.

2. STUDIES ON THE HISTORY OF REVISIONISM

Bar-Nir, Dov, *From Jabotinsky to Begin: Profile of a Movement*, Tel-Aviv, 1982. A hostile portrayal, which views Revisionism as a 'historical blunder'.

Bell, J.B., *Terror out of Zion: Lehi and the Palestine Underground, 1929–1949*, New York, 1972.

Goldstein, Yaacov, and Shavit, Yaacov, *The Agreement between David*

Ben-Gurion and Zeev Jabotinsky and its Failure (1934–1935), Tel-Aviv, 1979.

Goren, Yaacov, *The Decisive Conflict*, Tel-Aviv, 1986.

Orland, Nachum, *Israels Revisionisten: Die geistigen Väter Menachem Begins*, Munich, 1978.

Shavit, Yaacov, *Revisionism in Zionism: the Revisionist Movement – the Plan for a Colonization Regime and Social Ideas 1925–1935*, Tel-Aviv, 1978.

—, *The Mythologies of the Zionist Right Wing*, Tel-Aviv, 1986. A collection of 7 articles, which provided the background for several of the themes of this study.

3. BIOGRAPHIES

In addition to the many complimentary articles, several admirers have written biographies of Jabotinsky. Some of these are:

Ben-Ari, Yehuda, Z. *Jabotinsky: his Vision and Battles (On the occasion of his 100th Anniversary)*, Tel-Aviv, 1980. A short biographical survey.

Jabotinsky, Eri, *My Father, Zeev Jabotinsky*, Tel-Aviv, 1980. Biographical narratives about chapters in Jabotinsky's life, written by his only son.

Nedava, Joseph, *Jabotinsky in the Eyes of his Contemporaries*, Tel-Aviv, 1944.

Remba, Isaac, *Jabotinsky, as seen by the World and by his People*, Jerusalem, 1940.

—, *The Defender and the Prisoner*, Tel-Aviv, 1960.

Schwartz, Shalom, *Jabotinsky, a Fighter for his Nation* (2nd ed.), Jerusalem, 1943.

Schechtman, Joseph B., *The Vladimir Jabotinsky Story: Rebel and Statesman*, 2 vols., New York, 1956–1961. A three-volume Hebrew translation was published in 1959. This work is so far the most comprehensive and most authoritative biography of Jabotinsky, even though it is written by a close collaborator and admirer. Another biography is being written by Shmuel Katz.

Since 1977 several biographies have been written about Menachem Begin, the best of which are:

Haber, Eitan, *Menachem Begin: the Legend and the Man*, New York, 1978.

Perlmutter, Amos, *The Life and Times of Menachem Begin*, New York, 1987.

Silver, Eric, *Begin: a Biography*, London, 1984.

There is a wealth of articles and studies about Greenberg available, but as yet no complete biography.

Hever, Hann (ed.), *Uri Zvi Greenberg. On his 80th Anniversary; Exhibition at the Jewish National and University Library*, New

York, 1977. This is the most comprehensive biography so far.
Lindebaum, Shalom, *The Poetry of Uri Zvi Greenberg (Hebrew and Yiddish): an Outline*, Tel-Aviv, 1984.
Yevin, Yehoshua H., *Uri Zvi Greenberg, Legislative Poet*, 1937.

Books about Avraham Stern:

Amichai-Yevin, Ada, *In Purple: the Life of Yair – Avraham Stern*, Tel-Aviv, 1986. A biography by an admirer of Stern.
Sherman, Arnold, *Kindling: Biography of Arye Ben-Eliezer*, Jerusalem, 1986.
Yevin, Yehoshua II., *The Blood on the Verge*, Tel-Aviv, 1957.

A considerable amount of important and valuable material on the history of Revisionism is contained in the books, articles, memoirs and correspondence of various personalities belonging to the Labour movement and various other Zionist currents and organizations. In this context we must mention in particular Chaim Weizmann, David Ben-Gurion, Moshe Sharet, Eliyahu Golomb and Berl Katznelson. Ben-Gurion devoted considerable attention to the struggle with Revisionism in several of his writings. This struggle has received particular attention in Ben-Gurion's biography by Shabtai Tevet (see volumes II and III, published in 1980 and 1986).

4. HISTORY OF THE JEWISH PEOPLE, ZIONISM AND ERETZ ISRAEL

A selected and annotated bibliography can be found in:

Porath, Yehoshua, and Shavit, Yaacov, *The History of Eretz Israel, Vol IX: The British Mandate and the Jewish National Home*, Jerusalem, 1982, pp.329–346.

A wide variety of literature, written from various points of view, is available for the English reader. For this reason we will confine ourselves to a number of works on subjects that are most closely related to this study. Most of the books mentioned in this section of the bibliography contain extensive bibliographical lists:

Arian, Asher, *The Chosen People*, Ramat-Gan, 1973.
—, *Politics and Government in Israel*, Tel-Aviv, 1985.
Avineri, Shlomo, *Varieties of Zionist Thought*, Tel-Aviv, 1980. The book was also published in an English version under the title *The Making of Modern Zionism: the Intellectual Origins of the Jewish State*,
New York, 1981.
Avizohar, Meir, *Militant Zionism: an Introduction to Ben-Gurion's Diaries and Memoirs, 1939*, Beer-Sheva, 1985.
Avneri, Arieh L., *From 'Velos' to 'Taurus': the First Decade of Jewish 'Illegal' Immigration to Mandatory Palestine, 1934–1944*, Tel-Aviv, 1985.

Cohen, Mitchell, *Zion and State: Nation and Class in Shaping Modern Israel*, London, 1987.

Dothan, Shmuel, *The Partition of Eretz-Israel in the Mandatory Period: the Jewish Controversy*, Jerusalem, 1979.

—, *The Struggle for Eretz Israel*, Tel-Aviv, 1981.

Friesel, Evyatar, *Zionist policy after the Balfour Declaration, 1917–1922*, Tel-Aviv, 1972.

Gal, Allon, *David Ben-Gurion: Preparing for a Jewish State*, Beer-Sheva, 1985.

Galadi, Dan, *Jewish Palestine during the Fourth Aliya Period (1924–1929)*, Tel-Aviv, 1973.

Goldstein, Yaacov, *Mapai, the Factors leading to its Establishment*, 1975.

—, *The Road to Hegemony: Mapai, the Crystallization of its Policy 1930–1936*, Tel-Aviv, 1980.

Gorny, Joseph, *Achdut Haavoda 1919–1930: the Ideological Principles and the Political System,*1973.

— *Partnership and Conflict: Chaim Weizmann and the Jewish Labour Movement in Palestine*, Tel-Aviv, 1976.

—, *The Arab Question and the Jewish Problem*, Tel-Aviv, 1985.

Halperin, Ben, *The Idea of the Jewish State*, Cambridge (Mass.), 1961.

Harkabi, Yehoshafat, *Fateful Decisions*, Tel-Aviv, 1986. A polemical and critical study of the Revisionist mentality.

Heller, Joseph, *The Struggle for a Jewish State, Zionist Politics, 1936–1948*, Jerusalem, 1985. Contains a lengthy introduction and a broad selection of documentary material.

Horovitz, Dan and Lissak, Moshe, *The Origins of the Israeli Polity: the Political System of the Jewish Community in Palestine under the Mandate*, Tel-Aviv, 1972. [Eng. trans. *Origins of the Israeli Polity*, Chicago U.P., 1978] The most comprehensive and systematic study of the political system of the Jewish community in Mandatory Palestine.

Isaac, Raoul Jean, *Israel Divided: Ideological Politicism in the Jewish State*, Baltimore, Md., 1976.

Kleinman, Aharon, *Divide and Rule, Britain, Partition and Palestine, 1936–1939*, pp.129–142, Jerusalem, 1983. Contains an extensive bibliography on British policy in Palestine.

Laqueur, Walter, *The History of Zionism*, London 1972.

Liebman, Charles S. and Don-Yehiya, Eliezer, *Civic Religion in Israel: Traditional Judaism and Political Culture in the Jewish State*, Los Angeles, 1983.

Mossek, Moshe, *Palestine Immigration Policy under Sir Herbert Samuel*, Cass, London, 1978.

Oppenheim, Israel, *The Pioneer Movement in Poland 1911–1929*, Jerusalem, 1982.

Raanan, Zvi, *Gush Emunim*, Tel-Aviv, 1980.

Schatzberger, Hilda, *Resistance and Tradition*, Ramat-Gan, 1985.

Shapira, Anita, *Futile Struggle: the Jewish Labour Controversy 1929–*

1939, Tel-Aviv, 1972.

Shavit, Yaacov, *The 'Open Season': the Confrontation between the 'Organized Yishuv' and the Underground Organizations 1937–1947*, Tel-Aviv, 1976.

—, *The New Hebrew Nation: a Study in Israeli Heresy and Fantasy*, Cass, London, 1986.

Yisraeli, David, *The Palestine Problem in German Politics 1889–1945*, Ramat-Gan, 1974.

Vital, David, *The Origins of Zionism*, Oxford, 1975.

—, *The Formative Years*, Oxford, 1982.

5. THE JEWISH PEOPLE AND ZIONISM IN EASTERN EUROPE

For a detailed bibliographical list of studies about the history of Eastern European Jewry, with the emphasis on Poland, see:

Mendelson, Ezra, *The Jews of East-Central Europe between the two World Wars: a Select Bibliography*, Jerusalem, 1978.

Several recent studies on the subject are:

Heller, Celia, *On the Edge of Destruction: the Jews of Poland between the two World Wars*, New York, 1977.

Mahler, Raphael, *Polish Jewry between the two World Wars*, Tel-Aviv, 1968. A socio-economic history based on extensive statistical data.

Maor, Y., *The Zionist Movement in Russia*, 2nd ed., Jerusalem, 1975.

Melzer, Emanuel, *Political Struggle in a Trap: the Jews of Poland 1935–1939*, Tel-Aviv, 1982.

Mendelson, Ezra, *Zionism in Poland: the Formative Years 1915–1926*, New Haven, Conn., 1981.

—, *Zionism in the Jewish Community of Poland during the Twenties*, Tel-Aviv, 1982 (English).

Vago, Bela and Mosse, George (eds.), *Jews and Non-Jews in Eastern Europe 1918–1945*, New York, 1974.

6. BACKGROUND LITERATURE

Bullock, Alan and Shock, Maurice, *The Liberal Tradition: from Fox to Keynes*, Oxford, 1962.

Buckle, H. Thomas, *Introduction to the History of Civilization*, London, 1856–1861.

Carsten, F.L., *The Rise of Fascism*, London, 1967.

Cole, G.D.H., *The History of Socialist Thought*, Vol. III, Part II, London, 1956.

Cross, Colin, *The Fascists in Britain*, London, 1961.

Davies, Norman, *God's Playground: a History of Poland*, Vol. II, 2nd ed., Oxford, 1982.

Dorion, Yisrael, *The Teaching of Joseph Popper-Linkeus*, Jerusalem, 1953.

Duff, R. Palme, *Fascism and Social Revolution*, 1934.

Duverger, Maurice, *Political Parties: their Organization and Activity in the Modern State*, New York, 1967.

Einzig, Paul, *The Economic Foundations of Fascism*, London, 1933.

Eley, Geoff., *Reshaping the German Right*, Newhaven, Conn., 1980.

Epstein, B.R., *The Radical Right*, New York, 1967.

Fein, J. Leonard, *Politics in Israel*, Boston, 1962.

Fraser, Derek, *The Evolution of the British Welfare State*, reprint, London, 1975.

Goad, H., *The Making of a Corporate State*, London, 1932.

Gregor, James, *The Interpretations of Fascism*, New York, 1974.

Hamilton, Alistair, *The Appeal of Fascism: A Study of Intellectuals and Fascism 1919–1945*, London, 1971.

Harrison, J.R., *The Reactionaries*, London, 1966.

Ivianski, Zeev, *Individual Terror, Theory and Deed*, Tel-Aviv, 1977.

Kassalow, Everett M., *Trade Unions and Industrial Relations, an International Comparison*, London, 1969.

Kirk, R., *The Conservative Mind*, Chicago, 1953.

Kohn, Hans, *Pan-Slavism: its History and Ideology*, New York, 1960.

Kolitz, Zvi, *Mussolini, his Personality, his Teaching*, Tel-Aviv, 1936.

Labriola, Antonio, *Essay on the Materialistic Conception of History*, Chicago, 1904.

Laqueur, Walter (ed.), *Fascism: a Readers' Guide*, Los Angeles, 1976.

Laqueur, Walter and Mosse, George L. (eds.), *International Fascism, 1920–1945*, New York, 1966.

McClelland, J.S. (ed.), *The French Right from de Maistre to Maurras*, New York, 1971.

Michels, Roberto, *Political Parties*, New York, 1959.

Nolte, Ernest, *Three Faces of Fascism* (transl. from German), New York, 1966.

Rogger, Hans and Weber, Eugen (eds.), *The European Right*, Los Angeles, 1965.

Rothschild, Joseph, *East Central Europe between the two World Wars*, Seattle, 1974.

Rudin, W.A., *The Growth of Fascism in Great Britain*, London, 1935.

Ruggiero, Guido de, *The History of European Liberalism* (transl. from the Italian), Boston, 1959.

Schneider, H.W., *Making the Fascist State*, New York, 1933.

Schorske, Carl G., *Fin-de-Siècle Vienna: Politics and Culture*, New York, 1981.

Selinger, Martin, *Ideology and Politics*, London, 1976.

Sereni, Anzio, *The History of Italian Fascism*, Tel-Aviv, 1951.

Talmon, Y.L., *Political Messianism: the Romantic Phase*, London, 1966.

Thomson, A. Raven, *The Coming Corporate State*, 1935.

Ulman, Lloyd and Flanagan, Robert, *Wage restraint: a Study of Incomes Policies in Western Europe*, Los Angeles, 1971.

Walicki, Andrzej, *Philosophy and Romantic Nationalism: the Case of*

Poland, Oxford, 1982.
—, *The Slavophile Controversy*, O.U.P., New York, 1975.
Woolf, Stuart (ed.), *The Nature of Fascism*, New York, 1969.

Index

in Eretz Israel, 47–8, 81
  Central Committee, 45
  development in, 45–6
  and *Hazit ha-Am*, 89
  leadership of, 47–8
  socio-demographic structure, 83
  voting strength in, 42–3
emergence, 279, 325
and Fascism, 363
financing of, 57
on future Jewish Legion, 95
growth of, 35–6
importance of *hadar* in, 89
headquarters in Warsaw, 70
'impressionism', 89–90
and IZL, 98
Jabotinsky's suspension of the
  Executive, 62
and Jewish Agency enlargement,
  193
and labour exchange demands, 294
and labour relations, 293
labourers in, 92
and Mapai, 400n1
and middle-class orientation, 78,
  278–81
and national Jewish loan idea, 193
nationalist views of members of, 83
platform, 20, 29, 185, 192–3
in Poland, 38
  growth of, 70
plebiscite of April 1933, 61–2, 63, 69
on public funds, 329
rival to workers' parties, 328
state as goal of, 188
Stern's opposition to, 153
structure of, 49–51
World Conferences of, 50, 59
  1925, 278
  1927, 278
  1932, 60–1, 68–9, 208
  1934, 55
  1938, 223
World Council, 49–50
World Executive, 45, 47, 50, 98
  Berlin, 50
  London, 44, 47, 50, 69
  meeting in Katowitz, 61, 62, 65
  Paris, 47, 50
and Zionist Congress elections, 37,
  69
and Zionist Organization, 62, 72
  see also Revisionism; Revisionist
  movement
Hebrew Committee for Jewish

Liberation, 376
Hebrew culture, 108, 159
Hebrew labour, 344
  ideology of organized, 348
Hebrew language, 26, 48, 122, 137,
  150, 155, 265
Hebrew visionary literature, 138
Hebrew revolution, 137, 227
  rule over minorities, 138
He-Halutz (pioneering org.), 70
Heller, P., 392n14
Helsingfors Programme, 258, 260
Hentzig, Otto von, 231
Herbert, Johann Frederick, 111
Herder, J.G., 111, 115
Herut movement, xii, 383n5
  call for compulsory arbitration, 308
  as continuation of Revisionism, 315
  demands on the Histadrut, 308
  etatist principles in platform, 315
  former underground members in,
  314
  and IZL, 319
  first platform, 265
  opposition to military government
  over Arabs, 269–79
  on social function of a state, 307
  and Revisionist socio-economic
  theory, 308
Herut (newspaper), 265
Herzl, Benjamin Ze'ev, 19, 20, 30,
  386n37
  Altneuland, 281–2, 287
  influence on Jabotinsky, 305
  concept of 'new Jew', 22
  idea of the 'Charter', 182
  ideas of, in Revisionism, 108
  and ultimate goal of Zionism, 296
Heschel, Michael, 47
Hevrat ha-Ovedim, 46
Hibbat Zion movement, 19, 183
Histadrut (Labour Federation), 44,
  48, 68, 75, 76, 80, 173, 280, 325,
  376
  conflict with Revisionists, 92, 94,
  292, 344–8
  dominance of labour exchanges and
  markets, 77, 95, 291, 292, 336, 345
  as employer and trade union, 347
  rejection of compromise
  referendum, 348
  welfare system of, 46, 85
Historiography, Zionist, xiv
History, Jewish, place in general, 2
Hitna'arut (Awakening), 72

Jewish Liberation, 376
UNSCOP Commission (1947), Lehi
memorandum to, 253
Unser Welt, 224
Upper Galilee, 375
Urban development, 290

Vienna, 385n25, n26
Ha-Zohar World Conference, 50
von Weisl, Ze'ev, 44, 45

Wars of Liberation, 214
Warsaw, 15
Jewish, 38–9
Warsaw Ghetto uprising, 397n47
Washitz, Ephraim, 44
Weimar Republic, 352
Weinshal, Avraham, 44, 72, 386n41
Weinshal, Jacob, 44, 45
Weinstein, Baruch, 44, 45
Weizmann, Chaim, 30, 32, 71, 84,
211, 279, 330
and British Zionist policy, 183
Greenberg on, 148–9
and Jewish Agency enlargement,
193
on methods for Zionism, 191
minimalist declarations, 185
and removal as chairman of Zionist
Movement, 60
Weltanschauung, definition, 6, 8
White Papers,
immigration regulations, 234
of 1922, 192, 197
of 1930, 58, 185, 210, 211, 331
of 1939, 17, 188, 189, 207, 215, 216,
218, 237, 239, 240
Wilson, Woodrow, 182
Work Brigades *see* Labour Squads
Working class,
Jewish, 279
Revisionist, 76, 77, 91–2
Workers' parties, Zionist in Eretz
Israel, 74
and ideology of class struggle, 343
and Jabotinsky, 329, 351–2
and Partition Plan (1947), 335
rivalry with Revisionism, 350, 357
solidarity of working class, 344

Xerxes, 205, 395n2

Yair *see* Stern, Avraham
Yavne ve-Yodefat (National Union of
Zionist Academics), 87

Yehuda Halevi,
Ha-Kuzari, 392n11
Yellin-Mor, see Friedman-Yellin
Yevin, Yehoshua Heschel, 44, 45, 61,
68, 88, 90, 136–8, 333–4, 341
on aim of Zionism, 137
and 'Bar Kochba' ethos, 137
dismissal from *Ha-Yarden*, 89
Jerusalem Waits ... (novel), 80, 345
Jewish state, view of, 137
on messianic movements, 152
and nationalist ideology, 137
and revolutionary trend in Zionism,
136
Second Temple period as model, 137
'12 Principles of the Constitution of
Freedom', 137–8
*Uri Zvi Greenberg: Meshorer
Mehokek*, 137
Yiddish language, 26, 48
Yiddish press, 56
Yishuv (Jewish community in Eretz
Israel), 346
and immigrant absorption, xix
leaders' attitude to counterterror,
333
middle class in, 74
rightist political programme in, 29
social relations system of, 293
Young Turks, 399n16
Yovel (Jubilee year), 300, 301
Yunitchman, Shimshon, 55, 227, 237
and Begin, 228

Zaltzman, 44
Zangwill, Israel, 264
Zemach, Shlomo, 351
Zion Sejm Scheme, 42, 219
Zionism,
and British cooperation, 33
divisions between Right and Left, 4–
6
ideological currents in, 160
maximalist, 254
messianic element in, 140, 391n4
militancy of, 217
as national mass movement, 374
political, 182–4
as reactionary movement, 3
and rescue schemes, 201
and rights to Eretz Israel, 268
settlement effort of, 290–1
territorial romantic dimension in, 6
trends in,
Herzlian, 31